# LITERARY THEORY AND CRITICISM IN THE LATER MIDDLE AGES

This collection makes a new, profound and far-reaching intervention into the rich yet little-explored terrain between Latin scholastic theory and vernacular literature. Written by a multidisciplinary team of leading international authors, the chapters honour and advance Alastair Minnis's field-defining scholarship. A wealth of expert essays refract the nuances of theory through the medium of authoritative Latin and vernacular medieval texts, providing fresh interpretative treatment to known canonical works while also bringing unknown materials to light.

ARDIS BUTTERFIELD is Marie Borroff Professor of English and Professor of French and Music at Yale University. Her books include *Poetry and Music in Medieval France* (Cambridge University Press, 2002) and *The Familiar Enemy: Chaucer, Language and Nation in the Hundred Years War* (2009), which won the R. H. Gapper prize for French Studies.

IAN JOHNSON is Professor of Medieval Literature and Head of the School of English at the University of St Andrews. The author of *The Middle English Life of Christ: Academic Discourse, Translation and Vernacular Theology* (2013), he edited *Geoffrey Chaucer in Context* (Cambridge University Press, 2019), recognised as a 2020 *Choice* Outstanding Academic Title, and, with Alastair Minnis, *The Cambridge History of Literary Criticism*, II, *The Middle Ages* (Cambridge University Press, 2005).

ANDREW KRAEBEL is Associate Professor of English at Trinity University, Texas. He is the author of *Biblical Commentary and Translation in Later Medieval England: Experiments in Interpretation* (Cambridge University Press, 2020), which was awarded the Ecclesiastical History Society's book prize.

# LITERARY THEORY AND CRITICISM IN THE LATER MIDDLE AGES

*Interpretation, Invention, Imagination*

*Essays in Honour of Alastair Minnis*

EDITED BY

ARDIS BUTTERFIELD
*Yale University*

IAN JOHNSON
*University of St Andrews*

ANDREW KRAEBEL
*Trinity University*

Shaftesbury Road, Cambridge CB2 8EA, United Kingdom

One Liberty Plaza, 20th Floor, New York, NY 10006, USA

477 Williamstown Road, Port Melbourne, VIC 3207, Australia

314–321, 3rd Floor, Plot 3, Splendor Forum, Jasola District Centre, New Delhi – 110025, India

103 Penang Road, #05–06/07, Visioncrest Commercial, Singapore 238467

Cambridge University Press is part of Cambridge University Press & Assessment, a department of the University of Cambridge.

We share the University's mission to contribute to society through the pursuit of education, learning and research at the highest international levels of excellence.

www.cambridge.org
Information on this title: www.cambridge.org/9781108716628

DOI: 10.1017/9781108698351

© Ardis Butterfield, Ian Johnson and Andrew Kraebel 2023

This publication is in copyright. Subject to statutory exception and to the provisions of relevant collective licensing agreements, no reproduction of any part may take place without the written permission of Cambridge University Press & Assessment.

First published 2023
First paperback edition 2025

*A catalogue record for this publication is available from the British Library*

*Library of Congress Cataloging-in-Publication data*
NAMES: Minnis, A. J. (Alastair J.), honouree. | Butterfield, Ardis, editor. | Johnson, Ian R. (Ian Richard), editor. | Kraebel, A. B. (Andrew Brock), 1983- editor.
TITLE: Literary theory and criticism in the later Middle Ages : interpretation, invention, imagination / edited by Ardis Butterfield, Yale University ; Ian Johnson, St Andrews University ; A.B. Kraebel, Trinity University.
DESCRIPTION: Cambridge ; New York, NY : Cambridge University Press, 2023. | Includes bibliographical references and index.
IDENTIFIERS: LCCN 2022050738 (print) | LCCN 2022050739 (ebook) | ISBN 9781108492393 (hardback) | ISBN 9781108716628 (paperback) | ISBN 9781108698351 (epub)
SUBJECTS: LCSH: Criticism, Medieval. | Literature, Medieval–History and criticism–Theory, etc. | Latin literature, Medieval and modern–History and criticism–Theory, etc. | LCGFT: Festschriften.
CLASSIFICATION: LCC PN88 .L58 2023 (print) | LCC PN88 (ebook) | DDC 801/.950902–dc23/eng/20221230
LC record available at https://lccn.loc.gov/2022050738
LC ebook record available at https://lccn.loc.gov/2022050739

ISBN   978-1-108-49239-3   Hardback
ISBN   978-1-108-71662-8   Paperback

Cambridge University Press & Assessment has no responsibility for the persistence or accuracy of URLs for external or third-party internet websites referred to in this publication and does not guarantee that any content on such websites is, or will remain, accurate or appropriate.

# Contents

| | |
|---|---|
| *List of Figures and Tables* | *page* vii |
| *List of Contributors* | viii |
| *Preface and Acknowledgements* | xi |
| *List of Abbreviations and Conventions* | xvi |
| *The Career and Contributions of Alastair Minnis* | xviii |
|     Vincent Gillespie | |
| | |
| Introduction: Criticism, Theory and the Later Medieval Text | 1 |
|     Andrew Kraebel | |
| 1  Access through *Accessus*: Gateways to Learning in a Manuscript of School Texts | 24 |
|     Marjorie Curry Woods | |
| 2  Scholastic Theory and Vernacular Knowledge | 42 |
|     Jocelyn Wogan-Browne | |
| 3  Poetics and Biblical Hermeneutics in the Thirteenth Century | 62 |
|     Gilbert Dahan | |
| 4  Robert Holcot and *De vetula*: Beyond Smalley's Assessment | 78 |
|     Ralph Hanna | |
| 5  The Inspired Commentator: Theories of Interpretive Authority in the Writings of Richard Rolle | 94 |
|     Andrew Kraebel | |
| 6  Guitar Lessons at Blackfriars: Vernacular Medicine and Preacher's Style in Henry Daniel's *Liber Uricrisiarum* | 116 |
|     Joe Stadolnik | |

| 7 | The Re-cognition of Doctrinal Discourse and Scholastic Literary Theory: Affordances of *Ordinatio* in Reginald Pecock's *Donet* and *Reule of Crysten Religioun* <br> Ian Johnson | 137 |
|---|---|---|
| 8 | Arts of Love and Justice: Property, Women and Golden Age Politics in *Le Roman de la Rose* <br> Jessica Rosenfeld | 159 |
| 9 | The Many Sides of Personification: Rhetorical Theory and *Piers Plowman* <br> Nicolette Zeeman | 180 |
| 10 | Encountering Vision: Dislocation, Disquiet, Perplexity <br> Mary Carruthers | 206 |
| 11 | George Colvile's Translation of the *Consolation of Philosophy* <br> Ian Cornelius | 220 |
| 12 | When Did the Emotions Become Political? Medieval Origins and Enlightenment Outcomes <br> Rita Copeland | 249 |
| | Bibliography of the Works of Alastair Minnis <br> Gina Marie Hurley and Clara Wild | 269 |

*Bibliography*     286
*Index*     316

# Figures

0.1 Alastair with his older daughter, Sarah, in Bristol, 1981 — *page* xiv
0.2 Berlin, Staatsbibliothek MS Lat. fol. 34, f. 47$^{rb}$ (selection). The opening of Book II in a twelfth-century commentary on Virgil's *Aeneid* — 2
0.3 Oxford, Bodleian Library MS Auct. F. 2. 9, f. 70$^r$. From a twelfth-century glossed copy of Lucan's *Pharsalia* — 7
0.4 Cambridge, Trinity College MS B.14.33, f. 10$^v$ (selection). The branches of knowledge (*sciencia*) in the *Ysagoge in theologiam* — 13
1.1 Munich, Bayerische Staatsbibliothek Clm 391, f. 18$^v$. Opening of the *Achilleid* of Statius, with *accessus* glosses — 35
5.1 Lincoln, Cathedral Library MS 139, f. 12$^v$ (selection) — 113
11.1 The title page of George Colvile's translation of Boethius's *De consolatione philosophiae*, printed by John Cawoode in 1556 — 222
11.2 The 1556 print, sig. B1$^r$, showing the opening of Boethius's *Consolatio* and Colvile's translation of it — 224
12.1 Giles's *De regimine principum*, misattributed to Aquinas — 260

# Table

2.1 The *Lumere as Lais* and the Aristotelian scholastic prologue — *page* 44

# Contributors

ARDIS BUTTERFIELD is Marie Borroff Professor of English, Professor of French and Music at Yale. Her books include *Poetry and Music in Medieval France* (Cambridge University Press) and *The Familiar Enemy: Chaucer, Language and Nation in the Hundred Years War*, which won the R. H. Gapper prize for French Studies. She is currently completing an edition of medieval English lyrics for Norton and a book on medieval song. She gave the inaugural lectures in the Princeton Bain-Swiggett Poetry and Poetics Seminar in 2022.

MARY CARRUTHERS, FBA, FAAAS, has research interests in the psychological, socio-cultural and textual aspects of medieval rhetoric in the Latin traditions, in reading and composition practices deriving from monastic meditation and prayer, and in questions of literacy and orality in various medieval literary cultures, clerical and courtly. Her many publications include *The Book of Memory* and *The Craft of Thought* (both with Cambridge University Press), as well as *The Experience of Beauty in the Middle Ages*.

RITA COPELAND is the Rosenberg Professor of Humanities and Professor of Classical Studies, English and Comparative Literature at the University of Pennsylvania. Her many books and articles include studies of translation, the arts of grammar and rhetoric, medieval education and intellectual history, literary theory, allegory and classical reception. Most recently she has published *Emotion and the History of Rhetoric in the Middle Ages*. With Peter Mack, she is General Editor of the five-volume *Cambridge History of Rhetoric*.

IAN CORNELIUS is Associate Professor of English at Loyola University Chicago. He is author of *Reconstructing Alliterative Verse: The Pursuit of a Medieval Meter* (Cambridge University Press) and of essays and articles on medieval English literature.

GILBERT DAHAN, directeur de recherches at the Centre national de la recherche scientifique, directeur d'études at the École Pratique des Hautes Études, Section des Sciences religieuses, Paris, works on Christian exegesis of the Bible in the Middle Ages and has published several books on that topic. He has organised several colloques and is one of the editors of the 'Etudes d'histoire de l'exégèse'.

VINCENT GILLESPIE, FBA, is Emeritus J. R. R. Tolkien Professor of English Literature and Language at the University of Oxford. He is Director of the Early English Text Society, and Series Editor of Exeter Medieval Texts and Studies. He writes on medieval poetics, medieval religious literature, Julian of Norwich, Syon Abbey and medieval book history.

RALPH HANNA is Professor of Palaeography (emeritus) and Emeritus Fellow of Keble College, Oxford. He's a library-rat, these pandemic days working at it online. His most recent major publication is *Robert Holcot, Exegete*.

GINA MARIE HURLEY received her PhD in Medieval Studies from Yale in 2020. She is currently the assistant director of graduate and postdoctoral teaching at the Poorvu Center for Teaching and Learning, and is also at work on a monograph on the ways reputations are made and broken in Middle English literature. Her work has appeared in the *Journal of English and Germanic Philology*, *Chaucer Review* and *Medium Ævum*.

IAN JOHNSON is Professor of Medieval Literature and Head of the School of English at the University of St Andrews. He specialises in Middle English literature, medieval literary theory, translation and devotional textuality. The author of *The Middle English Life of Christ: Academic Discourse, Translation and Vernacular Theology*, he edited *Geoffrey Chaucer in Context* (Cambridge University Press), recognised as a 2020 *Choice* Outstanding Academic Title, and, with Alastair Minnis, *The Cambridge History of Literary Criticism*, II, *The Middle Ages* (Cambridge University Press).

ANDREW KRAEBEL is Associate Professor of English at Trinity University. He is the author of *Biblical Commentary and Translation in Later Medieval England: Experiments in Interpretation* (Cambridge University Press), which was awarded the Ecclesiastical History Society's book prize, and he is currently at work on a new history of literary theory and criticism in the Middle Ages. With Alastair Minnis, he is preparing a revised and expanded edition of the anthology *Medieval Literary Theory and Criticism* for Oxford University Press.

JESSICA ROSENFELD is Associate Professor of English Literature at Washington University in St Louis. She is presently co-editor of *Exemplaria: Medieval/Early Modern/Theory* and associate editor of *The Chaucer Encyclopedia* (forthcoming). She is the author of *Ethics and Enjoyment in Late Medieval Poetry: Love after Aristotle* and co-editor with Thomas Prendergast of *Chaucer and the Subversion of Form* (both with Cambridge University Press).

JOE STADOLNIK took his PhD at Yale and has had research fellowships at the Institute of Advanced Studies at UCL and the Institute on the Formation of Knowledge at the University of Chicago. He has published research on medieval English literature, medicine, alchemy and manuscript culture in multilingual, international contexts. With Jenna Mead, he is editor of *A Treatise on the Astrolabe* for the Cambridge Complete Works of Geoffrey Chaucer.

CLARA WILD has recently completed her PhD at Yale, with Alastair Minnis as her dissertation advisor. She is currently a visiting instructor at Georgia Southern University. Her research focuses on late medieval devotional writing.

JOCELYN WOGAN-BROWNE has taught in Australia, the UK, Italy and America. She is emerita Thomas F. X. and Theresa Mullarkey Chair in Literature, Fordham University, New York, emerita Fellow of the Medieval Academy of America and former Professor in Medieval Literature, University of York, UK. She publishes mainly on medieval women's literary cultures and on francophone medieval vernacularity. She is due to give the James Ford Lectures in British History at Oxford in 2024–25.

MARJORIE CURRY WOODS, former Sue Goldston Lebermann Professor of Liberal Arts, has retired from the University of Texas at Austin. Her research into teaching methods in medieval school manuscripts has resulted in three monographs: *An Early Commentary on the Poetria nova of Geoffrey of Vinsauf*, *Classroom Commentaries: Teaching the Poetria nova across Medieval and Renaissance Europe* and *Weeping for Dido: The Classics in the Medieval Classroom*. She lives in Hawai'i, where she first encountered the classics and wrote an ethopoeia in fifth grade at Hanahau'oli School.

NICOLETTE ZEEMAN is Professor of Medieval and Renaissance English at King's College and in the Faculty of English, University of Cambridge. Her most recent book is *The Arts of Disruption: Allegory and Piers Plowman*. She has long been interested in medieval literary theory and, amongst other things, the work of Alastair Minnis.

# *Preface and Acknowledgements*

These essays are offered in honour of Alastair Minnis, and they are meant as an expression of the contributors' sincere and profound gratitude for all he has done for us – and for the field of medieval literary studies – as our teacher, editor, colleague and, more broadly, our guide to what he called scholastic literary attitudes. From his pathbreaking work in *Theory of Authorship*, to his editing (with Ian Johnson) of the massive medieval volume of *The Cambridge History of Literary Criticism*, to monographs on Chaucer and the *Rose* and on medieval ideas of Paradise and Hell, to the anthology of materials which his students affectionately call 'Minnis and Scott', to seminal articles on texts and topics too varied to enumerate here, Alastair has done more than anyone to create and foster the study of medieval literary theory and criticism and to demonstrate how richly rewarding such study can be for readers of later medieval literature. Throughout his scholarship, Alastair models a way of reading – reading works of medieval literature, reading commentary, reading scholastic philosophy and theology, reading manuscripts, reading works of intellectual history – that unerringly points to his training at the hands of his beloved mentors, Beryl Smalley and Malcolm Parkes. This kind of reading is, inevitably, a tall order, but Alastair wears his learning with humility – and with generosity and joviality – and he thereby encourages the rest of us to make the attempt for ourselves. And, for more than three decades, those attempts have found a home and ample and rigorous support, feedback and commentary in the series which Alastair founded and edited, Cambridge Studies in Medieval Literature.

We look back, now, through the prism of that firmly established series and, of course, through the dauntingly huge and influential corpus of Alastair's published work at what looks like a well-settled narrative of unopposable and naturally flowing achievement, starting, as everyone knows, in 1984 with *Theory of Authorship*. The shock waves and intellectual excitement that *Theory of Authorship* caused in the mid-1980s have had no equal in the trade since. But, despite the hugely positive reaction to the book, it was not all plain sailing in those early years – as Alastair himself has stressed to each of us. In the 1970s and 1980s, mainstream academic attitudes to medieval literary theory – or even the idea of the possibility of the existence of medieval literary theory – were all too often rather inhospitable. It was a common experience to hear otherwise well-informed literary academics declare that, apart perhaps from rhetoric, there was no such thing as medieval literary theory. It may be surprising, in retrospect, to recognise just how much Alastair had to work against the grain in those early days. It is a testimony not only to the sheer power and weight of his scholarship, but also to the tactful persuasiveness of his personality, that his achievements are now a central pillar of medieval studies.

Alastair's writing is also exemplary insofar as he refuses to imagine the Latin and vernacular materials he studies as existing in any overly simplistic relationship. While attending to the various ways in which some texts and writers are invested with authority (itself a 'waxen nose'), and to the various directions of influence across linguistic boundaries, Alastair persistently refuses to treat Latin material as an inert body imitated (or mined, or whatever metaphor one wants) by the 'lowly' vernacular, just as he seems to have little patience for antagonistic narratives of the 'upstart' vernacular straining against the chains of 'repressive' Latin scholasticism. He does, however, persistently value scholastic Latin material for its cosmopolitanism, its potential to cross national borders and carry ideas across linguistic traditions. It is no accident that his writing takes up major authors in Middle English, French and Italian, while also exploring the appearance of scholastic texts and ideas in medieval Spain, Sweden, Germany and the Netherlands. Where medieval scholasticism is, there Alastair's heart will be also, and medieval scholasticism was seemingly everywhere.

### Ian writes:

There is more – much more – to Alastair's personality than persuasiveness. I recall vividly my own (very cordial) first meeting with Alastair, in Malcolm Parkes's room – permanently smoke-filled, as Vincent Gillespie describes below. Malcolm, realising that one of his undergraduates was developing a taste for medieval literary thought, lent me his copy of Yer Man's PhD thesis – the precursor to *Medieval Theory of Authorship*. I was hooked: next stop the University of Bristol with AJM as PhD supervisor. Every meeting with Alastair was a real treat, not only because he was such an inspirational and entertaining supervisor, but also because he shared his current work with me. During those years in Bristol, I watched my preternaturally energetic mentor, apparently fuelled only by Mars Bars and coffee, rise to the challenges of putting together *Medieval Literary Theory and Criticism* – to say nothing of carrying out a wealth of foundational work on theory of imagination or the massive ground-breaking project (with Tim Machan) on the Latin, French and English traditions of the text of, and commentaries on, Boethius. Well into my fifth decade of knowing him, I still don't know how he does it.

### Andrew writes:

I want to dwell on Alastair's generosity and joviality. For me, as I think for many of his students, Alastair has made the task of working at the intersection of literary history and the history of ideas not just intellectually rewarding, but also both exciting and remarkably good fun. Recovering the odd mix of the strange and familiar from this material, not shying away from the complexity of it all but taking delight in the contradictions that inevitably arise, and being at once critical and generous with later medieval writers as they worked through sources and ideas that were, similarly, both strange and familiar to them, and as they themselves took intellectual risks – all of this was brilliantly modelled and encouraged, over meals and drinks, at conferences, in the classroom, through countless hours in his office, in New Haven and now in the Scottish Borders. (I am reminded in particular of a recent visit to the Borders, where Florence and Allie found us carrying on, animatedly discussing various points of medieval literary theory, though in the dark – the sun having set at some point in the conversation without our noticing.) I remember Alastair speaking of his wonder at encountering medieval English poetry as an undergraduate studying with Éamonn Ó Carragáin at Queen's University Belfast. The wonder of those early encounters is still, I think, evident in Alastair's research and writing today, impelling him to cast yet more light on the obscurities of later medieval literary and intellectual culture, and inspiring his students to follow his example, aspiring to the virtues of our good, kind and boundlessly curious teacher.

### Ardis writes:

My earliest meeting with Alastair was as an MA student in Bristol, where Ian had just started working on his PhD. Alastair's formidable energy burst

Figure 0.1  Alastair with his older daughter, Sarah, in Bristol, 1981.
Photograph by Florence Minnis.

out of his lectures on medieval authorship and it was thrilling to realise that he was sharing brand new research almost as quickly as he was creating it. That short year in Bristol, with Myra Stokes, Ian Bishop and the calm, brilliantly urbane John Burrow, managed to turn me into a medievalist, as well as introduce me to the dramatically beautiful Bristol hills, a healthgiving alternative to fenland life in Cambridge (see, for a beautiful example of the former, Figure 0.1). In the years since, Alastair generated constant collegiality and friendship from afar, and it was a huge pleasure to reconnect in closer circumstances when, in one of those unexpected life events, I found myself at Yale.

Andrew and Ian have written eloquently of Alastair's research and scholarship in terms which I entirely share and cannot better. So let me comment instead on the small but vital ways he helped a fellow Brit negotiate life on the East Coast, always with encouragement, often over lunch or dinner, and with a plentiful supply of hilarious anecdotes to add spice and cheerful wisdom to the tasks at hand. As a colleague he was a rock, tireless in his teaching, which included a popular lecture course on medieval literature and the movies – one of Alastair's less well-known areas of fun expertise – and dedicated in his efforts to promote medieval studies. Who of the medievalists at Yale will forget the sight of a beaming Alastair climbing onto a chair to welcome new graduates and faculty to the Medieval and Renaissance Studies program, wine glass perilously in hand? His gift for supportiveness is phenomenal. And since retirement, if it were possible, it has even increased, as Alastair has learned to wield the communicatory powers of Zoom from his cockpit in the Borders.

To conclude, we are only three amongst many others who are deeply grateful for all that Alastair has so kindly and brilliantly given. The range and depth of his contribution are stupendous – whether, for example, it may have been his invaluable assistance with a book proposal for those (not necessarily from Alastair's own institution) with a newly-minted doctorate; or his subtle negotiating of complex national or international duties; or his unwavering practical-minded support for colleagues or students going through tough times; or, behind the scenes, his delicate solving, with typical finesse, resourcefulness and good humour, of the crises and awkward tangles afflicting various organisations over many years. So many people know that they owe Alastair a great deal. There are many too who don't know quite how much they really owe him. Alastair's intellectual legacy, both acknowledged and unacknowledged, is colossal and generative, and will continue to grow beyond all our lifetimes. This collection's editors and contributors would like to think that this volume will play its own part in (and serve as testimony and tribute to) the continuing tradition sparked by the individual talent of Alastair Minnis.

As all of that would suggest, it would be hard to do justice to Alastair's contributions to the field with any single volume. We have decided to focus ours on the subject that was at the heart of his intervention – medieval literary theory and criticism. More tributes are surely possible, but we hope that ours reflects the unique and singular effect that he has had on medieval literary studies. It is offered with deep admiration, gratitude and affection.

The editors would like to express their warm gratitude to Linda Bree, who responded with such alacrity to our initial idea, being keen to honour Alastair's longstanding work as General Editor for Cambridge University Press with this special volume, and to Emily Hockley, who continued that encouragement as the book was prepared for publication. Grateful thanks also to the contributors for their collegiality and patience with the process of getting the volume into print, to Gina Hurley and Clara Wild for their meticulous research into the breadth and depth of Alastair's fast-moving publication output, and to Florence, for her expert help with the photos. Ian and Ardis want to extend particular thanks to Andrew, who was instrumental in taking care of so much, and for gracing the whole enterprise with his limitless cheerful efficiency over every detail.

# Abbreviations and Conventions

| | |
|---|---|
| *AND* | *Anglo-Norman Dictionary*, ed. Louise W. Stone, William Rothwell et al., 7 vols (London: Modern Humanities Research Association, 1977–92) |
| ANTS | Anglo-Norman Text Society |
| CCCM | Corpus Christianorum, Continuatio Mediaevalis |
| CCSL | Corpus Christianorum, Series Latina |
| CSEL | Corpus Scriptorum Ecclesiasticorum Latinorum |
| *DMLBS* | *Dictionary of Medieval Latin from British Sources* <logeion.uchicago.edu> |
| *EFA* | Beryl Smalley, *English Friars and Antiquity in the Early Fourteenth Century* (Oxford: Blackwell, 1960) |
| EETS es/os | Early English Text Society, Extra Series/Original Series |
| *GW* | *Gesamtkatalog der Wiegendrucke* (Leipzig: K. W. Hiersemann, 1925–) |
| *IA* | *Index Aureliensis: catalogus librorum sedecimo saeculo impressorum* (Baden-Baden: Valentin Koerner, 1965–) |
| LCL | Loeb Classical Library |
| Minnis and Scott | A. J. Minnis and A. B. Scott (eds), with the assistance of David Wallace, *Medieval Literary Theory and Criticism, c. 1100–c. 1375: The Commentary Tradition*, rev. ed. (Oxford: Clarendon, 1991) |
| *MÆ* | *Medium Ævum* |
| *MED* | *Middle English Dictionary* <quod.lib.umich.edu/m/middle-english-dictionary/dictionary> |
| *MTA* | Alastair Minnis, *Medieval Theory of Authorship: Scholastic Literary Attitudes in the Later Middle Ages*, reprinted 2nd edn (Philadelphia: University of Pennsylvania Press, 2010) |
| *ODNB* | *Oxford Dictionary of National Biography* <www.oxforddnb.com> |

| | |
|---|---|
| *OED* | *Oxford English Dictionary* <www.oed.com> |
| *PL* | *Patrologia Latina*, ed. by J.-P. Migne |
| STC | A. W. Pollard and G. R. Redgrave (eds), *A Short-Title Catalogue of Books Printed in England, Scotland and Ireland, and of English Books Printed Abroad, 1475–1640*, 2nd edn, 3 vols (London: Bibliographical Society, 1976–91) |
| USTC | Universal Short Title Catalogue <ustc.ac.uk> |
| *VLT* | Jocelyn Wogan-Browne, Thelma Fenster and Delbert W. Russell (eds), *Vernacular Literary Theory from the French of Medieval England: Texts and Translations, c. 1120–c. 1450* (Woodbridge: D. S. Brewer, 2016) |
| *YLS* | *Yearbook of Langland Studies* |

Printed sources cited in full here are not repeated in the bibliography at the end of the volume. Decisions concerning Latin orthography have been left to individual authors. Apart from those listed here, the works of Alastair Minnis are cited by short title and year. Citations of the works of Chaucer refer to *The Riverside* edition, unless otherwise noted.

# *The Career and Contributions of Alastair Minnis*

## Vincent Gillespie

In the prologue to his commentary on Hosea, the fourteenth-century English 'classicising friar' Robert Holcot borrows from John of Salisbury's *Polycraticus* and Hugh of St Victor's *Didascalicon* to list seven keys to knowledge. The first six are often listed in mnemonic verses from the medieval schools: 'A humble mind, eagerness for inquiry, a tranquil life, silent examination, poverty, a foreign land', and Holcot comments that 'these customarily open the way for many in their reading of difficult materials'.[1] The seventh key, borrowed from Quintilian, is 'love of one's teachers, for they should be loved and honoured as one does parents'. One should not perhaps be surprised that in his remarkable career Alastair Minnis has deployed all seven of these keys to striking effect, nor that this remarkable career and his storied achievements should map so closely onto Holcot and Hugh's understanding of the three kinds of humility necessary in the search for knowledge: 'First, that one should consider no knowledge, nothing written, worthless; secondly, that one should not be ashamed to learn from anyone ... because it is possible that someone simple knows what you do not; thirdly, that, when one has become skilled in knowledge, one should not disdain others'.[2] This sort of intellectual humility (surely one of the most powerful virtues in many modes of medieval writing) is not material impoverishment, but rather a lack of ego and a sense of modesty in the face of the works of intellectual giants of the past, a kind of beatitudinal poverty of spirit. Alastair's professional life conforms to Holcot's prescriptions remarkably well. Throughout his career he has taught literary scholars the importance of reading deeply, widely, attentively and comprehensively in 'difficult materials', the copious texts

---

[1] Holcot, *Selections on Minor Prophets*, ed. by Hanna, p. 29. For the verses, see Hugh of St Victor, *Didascalicon*, III.13, tr. by Taylor, p. 94 and n. 61 (at p. 214).
[2] Holcot, *Selections on Minor Prophets*, ed. by Hanna, p. 29, still citing *Didascalicon*, III.13.

and commentaries that underpinned medieval exegetical activity and that flowed into and decisively shaped the formation of secular and vernacular attitudes to the arts of imaginative stimulus written in the medieval period. By drawing our attention to the *multiplex modus* of Scripture, and the ways that medieval commentators reacted to the modes, Alastair built a sturdy and robust bridge between the worlds of exegesis and literary criticism which many subsequent scholars have crossed.[3]

His academic career, driven by Holcot's 'eagerness for inquiry', has taken him from The Queen's University, Belfast to Oxford as a recognised student, and to teaching posts at Queen's, Bristol, York and the 'foreign lands' of Columbus, Ohio and New Haven, before returning in retirement to the Scottish Borders, a geographical liminality that stylishly reflects the way in which, intellectually, Alastair has led the scholarly community into the margins of scholastic discourse and the liminal and overlapping spaces of Latin academic commentary and vernacular literary experiment. His 'silent examination' of manuscripts, containing often difficult and sometimes rebarbative texts, led him to listen to the voices of pages rarely turned by literary scholars, pages written by commentators and exegetes in academic and pastoral contexts, as well as commentators on classical texts as they were read and studied in medieval schools of all levels.

As he says in the preface to his great early monograph, *Medieval Theory of Authorship: Scholastic Literary Attitudes in the Later Middle Ages* (1984), he benefited from the existence in Queen's Belfast of a unique department, the Department of Scholastic Philosophy, where Theodore Crowley and James McEvoy guided and shaped his early exposure to those materials. Another colleague at Queen's, A. B. Scott, encouraged and supported his work on later Latin commentaries on classical texts. These scholars were obviously foundational in shaping Alastair's worldview, but it may be his time in Oxford in the 1970s that gave his understanding of the potentials of these materials its distinctive form.

Alastair's love of his teachers is always generously on display in his books and articles, but his Oxford mentors may have had a particularly powerful effect in colouring his scholarly approach and academic methodology. In the mid-1970s, the palaeographer and cultural historian Malcolm Parkes had made his pipe-smoked room over the lodge in Keble College an essential place of resort for visiting medievalists from all over the world. His graduate course on palaeography, for which he kept meticulous registers that now read like a rollcall of international medieval studies from

---

[3] *MTA*, pp. 126–29.

the 1960s through to the 1990s, were frequently audited by scholars on sabbatical or research visits. In the mid-1970s Parkes was developing his thinking about the concepts of *ordinatio* and *compilatio* and their profound influence on the *mise-en-page* of medieval books and on the structural *imaginaire* of medieval authors, thoughts which resulted in his now classic 1976 essay.[4] At the same time, Mary and Richard Rouse were often in Oxford, and Richard Hunt, Keeper of Western Manuscripts in the Bodleian, an expert on medieval grammar teaching, *accessus* and secular commentary, was also talking, teaching and occasionally writing on these materials.[5] So, Alastair's own developing thinking about the nature and *modus agendi* of compilation as an intellectual and bibliographical process was refined in the crucible of lively and high-powered discussions late into the night in Parkes's room, often fuelled by modest quantities of good single malt whisky. The Rouses did not always agree with the Parkesian view, and Alastair was able to calibrate his thinking by reference to both these adamantine intellectual forces.

Though Alastair venerated Malcolm in suitably Holcotian fashion as an academic foster parent, Oxford was also home to another major influence on his intellectual development: the great scholar of biblical exegesis, Beryl Smalley. Smalley's work on the classicising friars, *English Friars and Antiquity* (1960), and on Bible commentary more generally, *The Study of the Bible in the Middle Ages* (1940), had brought many medieval exegetes blinking shyly into the light of modern critical scrutiny, and had recognised (sometimes rather disapprovingly) that they were writing commentary inflected with literary taste and imaginative flair. Smalley saw in the younger Minnis someone with a natural affinity for the exegetical mode of thought. Parkes delightedly reported her saying to him: 'Alastair thinks he is a literary critic, but he is really an historian of exegesis'. The reality was, of course, that he was both, and his subsequent career has shown him to be a genuine pontifex, crafting hugely productive conversations between both scholarly disciplines. A third figure of great influence in these Oxford years was Pamela Gradon, whose remarkable *Form and Style in Early English Literature* (1971) is now unjustly neglected but was widely read in those Oxford years. Gradon brought high intellectual seriousness and sublime learning to bear on vernacular texts and their *modi tractandi* in ways that in some respects anticipated Alastair's more extensive thoughts on these subjects.

---

[4] Parkes, '*Ordinatio* and *Compilatio*'.
[5] See, e.g., Rouse and Rouse, *Preachers, Florilegia and Sermons*.

## The Career and Contributions of Alastair Minnis    xxi

It would have been during these mid-1970s years that I first met Alastair. I was an undergraduate at Keble, and in 1975 began graduate work with Douglas Gray and with the assistance of Parkes's rumbustiously iconoclastic but often acutely insightful interventions. Alastair was already showing the intellectual generosity that has shone throughout his career, and displayed a Holcotian humility in his willingness to talk to a very uncertain new graduate as I took my first tentative and unstable steps into research. What struck me then still strikes me today, decades later: his gentle willingness to listen intently to what one has to say without any desire to foist his point of view or to prejudge the outcome of a scholarly enquiry. This is indeed intellectual humility of a very high order. Despite already establishing himself as a young scholar who Knew Things, he would listen and talk as an equal, open to the idea that his interlocutor might know something he didn't or might benefit from something he did. Alastair's success as a teacher, mentor, administrator and scholar over many years and on several continents is founded on that same openness to conversation, learning, shared excitement and the spirit of enquiry and scholarly adventure. The range of topics explored in his many monographs reveals how productive that curiosity-led research can be when founded on attentive listening, silent reading and careful and highly discriminating questioning of his sources.

During the summers of 1976 and 1977, I was working as a night porter in Keble College. Malcolm Parkes, Alastair and other friends would often drop in for a chat and a coffee to pass the time. One evening has remained particularly vividly engraved in my memory. Many of my generation of graduates had become excited by the way that Parkes, Minnis and others (especially Judson Boyce Allen,[6] himself a frequent Oxford visitor and contributor to the informal King's Arms coffee seminar) were opening up new modes of thinking about medieval exegesis as a potential tool to use in the study of the vernacular literatures of medieval Europe. But the materials were hard to access, frequently only dabbled in superficially and often written in challengingly inaccessible Latin. The field needed an approach that was more rigorous and systematic. So, one balmy summer evening, Alastair and David Thomson (then a graduate working on medieval grammar and later Archdeacon of Carlisle and Bishop of Huntingdon) sat in Keble lodge with me while they drafted out a list of commentary texts that ought to be made available in translation for the use of scholars. In the event, Alastair had the motivation and momentum to see that

---

[6] See Allen, *Friar as Critic*, idem, *Ethical Poetic*.

project through to the hugely influential, ground-breaking anthology of translated materials, *Medieval Literary Theory and Criticism, c. 1100–c. 1375: The Commentary Tradition* (1988), co-edited with Brian Scott and assisted by David Wallace – a volume fittingly dedicated to the memory of Beryl Smalley. The origins and early shape of this volume were firmly rooted in the exciting intellectual milieu of Oxford in those years, and perhaps even in the less exciting and rather dingy milieu of a college lodge.

The preface to the 1988 second edition of *Medieval Theory of Authorship*, which drew from Alastair's doctoral thesis, argued that 'scholastic scriptural exegesis was a central force in the reshaping of literary values in the later Middle Ages' (p. vii). That whole preface is a valuable manifesto for Alastair's continuing literary agenda as it has spread and developed to encompass not just Middle English but also Old French, Italian and other European vernaculars. Like the medieval scholars and commentators he has done so much to illuminate, Alastair has moved around the intellectual centres and cultural synapses of medieval Europe with comfort and expertise, his Latinity (like theirs) ensuring a secure scholarly base-camp for his explorations of their vernacular literatures. His first monograph, *Chaucer and Pagan Antiquity* (1982), for example, offers the simple observation that, in the *Knight's Tale* and *Troilus and Criseyde*, Chaucer creates a powerfully disciplined and self-contained imaginative syllogism to explore what living and thinking like a pagan might entail in terms of the ethics and pragmatics of daily life. This allows Alastair to create an empathetic context in which to read the actions of the characters and to explore their ideological and emotional horizons. His later study, *Fallible Authors* (2007), similarly explores the interstices of literary authority and credibility, brilliantly allowing scholastic notions of sacerdotal authority and the *magisterium predicatoris* to create an intellectual scaffolding for explorations of the fallible utterances of the Pardoner and Wife of Bath.

His editorial labour with Ian Johnson on *The Cambridge History of Literary Criticism*, II, *The Middle Ages* (2005) required heroic reserves of patience and tolerance (and that was just with my chapter), but the volume is a landmark in the transformation of our understanding of the literary attitudes and cultures of the Middle Ages, and the contributors, drawn from a huge range of disciplines and languages, were shepherded and guided by editorial work that was not just enthusiastic and engaged, but also already in command of the field as well as the respect of the authors. If his book on the *Roman de la Rose* was called *Magister Amoris*, one might without exaggeration describe Alastair as *Magister Lectoris* and as, a *magister lectionis* – he has taught generations of students and scholars how to approach their texts with rigour, attentiveness and synthetic power, how to think across and between commentary traditions with discrimination and discernment. His work is full of a beautifully calibrated, rigorously controlled and intellectually hospitable understanding of the broader implications of medieval and contemporary acts of exegetical engagement and scholarly *lectio*.

It is perhaps not accidental that many of his favoured exegetical treatises are affiliated to members of the mendicant orders. In their interpretive synapse, created from a tension between fidelity to Scripture and tradition, on the one hand, and practical application of the resulting acts of interpretation, on the other, a tension so characteristic of the mendicant pastoral theology of the thirteenth-century schools, the *modi agendi* of such texts offer an intriguing parallel to the agile blend of magisterial command and open-minded attention to lexical and literary detail that one finds in so much of Alastair's writing. He too combines the rigorous and the pastoral, the theoretical and the applied, in his writing, speaking and teaching. All are characterised by acts of imaginative association nurtured in a rich tilth of a profound understanding of the broader intellectual, exegetical and pastoral trends and developments of the cultural and academic milieux underpinning (however remotely and indirectly) nearly all medieval vernacular literary production. It is entirely fitting that his 2009 monograph was called *Translations of Authority in Medieval English Literature: Valuing the Vernacular*.

Throughout his long career, Alastair has consistently modelled professional best practice: as a teacher, a graduate supervisor, a collaborator, an editor, an administrator, an academic politician, a defender of the discipline and a tireless advocate for our work. His work in York's Centre for Medieval Studies sustained and extended the pioneering interdisciplinary teaching and research of Derek Pearsall and Elizabeth Salter, perhaps especially the York Manuscripts Conferences, where many of us cut our paper-giving teeth. His role as General Editor of Cambridge Studies in Medieval Literature, from its inception in 1986 until very recently, established that series as one of the finest in the field, and his editorial midwifery gave sharper critical voices to several generations of scholars. He has rightly received most of the glittering prizes our profession can offer, given most of the starriest named lectures in the gift of our field and taught in Denmark, Iceland, The Netherlands, Belgium, France, Italy, Switzerland, Spain, Germany, Finland, Japan, Taiwan, China, Australia, New Zealand and Jerusalem.

Alastair's work is characterised by collegiality and communitarianism, and a lively sense of humour and fun always on display in person and occasionally in print. His work for the early days of the UK Council for College and University English (CCUE, now University and College English), charged with the defence of and advocacy for the subject, and his election in 2000 as a Founding Fellow of the UK's English Association speak to his early and ongoing commitment to the health of the subject. His later roles in the Medieval Academy of America and in the leadership of the New Chaucer Society show how that commitment continued to flourish after his move to the United States. (More recently, it has manifested itself in community involvement in his new home village in the Scottish Borders.) Throughout his career, Alastair has spoken up for medieval studies as a broad intellectual church, capable of powerful and innovative acts of interpretative synthesis, acts that he himself demonstrated by example as well as by precept. He is a tireless peace weaver in our profession and seeks to build consensus and a sense of common purpose. I have watched him at many conferences over the years, encouraging, supporting, gently redirecting generations of graduate students and early career scholars, and expressing enthusiasm as new corridors of thought open up to him. He listens intently, speaks deliberately and with care for the magisterial impact of his words, and can be as excited by the work of a new graduate as by that of an established master.

As part of his retirement from Yale, his beloved colleague Roberta Frank produced a touching tribute, and one story in particular beautifully illustrates the *fama* and renown of Professor Minnis.[7] As Professor Frank tells the tale, at the Kalamazoo conference a few years ago, Alastair and his old friend Terry Jones (of Monty Python fame) were chatting at a bar when three young people slowly and hesitantly, eyes wide in astonishment, approached the two of them. Terry sighed, used to this; they came closer: 'Are you?', one stuttered, ' . . . might you be . . . *Alastair Minnis*?' Although Alastair would probably maintain with his medieval *magistri* that the only good *auctor* is a dead *auctor*, he is most definitely an eminent *actor*, a primary efficient cause of much that is good in our discipline. And retirement shows no slackening of his productivity, as he addresses topics as varied as *From Eden to Eternity: Creations of Paradise in the Later Middle*

---

[7] Roberta Frank, 'Alastair J. Minnis, Douglas Tracy Smith Professor of English', Yale Faculty Retirement Tributes (2019), https://fas.yale.edu/book/faculty-retirement-tributes-2019/alastair-j-minnis (last accessed 23 January 2022). I am indebted to this account for some of the details included here.

Ages (2015), *Hellish Imaginations from Augustine to Dante: An Essay in Metaphor and Materiality* (2020) and *Phantom Pains and Prosthetic Narratives: From George Dedlow to Dante* (2021).

Leonard Boyle, the great Dominican palaeographer and Prefect of the Vatican Library, and another frequent visitor to the Oxford of the 1970s, has on his tombstone in the extraordinary Irish Dominican church of San Clemente in Rome another exhortation from Hugh's *Didascalicon*: 'Omnia disce: postea videbis nihil esse superfluum' ('Learn everything, and later you will see that nothing is superfluous').[8] Alastair's prodigious published output eloquently recalls his beloved Chaucer's repurposing in the *Retractions* of the Pauline dictum (Romans 15.4): 'All that is writen is writen for oure doctrine, and that is myn entente' (10.1082). In the *Didascalicon*, Hugh also says 'the wise student ... gladly hears all, reads all and looks down upon no writing, no person, no teaching'.[9] That enthusiasm, egalitarianism and joy of learning are the hallmark of Alastair as a teacher and a scholar, and we have all benefited richly from it. After a scholarly lifetime spent skilfully inserting the keys of knowledge into so many locked and forbidding texts and of personally embodying the Victorine and Holcotian ideals of scholarly humility, this volume allows some of Alastair Minnis's friends to say thank you to one of the good guys, someone that Cato and Quintilian would certainly recognise as *vir bonus dicendi peritus* ('a good man, skilled in speech').[10]

---

[8] *Didascalicon*, VI.3, tr. by Taylor, p. 137.  [9] *Ibid.*, III.13, tr. by Taylor, p. 95.
[10] Quintilian, *Orator's Education*, XII.1.1, ed. by Russell, v, 196.

# Introduction
## Criticism, Theory and the Later Medieval Text
### Andrew Kraebel

Hic respirat auctor.

Here the author takes a breather.

This neat little phrase appears in an anonymous twelfth-century commentary on the *Aeneid*, the first gloss in the exegete's treatment of Book II.[1] It is preceded only by the first words of the book, *Conticuere omnes*, 'All were silent', underlined in some surviving manuscripts to make them easier for a reader to pick out from the surrounding interpretive materials, and typically with the word-initial *C* spanning multiple lines, foregrounding the *ordinatio textus*, the formal division of the text. (See, for example, Figure 0.2, where space is left but no initial supplied.)[2] As the first break between books in the *Aeneid*, this is the exegete's earliest opportunity to discuss the phenomenon of the text's division. And so he offers this memorable gloss, implying that the break reflects a pause in the composition or – perhaps more likely – recitation of the author's work, a time in which he could catch his breath.

This note on poetic respiration is made even more intriguing by what comes next. The glossator continues, 'Hoc dicebat Magister Ansellus' ('This is what Master Anseau used to say'), evidently referring to the storied master of Laon (d. 1117), from whose school sprang the biblical *Glossa ordinaria*, one of the first major reference texts of scholastic exegesis.[3] We know this master better as Anselm of Laon, but some early sources give

---

[1] My quotations of this series of glosses on *Aen.* II.1 are taken from Berlin, Staatsbibliothek MS Lat. fol. 34, all on f. 47ʳᵇ. For discussion, see Kraebel, 'Twelfth-Century Expansion of Servius'. Appearing at the same time as that essay, Bognini, 'Aperçu d'une lecture séculaire', provides another useful reading. I am unpersuaded by arguments attributing the work to Hilary of Orléans (fl. *c.* 1125), first advanced by De Angelis, 'I Commenti Medievali', and followed in recent scholarship.
[2] Ideas of *ordinatio* are reviewed by Johnson in Chapter 7.
[3] Anselm was the hero of the early scholarship of Beryl Smalley, who argued for the place of his work in the creation of the *Glossa*. See esp. Smalley, 'Problem of the "Glossa ordinaria"', and her 'Quelques prédécesseurs'.

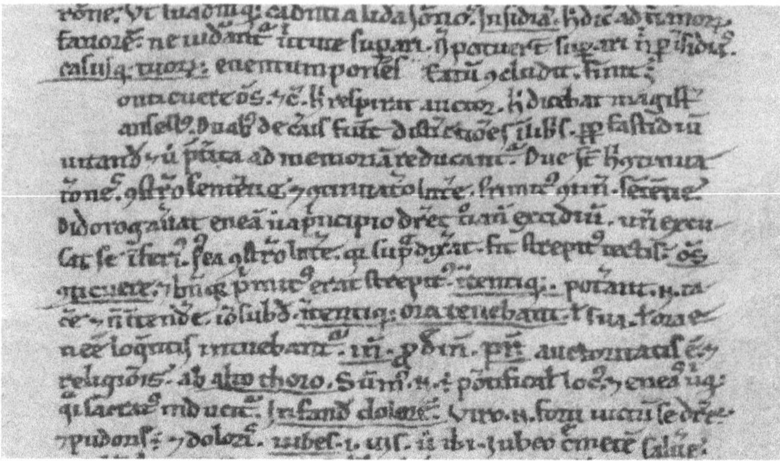

Figure 0.2 Berlin, Staatsbibliothek MS Lat. fol. 34, f. 47$^{rb}$ (selection). The opening of Book II in a twelfth-century commentary on Virgil's *Aeneid*. Reproduced by kind permission.

his name as Ansellus, modern French 'Anseau', and reference to him by this name has sometimes been taken as an indication of greater authenticity, reflecting 'insider knowledge' on the part of scribes and exegetes.[4]

This gloss, together with its knowing attribution, offers a tantalising view into the theories and practices of literary criticism in the later Middle Ages, and it may therefore serve as a useful starting-point for this collection as a whole. Across their different chapters, our contributors take up the question of how texts – poetic, biblical and philosophical, classical and medieval – were interpreted in the later Middle Ages, from *c.* 1100 to *c.* 1450, of how the composition of new poetry took part in – drew on, responded to or against, variously engaged with – this larger tradition of interpretation, and of the continuing influence of scholastic interpretation in later centuries. Here, by way of introduction to this vast and complicated field, I present what I take to be some typical examples of later medieval commentaries and the ways of reading they supported – how, that is, commentators tended to work. I then turn to consider the status of 'theory'

---

[4] E.g., in the case of the Psalter commentary discussed by Wilmart, 'Un commentaire restitué'. For further examples, see Giraud, 'Anselme de Laon', pp. 241 and 242, nn. 12 and 15. Baswell, *Virgil in Medieval England*, p. 339, n. 98, reports that most copies of the commentary register this ambiguity, reading 'Ansellus uel Anselmus'.

in this material, the forms that scholastic literary theory/-ies most often took and what this means for how we now study them. Throughout, my aim is to capture the current state of the field, and to explore ways in which this work may be taken further – some ways of thinking through and with medieval theory and criticism that are modelled in the chapters that follow.

To begin, then, I propose to read this Anselmian gloss, together with the series of glosses that come immediately after it, as illustrating some of the interpretive priorities and tactics commonly found in later medieval literary criticism. Putting this material alongside another twelfth-century collection of glosses will allow us to note some of the different forms of commentary, and especially some of the differences between commentary on classical and biblical material, as it was practised in this period – but it will also serve to emphasise the significant continuities across all of these texts, the major commitments of medieval criticism to testing received interpretations and creating new ones.

## Reading Medieval Criticism

Look again at Figure 0.2. The exegete follows Anselm's explanation of textual division with a second, and more detailed, account: 'Duabus de causis fiunt distinctiones in libris: propter fastidium uitandum et ut preterita ad memoriam reducantur' ('There are two reasons for dividing books: to avoid boredom and so that what has come before might be committed to memory'). In contrast to the purportedly Anselmian note, this second gloss reflects material found more widely in twelfth-century criticism. A similar account occurs, for example, in the commentary on Boethius's *De consolatione philosophiae* by William of Conches (d. *c.* 1155?), at the beginning of Book II, prosa 1 – again, the earliest obvious opportunity:

> *Post haec* etc. Hic incipit secundum uolumen. Mos erat antiquorum terminare libros suos per uolumina, ut daretur spatium lectori recolligendi praedicta, et ut ultaret fastidium, et ut citius aliquid, quod quaeretur, inueniretur.[5]
>
> *After these things*, etc. Here begins Book II. It was customary for the ancients to divide their works into books, in order to give the reader some space for committing what was said in the previous book to memory, to avoid boredom and to make it easier to find things.

---

[5] William of Conches, *Glosae super Boetium*, ed. by Nauta, p. 98.

Evidently it was not just authors who were thought to need time to gather themselves after a certain quantity of Latin verse or prose – and, as in the *Aeneid* gloss, William's iteration of this comment balances positive (an opportunity to digest the foregoing material) and comically negative (the threat of eyes glazing over) reasons for breaking works into smaller units. To which he adds the practical advantages for those who, without reading the whole from start to finish, need to find a particular passage.[6] Our glossator is thus introducing his readers to ideas about literature that can be applied more widely, to the remaining books of the *Aeneid*, and to other texts as well.[7]

Following these preliminaries, the glossator notes the continuities between Book I and Book II – that is, how Book II can be understood to pick up where Book I left off – and he then moves on to the task that occupies most of his attention, the word-by-word and phrase-by-phrase interpretation of Virgil's text. Here, as throughout his work, he draws the bulk of his interpretations from the late antique glosses associated with Servius, active early in the fifth century.[8] For example, in his treatment of the remainder of II.1–2 (with glosses numbered for ease of reference) –

> *Omnes conticuere.* [1] Et bene, quia primitus erat *strepitus* [*Aen.*, I.725]. *Intentique ora tenebant.* [2] Vel sua uel ora Enee loquentis intuebantur. *Inde* [3] pro deinde. *Pater* [4] auctoritatis est et religionis. *Ab alto thoro.* [5] Summus enim est pontificalis locus, et Eneas ubique quasi sacratus inducitur.

> *All were silent.* [1] And this is well-said, since before there had been *an uproar* (*Aen.* I.725). *And they held visages intent.* [2] This either refers to their own faces, or it means they stared at the face of Aeneas as he spoke. *Thereupon* [3] for 'then'. *Father,* [4] authoritative and revered. *From his high couch.* [5] For the highest place belongs to the pontiff, and Aeneas is everywhere presented as though he were holy.

– the first two glosses distil what were longer accounts in Servius, the third repeats Servius, though dropping his identification of this word as an example of apheresis, and the fifth is quoted verbatim from this source.[9] Only the fourth seems to be original to the twelfth-century writer,

---

[6] An idea more frequently discussed with regard to scholastic reference works: see Rouse and Rouse, 'Statim invenire'.
[7] For more on this kind of preparation for wider reading, see Woods's discussion in Chapter 1.
[8] On Servius, see Zetzel, *Critics*, pp. 319–24, and, in more detail, Kaster, *Guardians of Language*, pp. 169–97.
[9] Servius, *Servianorum in Vergilii carmina commentariorum*, ed. by Rand et al., II, 311.

# Introduction: Criticism, Theory and Later Medieval Text 5

apparently added in anticipation of the longer note that follows.[10] And so, as he had through Book I, the glossator continues through the remainder of Virgil's epic. Indeed, the methods and priorities evident in these opening glosses from Book II can be found informing the glossator's work on almost any page of his text. Distilling readings on offer in his authoritative source, he omits some material which he seems to have felt unnecessary, and these received and abbreviated interpretations are supplemented with his own insights, framed by more broadly applicable glosses that present ideas of literature then developing in the cathedral schools of northern Europe – in this case, notions of textual division – as well as, on occasion, the kind of memorable turn of phrase seen in the Anselmian scholion.

This snippet of glosses offers just one glimpse into the rich and varied phenomenon of later medieval commentary, and, though brief, it should already indicate some of the complex and at times contradictory forces that worked to shape such texts.[11] Above all, it points to later medieval commentaries as marked, persistently, by the desire to conserve and to supplement, to affirm the value of received readings, while questioning at least some of their claims and extending the possibilities of interpretation in light of new ideas, new sources and new audiences. By naming Anselm at the beginning of Book II – much as, at the very start of his prologue to the *Eclogues*, he had named Servius – the twelfth-century glossator affirms the value of these more recent interpretive insights.[12] That is, he canonises Anselm as yet another interpreter worthy of consideration and, indeed, citation. He asserts Anselm's status as a speaker of authority (*auctoritas*), someone whose words constituted 'a profound saying worthy of imitation or implementation' and whose opinions were fit to be preserved in the persistently accretive work of what we would now call literary criticism.[13]

But what of the content of that Anselmian gloss, its idea of the poet as breathless performer? How are we to read that understanding of textual division alongside those shared by William of Conches? To get at these questions, I want to consider another example. As Figure 0.2 illustrates,

---

[10] Neither the twelfth-century commentator nor Servius glosses the earlier instance of the phrase *pater Aeneas*, at I.580. Cf. ibid., II, 257; Berlin, Staatsbibliothek MS Lat. fol. 34, f. 46$^{va}$.
[11] To my focus on lemmatised commentaries and glosses, one could add, for example, commentaries written in more overtly homiletic styles, on which see the contributions by Hanna and Stadolnik in Chapters 4 and 6.
[12] For the *Eclogues* commentary, see Pellegatta (ed.), 'Edizione critica del commento *Testatur Servius*', here p. 121.
[13] *MTA*, p. 10, translating Huguccio of Pisa's definition of *auctoritas*.

the commentary on the *Aeneid* was written as lemmatised prose, with brief quotations from Virgil's text – the lemmata – incorporated into the attendant exposition and distinguished with underlining. Figure 0.3 therefore appears to reflect a different kind of interpretive accretion, the accumulation of layers of criticism in the form of many different glosses added by many different hands to a copy of the classical text. Taken from a twelfth-century manuscript of Lucan's *Pharsalia* or *Bellum civile*, here giving VIII.457–500, this page is perhaps most recognisable from its use on the cover of *Medieval Literary Theory and Criticism, c. 1100–c. 1375: The Commentary Tradition*, edited by Alastair Minnis and A. B. Scott, with David Wallace.[14] With wide margins and ample interlinear space, the manuscript seems to have been prepared in anticipation of glossing, which it received in abundance – at least six hands are discernible adding notes to this page. Some of their glosses are made up of single words meant to clarify meaning, as in the case of 'id est, astucior' ('i.e., more cunningly'), added over *melior*, VIII.482, 'better'. Others are written as paraphrases, another common technique in medieval criticism, e.g., explaining 'sic utile recto' (VIII.488):[15]

> Quod dii uolunt hoc uelis, et nolis fatis resistere. Quasi dicat: Rectum est ut recipiatur Pompeius, sed utilitas pocius sequenda est quam rectum.
>
> You should want what the gods want, and you should not want to resist the fates. As though he said: It would be right to welcome Pompey, but we should do what is expedient rather than what is right.

At least one gloss, in a box in the outer margin, supplies mythographic content relevant to the text at hand, in this case explaining the cult of Apis (cf. VIII.479):

> Absirtus frustratim interfectus a parentibus suis miseratione deorum ressuscitatus est, et postea Osiris uocatus, qui habuit Yo uxorem, postquam diis uacca mutata est. In hac Absirti suscitatione sacrificatus est quidam Apis, id est bos . . .
>
> Apsyrtus was killed in vain by his kinsmen and brought back to life by the mercy of the gods, and afterwards he was called Osiris. His wife was Io, after she had been turned into a cow by the gods. In the process of reawakening Apsyrtus, a certain Apis, i.e., a cow, was sacrificed . . .

---

[14] For descriptions, see Pächt and Alexander, *Illuminated Manuscripts*, II, 102 (no. 1046), and Munk Olsen, *L'étude des auteurs classiques*, II, 52–53.
[15] On paraphrasal glossing and the question of voice in commentaries, see Lawton, 'Eleanor Hull's Voices'.

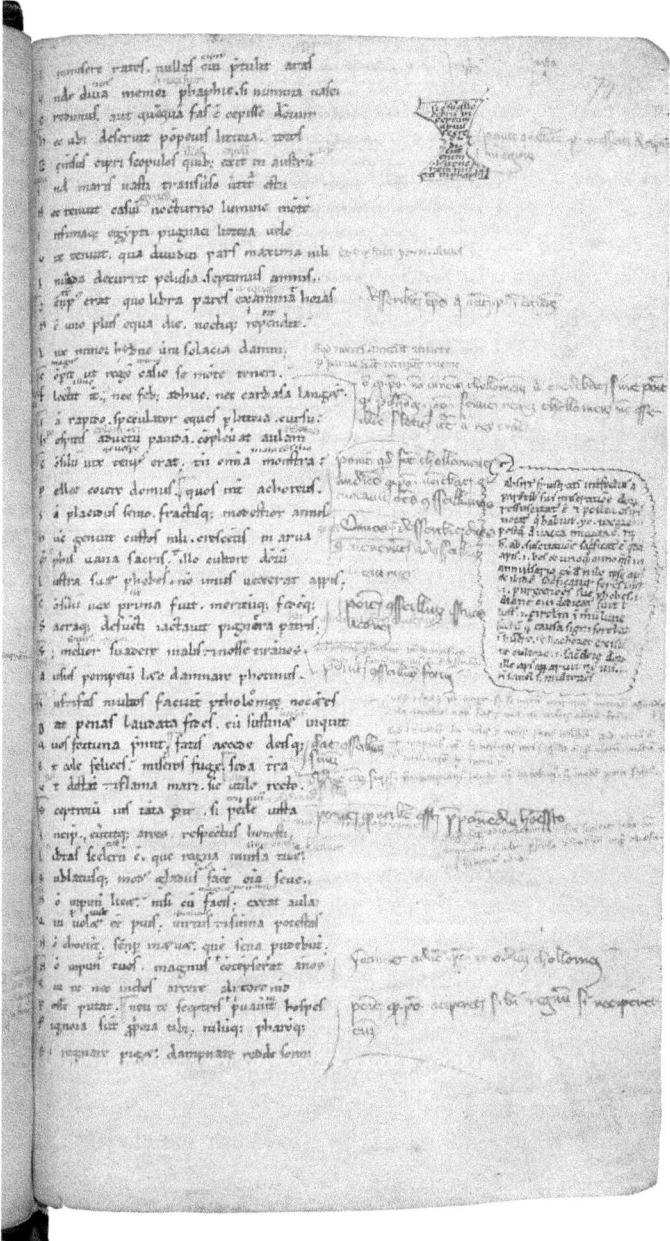

Figure 0.3   Oxford, Bodleian Library MS Auct. F. 2. 9, f. 70ʳ. From a twelfth-century glossed copy of Lucan's *Pharsalia*.
Copyright © Bodleian Libraries, University of Oxford, 2018. digital.bodleian.ox.ac.uk. Creative Commons Licence CC-BY-NC 4.0.

The conflation of the myths of Medea and Osiris, on the one hand, and Io and Isis, on the other, was relatively common in ancient and medieval commentary. On *Thebaid*, I.265, for example, Lactantius Placidus (d. *c*. 400) notes that Io was transformed into Isis after fleeing to Egypt, while a gloss on the same line in a twelfth-century copy of the *Thebaid* identifies Apsyrtus as the brother who dismembered Osiris, later reassembled by the Egyptians.[16] Our glossator contributes to this jumble. Yet another annotator, perhaps the last to add notes to this page, seems principally interested in dividing the text into summarisable units, writing, for example, 'Ponit consscillium Fotini' ('He sets out the counsel of Photinus'), with a corresponding bracket added before VIII.482, or 'Ponit quod Pompeius aciperet sibi regnum si reciperet eum' ('He sets out that Pompey would take the kingdom for himself if he welcomed him'), the final gloss on the leaf, with a bracket added in VIII.498.

Unlike the material on the *Aeneid*, none of these glosses can as yet be traced to an authoritative source, and some contradict interpretations found in more commonly available commentaries.[17] Almost certainly, each of these annotators crafted his glosses for himself, either seeking simple ways to clarify the text or providing more elaborate material – like the mythographic background – from memory. The result is a manuscript that, with each new layer of glosses, became more useful for its audience, in all likelihood a succession of grammar teachers seeking to lead a class of boys through Lucan's historical epic.

Yet, even as this glossed page clearly points to the status of medieval criticism as the cumulative work of many hands, its differences from the *Aeneid* commentary should not be exaggerated. Certainly, the latter is more obviously meant for study and consultation than classroom use – the fragmentation of Virgil's text into lemmata makes it more difficult to navigate on the fly, compared to the ready indexical function played by the central column of Lucan's verse. But these differences may be little more than after-effects of scribal handling, differences in *mise-en-page*, and they potentially obscure larger stylistic and formal similarities. Indeed, it seems to me very likely that the *Aeneid* commentary itself represents an attempt to record, in lemmatised prose, what had begun as a glossed copy of the epic. Notice that, like the glosses in the Lucan manuscript, each of the

---

[16] *Commentarios in Thebaida*, ed. by Jahnke, p. 32; London, British Library, Harley MS 2720. My thanks to Frank Coulson and Harald Anderson for supplying these examples. On Lactantius, see Zetzel, *Critics*, pp. 273–75, and, on Harley, Anderson, *Manuscripts of Statius*, I, no. 310.

[17] Cf. Hiatt, 'Lucan', p. 210, with further relevant studies cited at p. 223, n. 23.

interpretations in the *Aeneid* commentary is a discrete, readily isolable unit – reflected in my numbering in the selection above – each beginning with the bit of Virgil's text to which, in a glossed manuscript, it could be tied. If this is right, then the commentary would preserve, to at least some degree, the authoritative opinions recorded in what was presumably the master's (or successive masters') own copy.[18]

All of which might point to the humbler status of commentary on classical literature relative to biblical commentary – the other major vein of criticism composed in the medieval schools – or it might simply illustrate the different points in their education at which students would study classical and biblical texts. In contrast to the interpretive *bricolage* of these classical glosses, biblical commentaries tend to offer more sustained readings, with local insights tied to the larger interpretive claims articulated in the *accessus* or prologue, and they are more readily read as continuously unfolding prose. That is, the biblical commentary itself, rather than the commentated biblical text, is what structures the experience of reading – and this is true even when commentaries emerge from classroom lectures, as Herbert of Bosham (d. 1194) reports of the *Magna glosatura* on the Psalms and Pauline Epistles by his master, Peter Lombard (d. 1160).[19]

But the distinction between the styles of biblical and classical commentaries shouldn't be exaggerated either. I would be surprised to find a medieval biblical commentary in which the exegete was so focused on his argument that he did not preserve at least some received glosses extraneous to his larger designs, and of course the persistently consulted *Glossa ordinaria* is a collection of discrete and discontinuous scholia. Likewise, in the other direction, the allegorising commentary on *Aen.*, I–VI attributed to Bernardus Silvestris (d. 1178?) pursues with striking persistency a unified reading of the classical text.[20] Whether made up of discrete scholia or continuous prose, interpretively variegated or focused on a unifying notion of the text, the common feature in all of these works is the gloss, the reading that values the text's 'every single word', and medieval critics, however they arranged them, gathered up glosses from an ongoing

---

[18] Cf. Papahagi, '*Glossae collectae*'. The same situation likely pertains for other commentaries on classical literature attributed to specific masters, e.g., Arnulf of Orléans on the *Pharsalia*. See *Arnulfi Glosule super Lucanum*, ed. by Marti.

[19] For Herbert's comments, offered in his copy of the Lombard's *Glosatura*, see Glunz, *History of the Vulgate*, p. 343.

[20] Bernardus Silvestris, *Commentum super sex libros Eneidos*, ed. by Jones and Jones.

interpretive tradition, while also generating new ones of their own, all in an effort to draw yet more meanings from the writings of the *auctores*.[21]

The possibility that the lemmatised *Aeneid* commentary represents an attempt to transcribe a glossed copy of the epic can help us, finally, to say more about the short Anselmian gloss that begins Book II. The suggestion that classical poets recited their works to a contemporary audience is itself commonplace, seen in Isidore of Seville's (d. 636) claim that authors of classical tragedies read their work from a raised stage (*orchestra*), while the players pantomimed the scene – an idea elaborated in Nicholas Trevet OP's (d. 1334) commentary on the tragedies of Seneca.[22] And the notion of Virgil, specifically, reciting his verses appears in Servian glosses, e.g., on *Aen.*, IV.323 (from Dido's speech accusing Aeneas), where the poet is said to have 'delivered these verses with great passion when he recited them to Augustus. For he recited in the finest voice the third and fourth books'. Even earlier, in the *vita* by Donatus, we find the account of Virgil (with the aid of Maecenas) reciting the whole of the *Georgics* to Augustus after Actium, a performance that was 'attractive and strangely seductive'.[23] The notion of an author pausing to catch his breath in between books extends this line of thinking. It might be tempting, then, to read this gloss together with what follows it – that is, while the poet catches his breath, his audience can take a break as well, and they can begin to commit what they have heard to memory. And yet, when the glossator describes the memorisation of the text and the threat of boredom, he surely has in mind the experience of medieval readers, not ancient auditors – a point made even more clearly in William of Conches's version of the gloss, where to these explanations are added the benefits of rapid (readerly) consultation. Here we have, in other words, what began (and should now be read) as two distinct scholia, perhaps added to the margins of the classical text at different times, perhaps even in different hands. They are two distinct interpretive options. The second gloss repeats what was becoming a more widely shared technical account of the *ordinatio* or *forma tractatus* of multi-book texts, one that evokes the study of the text as written object. The first, in contrast, while apparently assuming ideas of

---

[21] To borrow a phrase from Woods, *Weeping for Dido*, p. 4, whose approach has inspired much of this discussion.

[22] Isidore of Seville, *Etymologies*, XVIII.XLIV.1, ed. by Lindsay. See Kelly, *Ideas and Forms*, pp. 42–44 and 133–34.

[23] Translated in Ziolkowski and Putnam (eds), *The Virgilian Tradition*, pp. 165 and 192, the latter part of a larger catalogue of the poet's recitations.

the poet as performer, seems to me as likely to be a bit of colour as a sincere interpretive claim, a fanciful remark meant to keep the attention of Anselm's students. It was something that he habitually said (*dicebat*). Like the gloss that follows it, then, this one too could be exogenous, not necessarily originating in the exposition of the work at hand. Master Anselm, in other words, could have made his wry observation in between books or chapters of any number of texts – including the biblical books with the exposition of which he is more commonly associated – and one of his former students, adding glosses to a copy of the works of Virgil, preserved his master's humour. This gloss seems likely to be a student's fond memory of his beloved teacher.

## Theory and the Medieval Gloss

All of this provides abundant evidence for medieval traditions of literary criticism, traditions which were yet more extensive and diverse than this brief sampling can illustrate. But do they present anything that could be called theory? The term 'theory' (*theoria* or *theorica*, the latter used as both noun and adjective) reached later medieval writers as a calque of θεωρία, meaning 'contemplation', in such texts as Cassian's *Collations* and, in one significant instance, the Latin text of the *Celestial Hierarchy* of pseudo-Dionysius.[24] There, the contemplation enjoyed by the highest ranks of the heavenly host is set in contrast to 'Contemplatiuas ... uarietate sacre scribentis theoriae in diuinum reductas', a phrase glossed by Hugh of St Victor (d. 1141) as follows:

> *Reductas in diuinum*, hoc est in diuinam cognitionem, *uarietate*, id est multiplici doctrina, *theoriae*, id est diuinae Scripturae – *theoriae*, dico, *sacre scribentis*, quia scilicet de diuinis et sacris rebus scribit et loquitur.[25]

> *Led back to the divine*, i.e., to divine knowledge, *by the variety*, i.e., the manifold teaching, *of theory*, i.e., of sacred Scripture – *of theory*, I say, *of one writing sacredly*, i.e., because he writes and speaks of holy matters.

Hugh takes *theoria* to refer to the biblical text, and perhaps specifically the text as meditated upon, as part of a spiritual discipline by which the reader can strive for divine knowledge. This is a form of contemplation inferior to

---

[24] The term is discussed briefly, with reference to Cassian, by Leclercq, *Love of Learning*, tr. by Misrahi, pp. 99–100.
[25] Hugh of St Victor, *Super Ierarchiam Dionisii*, VII, ed. by Poirel, p. 582.

that of the seraphim, but by no means a bad one. Likewise, throughout the *Collations*, Cassian glosses various uses of *theoria* with reference to monastic contemplation. Hence the 'better part' chosen by Mary is identified as consisting 'in theoria sola, id est in contemplatione diuina' ('in theory alone, i.e., in divine contemplation'), while the third and highest form of renunciation (*renuntiatio*) is achieved 'per indesinentem diuinarum meditationem Scripturarum spiritalesque theorias' ('through unstinting meditation on Holy Writ and through spiritual theories').[26] But religious texts are not the only things that can be contemplated. In his account of Lady Philosophy's eyes, for example, described in *De consolatione*, I.p1, William of Conches writes, 'Et sunt oculi Philosophiae theorici, id est contemplatiui, qui ratione et intellectu considerant naturas rerum et earum proprietates, non docendo alios nec scribendo' ('And Philosophy's eyes are theoretical, i.e., contemplative, considering with reason and the intellect the natures of things and their properties, neither teaching others nor writing').[27] Here, William evokes not monastic contemplation or biblical study, but rather the use of *theoria* in the division of philosophy into practical and theoretical branches, the latter variously called *philosophia speculativa*, *inspectiva* or *theorica*.[28] In the hands of Bernardus Silvestris, in his epic *Microcosmus*, IX.6, this division is personified as Physis and her daughters, Theorica and Practica, and it is incorporated into a larger schematisation in another twelfth-century text, the anonymous *Ysagoge in theologiam* (Figure 0.4).[29] Perhaps under the influence of such schemas, in his commentary on *De consolatione*, Hugh of St Victor substitutes *theoria* in place of *physica* in the traditional Hellenistic or 'Stoic' division of philosophy, with the other two branches being *logica* and *ethica*.[30] A different substitution occurs in a Psalter commentary attributed to Gilbertus Universalis (d. 1134), who notes that, while some biblical books pertain to physics and others to ethics,

> in quo loco seculares solent tractare de logica, ibi diuini de theorica, id est de contemplatiua uita intellectualiter – sicut in Canticis Canticorum, ubi agitur de altioribus mysteriis, id est de copulatione sponsi et sponsę, et sicut

---

[26] Cassian, *Cassiani Conlationes*, I.i.8 and I.iii.7, ed. by Petschenig, pp. 15 and 75.
[27] William of Conches, *Glosae super Boetium*, ed. by Nauta, p. 27
[28] William supplies this division later in his comments on the same prosa: see ibid., 31, and cf. *ed. cit.*, plate 5.
[29] Bernardus Silvestris, *Poetic Works*, ed. and tr. by Wetherbee, p. 134. For the *Ysagoge*, see Landgraf, *Écrits théologiques*, pp. 70–73.
[30] Hugh of St Victor, *Super Ierarchiam Dionisii*, I.prol., ed. by Poirel, pp. 403–4. The Hellenistic division was transmitted by Isidore, *Etymologies*, II.xxiv.3, ed. by Lindsay.

Introduction: Criticism, Theory and Later Medieval Text        13

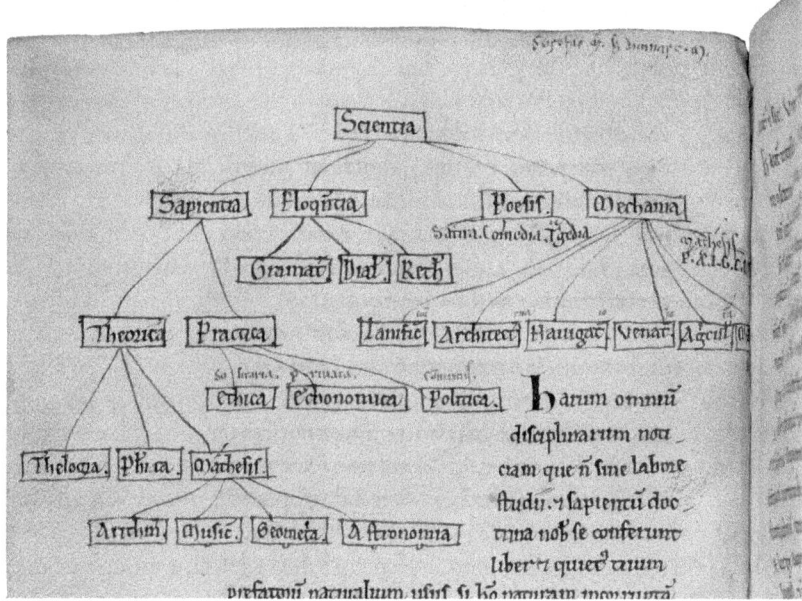

Figure 0.4   Cambridge, Trinity College MS B.14.33, f. 10ᵛ (selection). The branches of knowledge (*sciencia*) in the *Ysagoge in theologiam*.
Reproduced by kind permission of the Master and Fellows of Trinity College Cambridge.

> in hoc libro uere agitur de mysteriis, id est de incarnatione et passione et reparatione humani generis.[31]

> where secular texts typically treat logic, divine books treat theory, i.e., the contemplative life intellectually – as in the Song of Songs, where he writes of more profound mysteries, i.e., the union of the Bridegroom and Bride, and as in this book, where he writes about mysteries, i.e., the Incarnation and Passion, and the restoration of humankind.

Gilbertus concedes that some psalms pertain to ethics, but most of the Psalter is theoretical. Here, then, we seem to have a merging of the two major associations of the term, *theoria* as the rarefied contemplation that was the goal of monastic life, and as a branch of philosophy.

*Theoria* describes a field of study, then, one focused on abstractions, profound mysteries or things lacking material existence, and in at least some cases the term is used to describe texts – especially the Bible – with

---

[31] Laon, Bibliothèque municipale MS 17, f. 1ᵛᵃ. See Smalley, 'Problem of the "Glossa Ordinaria"', 8:51–60.

which one can plumb these depths. That is, for later medieval writers, 'theoretical' knowledge can be supported and explored *by means of* texts, including poetry like the Psalms, but the study of texts themselves is not within *theoria*'s ambit. For that kind of 'theory', the division of the sciences labelled *poesis* in Figure 0.3 would seem to be closer to the mark. Yet the *Ysagoge*-author's treatment of this branch of knowledge is frustratingly vague, and his subdivision of *poesis* into satire, comedy and tragedy seems simply to name – and that only partially – the varieties of poetry that one might study or compose, rather than identifying different groupings of ideas about such literature and its interpretation. Indeed, sustained discussions of 'poetics' in later medieval texts tend not to take up questions of interpretation, but rather to prescribe and offer guidance on composition, seen too in those *divisiones* that place poetics under the heading of rhetoric.[32] And, as Minnis observes, while we might expect the advent of Latin translation(s) of Aristotle's *Poetics* to have changed this situation, that text was generally read as fitting with or supporting already-circulating ideas of poetic language.[33]

And yet, though they are not collected or discussed as a unified field of study, ideas about literature – its interpretation and its effects on its readers, among many other things – may of course readily be found in later medieval sources. We have already seen some of them in the commentary on *Aeneid*, II – e.g., that the division of longer texts into books is meant to aid memorisation and to fend off boredom, to keep readers attentive. A similar interest in the affective response to poetry – to the relationship between form and the experience of reading – can be found, for example, in a glossed copy of Horace's *Odes* prepared *c.* 1100, where the lyric poet is said to have composed his collection 'de diuersa materia carminum et uariatione mellita' ('with many different subject-matters in his songs and with sweet variation') – that is, variation in his metres. This diversity is comparable to the different strings (*diversae cordae*) of the lyre itself, which 'uarie sonant ad maiorem audientium delectationem'

---

[32] On the place of poetics in later medieval divisions of the sciences, see Dahan, 'Notes et textes sur la Poétique', as well as Chapter 3. On *artes poetriae* and rhetorical traditions, see Woods, *Classroom Commentaries*.

[33] On the 1256 translation by Hermannus Alemannus, Minnis, 'Acculturizing Aristotle' (2005), p. 238, observes: 'It made sense to medieval culture, and medieval culture made sense of it'. And cf. Minnis, 'Medieval Imagination' (2005), p. 252: 'Medieval thinkers found the Averroes/Hermann treatise more comprehensible' than the more literalistic rendering of William of Moerbeke (1278) 'within their hierarchies of the sciences and in respect of ... [the] ethical aims of poetry'. For more on Arabic-to-Latin translations of Aristotle, see the contributions by Rosenfeld and Copeland, Chapters 8 and 12.

('produce different pitches, all for the greater delight of those who listen').³⁴ Likewise, Gilbert of Poitiers (d. 1154) suggests that the Psalmist 'metrice scripsit et diuersis loquendi generibus opus ornauit' ('wrote in metre and adorned his work with different ways of speaking'), specifically in order 'affectum carnalium hominum ... trahere' ('to draw the emotions of fleshly people') to the praise of God.³⁵ Approaching the question from a different angle, in the *Magna glosatura*, Peter Lombard claims that repetition is used in the Psalter not only to clarify or emphasise a point, but also to convey the affective state of the biblical *auctor*, his sorrow or his sense of wonder.³⁶

Medieval literary theories were not, then, typically developed in standalone essays, treatises or books – as is more familiarly the case with literary theories of the last century, or, indeed, in Aristotle's *Poetics* or Longinus's *On the Sublime* – but they are nevertheless there, if you know where to look for them. And one of the best places to look is in the glosses.³⁷ This was, among other things, the great innovation of *Medieval Theory of Authorship*. Minnis turned his attention not to the practical how-to guides of the *artes poetriae*, but instead to the ideas of poetry, and of literature more generally, that appeared in commentaries and glosses, and – following the lead of R. W. Hunt – he found the *accessus* or commentary prologues to be particularly rich sources.³⁸ Neither is it the case, for Minnis, that the *accessus* are to be taken as brief theoretical excursus independent of the larger commentary. As the discussions of *divisio* at the start of *Aeneid*, II and *De consolatione*, II pr. 1, should remind us, glossators developed and deployed theories not just in prologues, but also within their commentaries, as those theories were germane to the interpretive task at hand, and their *accessus* are functionally, then, large initial collections of such glosses.

This point – essentially a formal one – is significant for the larger shape of the discursive field which we can, in retrospect, call medieval literary theory. In part because they are generally pursued in various glosses rather than in sustained discussions independent from the work of criticism, later

---

³⁴ Paris, Bibliothèque nationale de France MS lat. 17897, f. 1ʳ.
³⁵ De Bruyne (ed.), *Préfaces*, p. 111.
³⁶ E.g., *PL* 191, 501c (on Ps. 52.4) or 1037b (on Ps. 117.16). On the wondering poet and the process of composition, see Carruthers's discussion in Chapter 10.
³⁷ For Aristotle, Longinus and other examples of ancient literary theory taking this form, see Russell and Winterbottom (eds), *Ancient Literary Criticism*.
³⁸ A point borne out by Woods in Chapter 1. In this regard, Minnis was a fellow-traveller with the American scholar Judson Allen, also influenced by Hunt's work, and whose *Ethical Poetic* appeared two years before *MTA*. Their affinities and disagreements are signalled in Minnis's review (1984).

medieval ideas of literature and its interpretation tend to be more varied, more suggestive, even – as in the Anselmian gloss on authorial breath – more aphoristic than what we might now expect.[39] When offering such glosses, whether in their *accessus* or elsewhere in their commentaries, later medieval critics seem only rarely to have meant for them to 'add up' to a consistent or coherent theoretical statement. Admittedly, my examples so far have focused on twelfth-century material, but the same point could be made for later works, which are similarly built of more-or-less independent glosses. Hence, for example, discussing the *forma tractatus* of the Canticle, Giles of Rome (d. 1316) notes that 'the order of the chapters in relation to each other, if properly understood, soothes the mind and gives pleasure' – a discrete comment, tied to his preceding account of the *forma tractandi* only through its shared reference to the word 'sweetness', taken from the pericope at the start of the prologue (Cant. 2. 14).[40] Such ideas about the text might best be considered useful notes for a reader to bear in mind while making their way through the commentary that follows, and they may help to draw meanings out of the text at various points, though not – I think – everywhere and always in the same ways. Viewed in these terms, the medieval habit of collecting ideas about literature and interpretation as a series of discrete glosses may have some potentially compelling and largely unappreciated affordances. That is, the freedom to collect and mix such glosses, in almost every case tailored to reflect the idiosyncrasies of individual critics or new circumstances of interpretation, to put these glosses together in new combinations and to bring them to bear on different works of literature, without concern for the creation of an overarching, internally consistent or totalising thing called 'theory' – all of this can make later medieval ideas about literature and interpretation surprisingly perceptive, sometimes startlingly novel and creative. When approached as a larger and variegated field, marked by the same accretive and supplementing impulses as later medieval criticism more generally – and a field that, to be sure, includes glosses of seemingly prescient sophistication – later medieval literary theory emerges as an especially complex and robust intellectual tradition.[41]

---

[39] I suspect, for example, that many interpretive theories set out in commentaries could also be found by a careful reading of Walther (ed.), *Proverbia sententiaeque*.
[40] Minnis and Scott, p. 246.
[41] As a large and growing body of scholarship has made it clear, medieval ideas of literature have exerted influence far beyond the Middle Ages, in some cases informing works of twentieth-century theory as well. See Holsinger, *Premodern Condition*, and Cole and Smith (eds), *Legitimacy of the Middle Ages*. And Ardis Butterfield usefully reminds me of the accretive and non-narrative quality of

Introduction: Criticism, Theory and Later Medieval Text 17

And all of this means, too, that ideas of literature recovered in the study of medieval theory and criticism are not to be treated as definitive or exhaustive in our own interpretations of medieval texts. As Denis Feeney warns of ancient commentary, 'We are not dealing with a problematic body of material ("literature") which can be explained with the aid of a less problematic body of material ("criticism"): we are dealing with numerous, often contesting, strands of problematic material which interact with each other in innumerable categories of time and space.'[42] Indeed, modern efforts to 'apply' ideas from medieval commentaries in the interpretation of medieval literature with a kind of dogmatic consistency will almost inevitably founder – hence, for example, the fate of the senses of Scripture in the hands of Robertsonian critics.[43] The historicised attitudes and interpretive approaches recovered from medieval commentaries should be studied in their own right, and they should help us draw yet more meanings from later medieval poetry and prose – but they do not exhaust the interpretation of these texts.

### Interpretation, Invention and Imagination

By recognising medieval literary theory and criticism as a diverse and highly variable body of ideas, shifting to fit the needs of divergent interpretive settings, this volume stakes a claim for the potentially broad appeal of this material – in literary studies, certainly, in Latin and in the many European vernaculars, but also in the history of ideas, the history of philosophy and theology, and the history of emotions, to name just a few. This breadth is reflected in the wide variety of sources taken up in the chapters that follow. Some contributors focus on exegetical prose and glosses like those discussed in the foregoing sections, while others trace the ends to which the ideas and practices of medieval commentary were put in pastoralia, medical texts, mirrors for princes or theological-scientific encyclopaedias, and others tease out the ways in which later medieval vernacular poetry contributed to these critical discourses. Diverse in

---

some twentieth-century theory. For more on the post-medieval influence of scholastic theory and criticism, see the contributions by Cornelius and Copeland, Chapters 11 and 12.
[42] Feeney, 'Criticism Ancient and Modern', p. 444.
[43] In this regard, it bears emphasising that the great twentieth-century work on the four senses, De Lubac's *Exégèse médiévale*, transforms a common but flexible medieval idea into something far more rigid and systematic. De Lubac's doctrine of the four senses is very much his own creation, though frequently treated today as an historical project. See, for example, Fredric Jameson's 'use of the patristic and medieval system of the four levels', for which, he says, he has relied on De Lubac. Jameson, *Allegory and Ideology*, p. xv and n. 10.

content, these materials are all also diversely interrelated, and their status as a more-or-less loosely unified field is captured, I think, in the three terms that make up our volume's subtitle: interpretation, invention and imagination.

Of the texts discussed in the following chapters, the commentaries and glosses quite clearly fit under the heading of *interpretation*, a term which – in its medieval Latin form – generally referred to the careful exposition of authoritative sources, including the translation of those sources into new languages, under the notion of translation as *expositio per aliam linguam* (interpretation by means of a different language).[44] In contrast, vernacular poetry offers clear examples of *invention* – 'the "creation of something new" (or at least different)', including 'ideas or material objects, ... works of art, music and literature'. But, of course, that definition could quite easily include the inventive work undertaken by exegetes, and, as Mary Carruthers – whom I've just been quoting – reminds us, medieval Latin *inventio* also has some of the sense of its other modern English derivative, 'inventory', the 'storage of many diverse materials' that can be brought out, re-arranged and worked up in the process of creative invention.[45] What else is a commentary, if not a carefully organised inventory of ideas, waiting for such creative deployment? And, of course, in the other direction, medieval vernacular poets were eager to present their work under the general heading of *interpretatio* and, relatedly, *compilatio*.[46] Our third term, then, *imagination*, attempts to capture some of the overlap between the other two, to articulate the intellectual work they have in common. Admittedly, such interpretive and inventive creativity is perhaps more in keeping with Romantic ideas of imagination than medieval ones of *imaginatio* or *phantasia* – a cognitive faculty often regarded with suspicion, prone to wander and open to all sorts of unsavoury influence. Yet, as Minnis notes, for at least some late medieval thinkers, poetry's 'imaginative power can help the human mind to formulate charitable possibilities in areas of enquiry wherein a mere mortal cannot expect to reach firm conclusions'.[47] That openness to new and seemingly boundless possibilities, and the role of written texts – especially poetry – in encouraging and enabling it, can serve as a neat summary of this volume as a whole.

---

[44] See Kraebel, *Experiments in Interpretation*, pp. 106–7, with further references.
[45] Carruthers, *Craft of Thought*, pp. 11–12.
[46] See Kraebel, 'Modes of Authorship', esp. pp. 99–100, and see Johnson's discussion in Chapter 7.
[47] Minnis, 'Medieval Imagination' (2005), p. 252.

The collection opens with studies of later medieval interpretation, beginning with two chapters on *accessus*. In Chapter 1, Marjorie Curry Woods presents Munich, Bayerische Staatsbibliothek MS Clm 391, an early thirteenth-century collection of common Latin school texts, each prefaced by glosses providing material associated with the form of *accessus* which Hunt dubbed 'type C'.[48] As Woods observes, the quality and quantity of these glosses are inconsistent across the manuscript, suggesting at once the exegete's (or exegetes') differing understandings of the interpretive categories germane to these various texts, and a sense of knowledge accumulating across the book. This manuscript – in Woods's hands – can thus cast more light on how *accessus* were used in teaching Latin literature. By the end of the thirteenth century, the *accessus* form seen in Clm 391 was giving way to a model deriving from the works of Aristotle, according to which the text was assessed in terms of its four causes (*efficiens, materialis, formalis, finalis*). In Chapter 2, Jocelyn Wogan-Browne explores the deployment of that form in the prologue to an insular French poetic text, the *Lumere as lais* (*Light for Laypeople*) of Pierre d'Abernon de Fetcham (fl. 1267–76). As Wogan-Browne emphasises, Pierre's work was part of a larger trend in French-language encyclopaedism, compiling specialist material from works in both Latin – some only recently translated from Arabic – and the vernacular, and reflecting not just the 'insider knowledge' of Latinate clerics, but also the interests, authority and patronage of the laity.[49]

Chapters 1 and 2 focus on trends in the interpretation of secular material, classical and technical/scientific writings. With Chapter 3, the collection turns to the other major locus of later medieval interpretive attention, the Latin Bible. Gilbert Dahan takes up the question of how thirteenth-century exegetes accounted for biblical authors' recourse to poetic language – potentially troubling, in light of the greater precision and clarity of scientific language. Dahan charts the gradual development of a surprisingly consistent response to this problem, which – he argues – can be found in approaches to the variegated *modi* (literary styles) adopted by biblical writers and, finally, in the need to convey inexpressible spiritual truths within the limitations of human language. Dahan highlights the recurrent use of the ps.-Dionysian terms *manuductio* or *manuducere* – a

---

[48] Hunt, 'Introductions to the *Artes*'. See too Minnis and Scott, pp. 12–36; *MTA*, pp. 15–28.
[49] The collaborative nature of vernacular scholasticism and the notion that what was made available and in what form reflected the interests and preferences of audiences, has been emphasised by Waters, *Translating Clergie*.

kind of authorial handholding, whereby poetic language is used to draw the reader up to divine knowledge. This idea endured into the fourteenth century, seen, for example, in John Wyclif's (d. 1384) argument that the earthly text of Scripture is only called 'sacred' on account of 'the guiding (*propter manuduccionem*) by which it leads believers to the awareness of the heavenly Scripture'.[50]

The next four chapters focus on the complex relationship between, on the one hand, scholastic theory and criticism, typically carried out in Latin, and, on the other, the larger body of insular literary production, in Latin and the vernacular(s), recovering some of the major routes by which ideas of scholastic interpretation reached readers and authors outside the universities. In Chapter 4, Ralph Hanna explores Robert Holcot's (d. 1349) commentary on the biblical Book of Wisdom. Holcot was part of a group of exegetes Beryl Smalley identified as the 'classicising friars', and Hanna focuses on the colourful rehearsing of classical literary and philosophical material shared by members of this group. With particular attention to Holcot's quotations of the ps.-Ovidian *De vetula*, Hanna argues that this habit points to the exegete's goal of supplying a model for his university audience, a way of presenting theological insights that is at once arresting and challenging, leaving the reader/auditor with rich materials for further rumination. As he observes, the wide circulation of Holcot's work reflects not just the text's classroom performance as lectures, but also the exegete's aspirations for its use by preachers with only limited university training. My own chapter then takes up the Latin and Middle English biblical commentaries of Holcot's contemporary, the Oxford-trained hermit-mystic Richard Rolle (d. 1349), whose texts seem meant not for preaching, but for private meditation, with the ultimate goal of preparing the reader for the ecstatic experiences Rolle believed to be the pinnacle of contemplative life. I recover theories of exegetical authority from across Rolle's corpus, reading them alongside scholastic ideas about the relationship between the authority of inspired biblical writers and the ongoing work of their interpreters. Positioning himself in this tradition, Rolle is far from hostile to the ideas and forms of scholastic literature. Instead, the mystic's career is marked by a desire to turn the resources of the schools – especially lemmatised biblical commentary – to meditative and caritative ends.

Bringing together the focus on scientific literature and preacherly concerns seen in earlier chapters, in Chapter 6 Joe Stadolnik argues for the importance of medieval *artes praedicandi* in the creation of Henry Daniel

---

[50] Wyclif, *De veritate*, 6, ed. by Buddenseig, I, 115. Wyclif goes on to cite Grosseteste.

OP's *Liber uricrisiarum* (*c.* 1379), a guide to assessing health from the evidence of urine. As Stadolnik observes, Daniel drew on the rhetorical strategies recommended for the aspiring preacher to craft his clear and useful text – adopting a *stylus grossus* (simple style), persistently defining his jargon and keeping his role as compiler before the reader's eyes. Yet neither this emphasis on simplicity nor his status as *compilator* prevents Daniel from developing his own distinctive style, a writerly bedside manner that can, as it were, 'help the medicine go down'. In Chapter 7, by contrast, Ian Johnson presents an author working in the opposite direction, explaining basic catechesis in a series of increasingly elaborate configurations. Johnson's chapter focuses on Reginald Pecock (d. *c.* 1459), whose creative engagement with scholastic ideas of *ordinatio*, the division of a text into ever smaller pieces, offered various attempts to present Christian doctrine in Middle English. Johnson charts Pecock's ordinational reshufflings – in tables, dialogues, syllogisms and exhortations – *and* his efforts to present all of this in a coherent, usable text.

These chapters thus focus on some of the major texts of scholastic commentary and theory and on the transformation of those texts to convey specialised knowledge to audiences beyond the schools. The works discussed in Chapters 2 and 4–7 all exist to be read both within those learned communities and outside of them – to serve the needs of university masters in the composition of yet more commentaries, *and* to be studied, meditated upon and/or consulted by less well-educated members of the clergy, by vowed religious and by the laity, in any number of 'real world' contexts. (And note that this is true of texts composed in Latin and the vernacular alike.) Their study is therefore crucial to understanding the phenomenon addressed in the next three chapters, that is, the creative engagement with scholastic theory and criticism on the part of later medieval vernacular poets. Certainly, this is not to say that the authors of vernacular verse did not (or could not) consult the kinds of commentaries discussed by Dahan in Chapter 3, but rather that these less specialised texts are responsible for much more of the familiarity with scholastic ideas and forms encountered in that literature. In light of Hanna's chapter, for example, it should be unsurprising to find Thomas Hoccleve (d. 1423) citing what 'Holcote seith vpon the book ... / Of Sapience'.[51] And here Geoffrey Chaucer (d. *c.* 1400) provides another salutary example, with the Nun's Priest's reference (at VII.3242) to Thomas Bradwardine's *De causa Dei* invoking a

---

[51] *La Male regle*, 249–50, in Hoccleve, *'My Compleinte' and Other Poems*, ed. by Ellis, p. 71.

text that – like Holcot on Wisdom – seems to have been meant for study within the university and beyond it.[52]

The next three chapters take up different questions of vernacular poets' engagement with scholastic literary theory and criticism, all arguing not for the reception or deployment of Latinate scholastic ideas in vernacular literary invention, and *not just* for the importance of such ideas for our interpretation of that literature, but most fully for the sophisticated contribution of these authors to the larger discourse of later medieval literary theory.[53] In Chapter 8, Jessica Rosenfeld reads Jean de Meun's (d. *c.* 1305) portion of the *Roman de la Rose* as committed to exploring the intersections of the political and the erotic. As Rosenfeld observes, this project was enabled by the Latin translation of Aristotle's *Politics* by William of Moerbeke (d. *c.* 1286), a text that was almost immediately made the object of learned commentary at the University of Paris. Rosenfeld casts light on the unique contribution of the *Rose* to these intellectual trends, focusing especially on the poem's allegory and the poet's recurrent interest in the Ovidian image of the Golden Age. Focus on allegory continues in Chapter 9, where Nicolette Zeeman takes up ideas of personification in William Langland's (d. *c.* 1390) *Piers Plowman*. Zeeman explores the various techniques by which Langland achieves his prosopopoeial effects – for example, through structural contrast and contradiction, or through the complication of the abstracted personification with specific, naturalistic detail – as the poet pursues an unusually elaborate and experimental approach to a device which, as Zeeman sets out, was theorised at length in late antique and earlier medieval rhetorical treatises and *artes poetriae*. Some of the same ancient rhetorical treatises inform Mary Carruthers's study in Chapter 10, accounting for the role played by dislocation and distress – solitude, emotional agitation, sleeplessness, pacing, nail-biting – in creating the state of mind needed for literary invention. The mental states described by Carruthers inform Will's wandering in *Piers*, the monastic *cubiculum* of Bernard of Clairvaux (d. 1153) and the dreamy garden of the late fourteenth-century *Pearl*, and her essay thus serves as a reminder of the important role of monastic traditions in later medieval literature and scholastic thought, illustrating the ways in

---

[52] Minnis, *Valuing the Vernacular* (2009), pp. 41–42; and see too Leff, *Bradwardine and the Pelagians*, pp. 13–14.

[53] This is an approach, then, that our contributors share with other recent scholarship: see, e.g., Denery et al. (eds), *Uncertain Knowledge*, Morton, *Philosophical Context*, Knox et al. (eds), *Medieval Thought Experiments*, Morton and Nievergelt (eds), *Thirteenth-Century Thought*.

which the category of 'theory' can bring together a wide range of seemingly disparate works.

The book's final pair of essays trace the longevity of scholastic theory and criticism. In Chapter 11, Ian Cornelius presents George Colvile's glossed translation of *De consolatione*, printed in 1556. Attending to the textual tradition of Boethius's work, Colvile's handling of *metra* and *prosae* and his potential familiarity with Chaucer's *Boece*, Cornelius illustrates the continuing possibilities of scholastic translation – understood under the rubric of interpretation, as noted above – into the sixteenth century, and his survey of pre-1556 printed editions of *De consolatione* reinforces the ongoing importance of this text in the era of Renaissance humanism. Such legacies are pursued further still in Chapter 12, where Rita Copeland brings us back to the question of the later medieval reception of the newly-translated Aristotle. Copeland focuses on Giles of Rome, and in particular on his reliance on a variety of Aristotelian works – especially the *Rhetoric* – in his handbook of rulers, *De regimine principum* (*c.* 1277). By recovering Giles's notion of the ruler's awareness and regulation of his own emotions as crucial for the proper governing of the state, Copeland is able to trace an otherwise unrecognised scholastic theory far beyond the Middle Ages, in the writings of Thomas Hobbes (d. 1679) and Giambattista Vico (d. 1744). If scholastic literary forms were easily parodied in and after the Renaissance, the reach of individual scholastic ideas proves to be long indeed.

CHAPTER I

# *Access through* Accessus
## *Gateways to Learning in a Manuscript of School Texts*
### Marjorie Curry Woods

The world of medieval *accessus* is both puzzling and enlightening, for these formal introductions to texts produced for academic settings offer insights – but often only partial ones – into medieval analytical and critical practice. They were intended to precede texts, to provide a framework within which texts could be both encapsulated and introduced, and as a result they have become central to modern discussion of the history of teaching texts.[1] Especially familiar, in this regard, is a large collection of *accessus* copied together in a twelfth-century manuscript from Tegernsee, now Munich, Bayerische Staatsbibliothek, Clm 19475. Most of the *accessus* collected in this manuscript were translated and thus made available to a wide variety of scholars and critics in 1988 by Alastair Minnis and Brian Scott, who call them 'Literary Prefaces'.[2] More recently, Stephen Wheeler has edited and translated the complete run of Clm 19475's *accessus*.[3] This Tegernsee manuscript offers important access to what one teacher (or collector of teaching materials) composed or put together, revealing a varied but recognisable approach to medieval texts in the classroom at the time of its copying. While they vary greatly in length and amount of detail, each *accessus* in Clm 19475 answers a series of standard questions: what are the title, subject-matter, intention of the author, usefulness and part of philosophy under which the text is placed?[4] When we read through the

---

[1] The term *accessus* is both singular and plural (with a change in vowel length for the latter) in Latin. They are often referred to now as 'prologues', as in Hamesse (ed.), *Les Prologues médiévaux*, and Copeland, 'Academic Prologues', pp. 151–63. In the manuscript discussed here, however, one of the texts is described as containing its own *accessus* and other kinds of introductory materials are also found. Minnis's term 'Literary Prefaces' is the most attractive and best fits the texts whose *accessus* are examined here, but the same kind of semi-standardised introduction is used with non-literary texts as well (see *Les Prologues médiévaux*). I therefore retain the Latin term.

[2] Minnis and Scott, p. 12. Scott's translation is based on Huygens (ed.), *Accessus ad auctores*. See also the earlier translation of Ovidian material in this manuscript by Elliot, '*Accessus ad auctores*'.

[3] Wheeler (ed. and tr.), *Accessus ad auctores*.

[4] These categories are identified by R. W. Hunt as constituting his 'type C' *Accessus*. On Hunt's types A, B and C, see Minnis and Scott, pp. 13–16. Wheeler offers a slightly different taxonomy of

collection we learn these topics of inquiry ourselves and begin to anticipate their answers. As Wheeler notes, 'The order of these authors follows a graded course of study from simpler to advanced reading', and the cumulative effect is of repetition and variation within a standard but flexible paradigm.

While we have learned and can still learn much from the Tegernsee collection of *accessus*, I have wanted for some time to examine the sequence and content of *accessus* copied with the texts to which they provide the introduction, rather than – as in the Tegernsee manuscript – apart from those texts. I therefore searched for a school manuscript that contained some of the same texts, a volume that might serve as a fitting counter-example or complement to Clm 19475, and this search led me to a thirteenth-century manuscript now in the same library, Clm 391.[5] This book was owned by the famous fifteenth-century German bibliophile and humanist Hartmann Schedel (1440–1514),[6] but it is not one of those provocative and forward-thinking codices that were displayed in the 2014 exhibition of Schedel's manuscripts mounted by the library, or one of those he copied and annotated himself.[7] Rather, it is one that Schedel purchased, probably near the end of his life, and probably in France (according to Elisabeth Klemm) or Germany (according to Michael Baldzuhn).[8]

The contents of Schedel's manuscript are the six short classical and pseudo-classical school texts evoked many years ago by Marc Boas as the *Liber Catonianus*, among the most important in the medieval curriculum.[9]

---

'Servian, rhetorical, philosophical*, and *modern*', which correspond roughly to Hunt's, with the modern scheme as a modified version of the philosophical scheme, deploying three or four headings: '*subject matter, intention, utility* (optional) and *part of philosophy under which it is classified*' (p. 2). For the historical bibliography on *accessus*, see the references in Minnis and Johnson, 'Introduction' (2005), pp. 1–12, here p. 2, and Meyer, '*Intentio auctoris, utilitas libri*'.

[5] I first saw Clm 391, which was not available online at this time, in 2012, and then again in 2014, when I was working on manuscripts of the *Achilleid* (see Woods, *Weeping for Dido*, pp. 52, 60, 67–68). The further work for this chapter is based on a digitised microfilm.

[6] On Clm 391, see Klemm, *Die illuminierten Handschriften*, I, 193–94, and II, 168, pl. 503; Anderson, *Manuscripts of Statius*, I, 241–42; and Baldzuhn, *Schulbücher im Trivium*, II, 634–36. It was consulted in Osternacher (ed.), *Theoduli eclogam*, p. 20, and Öberg (ed.), *Versus Maximiani*, p. 66.

[7] *Welten des Wissens: Die Bibliothek und die Weltchronik des Nürnberger Arztes Hartmann Schedel (1440–1514)*, at the Bayerische Staatsbibliothek, Munich, 19 November 2014–1 March 2015. On a university manuscript copied and annotated by Schedel, see Woods, *Classroom Commentaries*, pp. 222–27 and pl. 12.

[8] Klemm, *Die illuminierten Handschriften*, I, 194; and Baldzuhn, *Schulbücher im Trivium*, II, 635.

[9] Boas, 'De Librorum catonianorum historia'. I have discussed the traditional content (and order, listed in the next note) of the *Liber Catonianus* in several earlier articles, the most recent of which is

Here, however, they are compiled in an order different from that in Boas, which is often considered standard.[10] As the list of their contents reveals, the amount of original introductory material varies and diminishes severely after the first two texts:

1. *Distichs of Cato* – several *accessus* on f. 1ʳ; text and glosses on ff. 1ᵛ–9ʳ.
2. *Eclogue of Theodulus* – two *accessus* and other introductory material on ff. 9ʳ–10ᵛ; text and glosses on ff. 11ʳ–18ʳ.
3. Statius, *Achilleid* – short *accessus* on f. 18ᵛ; text and glosses on ff. 18ᵛ–42ᵛ.[11]
4. Claudian, *Rape of Proserpine* – two later *accessus* on f. 43ʳ⁻ᵛ; text and glosses only on ff. 44ʳ–69ᵛ.
5. Avianus, *Fables* – short marginal *accessus* on f. 69ᵛ; text and glosses on ff. 69ᵛ–85ʳ.[12]
6. Maximian, *Elegies* – short marginal *accessus* on f. 85ʳ; text and very few glosses on ff. 85ʳ–98ʳ.

The texts themselves are all copied in a single hand, with each page prepared with room for ample marginal and interlinear glosses. The first two texts are preceded by more than one *accessus* copied separately from the text itself, which starts on its own page. Beginning with the third text, however, each work picks up immediately after the end of the preceding one, and any scribal *accessus* inserted from here on (as opposed to one added later, as we will see) is formatted as a long marginal comment.

As a complement to Minnis and Scott's invaluable treatment of the 'Literary Prefaces' in Tegernsee, in the pages that follow I alternately discuss and then edit and translate as much as possible of these scribal *accessus*. In the process, I hope to offer a mental journey through the approaches to the basic school texts in the manuscript.[13]

---

'Teaching of Poetic Composition', pp. 124–28. On the more flexible contents of the *Liber Catonianus* (especially in England), see Hunt, *Teaching and Learning*, pp. 66–79, and Cannon, *Literacy to Literature*, pp. 41–44.

[10] On the order of texts in this manuscript see Baldzuhn, *Schulbücher im Trivium*, II, 635. He suggests that the change in Clm 391 from the traditional order of *Distichs of Cato*, *Eclogue of Theodulus*, *Fables of Avianus*, *Rape of Proserpine*, *Achilleid of Statius* and *Elegies of Maximian* indicates a compiler (or source) out of touch with contemporary pedagogical interests. Baldzuhn finds little evidence of later use of the manuscript in the *Avianus* section and calls it 'a pure desk copy' (*reine Schreibtisch-Kopie*, p. 636), but the later *accessus* and glosses added in other parts of the manuscript suggest continued pedagogical concerns, whether the manuscript was used in a specific schoolroom or not.

[11] Anderson, *Manuscripts of Statius*, I, no. 362.   [12] Baldzuhn, *Schulbücher im Trivium*, I, 634–36.

[13] Later additions are therefore mentioned but not provided in my edited texts. For convenience the Latin will be included in the notes. Words that are indecipherable are marked with ***. All bolding,

These first *accessus* in Clm 391 introduce their texts using the same framework as in the *accessus* in the earlier Tegernsee manuscript, with the same basic categories of title, subject-matter, author's intention, usefulness and part of philosophy, although often varying the order. The secondary categories and information supplied in the *accessus* in Clm 391, however, are usually different: the *accessus* to the *Distichs of Cato* addresses the reason for undertaking the work and the structural divisions, and it provides a discussion of two kinds of justice; the *accessus* to the *Eclogue of Theodulus* introduces literary concepts and terminology, including character, argument, fable and history, types of authors' prologues and the four virtues; multiple intentions are provided for the *Achilleid* (an *accessus* to which is not included among those in Clm 19475); and a specific three-fold division of the beginning of a text is identified and applied to the *Achilleid*, and then applied but found wanting in the *accessus* to the *Fables* of Avianus and *Elegies* of Maximian. In the *accessus* to the *Fables* we find related but not identical terminology for tale, fable, story and history, while in the *accessus* to the *Elegies of Maximian*, the usefulness to the author is distinguished from the usefulness to the audience.

Within these *accessus* to texts in Clm 391 we find some material that appears unusual or especially revealing, therefore, as well as the kind of repetitions and redundancy common in manuscripts of school texts – and in some cases the manuscript offers multiple and not always consistent examples of a specific category. Just as important as these distinctions, though, is the reinforcing of the basic paradigm of access to texts shared by both Clm 391 and Clm 19475. We are consistently reminded that the terms discussed repeatedly in the *accessus* in both manuscripts provide a lens through which the literary works that follow are to be viewed.

### *Distichs of Cato*

On the first numbered folio of Clm 391 are two complete columns of loosely organised and somewhat repetitive academic prologues to the *Distichs of Cato*, with the text itself beginning on the verso. In this work we are immediately immersed in the medieval literary world of proverbial statements about conduct and behaviour – hence the alternate title, *Ethica*. These comprise one of the most important building blocks of medieval composition practice, as we see at the end of the second *accessus*.

paragraphing and line numbers are editorial and abbreviations have been expanded silently. Spelling, capitalisation, underlining and punctuation are retained from the manuscript.

The **first** *accessus* to **Cato** begins by quoting the initial word of the text, where the author notices 'the very great number of those who go seriously astray in the path of conduct' (Prol.).[14] This *accessus* offers a double perspective based on the author's personal and universal audiences.

> *As I noticed* (Prol.). This book is **divided into four parts** [= books]. In the **first** he writes about God's justice. Justice is twofold: natural and positional. Natural justice is what is just in itself; positional [justice] is a condition coming out of a specific reason limited to itself. In the **second** [book] he writes about prudence. Prudence is the distinguishing of good and evil with the magnifying of the one and the dismissal of the other. Alternatively, prudence is the foresight of future things. . . . In the **third** [he writes] about fortitude: fortitude is the strength of engaging with difficulties. In the **fourth** about self-control.[15] First, therefore, he shows the **reason for undertaking the work**, which is two-fold: universal and personal. The universal reason is the general instruction of all, which is noted where he says 'to the aid of their belief'; the personal reason is [the instruction] of his son . . . which he notes where he says, 'dearest son' (Prol.). The **subject-matter** in the book is this: they are the good morals (*mores*)[16] of Cato. The **intention** turns on the subject-matter,[17] for he intends to recall not only his son, but also, as I have said, all men in general from the wandering ways of vices to good morals (*mores*), and to sweetly inculcate in them the intention to live well. The **usefulness** is that, once this work has been read *** . . . [Thereafter follows a damaged and largely illegible section on the **author**, involving a discussion of the two historical Catos, arguing that neither could be the author of this text. It concludes as follows:] I have said that Tullius [Cicero] composed this work, and he put a title to his work from the name of a more authoritative person. **It is put under** [the part of philosophy called] **ethics**, for it discusses behaviour (*mores*) in any situation you like – except in the beginning of the second book, 'If perchance [you would fain acquaint yourself] with farming', etc. (2.1) with seven verses following, which, as some say, are not originally part of this book.[18] Having seen these things, let us turn to the text.[19]

---

[14] Quotations are taken from Duff and Duff (eds and trs), *Minor Latin Poets*, pp. 585–639.
[15] Cf. Roos, *Sentenza e proverbio*, p. 203.
[16] For Cato, 'morals' is correct, but in the medieval manuscripts of literary and rhetorical texts with which I am familiar, this term is used as the reason for putting almost every literary text (including those in this manuscript) under the category of ethics. It often means something more negative or simply descriptive, like 'behaviour', as it is translated a few lines below.
[17] Cf. Munk Olsen, 'Accessus to Classical Poets', p. 137: 'The "intentio" (intention) is closely connected with the subject-matter because they cannot exist without each other'.
[18] For these lines as possibly spurious, see Duff and Duff (eds and trs), *Minor Latin Poets*, p. 604, n. 1; also Roos, *Sentenza e proverbio*, p. 202.
[19] Clm 391, f. 1ra: '*Cvm animaduerterem* (Prol.). Iste liber **diuiditur in <quatuor>** [*** MS] **partes**. In prima agit de dei iusticia. Iusticia autem duplex naturalis et positiua. Naturalis est iusticia que in

This last phrase usually signals the end of an *accessus* and the beginning of glosses on individual words and phrases. Here, however, we have immediately afterward a **second** *accessus* **to Cato** with overlapping topics addressed in roughly the same order, but somewhat condensed:

> In the beginning of this little work five things are to be considered: the **reason** [for undertaking it], **title**, **subject-matter**, **intention**, **under what part of philosophy it is placed** ... [The **reason** again concerns his son:] fearing lest he follow the bad behaviour of certain Romans, he wrote this book by which he instructs in good behaviour (*bonos mores*) primarily his son but universally every man ... The **title** is 'Here begins Cato', and 'title' is derived from *tyto*, which is 'sun'. For just as the sun illuminates all the world, so the title illuminates the whole work to follow.[20] The **intention** is to instruct his son and all men (in) good behaviour/morals (*mores*). [The section discussing **under what part of philosophy it is placed** is damaged and not transcribed. On **prologues**:] One [kind of] **prologue** is said to anticipate the topic, the other to be outside the topic. A prologue which is said to anticipate the topic briefly touches on what [the author] says in what follows, such as the prologue of Cato here. A prologue outside the topic therefore speaks [not] about what follows, as in Sallust's prologue.[21] In the title is indicated the intention,[22] which is the following: the **intention** of the things in this work is to give the precepts of the poetic art. The poetic art is instruction that provides a specific path and rationale; practical knowledge of writing poetically is called the poetic art.[23]

---

suis consistit. Positiua est habitus ueniens ex ratione uniquique quod suum est distribuendum In **secunda** ait de prvdencia. Prudencia autem est discretio boni et mali cum dilacione unius et abiectione alterius. Vel aliter prvdencia est futurorum prouidencia ... In **tercia** de fortitudine fortitudo autem est uis aggrediendi ardua. In **quarta** de temperancia. Primo ergo ostendit **causam suscepti operis** que duplex est. Communis et priuata. Communis est instrvctio omnium generaliter que notatur vbi dicit opinioni eorum Priuata est filij sui a quolibet fidelis subpernosa filij instrvctio quod notat vbi dicit fili carissime. **Materia** in opera est hoc sunt boni mores catonis **Intencio** vesatur circa materiam intendit, enim non tantum filium suum sed sicut dixi vniuersos homines generaliter a uia viciorum erronea ad bonos mores reuocare et eis intencionem bene uivendi dulciter insinuare. **Wtilitas** est ut perlecto hoc libro \*\*\* ... dici quod Tullius hoc opus composuit. Et a nomine persone magis autentice opus suum intitulauit. **Ethice supponitur**, loquitur enim de moribus in qualibet sui distinctione nisi in principio secondi libri 'Telluris si forte' etc. (2.1) bene infra vij versus quod sicud quidam dicunt non est de libro. hiis visis ad litteram accedamus'.

[20] A common gloss; cf. Allen, *Ethical Poetic*, p. 57, n. 24.
[21] That is, one summarises, the other discusses a separate, more general issue, as in both of Sallust's prologues.
[22] See also n. 17.
[23] Clm 391, f. 1^{ra–b}: 'In principio huius opusculi v inquiruntur. **Causa**. **Tytulus**. **Materia**. **Intencio**. **Cui parti philosophie supponitur** ... de quo timens ne ipse malos mores assequentur ceterorum Romanorum scripsit hunc librum a quo instrvit bonos mores principaliter filium suum sed vniversaliter <per omnem> [\*\*\* *MS*] hominem ... **Tytulus** est Incipit Cato et dicitur titulus a tyto quod est sol quia sicut titan illuminat totum mundum sic titulus illuminat totum sebsequens opus. **Intencio** est filium suum <et omne>s [\*\*\*s *MS*] homines bonos mores instruere'. **Cui parti**

This second and very different discussion of the intention and title implies that this *accessus* itself may be the result of some effort at compilation, and I wonder if it might even have been copied by mistake from the *accessus* to another work. I hope not, though, since this somewhat casual identification of teaching the *Distichs of Cato* with writing poetically would underscore the centrality of proverbial wisdom to medieval composition theory, and to verse as the assumed form of composition.

Following the second *accessus*, the scribe copies three more paragraphs of ***accessus*-like material**, the first two of which also discuss the identity of the author, and – like the first *accessus*– reject the attribution to Cato. The first paragraph (much marred): 'We say therefore that whoever was the author of the book named it after someone else'.[24] The second says that the text is a 'hipograph, i.e., by an unknown author'.[25] The third of these paragraphs is actually a **mini-*accessus* to Cato**, repeating in more condensed form material seen in the longer *accessus*, presumably taken from another source but also providing an efficient review:

> *As I noticed* (Prol.). The four cardinal virtues are the **subject-matter** of this [work], and the **intention** revolves around this subject, namely the aforementioned virtues and their types. The **usefulness** is twofold: specific and universal. The specific is the usefulness to his own son; the universal is to all those listening, whom he vicariously calls sons. It is **placed under ethics** since it treats of behaviour/morals (*mores*). The **title** is, 'Here begins the *Ethics of Cato*'.[26]

## *Eclogue of Theodulus*

The *Eclogue of Theodulus* often follows the *Distichs* in medieval manuscripts of school texts, and in this regard Clm 391 is no

---

philosophie supponatur *** ... **Prologus** dicitur alius ante rem, alius praeter rem. Ille dicitur ante rem qui breuiter tangit quod in sequentibus dicit vt prologus istius catonis. Ille autem preter rem igitur de sequentibus <non> dicit vt prologo salustij. In tytulo notatur intencio quia talis est: **intencio** horum in hoc opera est dare precepta de arte poetica. Poetica ars est precepcio que dat certam uiam et rationem poetice noticia scribendi poetica Ars vocatur'.

[24] Clm 391, f. 1^rb: 'Dicimus ergo quod quicumque fuit auctor librum istum sub nomine alieno intitulauit'.

[25] Clm 391, f. 1^rb: 'Liber iste cuius lectioni insistimus dicitur ypocripho, idest ignote auctoris ...'.

[26] Clm 391, f. 1rb: '*Cum animaduerterem* (Prol.). **Materia** huius auctoris sunt quatuorum virtutes cardinales. **Intencio** versatur circa materiam, scilicet predictas uirtutes et earum species. **vtilitas** duplex est specialis et comunis Specialis est utilitas filii sui uel proprii Communis est omnium audiencium quos more uicarorum filios appellat. Ethice supponitur quia de moribus tractat. **Tytulus** est incipit ethica Katonis etc.'.

exception.²⁷ The *accessus* to this work begin immediately in the space left blank below the end of the double-columned text of the *Distichs* (f. 9^(ra–b)). The pseudo-classical *Eclogue* introduces students to quatrains (slightly longer units than the one- and two-line compositions comprising the *Distichs*) and, just as significantly, to great bodies of narrative material. Whereas the *Distichs* provide proverbial discourse to (re)use, the *Eclogue* provides a rich storehouse of matching and duelling exempla from pagan mythology and the Hebrew Bible.²⁸ The former are told by a young male shepherd 'born in Athens', Pseustis (Falsehood), the latter by Alithea (Truth), a shepherdess 'descended from King David's line'.²⁹

The **first *accessus* to the *Eclogue of Theodulus*** resembles that of the commentary by Alexander Neckham (d. 1219), described by Betty Nye Quinn, although at least one of the identifying cues does not appear to be present.³⁰ The scribe was evidently flummoxed by the more exotic terms, and I am indebted to Quinn's partial transcriptions for some of the conjectures that follow. Watch for the consistent use of threes throughout, a common medieval mnemonic and pedagogical device.³¹ There is also an emphasis in the second half of the *accessus* on the variety of aspects of style (*stilus*) that can be attributed to Theodulus. Rather than reflecting the three-fold rhetorical division of style into high, middle and low, alluded to earlier in the *accessus* with regard to Virgil, it here appears to refer to three different types of writing found in the text: argument (introduction at the beginning), fable (dialogue in the debate quatrains?) and history (in the conclusion). As often in the parts of *accessus* to school texts where terminology is introduced and dissected, there is a tendency toward acquisitiveness and compilation, which can result in redundancy and even contradiction. We see an example near the end of the *accessus*, where Theodulus is said to use two different kinds of argument (*argumentum*) in his work. Both are associated with the beginnings of texts, although the specific definitions are presented as distinct.

---

²⁷ In Clm 19475, however, the *accessus* to the *Distichs of Cato* is not the first, and there are *accessus* to other texts that intervene before that to the *Eclogue of Theodulus*.
²⁸ For who wins each set, see Herren, 'Reflections on the Meaning of the *Ecloga Theoduli*', pp. 217–30.
²⁹ For the balanced contrasts between the two characters, see, for example, the note in Rigg (tr.), *The Eclogue of Theodulus*, p. 13, on ll. 3–10.
³⁰ Quinn, 'Ps. Theodulus,' pp. 390b–98a. The commentary in Clm 391, however, lacks the etymologising gloss on 'distichs' (*distichii*, l. 288); see ibid., pp. 389b–90a. On Neckham and school texts, see Copeland, 'Curricular Classics', p. 27.
³¹ Cf. Camargo and Woods, 'Writing Instruction in Late Medieval Europe', p. 116.

There are **three kinds** of eclogues: some consist in the censuring of Cynics or bitter men, and Horace uses this type of eclogue in his *Sermones*. 'Eclogue' is named from *eglon*, which is a goat; a goat is a foul-smelling animal. Because it consists in the censuring of vices, it is called an eclogue,[32] that is, a goatish discourse. Another kind of eclogue consists in the low style (*humili stilo*), namely when someone introduces and belittles low-ranking persons in a short work. Virgil uses this [type of] eclogue. And there is a third eclogue which consists in humility. Theodulus uses this [type of] eclogue in his work when he directs us to humility, whence this book is thus **entitled**: 'Here begins the *Eclogue of Theodulus*'. 'Theodulus' means servant of God. In this work the author uses a three-fold **style** (and introduces three characters), namely **argument** (*argumentum*), **fable** (*fabula*) and **history** (*ystoria*). This noun 'argument' is taken three ways. An argument is a line of reason about something uncertain and creating trust, and [in this sense the word] is known to logicians. And 'argument' comes from *arguo* (to argue) or *ango, angis* (to cause distress). In addition it is a brief, comprehensive statement of what is to come, and it is according to this sense that Theodulus uses it in this book. In addition, an argument is a preface that [authors] put before their books before they advance to the principal work. This author [also] uses the argument of this [definition].[33] 'Fable' is named from *fando* (speaking), since the whole [fable] consists of spoken words (*sermonibus*). 'History' (*ystoria*) comes from *theoreo, -as*, which is 'to see', for it is written down just as it was seen. ... Likewise the author brings in three **characters**, namely Pseustis, Alithia, and Fronesis ...[34]

---

[32] According to Quinn, 'Ps Theodolus', p. 391a, Neckham's *accessus* includes 'et logos, quod est sermo' here.

[33] That is, Theodulus uses 'argumentum' in both the second and third senses.

[34] Clm 391, f. 9[ra–b]: 'Eclogarum **tres** sunt **diuersitates** quedam consistit in cynicis et in <amaris reprehensionibus> [*CTC*: panias(?) responsionibus *MS*] huius<modi> egloga usuus hor<a>cius in sermomibus suis. Egloga dicitur ab eglon quod est <caper. caper> [caperut. caput *MS*] autem fetidum animal est quod constat ex reprehensione uiciorum et inde dicitur agloga [*sic*] id est sermo caprinus. Est autem egloga alia que constat ex humili stilo scilicet quando aliquis induat humiles personas in opusculo suo et detractat. Hac egloga usus uirgilius Et est egloga tercia que consistit tantum in humlitate hac egloga uerum Theodulus in opera suo quando imnitauit nos ad humilitatem vnde liber iste sic intitulat Incipit egloga theodoli. Teodolus seruus dei interpretatur. Auctor in hoc opere utitur triplici **stilo** et tres inducit personas, scilicet **argumentum fabula** et **ystoria** Hoc nomen argumentum tripliciter tenetur Argumentum est racio dubie faciens fidem et est notum loycis. Et dicitur argumentum de arguo uel ab ango angis Item argumentum est breuis [est *expunc. MS*] comprehensio manere future et secumdum hoc usus Theodulus est in hoc libro Item argumentum est prefacio quam solent preponere operibus suis antequam agrederentur opus principale huius argumento usus est auctor iste. Fabula dicitur a fando quia tota consistit in sermonibus. Ystoria dicitur a theoreo as quod est uideo uides quia ita uidetur esse ut narratur ... Item introducit auctor iste tres **personas**, scilicet Pseustim in alithiam et fronesim ...'. The etymologies of these characters' names are omitted here, but see the next *accessus*.

The **second *accessus* to the *Eclogue*** continues in the same hand:

> *Like the land of the Ethiopians* (1). The **author** of this book was Theodulus, born of Christian parents, who when he studied in Athens saw Christians disputing with gentiles, and he gathered their reasonings into an allegorical Eclogue.[35] At the time of his death he had not fully revised some points of the text, such as at 'Now say' (319). The **title** is inscribed from name of the author, like Lucan: the work *of Lucan*, and thus Theodulus: the work *of Theodulus*. The title is as follows: 'Here begins the *Eclogue of Theodulus*'. Now 'eclogue' comes from goat: accordingly from *egle* which is goat and *logos* which is discourse, basically 'goatish discourse' ... 'Title' comes from *tytano*. For just as the sun illuminates the world so too does a title [illuminate] the work following.[36] ... The **subject-matter** are fables (*fabule*) and histories (*hystorie*). The **intention of the author** is falsehood conquered by truth. It is **placed under ethics** ... Ethics is divided into the **four cardinal virtues**, which are justice, temperance, fortitude and prudence. And two **characters** are introduced in this book, namely Pseustis and Alithia, who were herding flocks. One of them was a worshiper of idols and impugned the truth; 'Pseustis' means 'false' or 'falsehood'. Whence a 'pseudo-prophet' means a false one. Alithia in contrast spoke truly, and ['Alithia'] means the same as truth and comes from *alo, alis* (to nourish) since the truth nourishes us in faith. 'Theodulus' is named from *theos* in Greek which is *deus* (God) in Latin and *dolus, -li* (treachery, bad faith), hence 'Theodulus' is as it were speech about God and bad faith,[37] that is, composed of truth and falsehood ...[38]

The second *accessus*, at this point on the verso side, continues with two columns of glosses on the words of the prologue setting up the contest

---

[35] This *accessus* begins with the same narrative as that in Clm 19475, based on an earlier source; see Minnis and Scott, pp. 17–18; Wheeler (ed. and tr.), *Accessus ad auctores*, pp. 44–45 and 152–53. Later parts of this *accessus*, especially the etymologies, also resemble Clm 19475.
[36] The same etymology is cited in the second *accessus* to Cato.
[37] Note the alliteration in the Latin: 'de deo et dolo'.
[38] Clm 391, f. 9ʳᵇ⁻ᵃ: '*Ethiopum terrat* (1). **Auctor** huius libri fuit Theodulus parentibus xristianis editus qui cum athenis studeret xristianos cum gentilibus uidit ab alterantes quorum colligens raciones in allegoricam eglogam contulit preuentus mortem in quibusdam locis non emendauit ut ibi Dic et troyanum. **Tytulus** ex nomine auctoris liber prescribitur vt lucanus opus lucani. Sic Theodulus opus theoduli titulus est talis, Incipit egloga theodolui. Egloga enim capris transatum et ideo ab egle quod est caper et logus quod est sermo quasi caprinus sermo ... Tytulus a tycario dicitur quia sicut sol mundum illuminat ita titulus sequens opus ... **Materia** sunt fabule et hystorie. **Intencio auctoris** est falsitatem[est *del.*] deuictam a uirtute. **Ethice supponitur** ... Ethica diuiditur in **quatuor virtutes principaliter**. Que sunt Iusticia, temperancia, fortitude, prudencia. Et introducuntur due **persone** in hoc libro, scilicet pseustis et alathia, qui greges pascebant, quorum unus cultor ydolorum erat et veritatem impugnabat et dicitur pseustis falsus siue falsitas. Vnde pseudo prophete quasi falsus. Alathia vere affirmabat et interpretatur idem quod ueritas et dicitur ab Alo, Alis quia ueritas alit nos in fide. Theodulus dicitur a theos grece quod est deus lathine et dolus li vnde Theodulus quasi sermo de deo et dolo, id est ueritate et falsitate compositus'.

between Pseustis and Alithea, judged by Fronesis. In its attention to the questions of authorial biography, then subject-matter, intention and the part of philosophy to which the text belongs, this second *accessus* explores categories more familiar to us from the *accessus* to the *Distichs of Cato* than did the first.

But we are still not at the text. A second folio (f. 10$^{ra-vb}$) intervenes, consisting of six long paragraphs of background material on the subject of each part of three paired quatrains: on the floods, Hippolytus and Jacob, and Hercules and Samson. These paragraphs resemble amplified paraphrases of the type that a teacher might provide or, perhaps, ask students to compose. They are omitted here, but they are deserving of further study as examples of the manuscript compiler's interest in pulling together all manner of possible relevant pedagogical material.

## Statius, *Achilleid*

The third text in the manuscript, the *Achilleid* of Statius, focuses on the time young Achilles spends pretending to be a girl on the island of Scyros.[39] His mother, Thetis, has abducted him from the care of the centaur Chiron and deposits him among the daughters of King Lycomedes, whence he is rescued by Ulysses and Diomedes. Compared to the separate multiple *accessus* and other kinds of extended introductory material copied before the two preceding works, the *accessus* to Statius in this manuscript is skimpy indeed, signalling a severe shift in introductory attention to the text.[40] There are added small bits and pieces of introductory material different from what we have seen so far, but not uncommon in manuscripts of this text:[41] a separate list of *accessus* topics, a mythological preface, a note on Statius's name and a five-line summary-argument that continued onto a small unnumbered scrap written on both sides and bound into the manuscript.[42] After the first full page of glosses, the marginal comments drop off precipitously, a practice that continues with the remaining texts.

---

[39] Statius left the work unfinished, but during the Middle Ages a final line was often added, in this manuscript as an interlinear gloss above 'Explicit Stacius': 'Aura silet, puppis currens ad litora uenit' (f. 42$^v$).

[40] On the fewer marginal glosses in this manuscript from the *Achilleid* on, see Klemm, *Die illuminierten Handschriften*, I, 194a. She somewhat overstates the case, however, and the falling off that does not mean that the glosses on the *Achilleid* are not useful or revealing; see n. 5.

[41] See Jeudy and Riou, 'L'Achilléide de Stace'.

[42] For a complete list of this material, see Anderson, *Manuscripts of Statius*, I, no. 362.

Figure 1.1  Munich, Bayerische Staatsbibliothek Clm 391, f. 18ᵛ. Opening of the *Achilleid* of Statius, with *accessus* glosses.
Reproduced by kind permission.

The **short *accessus* to the *Achilleid*** is written in the margin next to the beginning of the text in the manner of later works in the manuscript. Discernible in Figure 1.1, it is squeezed somewhat awkwardly around the flourishes on the initial letter *M*.[43]

> The **intention** of Statius in this work is to dissuade a mortal altogether from wishing to contravene divine will, which Thetis attempted. Or his **intention** is to write about the strengths of Achilles nurtured by Chiron. Or his **intention** is to make his own spirit ready so that he himself might be able more perfectly to describe the actions of the emperor as he asked him.[44] Domitian and Titus were the sons of the emperor Vespasian. While Domitian's death was recorded, his deeds remained. The primary **subject-matter** of this book is Thetis and Achilles, but the secondary [subject is] Diomedes and Ulysses. Its **usefulness** is so that we do not stand in the way of divine will. Or its **usefulness** is that [one performing] a childish deception is brought to an upright and honest life. We say that it is **put under ethics** since it pertains to honesty of behaviour/morals (*morum*). In the manner (*more*) of other poets, he does three things in the work, namely he **introduces** (*proponit*), he **invokes** (*invocat*) and he **narrates** (*narrat*). He subtly combines the announcing with the invocation where he says, 'Bring back, O goddess, the great-hearted one' (ll. 3 and 1). The narration is at '[Paris] had set sail' (20). Indeed it should be noted that he invokes a god (8) and a goddess (3), asking for their aid, for because it is composed out of the god [Apollo] and the goddess Thetis, it is perfected. He invokes the goddess where he says, 'Bring back, O goddess' (3), the god where he says, 'Give me, Apollo, new springs' (8). *Bring back*, that is bring or say once more. For many say 'bring back' what is past and 'bring' what will be. Having said these things, let us go to the text.[45]

---

[43] There is no *accessus* to the *Achilleid* included in the *Accessus ad auctores* in Clm 19475.

[44] 'Often there are two or more intentions' (Munk Olsen, '*Accessus* to Classical Poets', p. 137).

[45] Clm 391, f. 18ᵛ: '**Intentio** stacii in hoc opera est dehortari quomodolibet mortalem ne uelit contraire diuine dispositionem quod nit<atur> [*** *MS*] thetis. Vel eius **intencio** est describere uirtutes achillis nutriti a chirone. Vel eius **intencio** est animum suum exercitatum reddere ut facta Domiciani imperatoris ut ipsum rogauerat posset perfectius describere. Domicianus vero et tytus errant fillij vaspasiani imperatoris. Mortuo autem domiciano inscripto mansuerunt eius gesta. Principalis autem **materia** huius libri est thetis et achilles. **Secundari**a vero dyomedes et vlixes. **Vtilitas** est ut non obstemus diuine dispositioni. Vel **utilitas** est pueliris edicio ad morieratam [= morigeratam] et honestam uitam. Dicimus eciam quod **ethice suponitur** quia ad honestatem morum pertinent. More aliorum poetarum tria facit in opere, scilicet **proponit, Inuocat, et narrat**. Hic autem subtiliter admisceret proposicionem inuocacioni, vbi didit Magnanimum etc. Diua refer. Narracio est ibi, <u>Soluerat</u>. Notandum eciam est quod inuocat deum ac deam ad operis sui commendacionem. Nam quod a deo et theti dea componitur perfectum est. Deam inuocat vbi dicit Diua refer Deum autem ubi dicit <u>Da fontes mihi phebe nouos</u>. Refer id est iterum fer uel dic. Quia multi dicunt refer quod preteritum est fer quod futuram. Hiis uisis accedamus ad textum'.

Here the *accessus* introduces the notion of a three-fold division of the first part of a text, dividing it into sections that introduce, invoke and finally narrate a story. This division is common in *accessus* to the *Achilleid*, and we will see that later in this manuscript it is considered (and discarded) in the *accessus* to the *Fables of Avianus* and the *Elegies of Maximian*.[46]

The *Achilleid* ends at the bottom of one verso, and the next text, the *Rape of Proserpine*, begins at the top of what seems originally to have been the next recto. Yet the main scribe provided no *accessus* to this stunning and evocative work. Claudian's poem is full of memorable passages in which the furies and other denizens of the underworld temporarily abandon their evil ways during the wedding, while the last lines describe Ceres's overwhelming guilt and frantic search for her daughter. Later, however, two *accessus* were copied on a folio apparently added between the end of Statius and the beginning of Claudian, one on each side; since they are later additions, these *accessus* are not copied here.[47] The first page of the text is heavily glossed like that of the *Achilleid*, although there is no *accessus* in the margin.[48]

Thus, there appears to have been some recognition that, by the end of the manuscript, considerably less introductory material was going to be added. The last two texts, the *Fables of Avianus* and the *Elegies of Maximian*, begin directly after the *Rape of Proserpine*, part way down the page, with no space in between. The introductory initial, however, is of the same kind as the earlier texts and easy to spot. While there is a short and simple *accessus* for each, there are few glosses at the beginning of each of the texts, in contrast to the two more amply glossed texts preceding. The *accessus* to these last two texts focus on the information that is most basic and hence most important what *has* to be noted about them.

### *Fables of Avianus*

The *Fables of Avianus* begin near the bottom of f. 69ᵛ with the four-line decorated initial '*R*' (from *Rustica*, 'peasant-woman') signalling a new text.

---

[46] E.g., Clogan (ed.), *The Medieval Achilleid*, *accessus* 45–48, p. 22; Anderson, *Manuscripts of Statius*, I, *passim*, e.g., nos 3, 13, 37, etc. For its application to the *Aeneid*, see Ziolkowski and Putnam (eds), *The Virgilian Tradition*, p. 720.

[47] The second added *accessus*, a single paragraph on f. 43ᵛ, shares a few similarities with that of Geoffrey of Vitry, *Commentary*, ed. Clarke and Giles. On Geoffrey's and later commentaries on Claudian, see Clarke and Levy, 'Claudianus', pp. 161a–71b. Like the *Achilleid*, the *Rape of Proserpine* is not one of the works for which an *accessus* is included in the *Accessus ad auctores* in Clm 19475.

[48] We do find, to the right of the text and below two long glosses, a gloss identifying the twelve-line preface to Book I as a kind of *accessus* and defining 'epigram' as a term to describe it.

The *Fables* commence (without the Preface) with the first animal fable, about a woman who had told her child that if he were not quiet, 'he would be given as a tit-bit for a ravenous wolf' (1.2). A hungry wolf overhears and almost starves to death waiting for his snack. The moral in the last lines states, 'Let anyone who believes in a woman's sincerity reflect that to him these words are spoken and that it is he whom this lesson censures' (1.15–16). The short **accessus** to *Avianus* is written in the left-hand margin:

> *A peasant-woman*, etc. (1.1). The fables taken from Aesop are the **subject-matter** of this work's author, who imitates Aesop in this work. Or, as others say, tales (*apollogi*) are the subject-matter. There is a difference between a **tale** (*apologus*) and a **fable** (*fabula*), a **story** (*argumentum*) and a **history** (*hystoriam*). A tale is a fiction handed down for the instruction of human life. A fable is a speech in which truth, along with things similar to the truth, are contained. A story is a created work but one that could plausibly take place, like the comedies of Terence. A history is a something already done, but on account of its age enshrined in the memory of men. The **subject-matter** in this work are tales. The author's **intention** is to describe fables so that out of these he can show the truth hidden under the cover of fables. The **usefulness** is instruction, or the **usefulness** depends on the proverbs put at the end of the tales.[49] The **title** is thus: '*The Book of Avianus the Tale-Teller begins*'. The word *apologus* comes from *apos*, which is 'correct', and *logos*, which is discourse/words, meaning words put at the end. This [author] does not proceed in the manner of other authors[50] since he does not **introduce** or **invoke** but only **narrates**, saying 'A peasant woman'.[51]

Note that the commentator reminds us of the three-fold paradigm of *proponit, invocat, narrat*, although this text exemplifies only the third. If we recall the academic and pedagogical functions of the *accessus*, this

---

[49] These morals are those included at the end of each fable, rather than the kind of additional morals like the list appended to the *accesssus* in Clm 19475.

[50] Cf. the *accessus* to Statius.

[51] Clm 391, f. 69ᵛ: '*Rustica* etc. (1). **Materia** auctoris in hoc opere sunt fabule ab esopo extracte. Inmitatur esopum in hoc opere uel ut alii dicunt, materia sunt(?) apollogi est <differentia> [*** MS] inter **apologum** et **fabulam**. **Argumentum** et **hystoriam**. Apologus est sermo fictus ad erudicionem humane uite traditus. Fabula est locucio in qua ueritas ut similes ueri continentur. Argumentum est opus fictum sed fieri potuit ut comedie terrencie. Historia est res gesta sed propter uetustatem ad memoriam hominum delata. Materie enim in hoc opere sunt apologi. **Intencio auctoris** est fabulas describere ut ex his ueritatem ostendat sub tegimine fabularum latentem. **Vtilitas** est instructio vel **utilitas** dependet a prou<er>biis in fine apologorum positis. **Titulus** talis est: auiani apollogarii liber incipit. Dicitur autem apologus ab apos quod est rectus et logus quod est sermo quasi sermo in fine positus. More aliorum auctorum iste non facit quia non **proponit** nec **inuocat** sed tantum **narrat** dicens. Rustica'.

highlighting of what is technically irrelevant comes better into focus. This kind of insistence on presenting an interpretive framework, even if it is only partially appropriate, is an example of pedagogical technique: sometimes one uses a text to teach what one wants to teach, whether directly relevant to the text or not.[52]

### Elegies of Maximian

The last work in the manuscript, the *Elegies of Maximian*, presents in verse an old man's recollection of his past loves and explicit sexual relationships and failures. The text of the *Elegies* begins with a three-line initial immediately after the end of the preceding work, several lines from the top of the page, and the *accessus* begins at the top of the margin to the right. It focuses on the horrors of old age more insistently than the even shorter *accessus* in the Tegernsee anthology (Clm 19475).[53] The ***accessus*** **to the *Elegies of Maximian*** here specifies the part of philosophy to which the text belongs as ethics because 'it treats of the *mores* of old men'. It does concede, however, that the work's secondary usefulness derives from its teaching the transitoriness of both youth and old age.

> The **subject-matter** of this author is old age and the misfortunes of old age, and, since his **intention** is centred around the subject, he intends secondarily for the misfortunes of old age to be conquered through the recollection of the honours that he had in his youth. The **usefulness [for] the author** is this, that through the publication of this book of the various evils that oppressiveness bestows on old age, it [the oppressiveness] is consigned to forgetfulness, according to that statement of Ovid, 'From it I win forgetfulness of my misfortune' (*Ex Ponto* 1.55[54]). The **usefulness [for] the audience** is twofold. First, that when this book has been read and one learns there the burden and difficulty of old age, we differentiate not a whit between regret for vices and penance for sins, and the lethargy and wasting away of debilitating dotage. Second, that our spirit not puff up in the flower of youth, since all things pertaining to both youth and old age are fleeting, just as the flower blooming in the morning droops and withers by evening. The **reason for undertaking the work** is that some say old age is to be desired, others not. Therefore, so that he might lessen the troubles of old

---

[52] There is a version of this technique in some university-level commentaries on the *Poetria nova*, a medieval rhetorical treatise sometimes taught at universities, where the text is used as an excuse to teach Aristotelian doctrine; see Woods, *Classroom Commentaries*, p. 176. Modern teachers have also been known to use a similar technique.
[53] Wheeler (ed. and tr.), *Accessus ad auctores*, p. 43. The *accessus* to the text in Clm 19475 is not included in Minnis and Scott.
[54] Ovid, *Tristia. Ex Ponto*, p. 295.

age, he tells through the troubles he describes that old age is not to be desired. **It is placed under ethics** since it treats of the *mores* of old men. The **title** is thus: 'The *Ethics of Maximian on the Impermanence of Life* begins'. And it should be noted that Maximian is the proper name of the author, or it could be made up, since he lived a long time [ago]. He is appropriately called Maximian [literally, the greatest] ... since he does not **propose** or **invoke** but rather **decries** old age in the manner of satirists, beginning 'Jealous [old age]!'(1).[55]

This *accessus* concludes with a startling description of the author's mode, playing on the three-fold sequence seen in the discussions of Statius and Avianus. It begins, as before, with *invocat* and *proponit*, but the version given here concludes not with the now expected *narrat*, but instead with a forceful *exclamat*, as well as the first mention of the satirists – writers whose works were typically studied after those in this manuscript. This surprising revision, apparently anticipating future readings and further study, is a variation of the pedagogical paradigm that I do not recollect having seen elsewhere.

## Observations and Conclusions

In the medieval volume of *The Cambridge History of Literary Criticism*, Alastair Minnis and Ian Johnson describe *accessus* as 'school prolegomena to the prescribed trivium texts wherein major critical issues are raised'.[56] We find in the various *accessus* in Clm 391 a repeated emphasis on the formulation and counting of categories and – especially in the *accessus* to the first two texts – the piling up of approaches dependent on these categories. Within even the much shorter *accessus* later in the manuscript,

---

[55] Clm 391, f. 85ʳ: '**Materia** huius auctoris est senectus et incomoda senectutis et quia **intencio** versatur circa materiam ideo hic intendit conqueri incommoda senectutis per recordacionem honorum que habuit in iuuentute. **Vitilitas** auctoris est hec quia per presentis libri edicionem diuersorum malorum que senectuti grauitas tribuit. Consequitur obliuione secundum illud ouidii Consequor ex illis casus obliuia nostri **vtilitas** audiencium duplex est primo ut hoc libro perlecto et ibi senectutis grauitatem et difficultatem experit penitenciam nostrorum viciorum et satisfactionem peccatorum torporem et desidiam ignaui senii nullatenus differamus. Secundo ut animus noster de flore iuuentituis non timescat quia transitoria sunt omia et iuuenia et senilia velud florens flos mane vespere decidat et arescat. **Causa suscepti operis** est quidam dicebant senectutem esse appetendam quidam vero non. Vt ergo eorum dissoluat incommoda senectutis enarrat per que non est senectutem appetendam demonstrat. **Ethice supponitur** quia de moribus senium tractat. **Tytulus** talis est. Ethica Maximiani de fragilitate vite incipit. Et notandum quod Maximianus est nomen propruim auctoris vel potest esse fictum quia diu uixerat. Dictus est maximianus recte scribentis more non scribit quia non **proponit** nec **inuocat** sed more satyricorum senectutem **exclamat** incipiens Emula'.

[56] Minnis and Johnson, 'Introduction' (2005), p. 2.

there are individual sentences that can illuminate a work, such as the conclusion to the *accessus* to the *Elegies* just discussed. Likewise, the description in the *accessus* to Statius of the subject-matter as Achilles and his mentors was for me a major insight into the medieval approach to this text, one which I have explored elsewhere.[57] These individual points are all the more memorable, insofar as they arise from an effort to prepare and reinforce a foundation with which to approach *any* text – in this case, a known grouping that, in various forms and combinations, was among the most widely taught in medieval schools.

In the Tegernsee manuscript, Clm 19475, it is the texts taught *later* in the presumed pedagogical sequence that receive the longer and multiple *accessus*.[58] But in Schedel's manuscript, Clm 391, much more attention is paid to the *first* texts to be taught. The multiple *accessus* to the *Distichs of Cato* and the *Eclogue of Theodulus* in Clm 391 provide reinforcing frameworks right at the very beginning of study, while the lack of any such original material for Claudian's *Rape of Proserpine* and the very brief *accessus* for the work preceding and two following it imply that what has already been learned is sufficient to introduce students at even a basic level to a range of issues of literary interpretation. Furthermore, it is the *Distichs of Cato* and the *Eclogue of Theodulus* that continue to be placed at the forefront of many medieval school manuscripts, even after the works to follow were at least partially replaced by the non-classical and more overtly Christian texts of the *Auctores octo*. The order of the remaining texts in Clm 391 remains a puzzlement, although the addressing of the *proponit, invocat, narrat* paradigm in the third, fifth, and sixth texts may have influenced moving the *Achilleid* to third place, since its *accessus* is the only one that perfectly exemplifies it. Even when explanations for them remain inaccessible, each change, like each idiosyncrasy and each adherence to the expected pattern, suggests a pedagogical point of view, the values of a teacher.[59]

---

[57] See Woods, *Weeping for Dido*, pp. 60–61.
[58] With the exception of the much longer *accessus* and morals added to the *Fables of Avianus*.
[59] I am grateful to Andrew Kraebel for help with manuscript readings, and to Abigail Adams, Rebecca Beal, Johanna Hartmann, Xinyao Xiao and Alexander Thomas for comments and corrections.

CHAPTER 2

# *Scholastic Theory and Vernacular Knowledge*

## Jocelyn Wogan-Browne

In posing the question of how literary theoretical texts and academic commentaries came to have their influence in late medieval literature and culture more generally, the editors of this volume rightly suggest that the answers will reveal entanglement and complicated interchange. This chapter explores late twelfth- and thirteenth-century texts in England to argue for a more complicated model than that of a Latin-vernacular(s) binary. One of the most powerful scholastic forms, for instance, is the *accessus ad auctores* prologue, an important and early identified template in the vast panoramas opened up by Alastair Minnis's scholarship. The *accessus*, as in his classic account, uses a set of (often slightly varied) categories for introducing authoritative writings: *intentio auctoris*, *titulus*, *modus agendi/modus tractandi* (i.e., stylistic and didactic mode of procedure), *ordo* (the structure by which the contents are arranged), *utilitas* (pedagogic and moral usefulness of the work), *materia* (subject-matter) and the branch of knowledge to which the work belongs (*cui parti philosophiae supponitur* ).[1] Coming into use over the course of the thirteenth century, the Aristotelian version of this template makes *accessus* both more compact and more comprehensive by adapting the four causes – efficient, material, formal and final – seen by Aristotle as responsible for all activity and change in the universe to the production of texts.[2] Derived not from the *Poetics* but the *Physics* and the *Metaphysics,* the Aristotelian prologue in medieval hands implies a Christianised cosmology in which writers and compilers exercise a second-level creativity and craftsmanship under God. This attractive and weighty template had high prestige from its association with the learned exegesis of important texts – biblical and scholastic. Yet the Aristotelian prologue is seldom used in French or Middle English works composed in later medieval England, though aspects of scholastic

---

[1] Minnis and Scott, p. 2; *MTA*, pp. 9–39.   [2] Minnis and Scott, pp. 3–4; *MTA*, pp. 28–29.

*accessus* are everywhere to be found informing approaches to texts.³ As Alastair Minnis's own work on vernacularity argues, if such a prologue structure is available, the idea that it will be used in a straightforward adoption of a Latin template is but the beginning of a more complicated story.⁴ This chapter will argue that the rarity of the full Aristotelian *accessus* speaks not to the paucity but to the richness and variety of vernacular engagement with traditions of learning, in which very specific choices about textual *accessus* can be made, and in which scholastics and clerics are specialists but not monopolists in knowledge.

The single extant French-language Aristotelian prologue is found in Pierre d'Abernon de Fetcham's *Lumere as lais* (*Light for Laypeople*) of 1267–68, composed at the height of the establishment of Aristotle in university curricula.⁵ The *Lumere* is a verse theological encyclopaedia of c. 14,000 lines, re-working Honorius of Autun's (d. 1151) *Elucidarius* and elaborating this principal source with material from the *Historia Scholastica* of Peter Comestor (d. 1178) and elsewhere.⁶ The verse *Lumere* seems to have been in demand: it is extant in twenty-two manuscripts of both clerical and lay ownership.⁷

Table 2.1 shows how closely the *Lumere* follows the elements of the Aristotelian *accessus* and how it differs in its addition of a fifth cause, 'l'entitlement' or title, a category typically addressed in R. W. Hunt's 'type B' *accessus*, a much older form.⁸ The 'title' is explained at the end of the *accessus* with a great deal of thematic weight attached to it (ll. 667–94). It connotes a double enlightenment of knowledge and love ('De saver e d'amer ensement', l. 678) working together for clergy and laity, in a language they share. Claire Waters has eloquently discussed the *Lumere*'s engagement with its audiences in a 'fiction of affectionate disputation', and she has shown the dynamism and range of written pastoralia in the

---

³ On vernacular versions of commentary and glosses, see Hanna, Minnis et al. (2005), 'Latin Commentary Tradition and Vernacular Literature'.
⁴ See especially his *Valuing the Vernacular* (2009). For a repertoire of francophone literary theory circulating in and from England, see *VLT*.
⁵ Jones, 'University Books and the Sciences'.
⁶ Hesketh (ed.), *Lumere as lais*, III, 12–18. For a text and translation of the *accessus*, see *VLT*, no. 19. Citations here are from Hesketh.
⁷ First charted in Lefèvre, *L'Elucidarium* pp. 269–329. For an updated list of versions, manuscripts and editions, see http://huwgrange.co.uk/elucidarium.html (last accessed 8 November 2022). There are also some dozen early prints. An early thirteenth-century prose French version has twenty-three extant manuscripts. For examples of ownership, see Sandler, 'The *Lumere* and Its Readers', and her 'Scribe, Corrector, Reader'. I thank Professor Sandler for generously sending offprints of these articles.
⁸ See *MTA*, pp. 15–16.

Table 2.1 *The* Lumere as Lais *and the Aristotelian scholastic prologue*

**Aristotle**

1. *Efficient cause*: the motivation or force bringing something from potential into actual being
2. *Material cause*: the matter or substratum of a thing
3. *Formal cause*: the essence or pattern that 'enforms' the thing
4. *Final cause*: the end or objective aimed at

(Definitions from *MTA*, pp. 8–9)

| **s. xiii Aristotelian Prologue: Four Causes** | | **Pierre de Fetcham *Lumere as lais*** |
|---|---|---|
| | | **Cinc choses** sout [em] ja enqu[e]re<br>Au commencement en livere fere:<br>Ki fust *autur*, e *l'entitlement*,<br>E *la matire* e *la furme* ensement,<br>E *la fin*, ce est par queu reisun<br>Fu fest la composiciun. (ll. 531–36). |
| *efficiens* | (author) | *autur*: God (human author is His instrument or notary, ll. 537–52) |
| | | *l'entitlement*: *Lumere as lais* (enlightenment for laity and clerics through knowledge and love, ll. 667–94) |
| *materialis* | (materials) | *matire* or *sujet*: Christ as creator and creature (ll. 553–74) |
| *formalis* | *forma tractatus* (arrangement, structure)<br><br>*forma tractandi* (treatment, style) | *furme*: Division into 6 books (from God and creation to sin, the incarnation, sacraments and judgement (ll. 575–614)<br>In each book the disciple raises questions, and the master answers them (ll. 615–26) |
| *finalis* | (ultimate objective or effect of the work) | *fin*: God, + *une fin generale* (all audiences amended by the work, ll. 655–58) + *une fin especial* (solace and amendment for *mes especiaus amis*, ll. 659–62) + the writer's own *propre fin* (remission of sin and grace to see God before his face, ll. 663–66) |

thirteenth century, as learning – *clergie* – is transferred in mixed lay-clerical francophone textual communities.[9] The *Lumere*'s own lexical innovations testify to the expanding registers of French, in this case into scholasticism and theology. Its editor, Glynn Hesketh, identifies 161 French neologisms, both morphological and semantic, only a very small proportion of them

---

[9] Waters, 'Loving Teaching', and her *Translating Clergie*, pp. 45–60.

direct calques on Latin terms.[10] They include the use of *sujet* in the sense of a theme or subject-matter, *conclusiun* in the sense not of an ending but as the conclusion of an argument, the *accessus causes*, *generaument* (*adv.*) generally, as a class, *proposiciun* as 'proposition of argument, premise', *ymaginer* (*v.a.*) to imagine, form a mental picture, and much else of interest. As Hesketh notes, the *Lumere* creates 'a whole web of terms based on the scholastic (ultimately Aristotelian) hierarchy of "genus", "species", "difference", and "property"', not all new words, but all acquiring 'a new technical meaning when used as part of a system in this way'.[11] The *Lumere*'s lexical innovation speaks to the presence of a mixed clerical and lay public, including reading and listening lay people, who are educated but not scholastic, and who, as in Waters's argument, are made partners in the *Lumere*'s work of understanding.

Already in 1212, Angier, a member of St Frideswide's Priory in Oxford, had seen that some transfer of learning from cleric to layperson was a crucial move. For his translation of Gregory's *Dialogues*, he writes a vernacular *accessus* of some 460 lines in which he details the necessity of engaging lay penitents' volition and knowledge in the work of salvation. Together with Angier's prologues to the individual books of the *Dialogues*, this is one of the most extensive insular vernacular discussions of textual access, supported by a specific *mise-en-page*.[12] His audiences – 'Qui qe tu soies, lais ou clerz' (*Introductio*, l. 1, p. 14), 'Seignors e dames, laie gent' (*Proemium*, l. 135, p. 28) – are put in charge of their own reading. Angier directs attention to his extensive list of *capitula* laid out in alternating columns in both Latin and French versions (see Paris, Bibliothèque nationale de France MS fr. 24766, ff. 3ᵛ–8ʳ), and he urges his audience to choose the chapters they want to read or review for themselves (*Introductio*, ll. 21–36, p. 15). That Angier expects a reading as well as a hearing public is manifest in his account of his *mise-en-page*: after explaining that dialogue is 'the speech exchanged between two people over two points when one responds and the other opposes', he adds that it has pleased him to 'pick out in different colours the name of each person [Gregory and his deacon Peter] where he speaks to the other' (*Proemium*, ll. 175–77, 199–201).

When Pierre de Fetcham writes for a lay public some fifty years later, his choice of French as the language that links clergy and laypeople, and much

---

[10] Hesketh, 'Lexical Innovation'.   [11] Ibid., p. 63. See also Waters, *Translating Clergie*, p. 54.
[12] Wogan-Browne, 'Time to Read'. For text and translation from Angier's *accessus*, see *VLT*, no. 24a, and pp. 424–26. Citations here from Orengo (ed.), *Les Dialogues de Grégoire*.

of his matter, continue the pastoral concerns embodied in Angier's *accessus* and the large francophone pastoral corpus in England, but his use of the Aristotelian prologue responds in an innovative way to thirteenth-century Aristotelianism's newly-intensified emphasis on the ordering of the world and the importance of understanding its underlying systematicity. This is appropriate to the nature of his work – a large and systematic compilation – and also a signal of the way underlying assumptions of the created world's intelligibility are shared between clergy and laity.

I want to set Pierre de Fetcham's *Lumere* in a wider context here, for he is writing both in a pastoral and dialogic tradition and amidst a general explosion of knowledge-writing and of writing in French. One cue is Pierre de Fetcham's term for his authorship:

> De cest livere si est autur
> Pri[n]cipaument nostre Seignur,
> Kar a ceo ne su jeo veraiment
> For sun *notur* e *estrument*,
> Kar ceo ke en pensee me fist lire
> Mis en cest livere par escrire. (ll. 537–42, my italics)

> The author of this book is firstly Our Lord, because as far as this is concerned, I am truly nothing but his notary and instrument. What he directed my thoughts to read, I have put down in writing in this book.

'God's instrument' is a standard enough concept for an earthly author, but *notor* (notary) is relatively rare, even in its more general sense of 'amanuensis'. This franco-latinate word, first cited in English *c.* 1340, regains new prominence in the thirteenth century for one dimension of its post-classical Latin meaning, that of 'shorthand writer, clerk, secretary, public clerk'.[13] To the older *escrivain* (scribe), *notor* adds an increased range of administrative functions, such as the ability to draw up contracts, administer oaths, etc.[14] There is debate over whether Pierre de Fetcham was an Augustinian canon with some university training who became a lawyer, or whether the canon was the lawyer's father (it is not clear which of them left

---

[13] Latin *notarius* becomes newly-prominent in British sources (*OED*, s.v. 'notary'; *DMLBS*, s.v. 'notarius') in the thirteenth century, and the word is refreshed in all the romance languages in the thirteenth and fourteenth centuries. Both *OED* and *MED* cite the *Ayenbite of Inwit* (c. 1340) as the first English use: 'Þe ualse notaryes þet makeþ þe ualse lettres and ualseþ þe celes'.

[14] For Pierre's contemporary, John of Howden (fl. 1268/9–1275), even in intensely lyrical Latin verse, love can be Christ's 'scriba ... et notarius', suggesting the greater specialisation of the notary. Raby (ed.), *Poems of John of Hoveden*, p. 239, st. 231.

a library of canon and civil law books).¹⁵ But the concept of a writer as God's notary suggests both the legal world and the world of notarial bureaucratic writing, whose best known exponent was Brunetto Latini, influential in England as elsewhere – and himself the author of a French-language encyclopaedia, *Li Livres dou tresor*.

In the later thirteenth century, French, an important meritocratic language in England, expands alongside Latin in bureaucratic as well as ecclesiastical writing and into records, administration and knowledge of all kinds. Alongside its use at court and in elite literary production, French adds to its domains technical writing, commerce, central and local government business, legal proceedings, correspondence and the professional codes and documents of sailors, soldiers, merchants and civic bodies.¹⁶ This is accordingly a period of vigorous vernacular experimentation with textual *accessus* and the valences of literary form across many different kinds of knowledge. Ruth Dean and Maureen Boulton's *Guide to Anglo-Norman Literature* lists 115 treatises and encyclopaedias in its chapters on scientific, technical and medical writing, and indeed further relevant texts appear in Dean and Boulton's other categories.¹⁷ Some of this corpus dates from the twelfth century, showing considerable overlap in text types with Old English, the established vernacular of learning from an earlier period, but most works are thirteenth- and fourteenth-century, with a few fifteenth-century examples.¹⁸ Their range of forms and subject-matters is striking. Medicine, for instance, includes prose, verse and mixed prose and verse treatises, and uses letters and other formal paradigms of organisation to create and perform a variety of relations to knowledge. In addition to medicine, there are treatises – verse, prose and mixed, framed and unframed – on geometry, chiromancy (prognostication by lines in the

---

¹⁵ See Russell (ed.), *La Vie seint Richard*, pp. 8–12; Martha Carlin's *ODNB* entry, s.v. 'Peter of Peckham'; Fetcham, 'De la charte du diable fet a coveytous', ed. by Levy and Jeffrey (a legal parody from *Lumere* Book III that circulated separately; *Lumere*, ed. by Hesketh, I, 126–27).
¹⁶ See Ingham, *Transmission of Anglo-Norman*; Hinton 'French and Anglo-French'.
¹⁷ In Dean, with Boulton, *Guide*, see the sections on Science and Technology (nos 325–405), Medicine (nos 406–41), plus select works from Grammar and Glosses (nos 281–324) and Homiletic (587–719, which includes the *Lumere*, 630), and other works, e.g., no. 589 (sermon exegesis of Sunday gospels); 590 (treatise on the sacraments), 622 (Grosseteste's *Chasteau d'amour*), 628 (*Dialogue de saint Julien*), 629 (French version of Edmund of Abingdon's *Speculum ecclesie*), 631 (*Jerarchie* [ps-Dionysius] by Pecham), 632–34 (Teaching dialogues), 635 (*Manuel des pechiez*, a vernacular *summa confessorum*), 644–47 and 654, 671, 682 (*Compileisun* on the religious life), 648–49 (versions of *Tractatus de tribulatione*), 675 (vernacular *Speculum humane salvationis*), 695 (Friar Nicolas Bozon, *Contes moralisés*), 697 (trilingual *De quatuordecim partibus beatitudinis S. Anselmi*) and 702 (Guillaume le clerc, *Bestiaire divin*).
¹⁸ Tyler, 'From Old English to Old French'.

were unable to sin (no. 18)? – as well as a wide range of questions about the natural and social world, e.g., How many kinds (*maneres*) of creatures did God create (no. 106)? Why are some people white and others brown or black (no. 130)?[24] Do the poor get more pleasure out of their poverty than the rich out of their riches (no. 155)?[25] Will there always be war in the world (no. 320)? Do fish sleep as they swim in the water (no. 586)? In what language did Adam give names? (no. 803)?[26] But *Sidrac* returns to salvific and eschatological questions too: How can one save oneself (no. 705)? Which is bigger, sin or God's mercy (no. 910)? How will one recognise the Day of Judgement (no. 1161)? Once viewed by modern scholars as naïve, these questions have an underlying theological/doctrinal framework. As the prologue explains, *Sidrac* is a book about how to maintain honour of body and how to perfect the soul, about the various kinds of knowledge and authority in the world (*les sciences e les autorités du monde*), and whatever people need to know who 'want to know about the power of God and about the world in accordance with the intelligence God has given to humans' (*veut savoir de la puissance de Dieu et du monde selonc le sens que Dieu dona a home*).[27]

Clerisy and learning are the basis of *Sidrac*'s authority in his dialogue with King Boccus. But *Sidrac* represents learned authority in several ways. Its *accessus* includes a ranging transmission story, from India to Syria to Greece to Toledo to Tunis to Frederick II, to Antioch and back to Toledo, with translations into Greek, then Latin, then Arabic and then back to Latin.[28] This gives it a pedigree as a book wanted by senior ecclesiastics and by major courts, royal and imperial, in Europe and the Mediterranean. *Sidrac* exemplifies an important further source of knowledge and textual authority in franco-latinate culture – that of kings (even if, like Boccus, they are fictive kings). Medieval kings were usually intensely educated as part of their upbringing, with exemplary and informative 'Mirrors for Kings' and other conduct treatises aimed at them. Kings must have, sponsor or know how to use knowledge. Where modern rulers have a civil service or state departments on which they are supposed to rely for information and help in evidence-based decision-making, medieval kings have councils as well as chanceries and other bureaucratic departments.

---

[24] The answers here draw on humoral and environmental theory: children follow their father or mother depending on who is keenest in the conception, or, if the woman has a hot complexion, they burn in her belly and become brown, or if the surrounding air and earth are very hot they become black. Ruhe (ed.), *Sydrac*, p. 85.
[25] Answer: Yes, for the rich always want more.   [26] Answer: 'ebrieu'.
[27] Ruhe (ed.), *Sydrac*, 'L'argument de cest livre', p. 3.   [28] Ibid., pp. 1–3.

Whether through personal knowledge, privileged access to institutional knowledge or identification with specific bodies of knowledge, royalty has a long-standing profile as a textual guarantor. In a powerful variant of the patron and clerk relation, in which doctrinal knowledge is mutually constructed, kings – as with Sidrac and Boccus – are often represented in their relation to the institutions of knowledge by a personal *philosophus*. Many of the thirteenth-century examples have their roots in Latin tradition, but are equally well established in vernacular texts: Alexander the Great and Aristotle are one such pair, Arthur and Merlin another. The pseudo-Aristotelian *Secreta secretorum*, whose Latin translation in the early thirteenth century is ultimately from the Arabic, is an encyclopaedic mirror for kings on good government, framed as a letter to Alexander the Great from his tutor Aristotle. Its thirteenth-century re-workings in French and Latin all hammer home the indispensability of learning for kings. Pierre de Fetcham himself composed a verse vernacular *Secreta secretorum* as well as his *Lumere*, and his Alexander is urged by Aristotle to 'set up universities! Establish schools in cities!' (ll. 1158–59: 'Universitez apparaillez, / Estudie en citez establiez'), and to command his men to bring up their sons as lettered people, 'cognisant of the liberal arts and ethics'.[29] Authority is thus heterogeneous, and its vernacularity, even when this is authorised by claims to Latin (and sometimes Greek or Arabic) sources, speaks to the socio-economic powers and the investments of laypeople in specialised knowledge and relations with *clergie*.

One kind of treatise for which kings are a source of authoritative knowledge is the lapidary, ultimately going back to Jewish commentary on the breastplates of Aaron and Moses. The many French-language lapidaries of the twelfth and thirteenth centuries frequently follow Marbode of Rennes's influential eleventh-century *De gemmis* in making 'King Evax of Arabia' their authority, while in the fourteenth century 'King Philip' (Philippe VI de Valois, r. 1328–50) becomes a sponsoring authority for lapidary knowledge.[30] At the request of the Emperor Nero, Evax personally composes a book for him written in his own hand (*k'yl meïsme de sa main fist*).[31] This physical association with the book endows it

---

[29] Beckerlegge (ed.), *Le Secré de Secrez*, 1162–64: 'Ke lur fiz apreignent de lettrure, / E ke d'estudie preignent cure / En les arz e en morautez / Si ke seient clers esprovez'.
[30] For the Evax prologue, see, e.g., the 'First French Version', 1–46, in Studer and Evans (eds), *Anglo-Norman Lapidaries*, pp. 28–29, and the 'Anglo-Norman verse adaptation', 1–58, in *Anglo-Norman Lapidaries*, pp. 71–73. (The latter is Dean, with Boulton, *Guide*, no. 348). For King Philip's lapidary, see Pannier (ed.), *Les lapidaires français*, pp. 286–97 (text at pp. 291–97).
[31] 'Anglo-Norman adaptation', 24, in Studer and Evans (eds), *Anglo-Norman Lapidaries*, p. 72.

with extra charisma: kings have the power to heal through touch, and precious stones can heal various physical ills, if they are touched, worn, looked at or scraped, powdered and drunk.[32] From the twelfth to the fourteenth centuries, kings and precious stones remain intimately associated, such that royal authority in lapidaries becomes an aesthetics of appropriateness. Albertus Magnus (d. 1280), structuring his *De mineralibus* according to Aristotelian *causae*, continues to cite Evax as authority for the agate's power to make a man 'agreeable and persuasive ... of good color, and eloquent', and to 'protect him against adversity'.[33]

The material culture of precious stones unites secular and sacred knowledge. Like relics, precious stones are found both in church and royal treasuries, where they act as material contacts both with exotic earthly realms and with the numinous. They are objects of meditation, bridging the material and the spiritual through the emotion of wonder at their charismatic and mystical beauty, and also objects displaying the power and connoisseurship of their proprietors.[34] Like relics, too, precious stones blur the boundaries of the animate and inanimate: in Aristotelian terms, stones display will and volition normally assigned only to human consciousness. By fundamental principles of motion and causation, stones, if thrown, seek to return to earth, just as seeds seek to grow. Stones are thus to be located within a systematic and total Christian reality: as the lapidaries agree throughout their tradition, God has put some of his own virtue in them, so that they become signs of his creation with their active and beneficent powers.[35]

Rather than simply characterising lapidaries as pre-scientific magical thinking, looking at their assumptions shows us a world in which stones and other non-human created things are linked with humans and can engage with them. They also offer a tradition in which a non-scholastic but powerful lay authority invests in systematic knowledge. Royal authority is an appropriate source of this knowledge, given the affinities between

---

[32] See, e.g., Phillippe de Thaun (attr.), 'Alphabetical Lapidary', 1695–98, in Studer and Evans (eds), *Anglo-Norman Lapidaries*, pp. 200–258 (at p. 258); Gontero-Lauze, *Sagesses minerales*; Cohen, *Stone*, pp. 195–252.
[33] Albertus Magnus, *De mineralibus*, II.II.1 (*The Book of Minerals*, tr. by Wyckoff, p. 72).
[34] Daston and Park, *Wonders and the Order of Nature*, pp. 67–69, 74–77, 88.
[35] 'Anglo-Norman verse adaptation', 41–45, in Studer and Evans (eds), *Anglo-Norman Lapidaries*, pp. 72–73: 'Deus les [the stones' *vertues*] i mist mult gloriuses, / Pur ce unt els nun precioses, / Iço vus di je ben pur veir / Ke ren ne poet vertu aveir, / Si Deus li veirs ne li consent /E si de li ne li descent'. Of Aristotelian thinking about stones, Kuhn remarks that 'contemplating a falling stone, Aristotle saw a change of state rather than a process' (*Structure of Scientific Revolutions*, p. 124).

kings and precious stones and the tangible powers exercised by both.[36] The fabulous figure of King Evax of Arabia is not a fiction used to supply a lack of systematic knowledge, but a figure of the social location, nature and function of a specific body of knowledge. And knowledge itself, as Rita Copeland and Ineke Sluiter have suggested, cannot be entirely dissociated from fictiveness. 'Scientific classification is by its nature', they argue, 'a kind of fictive form itself, an imagining of an integrated whole'.[37] This the lapidaries, like the Aristotelian prologue itself, seek to do.

The interaction of aesthetics and knowledge, the surprising literariness of didactic writing, can be still more striking:

> Dreit e reison e volenté
> Ferme de mon einzdegré
> M'ad le cueor suspris
> A dire ceo ke jeo ai apris ... (ll. 1–4)

> Right and reason and unwavering resolve, by my own free will, have given me the desire [*lit.* have overwhelmed my heart] to tell what I have learned.

This sounds like the beginning of a love lyric, secular or devotional. But it is the verse prologue of a treatise on falconry – one sense of *ferme* is 'a small cage for a hawk' (*AND ferme*[1]), so there may be a pun 'mewed up in my own volition/purpose' here.[38] Vernacular lyric tradition appropriately performs access to a body of knowledge sponsored by and identified with kings, and one that involves intense affectivity and intimacy. Insofar as falconry depends on extremely close relations between falconer, bird, and their mutual lord, the king, this is an art, so to speak, of the heart. As with King Evax and the lapidaries, falconry is a genre of royal composition, patronage and practice: Frederick II of Hohenstaufen's own treatise, composed in Sicily in 1244–50, is well known, and there are insular precedents.[39] Adelard of Bath (*c.* 1080–*c.* 1150) dedicated his falconry treatise, *De avibus tractatus*, to the future Henry II as a young prince, and

---

[36] For examples of royal jewels, see Evans, *Magical Jewels of the Middle Ages*, esp. pp. 114, 117–18.
[37] Copeland and Sluiter (eds), *Medieval Grammar and Rhetoric*, p. 13.
[38] Hunt edits the text from Cambridge, University Library MS Ff.6.13 (s. xiii²), f. 78ᵛ, in his *Three Anglo-Norman Treatises on Falconry*, p. 19 (here ll. 1–4). See also Burnett (ed. and tr.), *Adelard of Bath*, p. 242, for a small shed (*casam*) in which hawks are kept while their feathers firm up, 'quam vulgo *firmam* dicunt' (emphasis added).
[39] Willemsen (ed.), *De arte venandi*; Wood and Fyfe (trs), *Art of Falconry*. For other compositions by kings and at royal courts, see Hunt (ed.), *Three Anglo-Norman Treatises*, pp. 4–6.

he cites the books of King Harold (i.e., Godwineson) as a source.[40] The French treatise quoted above, like other thirteenth-century vernacularisations, is intensely concerned with the medicining of falcons, their physiology and regimen, necessary consequences of falconry's concern with the nature of the birds and how to form them. Much attention is paid to the bird's lungs: when birds are diseased, the falconer must in some cases suck out internal infection or phlegm with a straw.[41] Even allowing for that presence of animals at the heart of much human medieval life so vividly demonstrated by Susan Crane, falconry demands exceptional intimacy.[42] Adelard says, for instance, that men caring for hawks must be not only sober and chaste, but pleasant-smelling (*bene anhelantes*): bad breath (*fetidus anhelitus*) gives the hawks rheum and makes them hate humans.[43] This intimacy, with its exchanges of inhalation and exhalation, makes a lyric invocation a meaningful form of *accessus*, an in-spiration for a falconry treatise. Moreover, as Sara Petrosillo has recently shown, this particular lyric prologue appropriately performs a heart-stopping resolve to decisive action in its opening. The aesthetics of falconry, Petrosillo argues, have all to do with weight and balance, so that the ultimate point for which falconry's intimate relations are cultivated is the beauty of the stoop from on high. The perfectly fed and exercised falcon is trained to make this not for its own hunting needs, but for the aesthetic appreciation of falconry's art.[44]

These aesthetics are rooted in humoral theory, freshly infused with the thirteenth century's heightened attention to the structures of the natural world. Another thirteenth-century verse falconry treatise, associated with a nobleman, 'le cunte Simun', is extant in Winchester College MS 26, a late thirteenth-century manuscript of canonical Latin medical texts.[45] Its author, named only as 'Samsun' (l. 31), sets the treatise's knowledge within the laws of creation – 'Ki ben i met del tut sa cure / Primes enquere lur

---

[40] *De avibus tractatus*, in Burnett (ed. and tr.), *Adelard of Bath*, pp. 237–55 (both versions of prologue, at 238, 240). Haskins suggested that if Adelard was a royal tutor, as seems likely, he may have had access to Harold Godwineson's hawking books (presumably included in the Norman administration's spoils after 1066). This is another (posthumous) collaboration of *philosophus* and king. Haskins, 'King Harold's Books'.
[41] Burnett (ed. and tr.), *Adelard of Bath*, pp. 248 and 249, no 8.   [42] Crane, *Animal Encounters*.
[43] Ibid., p. 240.   [44] Petrosillo, 'Predatory Poetics', 204–5, 199, 202–3.
[45] Hunt (ed.), *Three Anglo-Norman Treatises*, pp. 40–81. Perhaps Lord Simon is Simon of St Liz, Earl of Northampton, recorded as receiving 5s from Gervasius Falconarius for every year when 'he does not mew a hawk for him' (Oggins, *The Kings and Their Hawks*, p. 60 and n. 73). The treatise mingles *accessus* elements (title, l. 1, authoritative sources, ll. 5–6, the *causa scribendi* ['l'achaisun / De quei est fet, e en ki nun', 21–22], 21–42) and courtly conventions (especially in its exclusion of *vileins* and praise of the patron, ll. 32–42).

## Scholastic Theory and Vernacular Knowledge 55

[i.e., the falcons'] nature' (ll. 45–46) – grounding social hierarchy on natural diversity. The prologue stresses a human dominance authorised by Genesis, but sets it amidst fundamental contiguity, explaining that birds are, like all created things, diverse:

>       Kar sicume de nous veuns
> 48    Que de nature diversuns
>       Les uns umbles, les uns orgoilus,
>       Alquez irais e envious,
>       Kar si nun veuns diverser,
> 52    Ben poüns par resun prover
>       Que diversent ces creatures
>       Sulunc lur murs e lur natures.
>       Furmez sumes de une matere,
> 56    Mais que la nostre out Dex plus chere,
>       Kar de sun saint Esperit demeine
>       En face de hume mist sa aleine.
>       A sun semblant, a sun ymage
> 60    Nus fist, ço dit divine page. (ll. 47–60)[46]

Just as we ourselves include the meek, the spirited, the fierce and the ill-natured, so birds are diverse in their nature and *mores*. We are all made of the same matter, but God cherishes our human matter more, for with his own Holy Spirit he breathed on the face of man and, according to the Holy Scripture, made us in his image.

So too, being hatched and raised in *aire* of *diverse qualité* (l. 73) in various regions, hawks differ in kind because of air, the element that is the theatre of hawks and their austringers. God's breath, humans and birds are hierarchically interconnected, and this treatise goes on to discuss diseases both shared by and particular to humans and hawks. *Tisis* or consumption (explained as a Greek name for weakness of the lungs 'en griu un nun / D'enfertez qui vent en polmun', ll. 81–2) is a prominent concern (ll. 75–98).

Different tropes, figures and modes of authority are thus deployed in this franco-latinate culture, with careful attention to the form and nature of the knowledge being textualised and its audiences. Among questions of form, the most pervasive is the continuing significance of verse itself as a form for knowledge in the thirteenth century, even alongside an increasing imputation of objectivity and self-sufficiency to prose. Adrian Armstrong and Sarah Kay make the point that for all the so-called rise of prose in the thirteenth century, verse encyclopaedias and treatises continue to be

---

[46] Hunt (ed.), *Three Anglo-Norman Treatises*, p. 44.

composed. However, they develop a specialised function in the economy of representation, much in the way, Armstrong and Kay suggest, that black and white photography and film acquire a different kind of authenticity and signifying capacity once colour photography is the norm.[47] Verse retains its crucial role and its performative narratorial presence, its suasive, socialising relation to its audience.

For an example, consider the following prologue:

>     De geste ne voil pas chanter
>     Ne veilles estoires cunter,
>     Ne [la] vaillance as chivalers
> 4   Ke jadis esteient si fers:
>     Mun sen, ceo crem, pas ne savereit
>     Lur valur descrivere a dreit.
>     De dire poi crendreie mult;
> 8   E, de autre part, aussi redut
>     Ke tant preisasse lur valur
>     Ke tenu fusse a mentur,
>     Kar mult i ad cuntes e fables
> 12  Ke ne sunt pas veritables.
>     Pur ceo de tele chose dirrai
>     Dunt verité vus musterai ... (ll. 1–14)

> I don't want to sing about great deeds or tell old histories or the valour of knights who were once so brave. I fear that my intelligence would not know how to describe their bravery properly. I would be frightened of saying too little and, on the other hand, worried that I would praise their bravery so much that I would be held a liar, for there are many stories and fables that are not at all truthful. Because of this I will relate to you something whose truth I can show you.

This could be a prologue to many kinds of literary texts – a romance, hagiography or a poem about Christ's passion and the redemption – but it is actually a verse treatise on computus, Ralph de Lenham's *Art de Kalender*.[48] Composed in 1256, it is occasioned, Ralph says, by his unnamed lord's commission (ll. 17–22). The *Art de Kalender* shares the prologue quoted here with a late thirteenth-century verse text, the *Marriage of the Nine Daughters of the Devil*, a genealogically organised moral satire on sin dubiously attributed within the text itself to the great

---

[47] Armstrong and Kay, *Knowing Poetry*, pp. 2–3. Thus, for example, prose French versions of the *Elucidarius* antedate the verse *Lumere as lais*.
[48] Hunt (ed.), *Rauf de Linham, Kalender*, p. 5. Hereafter cited by line number in the text. For the prologue, see *VLT*, no. 40.

scholar-prelate Grosseteste.[49] It seems more likely that the *Marriage* borrows the prologue than that the *Kalender* does. But, regardless of priority, a set of vernacular literary conventions is here deployed as a way to knowledge, and that the prologue should be recyclable speaks not to indifference about how texts are accessed but to the felt necessity of verse's social performance and its related need to be situated, whether generically and/or in terms of its patron and audience networks or audience interfaces. It is also a reminder that the prologue strategies familiar from what we call literary texts come from a wide repertoire of textuality.

In the *Kalender*, the prologue both invokes and places itself within and against a literary system. In ll. 2–4, it moves *chansons de geste* from affiliation with historiography to the realm of romance and to the non-verifiable. And it further claims that the truth value of old histories cannot be safely estimated, given their transmission through time. Against this, the prologue sets calendrical knowledge, but this is knowledge derived from two kinds of time, from Roman civilisation as well as Christianity. The treatise has to suture these two together carefully, as in, for instance, the change from Romulus's ten-month year to the Christian twelve months. The *Kalender* is preoccupied with diversity, with the way different groups reckon the beginning of the first day of the week. Jews count it from the evening, says the *Kalender*, because 'en lur lei … truvent une tele reisun / Escrite el Bible', ll. 421–3). Evening was made first, then day. Christians, on the other hand, begin at midnight because Christ was born then,

> E par sa nessance aparut
> Nostre jor, et nostre nut
> Passa. (ll. 433–5)

And in his birth, our day dawned, and our night passed.

Even though this is not a polemical contrast of the two, one might still think it an example of the standard move to reinforce Christian identity by othering Jews, but a third group is now cited: 'Le commun puple' say that 'en l'aube de jor / Est le commencement del jor' ('the day's beginning is the dawn'), and the day should be counted from when first light first illumines it (ll. 437–46). So, Ralph de Lenham concludes,

---

[49] See Dean, with Boulton, *Guide*, no. 686.

> Le jor, si cum vus ai cunté
> En diverse houre est comencé
> Pur la diverse gent del mund,
> Ke pas de une lei ne sunt. (ll. 447–50)

The day, as I have told you, begins at different times for the different peoples of the world, who are not all of one faith.

The diversity which any systematising of calendrical matter entails is managed by vigorous narratorial presence. Ralph lays out sets of names – days of the week, the months, groups of feasts – and mediates the failure of these sub-sets to cohere by deploying the voiced and figuratively embodied social presence of the narrator. As Armstrong and Kay argue, poetry is the privileged medieval interface with sociality (rather than, as in modern conceptions, with private experience).[50] Thus, the *Kalender* presents the organising force of calendrical knowledge as crucially dependent not on its objective status but on social agreement to use the calendar's non-cohering subsets of knowledge, to work with the gaps in the systems of classical and Christian inheritance. When you have heard or read the treatise, whatever else, you know that time and the world it regulates are not simply intuitively knowable. Ralph de Lenham's <u>Art de Kalender</u> (emphasis added) constructs a body of knowledge through vernacular arts of representation as much as through translating Latin technical matters.

My final example offers a verse prologue based on Genesis:

> [Q]uant Deus out la femme fete,
> De la coste Adam est traite.
> Bauté la duna perdurable,
> 4 Mes ele le perdi par le deble;
> Puis que ele out la pume gusté
> Mult en fu disonuré.
> E les dames que ore sunt,
> 8 Ke de ceo culpes ne hunt,
> Pur ceo que Heve forfist tant
> De lur bauté sunt mult perdant. (ll. 1–10)[51]

When God made woman, he took her from Adam's side. He gave her everlasting beauty, but she lost it by means of the Devil: once she tasted the apple, she was greatly dishonoured. And women living today, who are not themselves guilty of this transgression, have highly perishable beauty because of Eve's great sin.

---

[50] Armstrong and Kay, *Knowing Poetry*, p. 199.
[51] Ruelle (ed.), *L'Ornement des Dames*, with citations here from *VLT*, no. 32b.

Here, one might anticipate access to doctrinal or misogynistic writing: but the text is a thirteenth-century vernacular *Ornatus Mulierum*, a treatise on cosmetics in which beauty treatments and remedies are cunningly authorised as remedies for the Fall via theology, virginity doctrine and medicine. As authorities, the text cites Galen, Constantine, Hippocrates and a Saracen woman, Trota of Salerno ('une dame qi ert Saracine, Mires ... de sa lai', who would be 'mut ... valiant si ust fei', ll. 34–36). To inflect the usual medical authorities with credentials for women *practitioners* is significant in a treatise that embodies knowledge of women as its subject, mode and organisation. The prologue uses a top-down bodily taxonomy (*A prime des chevoilz dirai*, l. 21) familiar not only from medical treatises but from rhetorical top-down *effictio* and *notatio* in lyric and narrative: here it forms the framework for ordering the prose remedies offered in the treatise, from treatments for hair-loss downwards. These seem just as mixed a bag as their modern descendants, sometimes tempting and yet always a little dodgy in their seductive asseveration. No wonder that the prologue's invocation of authorities plays so much on credal adherence, faith and credibility. So too, in the prose recipes, as with Ralph de Lenham's narratorial presence in the *Kalender*, efficacy is constantly authenticated by narratorial witness and insistence. The doubling of narrative presence in both the verse and the prose of the *Ornatus* works hard to secure the knowledge deployed in this work *as* knowledge.

By the time of the *Lumere*'s 1267 completion, then, the world of francophone approaches to works of learning and bodies of knowledge is highly diverse. Other French versions of the *Elucidarius* translate Honorius's own prose prologue – none has a full scholastic *accessus*. Pierre de Fetcham's choice of verse indicates the performative nature of dialogue in his text and its importance in socialising his text's knowledge, and his substantial *accessus* speaks to the systematicity and the compilatory scope of the *Lumere*, but it also testifies to the nuanced choices made in franco-latinate writing of the period. Other choices were possible, as in Pierre de Fetcham's own version of the *Secreta secretorum* and in the prologues to other encyclopaedic works in this literary culture.[52] Few, apart from *Sidrac*, however, have the compilatory range and ambition of

---

[52] Beckerlegge (ed.), *Le Secré de secrez*. For other insular French encyclopaedic works, see n. 17; further choices are represented in the presence of continental works, such as *Sidrac* or Gossuin de Metz's *Imago mundi* verse treatise in insular versions.

the *Lumere*. Moreover, the *Lumere* is not just borrowing a powerful template, but commenting on and positioning it. The Aristotelian *accessus* is not the only element of the prologue: the first is a summary of Genesis, followed by Eve's speech looking to the redeeming fruit of the Virgin's womb (ll. 219–332) and narratorial comment and prayers (ll. 333–404), brief treatments of the world's inconstancy, fear of the envious and the importance of finding the right path (405–530). The Aristotelian *accessus* runs from l. 531 to l. 694. Armstrong and Kay suggest that the *Lumere* problematises the origins of human knowledge and its simultaneous loss and gain in the fall with its account of the tree in Genesis: although the fall means that 'knowledge (*science*) of God himself and the world ... is now lacking to us, in another sense eating the apple has brought us knowledge of that lack'.[53] I would add that, in the context of this thematising of Genesis, Pierre de Fetcham's Aristotelian *accessus* is positioned as a strategy of fallen knowledge, doing what it can with post-lapsarian lack, in contrast to pre-lapsarian natural knowledge. This sophisticated use of the Aristotelian template is all the more effective in the relational vernacular of French through which schoolmen and many others could converse or entertain common projects in a multilingual society. So full and so Aristotelian a form of the prologue is not to my knowledge used again in insular vernacular texts until Bokenham's *Legendys of Hooly Wummon* of 1447, where its presence has equally specific reasons, in a textual community embracing Cambridge scholars, East Anglian religious, nobility and gentry.

The poetics of vernacular knowledge in the thirteenth century engage a range of forms and genres previously equalled only in Old English prose, and they develop the vernacular as a domain of knowledge. They build in understanding of the cosmos as an element of the authority of texts and their authors. They subjectivise and socialise knowledge and narration. Performed relations between the authority of the text, narratorial presence and audience engagement lay the ground for the notion of the author's witnessing experience as an element of textual authority, an aspect of poetics that would become crucial in later fourteenth-century writing by Langland, Chaucer, Gower and others. Some thirteenth- and early fourteenth-century knowledge-writing turns narratorial biography into a conduit to cultural-geographical knowledge. Mandeville's *Livre* (probably first composed in insular French, *c*. 1356–57) is the obvious example, but

[53] Armstrong and Kay, *Knowing Poetry*, p. 112.

other less well known texts could also be cited.⁵⁴ In such works it is indifferent in one sense whether the narratorial presence is fictive or not: what matters is to have a representative subjectivising anchor for the compilations of knowledge being newly brought within textual scope and organised into formally accessed books whose *ordinatio* and performed narrative stances engage expanding and varied textual communities.

Late medieval poets and natural philosophers, to borrow Kellie Robertson's recent formulation à propos Jean de Meun, Chaucer and Deguileville, 'shared a vocabulary, and more important, an orienting set of questions about the moral authority of the natural world and the writer's ability to claim this authority when representing [human] experience'.⁵⁵ When these later writers construct narrative *personae* and include disquisitions on what they called *philosophie* (by which is meant something like our 'natural science'), they are not initiating but continuing and developing the dynamic effects of the co-habitation of thirteenth-century scholastic and vernacular knowledge.⁵⁶

---

⁵⁴ See, e.g., *VLT*, pp. 411–12; Franklin Brown, *Reading the World*, esp. pp. 307–8.
⁵⁵ Robertson, *Nature Speaks*, pp. 1–2.
⁵⁶ My thanks to Alastair Minnis for decades of stimulation provided by his work, to the editors of this volume and to audiences for earlier versions of this essay, especially to Caroline Jewers and the University of Kansas medievalists at Lawrence, KA, the Graduate Societies at CUNY and Notre Dame, and, as always, the Columbia Medievalists' discussion group, with particular thanks to Francis Ingledew for illuminating follow-up discussions and readings in the history of science. I am grateful to my own graduate classes, who have explored some of the texts discussed here with encouraging vigour and interest, and to Annalise Wolf, PhD candidate at Fordham, for valuable research assistance. For time and space to finish the work, I am grateful to the Institute for Advanced Study at Central European University, Budapest.

CHAPTER 3

# Poetics and Biblical Hermeneutics in the Thirteenth Century

### Gilbert Dahan

The integration of Aristotle's writings was crucial to the development of Latin intellectual culture in the thirteenth century, prompting the definition of theology as a science and, albeit indirectly, the creation of what are now called the 'human sciences' – fields that include, for example, politics. Of these writings, the last to have any impact was undoubtedly the *Poetics*, which remained untranslated into Latin until its rendering in 1278 by William of Moerbeke, though a translation of Averroes's 'middle commentary' had been undertaken in 1256 by Hermannus Alemannus.[1] Of course, poetics – or rather poetry – had found a place in schemas of the sciences long before the establishment of a 'science of poetry', that is, of poetics, properly so-called. What we will attempt to determine here, then, are the repercussions of this 'science of poetry' for biblical exegesis, focusing on a few key issues which can be summarised briefly. To be sure, techniques for analysing poetic figures had long been applied to biblical texts, though such interpretations were carried out under the banner of rhetoric, in particular following the work done by Cassiodorus in his commentary on the Psalms.[2] In contrast, the thirteenth century saw something distinctive, namely, the analysis of biblical language itself in light of poetics. Taking place at the same time as the establishment of theology as a science and the emergence of 'scientific' biblical exegesis, this shift is not unimportant.[3] Scientific language (and we will see how this is defined) is taken to be preeminent, and it is set in opposition to poetic language, typically defined as containing lies. Yet biblical texts quite clearly contain poetic language. Since Scripture is the word of God and thus the highest form of language, how are these poetic portions to be understood? Likewise, we must consider the extent of Aristotelian poetics' contribution

---

[1] Both texts are edited by Minio-Paluello; see his study, 'Guglielmo di Moerbeke'.
[2] Cassiodorus, *Expositio Psalmorum*, ed. by Adriaen; see Grondeux, *À l'école de Cassiodore*.
[3] See Chenu, *La théologie comme science*.

to the analysis of biblical language – and, as we will see, in this regard medieval thought sometimes goes beyond the approaches of modern exegesis. Since the mid-seventeenth century, sustained and careful attention has been given to 'biblical poetry', typically considered as a particular genre, but this has very frequently been limited to the analysis of specific forms (notably parallelism).[4] By focusing instead on the poetic language of the Bible, certain medieval exegetes and intellectuals appear to prefigure a different approach, perhaps similar to that of languages now considered 'mythical'.

In addressing this rich and complex material, we will take up the place of poetics in the classifications of the sciences, the definition of poetic language (from the perspective of biblical exegesis), and the general analysis – most often found in the prologues of commentaries – of the language of biblical books, followed by some brief examples of the study of poetic texts.

## The Place of Poetics in the Classifications of the Sciences

The twelfth and thirteenth centuries saw the composition of several works attempting to establish a way of ordering the various domains of knowledge, thus offering an inventory of the sciences and establishing their relation to one another.[5] Though this type of writing can already be found in the early medieval period, it was thoroughly transformed under the influence of Arabic thought, testifying to the extensive diffusion of Greek (especially Aristotelian) writings. There were four principal types of divisions of the sciences, and not all of them included a place for poetics. In the antique system of the *trivium* and *quadrivium*, the division of the *trivium* (grammar, rhetoric, logic) could include poetics under the heading of rhetoric. The 'Stoic' division identifies three branches of philosophy: physical, moral and logical, *a priori* leaving no place for poetics before logic was assimilated to the writings in Aristotle's *Organon*, to which we will momentarily turn. The division referred to as Aristotelian – mathematics, physics, theology – is in fact itself a subdivision of the schema dividing speculative philosophy, practical philosophy and poetics, where 'poetics' denotes the body of knowledge needed to create something (that is, a craft or art). A variant version of this schema adds the sciences of language

---

[4] Alter, *The Art of Biblical Poetry*, pp. 3–26, offers a historical survey, beginning with Robert Lowth's *De sacra poesi Hebraeorum* (1753).
[5] Dahan, 'Les classifications du savoir'.

(grammar, rhetoric, dialectic – the sciences of the *trivium*), in contrast to philosophy or wisdom. Finally, another scheme, concerned specifically with logic, follows the different treatises of the *Organon*. This is, of course, of particular interest for our purposes, since the *Rhetoric* and *Poetics* were typically added to the *Organon* proper (*Categories, On Interpretation, Prior* and *Posterior Analytics, Topics, Sophistical Refutations*, all preceded by the *Isagoge* of Porphyry), with the integration of these two under the heading of logic apparently originating with Arabic authors, al-Farabi (in the translation of Gerard of Cremona) and Avicenna.[6]

In light of its affiliation with the *Organon*, thirteenth-century discussions of poetics for the most part focused on its role relative to the procedures of logic – this is, for example, what we find at the beginning of Thomas Aquinas's commentary on the *Posterior Analytics*.[7] A certain *Quaestio in poetriam* supplied in a manuscript of Averroes's commentary on the *Poetics* (in the translation of Hermannus Alemannus) provides the basic elements of the issue.[8] Poetics constitutes a part of logic, but one distinct from the rest: it has to do with the practical intellect and, more precisely, acts directed toward oneself (while rhetoric considers acts directed toward others). It comes second-to-last in the hierarchy of logic, with only sophism ranking lower – and this same schema appears in the writings of nearly all the relevant authors.

Exceptions may be found in two texts, quite different from one another. The first is a certain *Ysagoge in theologiam* attributed to the school of Abelard but in some respects resembling works produced in the school of St Victor.[9] Here, science is divided into four parts: *sapientia, eloquentia, poesis* and *mechanica*. The place given to poetry is, at first, surprising, but this text predates the influence of Arabic and Aristotelian thought, and so it is not really concerned with poetics but rather with poetry, as its definition of the term confirms:

> Poesis autem est scientia claudens in metro orationem gravem et illustrem, que per satiram vicia eliminat et virtutes inserit, per tragediam tolerantiam

---

[6] See the texts cited in Dahan, 'Notes et textes sur la Poétique', pp. 188–90.
[7] *Expositio libri Posteriorum*, pr., quoting from the new Leonine edition by Gauthier, I/2, 7: ' ... Quandoque uero sola estimatio declinat in aliquam partem contradictionis propter aliquam representationem, ad modum quo fit homini abhominatio alicuius cibi si representetur ei sub similitudine alicuius abhominabilis; et ad hoc ordinatur poetica, nam poete est inducere ad aliquid uirtuosum per aliquam decentem representationem. Omnia autem hec ad rationalem philosophiam pertinent: inducere enim ex uno in aliud rationis est'.
[8] Edited in Dahan, 'Notes et textes sur la Poétique', pp. 206–19.
[9] Edited in Landgraf, *Écrits théologiques*, pp. 63–289; see Luscombe, 'Authorship'.

laborum et fortune contemptum. Communiter autem omne poema fortium et ignavorum exempla proponit.[10]

Poetry is the science of setting serious and noble speech in meter: through satire it eliminates vices and instils virtues, through tragedy the suffering of labour and the contempt of fortune. Commonly, every poem offers examples of brave people and of cowardly ones.

The *divisio* itself adds comedy to satire and tragedy. Second, and just as remarkable for our purposes, is the *Moralis philosophia* of Roger Bacon (d. 1292).[11] Unlike other contemporary writers, Bacon gives priority to the 'practical sciences' (ethics, politics and economics), which require more complicated methods than the speculative sciences, the latter being satisfied with demonstrative and dialectical arguments. The practical sciences, in contrast, make use of rhetorical argument, including poetics, which Bacon approaches in two different ways: the teaching of poetic composition and, especially, as a moral science. In his *Opus maius*, Bacon does not hesitate to consider poetics as the superior part of logic, and he laments the lack of a good translation of the work of Aristotle.[12] The entire fifth part of the *Moralis philosophia* takes up the issue of rhetorical argument, which consists of three *species*: one regarding faith and its proofs, one which incites people to justice and one which leads us to worship of the divine, to the law and the virtues. This last *species* is the proper object of poetics. In support of this position, Bacon cites Averroes's commentary in the translation of Hermannus, the *Ars poetica* of Horace and passages on the subject in the works of al-Farabi, Avicenna and al-Ghazali.[13] A poetic argument, he says, is composed of similitudes deriving from the properties of things.

---

[10] Landgraf, *Écrits théologiques*, p. 72.
[11] Bacon, *Moralis philosophia*, ed. by Massa; see Massa, *Ruggero Bacone. Etica e poetica*.
[12] Bacon, *Opus maius*, III, ed. by Bridges, I, 70: 'Etiam de logica deficit liber melior inter omnes alios [the *Poetics*] et alius post eum in bonitate secundus [the *Rhetoric*] male translatus est nec potest sciri nec adhuc in usu vulgi est, quia venit ad Latinos et cum defectu translationis et squalore'.
[13] *Moralis philosophia*, V.iii.6–10, ed. by Massa, pp. 254–56: 'Et quia sic est, ideo argumentum rethoricum habet tres species. Una est circa quae fidei sunt et secte fidelis probande ... Secundum genus argumenti rhetorici est circa que flectunt ad compassionem iusticie, que in Rhetorica Tullii edocentur. Tercium est in hiis que nos flectunt ad opus in culto divino, legibus et virtutibus. Et duo prima nunc tacta vocantur absolute rethorica nec mutant hoc nomen; tercium vero argumentum, quod flectit ad ea que hec quinta pars considerat [moralis philosophia], rethoricum quidem est, sed vocatur proprio nomine 'poeticum' ab Aristotile et ceteris philosophis... Quoniam vero non habemus in latino librum Aristotilis de hoc argumento, ideo vulgus ignorat modum conponendi ipsum ; sed tamen illi qui diligentes sunt possunt multum de hoc argumento sentire per Commentarium Avenrois in [*ed.* et] librum Aristotilis, qui habetur in lingua latina... Poetica eciam Oracii multum operatur in hoc atque dicta Alpharabii in libro De sicentiis et Avicenne in principio Logice, quam habent Latini, et Algazelis in suo Tractatu logicali'.

The utility of philosophy is measured only in relation to divine things, and this part of philosophy can be put to remarkable use in the service of the divine, as the saints (especially Augustine) teach. Bacon then gives several examples of different styles: e.g., the simple (Galatians, 1 Timothy, etc.) and the grandiose (1 Corinthians, Romans, etc.). In this regard, his comment on the Prophets is quite interesting:

> Nam in prophetis, ubi sensus Dei miris enigmatibus concluditur, tanquam radius solaris nubis obumbracione tempereatur, quatinus oculus noster ipsum valeat contueri. Sic enim altissime veritates divine, nostris mentibus improporcionales, fiunt per huiusmodi sermones propheticos nobis conformes. Nam aliter misteria Dei non possunt nobis declarari, nisi primo manu ducamur per huiusmodi sacra velamina Legis et Prophetarum, sicut docet beatus Dionisius in libris suis et ceteri sancti idem contestantur et ex libro Tullii de condicione mundi [patet], ubi officium oratoris elegancius quam alias describit.[14]

> In the writings of the Prophets, where God's meaning is enclosed in marvellous enigmas, it is as though the sun's beam is tempered by the covering of a cloud so that our eye is able to gaze upon it. For thus the profoundest of divine truths, themselves out of proportion to our minds, are made proportionate to us by these prophetic words. We would otherwise be unable to expound the mysteries of God, unless we are first led by the hand through this holy veil of the Law and Prophets, as blessed Dionysius teaches in his books, and all of the saints bear witness to the same, and it is clear, too, from the book of Tully, *On the condition of the world*, where, more elegantly than elsewhere, he describes the role of the orator.

Though certain authors classify it as the lowest of the sciences, it is thus clear that poetics is still in a position to contribute to the understanding of holy books and divine mysteries.

## Scientific Language and Poetic Language

When scholastic writers sought to define the language of biblical texts, and its potential uniformity, their most pressing concern was to determine whether Scripture presents the best of all possible languages, that is, whether it is scientific. In the prologue to his commentary on the *Sentences*, Thomas Aquinas sets this out quite clearly:

---

[14] Ibid., V.iv.13–14, ed. by Massa, p. 261. The editor identifies the work of Cicero as *De optimo genere orationis*, I.3. The phrase *manu ducamur* suggests the ps.-Dionysian affiliations of the passage, discussed further below.

> Nobilissimae scientiae debet esse nobilissimus modus [i.e., procedendi]. Sed quanto modus est magis artificialis, tanto nobilior est. Ergo, cum haec scientia sit nobilissima, modus eius debet esse artificialissimus.[15]
>
> The mode of procedure of the most noble of the sciences [i.e., theology] ought itself to be most noble, and the more artificial [i.e., scientific] a mode is, the more noble it is. Therefore, since this science is the most noble, its mode ought to be the most artificial.

As should be apparent, the difficulties presented in this text are numerous. This is precisely the moment at which the consideration of theology as a science is coming to the fore – the commentary on the *Sentences* dates to Thomas's first Parisian tenure, 1252–56. The term 'theology' is still ambiguous, at once denoting the Word of God (i.e., Scripture and its interpretation) and the study of that Word (our use of the word 'theology'). Similarly, the adjective *artificialis* presents another difficulty, this involving the equivalence of *ars* and *scientia*.[16] But underlying all of this is the larger problem that the Word of God is, quite clearly, not consistently 'scientific', and, in line with our present concerns, its poetic portions are easy to identify. It will be useful to review, albeit quickly, some of the stages in the development of this line of reasoning, which seems to begin with the *Summa theologica* attributable, in part, to Alexander of Hales. It is thereafter found in the prologues to *Sentences* commentaries or theological *summae*, with authors in both categories of texts going on to examine the 'proper mode' of theology.

The opening tract of the *Summa fratris Alexandri* is unusually wide-ranging, including a question addressing 'An modus sacrae Scripturae sit artificialis vel scientialis' ('If the mode of sacred Scripture is that of an art or science') – as we have seen, these last two terms are equivalent, and it should be noted that he uses the term 'sacred Scripture', not 'theology'.[17] (The *Summa* dates to 1235–45, the early stages of considering theology as a science.) Alexander begins by opposing the scientific mode to the poetic one, the latter being the mode of theology and including narrative – in its literal and figurative senses (*modus historicus vel transumptus*) – and parable. Alexander then describes the scientific mode: it is based on definition, analysis and synthesis (*definitivus, divisivus et collativus*).

---

[15] Aquinas, *Scriptum super libros Sententiarum*, prol., q. 1, art. 5, t. I, ed. by Mandonnet and Moos, p. 16; see Oliva, *Les débuts*, p. 328.
[16] Cf. Chenu, *La théologie comme science*, p. 40.
[17] *Summa fratris Alexandri*, tract. int., q. 1 ('De doctrina theologiae'), c. 4 ('De modo traditionis sacrae Scripturae'), art. 1, 1, 7–9.

Further, the scientific mode makes use of clear language (*per sermones manifestos*), while Scripture uses 'mystical speech'. The mode of sacred Scripture is not, then, that of science, at least as it is understood by human beings, but it arises from a divine tendency to teach the soul about its salvation. Rather than resolving these arguments with a response *ad obiecta*, Alexander goes on to offer an explication which qualifies the negative response and includes several interesting arguments, in the end appearing to concede the presence of a scientific mode in Scripture. He first has recourse to pseudo-Dionysius the Areopagite, who tries to overcome the difficulty posed by the transcendent quality of the truths of Scripture through the analysis of a poetic mode moving from material realities to spiritual truths.[18] To definitions by analysis and synthesis he opposes the particular character of biblical texts, the mode of which is different in different books (*praeceptivus* in the Pentateuch and Gospels, *exhorativus* in the books of Solomon and the Epistles, etc.). Finally, the mystical quality of scriptural discourse is explained in terms of the virtue of faith, the need for study and the concealing of mysteries from those who are not worthy of this teaching. The text is of considerable interest, but it undoubtedly represents the early stages of a line of thought, with Alexander yielding, in a somewhat forced way, to the requirement of an ideally scientific language for sacred Scripture. In any case, the opposition between scientific language and poetic language is clear.

The treatment of this issue in the prologue to the *Sentences* commentary of Thomas Aquinas likewise implies a positive response – the mode of theology is scientific, despite arguments to the contrary, including the claim that 'poetics, which contains very little truth, differs from this science [i.e., theology], which is the epitome of truth. Therefore, since poetics proceeds by metaphoric locutions, the mode of this science must not be such'.[19] Thomas then goes on to analyse the language of the Bible. The principles of theology are given by revelation, in response to which the language of the Prophets takes its form, and he then appeals to the evidence of miracles, the language of which is narrative. Most importantly – and here again we see the influence, though unnamed, of ps.-Dionysius – since these details surpass the ability of human reason in the present world, 'it is necessary for us to be led by the hand' (*manuducatur*, a

---

[18] See ps.-Dionysius, *De Hierarchia angelica*, chs. 1 and 2, tr. in Minnis and Scott, pp. 173–82.
[19] *Scriptum super libros Sententiarum*, ed. by Mandonnet and Moos, I, 17: 'Sed poetica, quae minimum continet veritatis, maxime differt ab ista scientia, quae est verissima. Ergo, cum illa procedat per metaphoricas locutiones, modus hujus scientiae non debet esse talis'.

Dionysian term) 'by means of similarities borrowed from the perceptible world', so that the mode of this science is metaphorical, symbolic or parabolic.[20] Here are three characteristics of poetic language, also apparently taken up and included in theology as a science. Though a certain hesitation is thus still discernible, Thomas seems to have made considerable progress in advancing this line of thought.

A question 'on the proper mode of theology' likewise appears at the beginning of the *Summa theologiae* of Albertus Magnus, along with a question concerning whether or not its mode is scientific (*si habeat modum scientiae vel artis*).[21] Here we are closer to the discussion of Alexander of Hales, but some change is still evident: though Albertus provides the same definition of a scientific mode (*definitivus, divisivus, collativus*), his elaborations reveal the influence of certain advances in logic. The three arguments are the same. Holy Writ does not use a scientific mode, instead making use of history and parable, 'or even metaphor', and ps.-Dionysius is quoted on the point that it 'poetice procedit sub integumentis metaphoricis' ('proceeds poetically under metaphoric coverings'). Yet it is a sin to have recourse to metaphoric or improper language in scientific problems.[22] Finally, he considers Scripture's use of mystical words and integuments. Albertus concedes all of this and still goes on to try to demonstrate that Scripture is a practical science (according to the classification making use of the *Organon*, discussed above), arguing that the scientific mode is not appropriate for everyone. The limits of human intelligence compel Scripture to make use of images and perceptible realities to direct us – the term *manuductus* is used once again – to invisible mysteries. He then posits an essential difference between human sciences and theology. The rules are different for these two categories, with theology treating the incomprehensible light and thus making use, in its proper mode, of images and figures, as described by the field of poetics. As with Alexander of Hales, the problem is resolved by insisting on a fundamental separation of theology and the other human sciences.

---

[20] Ibid., I, 17–18 (and cf. Oliva, *Les débuts*, p. 330): 'Et quia etiam ista principia non sunt porportionata humanae rationi secundum statum viae, quae ex sensibilibus consuevit [Oliva reads 'conuenit'] accipere, ideo oportet ad eorum cognitionem per sensibilium similitudines manuducatur ; unde oportet modum istius scientiae esse metaphoricum sive symbolicum, vel parabolicum'.
[21] *Summa theologiae*, lib. I, pars I, q. 5 ('do modo proprio theologiae'), c. 1, in *Opera omnia*, XXXIV:1, 16–17.
[22] Ibid., p. 16: 'Metaphoricis sive transumptis uti in problematibus peccatum est scientialis et artificialibus, ut in II Topicorum dicitur. Talibus autem maxime sacra Scriptura utitur ...'.

Further developments in the question of the mode of theology are evident in the *Summa quaestionum ordinarium* of Henry of Ghent, who poses the question differently.[23] Article 14 of his *Summa* is devoted to the form of theological science, i.e., its 'mode of treatment' (*modus tractandi* or *tradendi* – Henry says that this is the same thing as the *modus agendi*). He first takes up the 'multiform' or 'uniform' character of this mode. Based on the plural quality of divine wisdom and on the variety of people to whom it is addressed, some maintain that the mode of this science should be multiple. For Henry, however, its appropriate mode 'is such that under one and the same word diverse ideas are contained, touching on diverse subjects and diverse articles of faith'. This mode is thus specific to Scripture and transcends our language. He then turns to consider a topic that will be familiar from the earlier texts: 'Arguitur quod modus tradendi hanc scientiam debeat esse argumentativus sive doctrinalis sive rationativus sive inquisitivus, quod idem est' ('It is argued that the mode of transmitting this science should be based on argumentation, teaching, reason or inquiry – all of which amounts to the same thing').[24] Henry refutes this point, since this science surpasses the possibilities of human reason. He argues that its proper mode is narrative, and he mentions its use of metaphor. At this point, then, Henry appears to have taken us far afield from the question of poetics, but though he does not refer to ps.-Dionysius (preferring to cite Augustine), and though some of his positions appear to run counter to the prevailing opinions of his time (especially the uniqueness of scriptural language), his understanding of a language which transcends the possibilities of human reason certainly continues to develop this line of thought.

In this collection of texts, we can note an emerging opposition between scientific language and poetic language – much like what one finds in the work of Paul Ricœur.[25] Poetic language is defined by its three principal modes, as given for example by Thomas Aquinas: metaphor, symbol and parable. Of these three, metaphor is apparently the most important, since it entails the transfer of meaning and, therefore, immediately requires an active hermeneutic process. Symbol tends to involve ps.-Dionysian ideas, which also serve as the basis for a set reading of Holy Writ. Parable has recently been the object of several studies, the major question being whether or not its interpretation ought to be considered spiritual rather than literal. It seems that, despite a significant number of spiritual

---

[23] *Summa quaestionum*, I, ff. 99ᵛ–101ᵛ, 'De modo tradendi Theologiam'. [24] Ibid., f. 100ᵛ.
[25] See especially *La métaphore vive*, p. 325 ff.

interpretations of parables, several medieval theorists of exegesis wished to restrict them to the domain of literal exegesis.[26] The domain of the letter is thus immense: not only does this understanding go well beyond the threefold Victorine scheme of *littera–sensus–sententia*, itself a source of major progress in twelfth-century exegesis, but the field of spiritual exegesis finds itself reduced, since such a hermeneutic includes much more than a narrow literal explication of the biblical text, encompassing instead a detailed consideration of metaphor, a symbolic approach and consideration of paraphrase. We are thus at one of the major turning-points of thirteenth-century exegesis, and it seems that reflection on poetics has helped to set off this (admittedly slow) development, going far beyond the analysis of rhetorical figures and constituting one of the great riches of medieval exegesis.

With these theoretical considerations in mind, let us now turn to examine the practice of medieval exegesis, illustrated by some brief examples.

### Overarching Analyses: The 'Modi'

Without doubt, one of the major developments in medieval exegesis was the analysis of the *modi*, the 'modes' of language of the biblical book being studied.[27] The origin of this approach may be found in the scheme of the *accessus*, elaborated in the high medieval period and applied first to the secular literature studied in the schools and then, in the twelfth century, incorporated into the study of biblical books.[28] More specifically, it appears to derive from the heading of the *modus agendi* in these *accessus*, the 'manner of proceeding' of the works in question. In some cases, even in the thirteenth century, the analysis of the *modus agendi* amounts to little more than an outline or summary of the contents, particularly in the case of biblical books. Much more interesting, however, is the treatment of the *modus agendi* as the study of the style or language of the book under consideration. When the schema of the four Aristotelian causes came to

---

[26] See the summary of my *séminaire* for the École pratique des hautes études, Dahan, 'Les paraboles'.
[27] Dahan, *L'exégèse chrétienne*, pp. 416–23. For a different perspective, see Minnis's exceptional study, 'Literary Theory' (1979), as well as his '*Multiplex modus*' (2000).
[28] On the *accessus*, see the classic studies of Quain, Hunt and Silvestre. The earliest biblical commentaries to make use of this scheme seem to be treatment of the Psalms by Bruno the Carthusian and Roscelin of Compiègne, followed by Peter Abelard: see Dahan, *Lire la Bible*, pp. 63–66; Kraebel, 'School of Rheims'.

rival the *accessus*, these discussions were included under the heading of the 'formal cause'.²⁹

In some cases, the analysis of the *modi* illustrates what has been said above regarding the multiplicity of languages in Scripture (even if this notion was contested by certain medieval theorists), naming, for example, the narrative, exhortative, prayerful, etc., in the course of determining the dominant 'mode' in each book. The great majority of commentators define the mode of the historical books, for example, as 'narrative'. For considerations of poetic language, we may look in particular to the prologues to Job, Ecclesiastes, the Canticle of Canticles and the prophetic books. It is significant to find the mode of Job defined as poetic by Thomas Aquinas, whose commentary in many ways constitutes a break from the earlier tradition.³⁰ With regard to mode, earlier commentaries had essentially restricted their consideration to the beginning and end of the book, which are, indeed, narrative. Yet, in keeping with the judgements of exegetes today,³¹ Aquinas draws attention to Job's poetic character: 'Liber iste per modum poematis conscriptus est, unde per totum hunc librum figuris et coloribus utitur quibus poetae ut consueverunt' ('This book is written in the mode of a poem, and therefore, throughout this book, it makes use of the figures and rhetorical colours that were the common fare of the poets').³² For Ecclesiastes, the prologues often expound on the '*concionator* theory' that had been articulated by the Fathers: not everything in this biblical book is to be attributed to a single speaker, Solomon, but it instead gives the words of different interlocutors whose opinions do not always correspond to the truth. John of Varzy expresses this view clearly: 'Causa formalis est modus agendi, qui est per modum concionatoris. Proponendo enim diversas sententias procedit, modo sapientis, modo stulti, ut sic ex pluribus una veritas elucescat' ('The formal cause is the mode of proceeding, which is in the mode of a preacher. He proceeds by offering various opinions, sometimes those of a wise man, sometimes of a fool, so that from many opinions one truth shines forth').³³ For the Canticle, more than the book's numerous images,

---

²⁹ *MTA*, pp. 40–72, illustrates this point in detail.
³⁰ Here I repeat some material from my study, Dahan, 'Commentary of Aquinas'.
³¹ E.g., Alter, *Art of Biblical Poetry*, pp. 85–110.
³² *Expositio super Iob*, quoting from Dondaine's Leonine edn, XXVI, 3.
³³ I have printed this prologue in Dahan, *Lire la Bible*, pp. 96–101 (here p. 100). The same view is expressed by Bonaventure, *Commentarius in Ecclesiasten*, in *Opera omnia*, VI, 6: 'Habet modum agendi singularem inter alios libros: procedit enim ut concionator, diversorum sententias proponendo, modo sapientis, modo stulti, ut ex plurium sententiis una elucescat veritas in anima auditorum'.

it is its form as an amatory dialogue which is emphasised by, for example, William of Auvergne (d. 1249).³⁴ In the case of prophetic books, medieval exegetes draw attention to different poetic procedures: in his prologue to Isaiah, for example, Thomas Aquinas affirms that the prophet uses beautiful similitudes, which are necessary insofar as the prophet delivers a transcendent message surpassing the possibilities of human reason.³⁵ With the analogies they establish, these images give us a way to grasp the realities the prophet sought to convey. Like the great majority of writers who develop this theme, Thomas has recourse to the thought of ps.-Dionysius, and he makes use of the typical expression *manuducere* ('to take by the hand', i.e., in order to lead to a higher understanding). He offers the same assessment of Lamentations, emphasising the difficulties posed by this book: its verbal ornaments, the profundity of its mysteries and its variety of similitudes.³⁶ Hugh of St Cher's prologues to the prophetic books reveal the same thing: the prophecy of Ezechiel is sometimes clear and sometimes obscure, especially in its visions and, above all, at the beginning and the end, while the difficulties posed by Daniel require readers to remain alert.³⁷

All of these examples of the analysis of *modi* contribute to the study of Scripture's poetic language: some portions of the Bible are written in a language that is obscure, a poetic language. More than mere verbal ornament, the use of *similitudines* at once makes the language obscure and provides the means of understanding it. (This term, *similitudines*, is admittedly somewhat vague, but in at least some cases it should be translated as 'metaphors'.) The mechanism of metaphor is at the heart of medieval exegesis, especially in the thirteenth century, and it is defined by the idea of *transumptio* or the 'transfer of meaning', thus effectively

---

[34] Dahan, 'L'exégèse chez Guillaume d'Auvergne', p. 267: 'Modus agendi: siue sponsus, siue sponsa loquatur, ut amans loquitur, hoc est affectiones suas et desideria ceterasque amoris sancti sequelas exprimit; pene enim omnia que hic dicuntur mutua sunt sponsi et sponse alloquia ex ui et uehemencia amoris erumpencia'.

[35] *Expositio super Isaiam*, quoting from Dondaine and Reid's Leonine edn, xxviii, 3: '... pulcras et curiales similitudines, que sunt necessarie nobis propter connaturalitatem sensus ad rationem ...'.

[36] *In Threnos*, quoting from the Vivès edition by Fretté, xix, 199: 'In modo ostenditur difficultas; unde sequitur *In qua erat involutus* [Ezech. 2:9, the prologue's *thema*]. Est enim iste liber involutus ornatu verborum ... Est etiam involutus profunditate mysteriorum ... Est etiam involutus varietate similitudinum'.

[37] *Postilla in Ezechielem*, in *Opera omnia*, v, f. 2ʳᵃ: 'Modus agendi talis est: alicubi planus est, alicubi obscurus. Planus est in exhortationibus et comminationibus. Obscurus in visionibus, maxime in principio et in fine ...'; *Postilla in Danielem*, ibid., f. 145ʳᵃ: 'Et etiam difficultas Libri ostenditur, cum dicitur quod est in eo sapientia et scientia. Et sic modus agendi designatur, et etiam attentio auditorum excitatur, cum audimus scilicet difficultatem in Libro'.

permitting the shift from the perception of material realities to that of spiritual truths.[38] We will try to illustrate this interpretive habit with some concrete examples drawn from the commentaries.

## Reading Poetic Language

The exegetical system developed in these commentaries goes beyond the plurality of senses and even, in some way, beyond the opposition between letter and spirit. *A priori*, we remain on the level of literal exegesis, but the analysis of poetic language supports an exploration of all of the possibilities of this literal meaning.[39] It is, of course, hardly surprising that Thomas Aquinas offers the clearest and most persuasive examples, since we have seen that his consideration of the language of theology led him to reflect on the languages of the Bible, especially its poetic language. In this regard, his commentary on Job is especially revealing.[40] Again, many theoretical statements in the commentary confirm the importance accorded to poetic language, as in his gloss on Job 35.10, where God is discussed as 'qui dedit carmina in nocte' ('he who has given songs in the night'):

> *Ubi est Deus . . . qui dedit*, scilicet per revelationem, *carmina*, id est humanae instructionis dogmata, quae ab antiquis multotiens carminibus comprehendebantur, *in nocte*, id est ad litteram in somnio nocturno, vel in quiete contemplationis seu obscuritate visionis.[41]

> *Where is God . . . who has given*, i.e., by revelation, *songs*, i.e., the foundations of human teaching, which were often expressed by the ancients in songs, *in the night*, i.e., literally, in a nocturnal dream, in the quiet of contemplation or the enigma of a vision.

The poetic form has, traditionally, been used to transmit wisdom. One wonders what Thomas has in mind here – Platonic myths, perhaps, or the stories conveyed in Ovid's *Metamorphoses*. An identical statement appears in his gloss on Job 36.24, where it is said that certain men have sung (*cecinerunt*) the work of the divine:

---

[38] See Dahan, 'Saint Thomas et la métaphor'.
[39] In an earlier study, I have attempted to analyse this surfeit in terms of the idea of the symbol: see Dahan, 'Symbole et exégèse médiévale'.
[40] See too some of the discussion and analysis offered in my study, Dahan, 'Commentary of Aquinas', especially the section on 'The Analysis of Language'.
[41] Aquinas, *Expositio super Iob*, Leonine edn, XXVI, 186.

Dicit autem *cecinerunt* propter antiquam sapientum consuetudinem, qui metrice divina et philosophica describebant. Quantumcumque autem homines aliqui sint sapientes, non possunt pertingere ad cognoscendam et enarrandam essentiam eius, sed tota hominis cognitio et sermo est de Deo per opera eius, quae tamen neque Iob neque aliquis homo perfecte cognoscere potest, et ideo subdit: *Omnes homines vident eum*, scilicet per sua opera: nullus enim adeo in sapientia deficit quin aliqua divinorum operum percipiat, et rursus nullus est adeo sapiens cuius cognitio non multum vincatur ab excellentia claritatis divinae.[42]

He says *they sang* on account of the ancient custom of the wise, who wrote down divine and philosophical matters in meter. For however wise certain people may be, they cannot attain to comprehending and articulating his [i.e., God's] essence, and yet human knowledge of God, and all human discourse about him, are by means of his works, which neither Job nor any other person can perfectly know. He therefore continues: *All people see him*, that is, by means of his works: for no one is so lacking in wisdom that he cannot perceive at least some of the divine works, and, conversely, there is no one so wise that his knowledge is not overcome by the excellence of divine clarity.

Anchored in the description of the realities of this world, which is the work of God, poetry is thus a means of escaping the frailty of human reason. Many other examples of this kind of analysis could be cited – on Job 38.1, for instance, where the description of God speaking from the midst of the whirlwind is taken either according to its proper sense or as a metaphor,[43] or on the introductory story, understood not as a narrative but as a symbolic tale given in the form of an enigma.[44] Aquinas's commentary on Isaiah could supply other telling examples, but let us turn instead to the work of a Franciscan author, Peter John Olivi (d. 1298), whose approach to hermeneutic questions differs significantly from that of the Dominican. Glossing Cant. 1.3, for example, 'Curremus in odorem unguentorum tuorum' ('We will run in the odour of your ointments'),[45] Olivi makes the following remark:

---

[42] Ibid., p. 191.  [43] Ibid., 199.
[44] Ibid., p. 7, an extremely important passage in Thomistic hermeneutics: 'Hoc autem symbolice et sub aenigmate proponitur secundum consuetudinem sacrae Scripturae, quae res spirituales sub figuris rerum corporalium describit, sicut patet Is. 6[.1] *Vidi Dominum sedentem super solium excelsum et elevatum*, et in principio Ezechielis et in pluribus aliis locis. Et, quamvis spiritualia sub figuris rerum corporalium proponantur, non tamen ea quae circa spiritualiter intenduntur per figuras sensibiles ad mysticum sensum pertinent, sed litteralem, quia sensus litteralis est qui primo per verba intenditur sive proprie dicta, sive figurate'.
[45] The addition *in odorem unguentorum tuorum* is commonplace in the thirteenth century (notably in the Alcuinian tradition), and it is retained in the Clementine Vulgate.

> Nota quod obiectis delectabilibus quinque sensuum tam sponsus quam sponsa nituntur metaphorice exprimere varietatem et varias suavitates sensuum spiritualium, quae non possunt nobis humano ore exprimi nisi sub sensibilibus; et ideo videbis quod aliquando nominant suavia obiecta visus vel auditus, aliquando odoratus, aliquando gustus vel tactus. Unde non videntur per hoc intendere nisi quod sub variis deliciis sensuum et sensibilium varias exprimant delicias et efficacias spiritualium sensuum et obiectorum, quae in apparatu spiritualium nuptiarum ineffabiliter et incomprehensibiliter redundant.[46]

> Note that both the bridegroom and the bride rely on objects agreeable to the five senses to express, metaphorically, the variety and the different charms of the spiritual senses, which cannot be expressed to us with human speech except by means of perceivable things. And so you will see that sometimes they denote charming objects of sight and sound, sometimes of smell, sometimes of taste or touch. They do not thereby seem to intend anything other than to express by means of various delights of the senses and perceivable things the pleasing and efficacious qualities of spiritual senses and objects, which ineffably and incomprehensibly overflow in the trappings of a spiritual wedding.

Olivi is sensitive to the rich poetic detail of the Canticle, which he tends to interpret according to its primary meaning or what could be called its 'literal' sense, but these metaphors in turn express immaterial truths which only poetic language can attempt to grasp.[47] Though his Lamentations commentary is, admittedly, less innovative, here too Olivi reflects the approach taken by other late medieval authors (and, indeed, by some more recent exegetes as well), raising questions about the text's poetic form – which, he says, does not appear to be appropriate for its prophetic subject-matter, especially for this kind of lament. Still, as the Psalms in particular make clear, the wisdom of the prophets makes use of a variety of rhetorical modes, in both verse and prose, which are prone to elicit certain emotive responses from their readers.[48]

These different examples confirm the function of poetic language in the Bible – in an immediate and banal way, it could be considered a matter of awakening certain feelings, a disposition of the spirit, in whoever reads it or hears it read. This is the role attributed, traditionally, to rhetoric as well as to poetry. More noteworthy, however, is the surpassing suggested in

---

[46] Olivi, *Expositio in Canticum*, ed. by Schlageter, p. 120.
[47] This is made clear in his prologue, ibid., ed. by Schlageter, pp. 93–110, even if, in his account of the text's *forma* (p. 98), he seems to refer to three spiritual senses (moral or contemplative, allegorical and anagogical).
[48] See especially Olivi's preface, Olivi, *La Caduta du Gerusalemme*, ed. by Bartoli, p. 1.

poetry, its ability to express that which transcends human reason. The ps.-Dionysian tradition left its mark on medieval exegetes, and this is certainly where it is more relevant for the interpretation of poetry. I have not found uses of Aristotle's *Poetics* in biblical commentaries: its translation almost certainly appeared too late to generate citations of this text in the thirteenth century, and exegetes instead appealed to Ciceronian rhetoric or more generally to the Latin rhetorical tradition. Nevertheless, and especially through the study of language, the thirteenth century saw the development of a line of thought which we may rightly identify as 'poetic science'.[49]

---

[49] This chapter has been translated by Andrew Kraebel.

CHAPTER 4

# Robert Holcot and De vetula
## Beyond Smalley's Assessment

### Ralph Hanna

There is a fair likelihood that the most widely read work of a late medieval English author was Robert Holcot's (d. 1349) extensive *Super Sapientiam Salomonis*. More than 170 copies of this commentary, the standard late medieval entrée to the text, have been identified. Nevertheless, Holcot and the implications of his work have remained strangely uninvestigated, since Beryl Smalley first drew him to critical attention some sixty years ago.[1] Smalley was a great scholar of Christian exegesis, but her comments on Holcot (and others of her 'classicising friars', like John Ridewall) were handicapped by her very strengths: she could only identify their behaviour, an interest in classical culture, the display of which she found tedious, as exegetically divergent. I take up this issue – what did Holcot think he was doing? – in hopes of teasing out those features that rendered him an attractive resource in the later Middle Ages, their characteristics and how they might have been used by readers/auditors.[2]

I begin with a moment from Holcot's prologue to *Super Sapientiam*, originally the introduction to this protracted sequence of lectures designed to introduce beginning Oxford theologians to the glories of this text. In certain ways, Holcot here takes up gambits rather traditional for such an occasion. Generically, this introductory sermon (and all Holcot's lectures are cast as *sermones moderni*, not as verbal or phrasal glosses) is supposed to be a *laus theologiae*, a whetting of interest in the spiritual marvels to be revealed by the biblical text.[3] And to a very large extent, Holcot delivers,

---

[1] See particularly her 'Robert Holcot OP', a good deal more extensive and pointed than her later treatment, *EFA*. Allen's study of Holcot's colleague John Ridewall, *Friar as Critic*, Clark, 'Friars and the Classics', and Slotemaker and Witt, *Robert Holcot*, have all tended to repeat Smalley's contentions.

[2] All my citations come from the 1476 Cologne edition of Holcot, *Super Sapientiam Salomonis*. I have used the online copy from Düsseldorf, which has extensive MS corrections.

[3] This performance thus bears comparison with Wenzel's 'Academic Sermons'. There Wenzel analyses several analogous sermons, his examples offering introductions to Oxford graduate lecture courses dedicated to Peter Lombard's *Sentences*.

albeit with a difference. As he says near the opening, 'the subtlety of holy Scripture, divinely inspired for man's use, has a certain unique and prior privilege. It justly claims for itself four reasons' – which Holcot has outlined – 'to be honoured and glorified above all other studies'.[4]

Rather early on in this performance, Holcot builds his argument with a reading of Esther 15.5–7. The passage describes Esther's heroic, daring and terrifying approach to Assuerus to plead for her people. The Vulgate says that, as Esther approaches, 'super unam [famulam] quidem innitebatur, quasi *pre deliciis* et nimia teneriturdine corpus suum ferre non sustinens' (15.6, emphasis added: 'Upon one of [her two maids] she leaned, as if *for delicateness* and overmuch tenderness she were not able to bear up her own body'). It is taken as typical for such opening lectures to present unqualified praise for the discipline supposed to be on offer, but this verse does no such thing. Rather, it suggests the possible dependence of theological reading (Esther) on other forms of knowing (the supportive *famula*). This first servile figure Holcot identifies as essentially classical, the philosophical pursuit of wisdom alone ('vana metaphysica', not divinity), citing Aristotle as master of argument. A second *famula*, who follows Esther and holds up her train, is law, both canon (including sacramental practice) and civil, which theology actually should counsel and on whom it is thoroughly dependent. Holcot's rejection of the first, most explicitly Aristotelian metaphysics, is predicated upon a passing undeveloped reference to some derivative of the *Glossa ordinaria*, its purport being that at bottom theology is a matter of faith, denied to pagan philosophers.[5]

Holcot's developing argument analyses the claims of both of Esther's *famule*. Of the two, that of her supporting handmaid is more succinct:

> Supra primam [famulam] sacra theologia, cum sit sibi ipsi sufficiens et robusta, *pre deliciis* tamen simulat se inniti, quasi dictis et modis eorum loquendo, opponendo, respondendo, probando et reprobando. Non per necessitate, sed *pre deliciis* vtitur sicut placet. (sig. A2ʳᵃ, emphasis added)

> Holy theology, although she is completely sufficient and powerful in herself, nevertheless pretends that she leans on this first maid *for delight*,

---

[4] 'Sed sacre Scripture subtilitas hominibus inspirata diuinitus per cuiusdam prerogatiue priuilegium singulare quatuor istas causas honoris et glorie sibi vendicat merito super omnes [sc. artes]' (sig. A1ʳᵃᵇ).

[5] Cf. 'sicut dicit glossa quedam interline[aris] Leu' 2' (sig. A1ᵛᵇ). Holcot's citation appears to paraphrase the gloss on Lev 2.2 'similiae' *gen.* (of the fine flour); see *PL* 113:302. Although customarily deprecated, Migne here, as fairly frequently, is reproducing what one will find in any version of the text. Here I have checked against Feruardent (ed.), *Biblia sacra*.

as if she spoke, argued, responded, proved and refuted through philosophers' words and methods. She uses these as she pleases, not from necessity but *for delight*.

For its communication or demonstration, theology accepts the 'delights' mandated by Esther and originally developed elsewhere and in a different cause, as the sole content of classical philosophy.

This reading, of course, is predicated directly on the text, as the repeated *pre deliciis* shows. And yet not quite: Esther's seemingly 'delicate nature' has been wrenched from context ever so slightly, lexically transformed into 'delights', joys that might be associated with theological discussion or debate, which is, apparently, supposed to be fun, not just soberly uplifting.[6] One should also note Holcot's use of *simulare*: rather than exactly textual, the verb represents Holcot's dramatic response to Esther's situation – she is not in actuality so dependent as she appears, only adopting this posture (*quasi*). Like that other woman of valour, Judith, she is a master of deceit. Esther here follows or adapts herself to court ceremonial, simulates fearful deference, precisely so that she can command, wheedling her husband/monarch Assuerus into doing what she wants.

Holcot's account here expects the standard symbolic reading of the biblical source of his example. In this, quite against some aspects of the literal text, Assuerus figures God – and Esther is thus indeed a proper figure for the theologian approaching the divine text.[7] However, the use of *simulare* modifies the deference of this moment, and in a manner strikingly self-reflexive. After all, Holcot's entire argument at this point is predicated upon – however shifting they will be – figural readings, rhetorical *similitudines*, engaging appearances, rather than substantial identities. Moreover, there is his cannily knowing sense, which Smalley found only irritating, that, in some way, whatever the divine majesty and mystery one approaches, the engaged theological reader is indeed an Esther, controlling the text, coercing it to his will for argumentative purposes, and not necessarily in an open or ostensibly principled fashion (*sicut placet*). In essence, if following his earlier arguments, Holcot's faith is to be seen as driving his theological reading, his reader is called upon to accept his apparently deferential *magisterium*, to have faith in his faith, however

---

[6] Analogously, cf. 'Conuenienter autem sacre scripture difficultati suauitas dulcis et vtilis est annexa' (sig. A 2$^{va}$: 'For properly, both sweet and useful pleasure is joined to the difficulty of holy Scripture'), with subsequent citation and discussion of the obvious Horatian parallel.
[7] Cf. Hanna, *Patient Reading*, esp. pp. 84–87.

capricious it might seem – a generosity of reading Smalley found herself unable to extend.

One might unpack Smalley's difficulties here. Smalley thought such moralisations absurd in the context of scriptural discussion, alien to what she considered 'proper exegesis'. But, just as she largely ignored Holcot's sermon form, she also failed to recognise that – as the great variety of his citations would suggest – this behaviour was to be recognisable to his audience as coming, not from learned glossing, but from a rather different discursive site. One needs to read contextually around Holcot's practices – on this occasion I choose his handling of pseudo-Ovid's *De vetula* – to qualify views like Smalley's and arrive at some sense of what 'exegesis' meant for Holcot. After all, few of the immediate audience in his cloistered Oxford lecture hall were destined to pass on to the glories of a DTh. Most, in fact, would be engaged in hands-on *cura animarum*, and Holcot sought to stimulate their imaginations so that they might be effective in this activity, particularly through sermons. Rather than theology-school engagement, he sought to foster a public effort to bring biblicised thinking to bear on communal reformation.

Moreover, Holcot's ultimate source for such activity is well known – and, frequently, often silently, pillaged throughout *Super Sapientiam*. This is John of Salisbury's *Polycraticus*, always seen as an enabling text for Holcot's greatest precursor, John of Wales. There is a lengthy and extremely detailed scholarship outlining the *sicut placet* behaviour of John's argumentation: his capacity for misreporting his sources and deriving arguments inobvious yet wittily compelling from his misreported versions. Like both the Johns who preceded and inspired him, Holcot has an eye, not to the lecture hall, but to reforming social practice in what all three designate as a Ciceronian 'res publica'. Holcot's lectures imagine taking imaginative reading practices, biblically predicated, out of a theology classroom to attract and influence a broad public audience.[8]

To return to the argument of Holcot's first lecture. Following upon his evocation of Esther, Holcot moves to a considerably more extended discussion, taking up Esther's second *famula*. She has now morphed a bit, into an *ancilla*. I think this a synonymous slippage that exposes some of Smalley's difficulties with this and similar texts. Smalley viewed exegesis

---

[8] On John of Salisbury and John of Wales, see Pantin, 'John of Wales'. On John's argumentative moves, see von Moos, 'Use of *Exempla*', with abundant further references. For a further example, see my discussion of John of Salisbury's absurd yet productive discussion of Noachic dietary restrictions, Hanna, 'Wisdom of Poetry'.

as substantially text-bound, and her interest was concentrated on the methods various commentators sought in order to explain some particular moment in the designated authority. Generally, her main interest, displayed with careful sophistication, was in finding patterns of repeated practice predicated on such local readings. Here, however, Holcot does not respond to the text *per se*, but to biblical language, always being denatured by its gloss. (The standard introductory *id est* always seems to tell the reader that a paraphrase might serve just as well as the text itself.) Nor is Holcot here practising the standard concordance-thinking mandated as customary exegetical and homiletic practice: find the same word somewhere else in a provocative passage that makes the point to be argued with utter directness.[9] Rather, the transition depends upon a synonym, and Holcot is counting on what we might recognise as literary imagery to construct a driving argument.

Here, in other words, Holcot appears to have 'righted himself', subordinating alien studies to theological truth. Except ... It is a qualified subordination, limited to an attack on a specific discipline, not in fact his earlier target (classical philosophy), but Esther's second *famula*, as if she were a personification of legal studies. The discussion ultimately finds its authority, not in a biblical text (although it begins there), but in an unexpected source, a piece of poetry.

While Esther's first *famula* has qualified value, Holcot argues that the second might be mirrored by Hagar as a dissolute *ancilla* (sig. A2$^{rab}$). Too many modern clerics, he says, are interested in the potential emoluments of their position, not in the pursuit of wisdom (*sapiencia*); this they forsake especially for legal studies, which bring *delicie* and *dignitates*. There is, of course, a further semantic slippage built into the argument here: a moment ago, some *delicie* were in fact licit, largely because they were figurative and mental 'delights', ones which involved intellectual activity, the disputation undergirded by Aristotelian logic. Literal delights, at least if resolutely pursued to the detriment of higher things, are not so. And a further slippage occurs, too, since – and this provides another logic for the subsequent provision of poetry – Holcot does not here defend inspired theology, but wisdom (philosophy more generally), against modern practice.

---

[9] In the later Middle Ages, such 'concordantial exactitude' (even extending to such a question as 'Can one licitly explain a passage by the same noun in a different case, or same verb in a different tense?') is mandated universally in the instructions for the most ubiquitous and most public exegetical occasions, sermons. See Wenzel's magisterial *Medieval* Artes Praedicandi, *passim*.

Such men, off hunting delicious pelf through legal studies, resemble the *ancilla* Hagar, to whom the angel said thrice, 'Reuertere ad dominam tuam et humiliare sub manibus eius' (Gen. 16.9: 'Return to thy mistress and humble thyself under her hand'). The argument then develops, initially through the claim that 'Leges enim et canones istis temporibus mirabiliter fecunde concipiunt delicias et pariunt dignitates' (sig. A2va: 'Today, civil and canon law with a wonderful fertility conceive delights and give birth to positions of power'). The figurative language underpinning this sentence, otherwise unexplicated, forms another example of Holcot's responsiveness to the dramatic situation embodied in the literal text. It alludes to the enmity created by Hagar's pregnancy and Sarai/Sarah's barrenness. And of course, Holcot is implicitly considering, and reapplying in his own situation (*istis temporibus*), the great scriptural model for figural reading, Paul at Gal. 4.22–31. He continues:

> Et ideo sacra Scriptura que est omnium scientiarum domina derelicta est; ad illas confluit quasi tota multitudo scolarium his diebus, et flebilis adimpletur lamentacio Ieremie, Trenorum primum, 'Facta est quasi vidua domina gencium'. Hec est eciam causa quare non solum illa ymmo ancilla prima, philosophia videlicet, a paucis respectiue modernis temporibus frequentatur, sicut plangit Ouidius, *De vetula*, libro primo, sic dicens:
>
>> Omnes declinant ad eam que lucra ministrat,
>> Vtque sciant discunt pauci, plures ut habundent.
>> Sic te prostituunt, o virgo scientia; sic te
>> Venalem faciunt castis amplexibus aptam,
>> Non te propter te querentes, sed lucra per te.
>> Ditarique volunt potius quam philosophari.
>
> Et infra: 'Sic [p]hilosophia / exilium patitur et philopecunia regnat'. Sed caueant sibi ne dominam hanc contempnant, quia ad eam oportet omnes finaliter reuerti et sub manibus suis humiliari cum velint saluari.[10]

Therefore holy Scripture, the ruler of all the sciences, is abandoned; today the whole pack of scholars rushes toward those other disciplines, and Jeremiah's tearful lament is fulfilled, 'The mistress of the gentiles has become as a widow' (Lam. 1.1). That is why today relatively few of them gather round even the first handmaid, philosophy, just as Ovid laments in *De vetula* I.691–96, saying:

---

[10] Holcot, *Super Sapientiam*, sig. A2[rab]. I correct the print, which has reversed *exilium* and *philosophia*; for the ps.-Ovidian text, see ps. Ovid, *De Vetula*, ed. by Klopsch.

> All turn aside to [Fortune] who provides them with pelf, and few learn in order to know, but most learn to get rich. Thus they whore you, O inviolate wisdom; you thus they render, with your chaste embraces, open to money. They don't pursue you for yourself, but money through you, and they want to be rich, rather than to be philosophers.
>
> And Ovid adds (735–36): 'Thus Philo-sophy endures exile and Philo-lucre rules the roost'. But they should beware disdaining this ruler, because everyone who wishes to be saved must, in the end, return to her and humble themselves under her hand.

Slippery stuff: at the start of the argument, the *domina* is, like Esther, theology, the study of holy Scripture, and yet, by its end, it is not clear whether it is still the queen herself or philosophy, who began this argument, like legal studies, as subordinated *famula*. That might well explain why, if one wishes to discuss exilic destitution and abandonment, one might stop citing the scriptural model of Lamentations and subordinate its single verse to eight extra-scriptural ones. If this is your topic, what better poet than the exiled Ovid? But he is, although apparently a spokesman for philosophy, after all, still a poet. 'Delight'-filled moments like this one drove Smalley to despair – not to mention to some particularly inperspicacious readings of what Holcot might have been about.

*De vetula* doesn't have much of a scholarly profile these days, and it therefore merits a brief introduction. It is not exactly a well-known monument of the canon – indeed it was created to be foisted on Ovid, likely in the second quarter of the thirteenth century. The poem is generally ascribed to Richard de Fournival, chancellor of Amiens and author of *Le bestiare d'amours* and *Biblionomia*, the catalogue of his library. The poem is divided into three books, diverse in tone. The first describes the life of 'Ovid' after he had given up love and had to seek some other pursuit; it is largely a satire on intellectual life, of a sort familiar from the earlier *Speculum stultorum* and *Architrenius*. The lines Holcot cites here are utterly integral to the argument of Book I: the theologian proves just as responsive to the detail of his non-biblical sources as to his biblical ones. This portion of the poem is marked by a monumental attack upon (and yet, amusingly enough, what amounts to instruction in) dicing, to much the same point as Holcot is making here. For 'Ovid', gaming is indulged only from a foolish desire for profit, whereas actually Fortune and nothing else rules the (inherently anti-providential) pursuit. The gambler thus resembles Holcot's bad scholar (ll. 396–576). In contrast, 'Ovid' prefers chess, invented by Ulysses at Troy to keep wits sharp during the lengthy siege. Further, he 'demonstrates' that this game's varying moves offer what amounts to 'philosophical' material – instruction in creation, since they mirror the movements of the heavens (ll. 577–635). Book II, which inspires the title (and is, in turn, licitly Ovidian in inspiration; cf. *Amores* I.8), explains the circumstances of the poet's renunciation. The amorous 'Ovid' is converted from love because of the tricks played on him by the aged go-between whom he thinks he is employing to facilitate a seduction. Instead, she herself, and not the girl, ends up in his bed. (And ultimately, though with enough of a delay that she too has become a *vetula*, 'Ovid' gets the girl as wife.) Both intellectual and amatory endeavours having proven barren, Book III comprises the poet's full recantation and movement toward heavenly love through more scholarly pursuits and, eventually, commitment (as we will see) to the Virgin.[11]

As this bald summary will indicate, *De vetula* might be perceived to be a good deal more germane to Holcot's argumentative situation than the biblical Lamentations. The grieving widow is, after all, a victim, an image of abandoned philosophical-theological studies as Babylonian captive, while Fournival's reconstructed 'Ovid' directly figures the to-be-humbled Hagar. Like the classical roué, prideful in her (productive) sexuality – all of it just *delicie* – she needs to be subjected to theological discipline. Indeed, simply the allusion to the title *De vetula* is telling, for in the central episode, 'Ovid' thinks he is getting true delights – and ends up with a repellent death's head (twice: the boy's a slow learner). He needs to find, as he will, later in Holcot's explication of Wisdom, a truly fecund image, the thoroughly desexualised but redemptively productive Virgin (the faith that underpins indulgence in [intellectual] delights).

In passing, I note a topic to which I will return. Holcot really liked this passage from *De vetula*. The lectures that comprise *Super Sapientiam* were delivered in the mid-1330s. But Holcot returned to this same passage and cited it in exactly the same form and in the same argumentative context in a work securely dated 1342. Although this text travels under the name of the Durham bishop Richard de Bury, Holcot was a member of his household and, rather generally, both in the Middle Ages and today, is

---

[11] For the fullest list of the very few studies, see www.arlima.net/uz/vetula.html (last accessed 8 November 2022). This also includes a manuscript list: about fifty copies, thirteen of them English (three of these excerpts), half the full copies Book III only. To this account, add Hexter, 'Shades of Ovid', pp. 304–8, with further references.

believed to have ghost-written at least portions of the work for his patron.[12]

This is, as I have suggested, not the only citation of *De vetula* in *Super Sapientiam*. Holcot returns to the poem – and extensively so – in his sixty-first lecture, providing his reading of Wis. 5.6, 'Sol intelligentiae non est ortus nobis' ('The sun of understanding hath not risen unto us'). Of course, the comparison of Christ to the sun is utterly commonplace, and the body of the sermon/lecture is given over to a lengthy discussion exemplifying 'quod Christus soli comparatur propter ... declaracionem manifestantem' (sig. N4$^{ra-vb}$: 'Christ is compared to the sun because of his open testimony', i.e., to his divinity). This illustration, 'qualiter iste sol moraliter complet et peragit motum suum' (sig. N4$^{vb}$: 'a moralised explanation of how the sun carries out and completes its motion'), involves a lengthy double comparison between Christ's salvific acts as illustrating the sun's passage through the zodiac signs in the course of the solar year and the redeemer's developing relationship with man through all salvation history.

Like many medieval sermons (and many of Holcot's lectures), this demonstration involves selective over-development of apparently analogous argumentative 'parts' at the expense of others. Here the complicated and hyper-divided (twelve-part, of course) argument consumes most of the lection. But one portion is easily four times as long as the discussion of any other zodiacal sign:

> De Leone transiuit in Virgine. Toto enim tempore medio inter resurrectionem suam et ascensionem, doctrina et fides ecclesie in beata Virgine potissime conseruaba[n]tur. Hec interim apostolos et discipulos docuit, monuit, consolata est. Vtpote illa que repleta fuit Spiritu sancto plenissime in verbi Dei concepcione, et ideo tunc temporis mansit in signo, id est in fide Virginis. De qua Ouidius, 3 *De vetula*, capitulo vltimo:
>
> > O virgo felix, o virgo significata,
> > Per stellas vbi Spica nitet, quis det michi tantum
> > Viuere quod possim laudum fore preco tuarum?
> > Nam nisi tu perfecta fores, non eligeret te
> > Hic Deus omnipotens vt carnem sumeret a te.
>
> Vbi prophetat diffuse quod Deus omnipotens sumeret de ea carnem et quod resurgeret a mortuis, quod matrem suam virginem assumeret in corpore et anima in celum. Vnde dicit sic in fine:

---

[12] See (ps.-) Richard de Bury, *Philobiblon*, IX.148 (p. 83); on the authorship, see *ed. cit.*, pp. xliii–vii, and Sharpe, *Handlist*, pp. 462 and 556.

> Non opus est vt eam velit exaltare gradatim,
> Sed simul assumet et eandem concatedrabit.
> Illic esto tui memoris memor, optima virgo,
> Illic cum fueris pro nobis tracta trahendis.
> Pro nobis non te pigeat suadere quod a[d] se
> Nos trahat is per te qui per te venerat ad nos,
> [Maxima quem per te dilectio traxerit ad nos,]
> A nobis ipsi sit gloria laudis; ab ipso
> Grati[a] sit nobis et mete nescia vita. (sig. N5$^{vab}$)

From Leo Christ passed into Virgo. For during the whole interval between his resurrection and his ascension, the church's doctrine and faith were most powerfully preserved in the Blessed Virgin. For this whole space, she taught, admonished, and consoled the apostles and the disciples. As one might expect, she was most fully filled with the Holy Spirit in conceiving the Word, and thus he remained at that time in this sign, that is in the faith of the Virgin. Ovid talks about this in the last chapter of *De vetula* (III.772–76):

> O blessed Virgin, O Virgin en-signed in the stars where your star Spica shines, who may give me so much life that I might be the spokesman of your praises? For had you not been perfect, God almighty would not have chosen you so that he could take on flesh from you.

There he amply prophesies that almighty God should take on the Virgin's flesh and that he should rise from the dead so that he might raise up his mother the Virgin into heaven, both in body and in soul. And so he says this in his conclusion (III.803–11):

> His purpose is not to wish to exalt her by stages; rather all at once, he will raise her up and enthrone her with him. May you there be mindful of one who remembers you, O greatest Virgin, when you have been drawn up to draw us there. May He not be slack in encouraging you on our behalf, so that He may draw us to Himself through you – He who through you had come to us and whose surpassing love has drawn him to us through you. May we praise Him in His glory; may He extend his grace to us and a goal in that life we do not yet know.

Holcot then continues:

> An sit liber Ouidij Deus nouit, quamuis a Leone, prothonotario sacri palacij Vastacij principis, referatur liber ille extractus de sepulchro Ouidij. Vnde *Testamentum Ouidij* nuncupatur. Dicit enim quod inuentus fuit in cimiterio publico in quodam sepulcro in suburbio Dioscori ciuitatis, que est caput regni Colcorum. Et quia ibi non erat copia Latinorum, eo quod Armenici linguam Latinam non intelligunt, rex Colcorum misit illum librum Constantinopolim, vbi tunc erat copia Latinorum. Refert etiam

> quod inter antiquorum sepulchra vnum inuentum est in cuius epigrama fuit sculptum litteris Armenicis, cuius interpretacio sic sonabat, 'Hic iacet Ouidius ingeniosissimus poetarum'. Obijt autem anno Christi decimo octauo, sicut refert Guilhelmus de Vang' in Cronica sua, tercio anno Tiberii. Vnde constat quod si liber veraciter suus erat, fuit pulcherrima prophecia. Sed hec sunt extra propositum.[13]

> Only God knows whether this book is really Ovid's, but Leo, the prothonotary of the holy palace of emperor Vastacius, says the book was taken from Ovid's tomb, and it is thus known as *Ovid's Testament*. Leo says it was discovered in the public cemetery in an outlying district of the city Dioscurus, the capital of the Colchians' kingdom. Because there were not many Latin speakers there, since Armenians do not understand Latin, the Colchian king sent the book to Constantinople, where there were plenty of Latin-speakers. He further reports that a tomb was discovered among those of the ancients, and it had an epitaph in Armenian letters that is translated, 'Here lies Ovid, the most imaginative of the poets'. He died in 18 A.D., the third year of Tiberius's reign, as William de Vang' reports in his chronicle. And thus, if this book was truly Ovid's, it was a most beautiful prophecy. But this is not to the point.

This extensive romp through the purported transmission-history of *De vetula* puts us in territory well plumbed and authoritatively explained to us by our honorand.[14] And I would suspect we even know where Holcot got this material. There are two copies of *De vetula*, both certainly produced from the same exemplar by named Durham scribes in the early- to mid-fifteenth-century: Cambridge, Sidney Sussex College MS 56, and Cambridge, Jesus College MS Q.G.22 (70). Both represent the same, relatively frequent reduced form of the text, with only its redemptive Book III. Both offer the same explanatory colophon, noting that 'duobus primis hic omissis propter multa que inseruntur scurilia' ('The first two books are left out here, because of the many offensive bits they include'). This mutually inherited note presumably reflects the scribes' common exemplar, but it equally implies that that exemplar had been derived, with deliberate selectiveness, from an earlier full text, presumably also an earlier Durham book and inferentially Holcot's source.

---

[13] Holcot, *Super Sapientiam*, sig. N5$^{vb}$. I have silently corrected the print's *Colt-* to *Colc-*. I assume the historical reference near the end is to the lost 'Vnus omnium' of William de Bougevilla OSB of St Neots, a text still extant in the sixteenth century; see Sharpe, *Handlist*, p. 756. Dioscorus, the purported site of Ovid's tomb, is now Sokhumi in Georgia.

[14] One scarcely needs a footnote to draw attention to *MTA*, or to Minnis and Scott, or to Minnis and Johnson (eds), *Cambridge History of Literary Criticism*, II, *The Middle Ages* (2005).

But more germanely for this transmission-history, both books share textual appendages. Following the colophon, both offer, first, an extensive *accessus* to Ovid (but mainly to *De vetula*, with a detailed summary of the whole): 'At the heads of books, people are accustomed to ask seven questions ... Troy having fallen ...' ('In librorum initiis septem solent inquiri ... Capta Troia ...'), and then a poem to introduce *De vetula*. The poem is headed 'prefatio Leonis protonotharii sacri palatii Bizantei sub Vacacio principe', which more or less dates this discovery-'history' to the period 1222 × 44, when John III Vatatzes was emperor in Nicaea – obviously the source of Holcot's opening explanation. The remainder of his account is equally derivative, more-or-less closely quoted from the *accessus*'s introduction of *De vetula*, there offered as the tenth (and last) of Ovid's works.[15] Thus, this material is legitimately protreptic, invitational. Holcot here provides the basic knowledge that ought to guide one to and in *De vetula*. Yet, simultaneously, this explanatory material is wedged between disclaimers – Is it really Ovid? Is it really information relevant to reading Wisdom?

In a general way, this moment – and a great many others in Holcot's *Super Sapientiam* – corresponds to a fairly widely dispersed kind of instruction to preachers. This resonates with Holcot's invocation of *delicie* in his prologue: inventive novelty is important and audience-pleasing. For example, discussing the conclusion of a sermon, Robert of Basevorn avers:

> Tamen hic sciendum quod ita potest adduci historia alia, sicut historia Bibliae, ut puta aliqua narratio Augustini vel Gregorii, vel alicujus auctoris, vel Helinandi vel Valerii vel Senecae vel Macrobii. Et hoc modo magis acceptatur narratio Augustini, dummodo sit nova et inusitata, quam Bibliae; et magis Helinandi vel alicujus alterius qui raro habetur, quam Augustini vel Ambrosii. Cujus ratio non est alia nisi vana curiositas hominum.[16]

> Nevertheless, you should know that here you may add another exemplary story, like one from the Bible, or perhaps some narrative from Augustine or Gregory, or some other author, whether from the chronicle of Hélinand or

---

[15] The *accessus*, a common but far from necessary accompaniment to the text (twenty-seven copies, only five English), is Coulson and Roy, *Incipitarium*, no. 167 (pp. 63–64); the portions Holcot is quoting correspond to Klopsch's edition 281/87–282/101. For the prefatory verses ascribed to Leo, see Klopsch, pp. 193–94; James also cites them in full, *Descriptive Catalogue*, p. 107. I take this occasion to remember the gracious, and lamentably departed, Frances Willmoth, archivist and librarian at Jesus; deeply welcoming, patient and accommodating, Frances facilitated my numerous visits to look at the fifty-manuscript donation (1686) of the Fellow Thomas Man, of which MS 70 is one.

[16] Quoted in Charland, *Artes Praedicandi*, p. 316.

Valerius Maximus or Seneca or Macrobius. And in this process, a story from Augustine, so long as it is new and infrequently cited, is more satisfactory than one from the Bible; and likewise one from Helinand or someone else infrequently cited than one from Augustine or Ambrose. There's no logic for this, other than people's vain curiosity.

'Vana curiositas': Basevorn probably means the widely attested pejorative, 'over-ingeniousness', certainly an invocation of the resistant spirit in which Smalley approached Holcot. It is indeed hard to think of anything more outré, estranging and thus arresting than this account of the supposed transmission of 'Ovid''s text, with the frisson of extra-European orientalism in its references to Dioscurus and Constantinople.

Yet it is equally the case that this material forms a narrative relevant and evocative in the context. Holcot's *accessus*-derived materials offer a narrative analogue to the acts he ascribes to the Virgin: the unknown resurrected, the 'good news' transmitted. (The gospels are, after all, equally as much as 'Ovid''s rendered biography, a *testamentum*). And of course, the linguistic permutations necessary to recuperate 'Ovid' echo the propagation of the gospels themselves, the tongues of fire that will convert the apostles into missionaries speaking all tongues. Moreover, through his textual citations, Holcot displays 'Ovid''s materials explicitly as transmitted through Marian intercession, resurrecting him from his philandry, and they render him prophetically in the same position as the unknowing apostles, also sustained by the Virgin.

The presentation thus resonates with that of Holcot's prologue, in which pagan philosophy does not display truth but offers a mode of presenting it attractively. Here 'Ovid', just like the apostles, graduates into what he wasn't, an instructive vehicle for salvation history. The resemblance is extensive, right down to the implicit demonstration that a recognisably *Metamorphosean* narrative of 'stellification' inherently resembles the Assumption (the latter not just a physical apotheosis, as is the star, but 'in corpore et anima'). Implicitly, Ovid is transformed into a serious epic poet, capable of something analogous to Virgil's fourth eclogue, always read as the prophecy of a crypto-Christian author. 'Ovid' is a model of a redeemed or redeemable classicism and of finding delightful truth in what conventionally might be seen as all the wrong places.

That reading, of course, raises a second, more constructive sense of Basevorn's 'curiositas', simple intellectual enjoyment, a delight in knowledge and manipulating it a pleasurable act (recall *sicut placet*). On the one hand, the argument here – while it involves a useful moral doubling exercise – is truly excessive. As Holcot's concluding sentence indicates

(I would take it as Estherian 'simulation'), for the purpose of praising the Virgin or mapping the diffusion of Christ's grace, simple citation of the title *De vetula* could have been entirely sufficient. Moreover, reducing the discussion to that citation would render the discussion of Virgo pretty much homologous in detail and extent with the other eleven parts of his division.

The logical inference is that this was stuff too good, potentially too edifying, to pass over. One doesn't surrender one's lectern simply to textual attentiveness, but one offers potentially edificatory nuggets, not apparently recuperable as theology, as well. But they are constantly and perpetually analogues to theology, in essence implicit textual *similitudines* rendering the biblical text approachable and resonant, while never integral to it – nor ever, in Holcot's practice, entirely or explicitly moralised in their relationship.[17] A large part of Holcot's performance as exegete is, as the prologue promises, 'simulative', pretending an intellectually delightful dependence. As he promises, the normal relations are reversed: scriptural reading demonstrates delights hidden, latent, unknown to their authors (why Ovid's death date, which renders his account prophetic, matters) but lurking in disparate materials and supportive of Scripture's ultimate truths.

This is very far from an isolated moment, either in Holcot or among Smalley's 'classicising friars' generally. I offer a couple of brief examples from the movement's enabling figure, John of Wales. These are all considerably less adept than Holcot's: John is a self-avowed mere *compilator*, and he does not offer implicitly moralised material but 'raw data' for others, as it were.[18] The first comes from the prologue to his *Communiloquium*:

> Predicator euangelicus etiam in priuata co[l]latione verba vite iugiter proponat pro loco et tempore, etiam in mensa ... Siquidem et inter comedentes Deus parabolas miscuit, prout dicitur in *Policrato*, libro viij, capitulo ix. Si[c] enim Diogenes et alij Cynnici (qui secundum Papiam sunt philosophi p[a]rcissime vite, nam cynos 'canis' dicitur qui est parcissimum animal) obuios monuerunt ... (sig. a1$^{rab}$)

---

[17] Cf. my reading of one of his mythological figures: Hanna, *Patient Reading*, pp. 263–67, with certain qualifications there introduced.

[18] For *compilator*, see *MTA*, pp. 94–95. My citations of John of Wales are from *Summa de regimine vite humane*. John's citations reveal his sources, passed on essentially intact (as a *compilator* is supposed to do). Both depend, as very frequently in John, on John of Salisbury's *Policraticus*, although in both instances the etymologies are original intrusions; see *Policraticus*, ed. by Webb, II, 282 (the whole discussion of VIII.8–10 here enabling) and (from IV.3) I, 242.

> A preacher of the gospel also ought to propound continually those words of life as is appropriate to place and time, even at the dinner-table ... For certainly God mixed his parables in, even to those who were eating, as it says in *Polycraticus*, VIII.9. Likewise, Diogenes and the other Cynics (according to Papias they are the philosophers most self-denying in their living, for the word *cynos* means 'a dog', the most self-denying animal) admonished passers-by ...

And another, this from the *Breviarium de virtutibus*, I.2:

> Narrat Trogus Pompeius, libro iij de Ligurgo, quod cum statuisset mandata et leges, quia dura Lacedemonijs videbantur, auctorem earum Apollin[u]m Delphicum finxit et se simulans proficisci ad oraculum Delphicum. Obligauit iuramento ciuitatem, vt nihil in legibus illis mutarent antequam ipse reuerteretur. Quo facto, [i]uit ad Cretam ... Et nota quod Delos est insula vbi erat templum Apollinis et locus diuinationis, prout dicit commentator Ethicorum i. Vnde dicitur Apollo Delphicus, et quia dicte leges erant honeste, ideo hic su[b]scribantur. (sig. C1$^{rb}$)

> Pompeius Trogus tells about Lycurgus in book 3. When he had established commandments and laws, because they appeared harsh to the Spartans, he feigned that Delphic Apollo was their author and pretended that he was setting out for the Delphic oracle. He also bound all the citizens by an oath that they would change nothing in those laws before he himself returned. Having done that, he instead fled to Crete ... Note that Delos is an island where there was a temple to Apollo and a place where divination went on, as the commentator says on Aristotle's *Nicomachean Ethics*, 1. Hence Apollo is called Delphic, and because these laws were virtuous ones, they are ascribed to that place.

Neither etymological note has anything to do with the point at issue, of course, and neither adds anything that underwrites either why one should offer instruction at dinner (or in the street) or why law should be (feigningly) blessed with divine authority. What they do accomplish, even in John's confounding the similar and synonymous epithets, *Deli(ac)us* and *Delphicus*, is to offer ready identifications of bits of fairly basic classical lore: What were the pagan schools of philosophy? Why is Apollo known as Delian/Delphian, e.g., at *Aeneid*, VI.12? 'Predicatores euangelici' are not limited to propounding 'verba vite', but potentially a good deal more besides. Here John provides a kind of information one might get in a somewhat less august surround than Holcot's theology lecture, an arts course lecture hall, where Holcot's fairly basic *accessus* material on *De vetula* would also be at home. But given both authors' wide dissemination, such information is open, not academically confined, and in the form both

Holcot and John are offering it, of greatest value in public sermon declamation.

As I hope I have demonstrated, Holcot brings a good deal more to the table, if you will. There is certainly novelty and delight here. But there is also, in Holcot's case, something of the meditative. Like the simulating Esther (or for that matter, John of Wales's Lycurgus), Holcot's moral claims on his audience are never quite overt. They appear only retrospectively, in rumination over the unexpressed analogies between his citations and their overt surround.[19]

This is, for one thing, great classroom teaching: Holcot's moves must have been hugely stimulating to his fledgling theologians. Assuming the lectures had the form we receive, these students will have puzzled over the unexpressed connectives, the moral lessons they might draw from his seemingly alien materials. And, of course, given the extensive circulation of *Super Sapientiam*, the lectures passed to a much wider cadre, who will have used their knowledge of the biblical text to 'concord' bits from Wisdom with the language of some other scriptural passage they were considering. This readership certainly included some very sophisticated people, capable of intuiting deep connections between extra-biblical lore, in which they probably already had expressed interests, and scriptural texts.[20] But equally, Holcot ceaselessly bestowed on his audience what the prologue's Esther promised, a demonstration of theology's capacity as integrative discipline, the power faith grants to find edification in the seemingly disparaged and worthless, if not pernicious.

---

[19] This is a particular difficulty for Smalley's literalistic reading strategy, always predicated on overt statement; cf. the analysis at Hanna, 'State of English'.

[20] This is certainly activity associable with the two Durham scribes of *De vetula*. In his Sidney Sussex copy, William Seton follows the text with Bersuire's *Ovidius moralizatus*; Robert Emylton's Jesus manuscript also presents William of Conches's commentary on Boethius's *De consolatione* and ps.-Seneca, *De remediis*. Among other similarly *au courrant* readers of *De vetula*, one could cite Fr William Herbert, Hereford OFM (the excerpt in London, British Library MS Royal 7 F. VII); John Erghome, York OESA (London, British Library MS Cotton Vespasian B. XXIII); and William Gray, bishop of Ely and benefactor of Balliol College (Royal 7 F. XII).

CHAPTER 5

# The Inspired Commentator
## Theories of Interpretive Authority in the Writings of Richard Rolle

### Andrew Kraebel

Sed ne videar statum meum superexaltare – quia solitarius sum qui hanc breuem exposicionem compilaui – 'solitudinem' mentis magis debetis intelligere quam corporis. Solitudinem mentis voco qua homo deserit tumultuosam cupiditatem et vanitatem istius mundi, et turbam malarum ac vanarum cogitacionum cum omnibus secularibus negociis perfecte relinquit, et se leuat in contemplacionem Dei et celestium gaudiorum, vt quamuis inter homines moretur, longe tamen a vita eorum distat.[1]

But lest I appear excessively to praise my own rank – for I who have compiled this short exposition am a solitary – you should understand 'solitude' as having to do more with the mind than the body. I call it solitude of mind when a person forsakes the tumultuous cupidity and vanity of the world and leaves behind the crowd of wicked and empty thoughts, along with all worldly business, and raises himself to contemplation of God and of heavenly joys, so that, though he continues to dwell among people, he is far removed from their life.

Richard Rolle (d. 1349) stands at the borders of scholastic discourse, drawing on the basic resources and conceptual framework of university exegesis, but producing insistently idiosyncratic texts. In this gloss on *solitudo* from his Latin commentary on the Psalms, quoted here in the revised form apparently prepared by Rolle himself, the widely influential Yorkshire hermit presents himself as a *compilator*, suggesting that he is the mere assembler and arranger of others' opinions.[2] As Alastair Minnis describes it, this writerly pose served to distance scholastics from the claims rehearsed in their texts, locating authority in the compiled material and

---

[1] London, Lambeth Palace Library MS 352, f. 124ʳ (on Ps. 54.8).
[2] On the versions of this commentary, see Kraebel, *Experiments in Interpretation*, pp. 191–202. The earlier version contains similar material but includes an attack on those 'qui suam tantum religionem commendant' (Oxford, Bodleian Library MS Bodley 861, f. 19ᵛᵃ).

thereby protecting the compiler from critique.³ Yet, after laying claim to this relatively humble role, the hermit immediately identifies the gloss that follows as offering not a *sententia* recorded in his major source, the *Magna glosatura* of Peter Lombard (d. 1160), but rather *his own* definition of mental solitude: 'I call it (*voco*) solitude of mind ...'. Though he avoids making himself the *materia* ('subject-matter') of the gloss, Rolle is still presented as an authority on solitaries and solitude. In this instance, then, to follow Bonaventure's well-known distinction, Rolle is acting not as a compiler, writing the words of others, but rather as a commentator, quoting the biblical text and adding interpretations of his own.⁴

Though certainly less prestigious than the last of the Bonaventuran categories, that of the author (*auctor*), the appeal and authority of the commentator could still be considerable, especially when the text being glossed was Holy Scripture.⁵ Indeed, throughout his writings, Rolle maintains that divine inspiration, typically associated with the biblical *auctores* themselves, is also necessary for anyone writing commentaries on their texts, and, without such inspiration, an exegete's glosses will necessarily tend toward error and heresy. These claims take a variety of forms, from general descriptions of the *sancti* who have the ability to interpret Scripture correctly,⁶ to more specific assertions that Rolle himself has received such inspiration,⁷ as well as prayers for divine aid before he begins to interpret what he considers especially difficult verses.⁸ Most of these references appear in his Latin works, but the hermit also makes his position plain in the vernacular, writing in his English Psalter commentary, for example, 'None suld be so herdy to translate or expone

---

³ Minnis, 'Discussions of *Compilatio*' (1979), pp. 385–421; *MTA*, esp. pp. 190–210; Minnis, 'Discourse of Compilation' (2006), pp. 47–63.
⁴ For Bonaventure, see Minnis and Scott, pp. 228–30; cf. Kraebel, 'Modes of Authorship'.
⁵ Recent work on scholastic theories of authority and literary production has focused on the status of the *auctor*: see, e.g., Bolens and Erne (eds), *Medieval and Early Modern Authorship*, and Partridge and Kwakkel (eds), *Author, Reader, Book*. Though Grondeux, '*Auctoritas* et glose', emphasises the derivative and anonymous quality of medieval glosses, her focus is on commentaries on early schoolroom texts, and it should be unsurprising that greater prestige and authority were to be found by exegetes glossing the more rarefied text of Scripture.
⁶ E.g., Rolle, *Melos*, 9, ed. by Arnould, p. 26/27–29.
⁷ E.g., Rolle, *Melos*, 15, ed. by Arnould, p. 47/16–18.
⁸ E.g., Cambridge, University Library MS Ii.1.26, f. 174ᵛ; cf. Moyes, *Introduction*, II, 254 (on Job 19.20): 'Dura verba hec sunt, et pene inpenetrabilia vt medullam pertingamus, vix quoque ab aliquo mortali ad liquidum exponuntur. Oportet ergo vbi vires succumbunt insipiencie mee ignoscere, presertim cum ea in quantum ipse qui aperit et nemo claudit michi reuelauerit studeam declarare'. See too, more briefly, Lambeth MS 352, f. 176ᵛ (on Ps. 118.34): '*Da michi intellectum* Scripturarum, quia per me ad hoc non possum attingere'.

Holy Wrytte bot if he felde þe Holy Gost in hyme, þat is enditere of Holy Writ'.[9]

Less sensational than his better-known accounts of inward fire and heavenly song, or their attendant sensation of sweetness, these claims of divine inspiration for his biblical exegesis are nevertheless crucial to Rolle's developing understanding of himself as a writer, and to the form and content of his extant writings more generally. Unlike those more fantastic mystical experiences, however, described at length in his *Incendium Amoris* and *Melos Amoris*, Rolle never attempts to expound upon what it meant for him to have felt 'þe Holy Gost in hyme' as the inspirer of his glosses, and consequently his thinking on the subject has either received passing treatment (as in Nicholas Watson's exceptional study of the hermit), or it has been unfortunately misrepresented and oversimplified.[10] In his magisterial survey of Christian mysticism, for example, Bernard McGinn has argued that 'it was important for the young hermit's claims to teaching authority that he be seen as an inspired commentator, one who, unlike the academic theologians of the schools, was given divine insight into the mystical meaning of the biblical text'.[11] McGinn's account begs a number of questions with regard to Rolle's theories of inspiration, suggesting that these ideas are especially associated with an early phase in his career, that they should be seen as setting Rolle apart from contemporary exegetes active in the universities, and that they are associated specifically with the mystical (or 'ghostly', 'spiritual') senses of Scripture, as opposed to the *sensus litteralis*. Though Rolle does not discuss these theories directly and at length, making it difficult to reconstruct his understanding of inspired commentary in any systematic way, careful consideration of his writings will nevertheless cast doubt on all these points. Certainly, Rolle's attempts to locate his exegetical authority in a form of divine inspiration differ in many respects from comparable theories found in the writings of his contemporaries in Oxford and Cambridge, but just as he makes use of the same basic sources as those schoolmen, so too are his ideas of inspiration consistent with at least some theoretical claims then current in the universities. As in his description of himself as a compiler, Rolle adapts standard scholastic theories of inspired exegesis in ways that reflect the particular demands of his larger project of writerly self-fashioning.

---

[9] San Marino, Huntington Library MS HM 148, f. 43[vab] (on Ps. 17.13); cf. Rolle, *Psalms of David*, ed. by Bramley, p. 61; cf. Alford, 'Biblical *Imitatio*', p. 7.

[10] Watson, *Invention of Authority*, e.g., pp. 5, 97–98 and 144. See too Clark, 'Rolle as Commentator', pp. 177–78.

[11] McGinn, *Varieties of Vernacular Mysticism*, p. 342.

Before turning to his different discussions of exegetical inspiration, it will be useful to note one major trend in the glosses which Rolle appears to attribute to the work of the Holy Ghost moving within him – that is, glosses not drawn from authoritative sources like the *Magna glosatura*. Though there are certainly exceptions, the glosses that Rolle does not borrow from other writers – that is, his own interpretive inventions – are frequently concerned with his favoured mystical experiences of heat, sweetness and song, as well as with the world-condemning wisdom which comes from them.[12] In his Latin commentary on the Psalter, such glosses are often brief and obviously motivated by phrases in the biblical text, e.g., '*Quoniam tu illuminas* luce gracie *lucernam meam*, id est cor meum, vt ferueat igne amoris tui' ('*For* with the light of your grace *you illumine my lamp*, i.e., my heart, so that it burns with the fire of your love'), or, '*Inflammatum est cor meum* igne diuini amoris ita, vt sentirem illud ardens et conuersum in flammam' ('*My heart has been inflamed* with the fire of divine love, such that I have felt it burning and turned completely into flame').[13] At other points in the same work, his departures from the *Magna glosatura* can be more elaborate and substantive, as well as less immediately relevant to the text being glossed – as when a perceived reference to the Holy Name prompts Rolle to write,

> Hoc cogitando in eo delectatus, vt non sapiam quicquam nisi nomine Iesu condiatur. In omni enim ore indulcabitur in quo retinetur, id est dulcifluum reddit palatum cordis et oris dilectoris sui, et mentem cogitantis se in canorum iubilum leuat.[14]

> I take such delight in this thought that I cannot taste anything unless it is flavoured with the name of Jesus, which sweetens every mouth that speaks it, i.e., it makes the palate of the heart and the mouth of his lover sweet, and it lifts to melodious song the mind of anyone thinking it.

Though interspersed among interpretations adapted from conventional scholastic sources in his commentaries on the Psalter, Lamentations and Apocalypse, novel glosses referring to his mystical experiences become the

---

[12] Cf. Rolle, *Incendium*, 14, ed. by Deanesly, pp. 184–85: 'Porro, ut potui in Scripturis perscrutari, inueni et cognoui quidem quod summus amor Christi in tribus consistit: in feruore, in canore et in dulcore'. The major exception to this trend is the *Postille super nouem lectiones mortuorum*, where Rolle works without an authoritative exegetical source, offering his own interpretations on a broader range of topics.

[13] Lambeth MS 352, ff. 96ᵛ (corrected) and 138ᵛ (on Pss 17.29 and 72.21); cf. *Magna glosatura*, *PL* 191, 198ac and 676d–678a.

[14] Lambeth MS 352, f. 177ʳ⁻ᵛ (on Ps. 118.55); cf. *PL* 191, 1071ab. See too the second gloss on Apoc. 1.14 (*oculi eius*) in Rolle, *Tractatus super Apocalypsim*, ed. by Marzac, p. 132.

near-exclusive focus of Rolle's later and more discursive exegesis, serving as the basis for sustained meditations on the ideal religious life. This approach is apparent in Rolle's gloss on the opening verses of the Canticle of Canticles, which he reads as expressing the desires of someone whose 'cor totum in desiderio Ihesu defixum in igne amoris conuertitur et dulcore deitatis funditus absorbetur' ('whole heart, planted firmly in the desire for Jesus, is turned into the fire of love and soaked with the sweetness of the godhead to its core').[15] Even more dramatically, in *Melos Amoris* the hermit assembles passages from various biblical books which he considers especially ripe for such interpretation, stringing his glosses (and related discussions) together to create a series of 'postils on the glory and perfection of the preeminent saints' ('de gloria et perfeccione sanctorum precellencium postillas').[16] *Melos* therefore lacks the larger structure of a commentary – it cannot easily be consulted to find Rolle's interpretation of a given biblical verse – but it nevertheless depends on his inspired ability to interpret Scripture.

Like the sensations of heat, sweetness and song described in these glosses, it seems possible that Rolle's exegetical inspiration itself could have been the result of (or begun with) some kind of ecstatic experience – but, if this were the case, the hermit never explains what that experience was or how it relates to other elements of his religious programme. Arguing that it must have occurred early in his career, Watson attempts to identify this inspiration with an event described in *Incendium*, where Rolle states that, almost three years after taking up the life of a hermit and a little less than a year before he felt 'the heat of eternal love' (*calor eterni amoris*), he witnessed 'apercionem hoscii celestis, ut reuelata facie oculus cordis superos contemplaretur, et uideret qua uia amatum suum quereret et ad ipsum iugiter anhelaret' ('the opening of the heavenly gate, so that, with the face unveiled, the eye of the heart contemplated the heavens and saw by which route it should seek its beloved and long for him continuously').[17] Later in *Incendium* he invokes the same progression, now describing this visionary experience as taking place when someone 'quasi

---

[15] Rolle, *Unprinted Latin*, ed. and tr. by Hanna, pp. 102–3.
[16] Rolle, *Melos*, 5, ed. by Arnould, p. 15, itself part of an assertion of exegetical inspiration, with Rolle claiming to write 'inspirante Spiritu'. As Watson, *Invention of Authority*, pp. 173–74 and 286–93, discusses, early sections of *Melos* adapt interpretations offered in Rolle's commentary on the Song of Songs. For a useful account of the form of *Melos*, see Albin, *Melody of Love*, pp. 10–15; on its relation to the commentary tradition, see Renevey, *Language, Self and Love*, pp. 91–101.
[17] Rolle, *Incendium*, 15, ed. by Deanesly, pp. 188–89. A similar description appears in Rolle, *Melos*, 8, ed. by Arnould, p. 23/18.

aperto celo supernos cives oculo intellectuali conspicit' ('catches sight of heavenly citizens with his intellective eye, when heaven is, as it were, opened').[18] Quite clearly, in neither of these accounts does Rolle overtly tie the *apertio caeli* to biblical interpretation. Watson, however, draws attention to a passage in his Apocalypse commentary, where the *ostium apertum in caelo* is glossed, 'Cum obscuritas Scripturarum in Ecclesia ostenditur, quasi ostium in celo aperitur' ('When an obscure point in the Scriptures is explained in the Church, it is as though a gate is opened in heaven'). This interpretation is taken from Rolle's major source, a commentary attributed to Anselm of Laon (d. 1117) or Anselm's brother Ralph, and it is followed immediately by a second gloss, original to Rolle, in which he claims that the opening of heaven also refers to mystical ascent, when the mind has been purged of impurities ('a sordibus purgetur') and the eye of the heart is raised up to contemplate the heavens ('ad celestia contemplanda suscipitur').[19] While flight to heaven and interpretive inspiration are thus in some way associated with one another, however, Watson's conflation of them is potentially misleading, especially when he concludes that 'the juxtaposition of these interpretations amounts to a claim that Rolle's experience of "Seeing into Heaven" enables him to penetrate the Scriptures as never before'.[20] Yet, as he does elsewhere in his commentaries – and, indeed, as is standard practice in scholastic exegesis – Rolle is clearly presenting these glosses as two distinct interpretive options (separated by 'Vel sic: ...'), alternative ways of reading the same material, and, absent some more overt indication, it would be highly unusual for two such glosses to constitute a single interpretive claim. Indeed, on various occasions in his Psalter commentary, Rolle repeats the first of these glosses, now elaborating on material found in the *Magna glosatura* and reading the opening of heaven as a metaphor, an indirect way for the Psalmist to describe inspired interpretation, without any suggestion of an accompanying mystical ascent.[21]

---

[18] Rolle, *Incendium*, 19, ed. by Deanesly, p. 202; for passing references to the *apertio caeli*, see pp. 239 and 246, and cf. p. 249.
[19] Rolle, *Tractatus super Apocalypsim*, ed. by Marzac, p. 156 (on Apoc. 4.1); cf. Watson, *Invention of Authority*, pp. 67–68 and 9. No English copies survive, but Leland appears to have seen one in the library of the Augustinians of Thornton-on-Humber (northernmost Lincolnshire): see Webber and Watson (eds), *Libraries of the Augustinian Canons*, p. 414.
[20] Watson, *Invention of Authority*, p. 97.
[21] Cf., e.g., Lambeth MS 352, f. 193ᵛ, where the *closing* of heaven is seen as the hiding of divinely-intended meaning: '*Qui operit celum* i.e. sanctam Scripturam *nubibus* id est figuris' (on Ps. 146.8), and his reading of Ps. 103.2, quoted in n. 27. The gloss seems to have been commonplace: see, e.g., *PL* 93, 545d–546a; *PL* 152, 1039cd; *PL* 167, 1017b; *PL* 194, 621d–622a; *PL* 196, 749a, etc.

While these references to the *apertio caeli* are brief and frustratingly vague, Rolle elsewhere returns to the interpretive options offered in his Apocalypse commentary, still holding them apart, but now giving a clearer view of how they relate. In *Contra Amatores Mundi*, as part of an attempt to clarify the claim that no one 'in hoc presenti seculo raptus sit ad perfectam visionem celestium' ('in this present age is taken up to perfect vision of heavenly things'), Rolle writes,

> Contemplativi vero viri, ut omnes asserunt, sunt sanctissimi, et illi quidem ad ipsam eterne claritatis visionem assidue suspirant ... Sed non dicunt se vidisse Deum, quem nemo unquam vidit. Sed quando dixerunt se vidisse secreta celestia, hoc intellige 'per speculum', quia revelata facie gloriam Dei contemplantur, et hoc fit aperto eis sensu ut intelligant Scripturas, aut aperto celo ut purgato cordis oculo celestes cives speculentur. Utrumque istorum magnum est, et nescio si dentur alicui nisi iusto et sancto.[22]

> As everyone agrees, contemplative men are indeed the most holy, and they ceaselessly long for that vision of eternal clarity ... But they do not say that they saw God, whom no one has ever seen. But when they have said that they saw heavenly secrets, understand them to mean 'through a glass', for with the face revealed they contemplate the glory of God. This takes place [i.e., they see heavenly secrets] either when the meaning has been opened so that they understand Scriptures, or when heaven has been opened so that, with the eye of their heart purged, they gaze upon heavenly citizens. Each of these two is august, and I do not know if they are granted to anyone but the just and holy.

The image of seeing into heaven is apparently a useful, though imprecise, way to describe two distinct phenomena, serving either as a figurative expression for exegetical inspiration, which of course has a heavenly source, or as a means of explaining mystical vision of heaven.[23] It is in this first sense that Rolle finds the *apertio caeli* deployed in various psalms, while the overlap in language (*oculus cordis*, *supernos* or *caelestes cives*, forms of *purgare*) suggests that the second corresponds to the mystical ascent he describes in *Incendium*. In yet another account of the same pair in *Emendatio Vitae* – with inspired interpretation and vision of *caelestes cives* now presented as two ways contemplatives 'gaze upon the Lord's glory' ('gloriam Domini speculantur') – the hermit explicitly marks them as distinct phenomena: only some people, he writes, are able to experience

---

[22] Rolle, *Contra Amatores Mundi*, 5, ed. by Theiner, p. 91.
[23] On the range of ecstatic experiences described as *visiones*, see Newman, 'Medieval Visionary Culture'.

both ('Quidam autum utrumque istorum acceperunt').²⁴ It is unlikely, then, that Rolle meant for this heavenly sight to be conflated with his inspired exegetical insights. His neglect to describe experiences associated with this inspiration makes it impossible to know when he came to believe he was thus inspired, and it could even be that this happened later than his perceptions of heat or song.²⁵ The composition of his early commentaries, in which those other experiences are described as the *sensus* of the biblical text, provides the only reliable indication of the point by which his ideas about inspiration were at least beginning to form.

Though he is largely silent with regard to the experience of inspiration, Rolle does provide some explanation of how his inspired interpretations compare to those of more familiar sources, especially the Fathers. In these cases, the hermit seems to position himself in the company of these ancient writers, thereby affirming his own authority as an exegete even as he maintains an obligatory pose of humility. Immediately after the passage in *Contra Amatores* quoted above, for example, having explained that no one can enjoy unmediated vision of God in this life, he continues,

> Attamen sancti patres magni fuerunt et mira sciencia prediti, itaque caritate non ficta insigniti. Ego vero parvus sum et in comparacione illorum minor. Nescio ostendere quam mira et quam magna Christus dignabatur eis revelare.²⁶

> Yet the holy Fathers were great men, endowed with wondrous knowledge and distinguished by unfeigned charity. Truly, I am small and, compared to them, of lesser status. I do not know how to show what wondrous and great things Christ deigned to reveal to them.

At least in part, Rolle is seeking to clarify that his previous comments were not meant to belittle saintly writers, that their lack of direct vision of God *in via* does not make them less holy than one might otherwise have believed. Yet he is also positioning his revealed knowledge in relation to theirs, already framed (in part) in terms of an ability to understand Scripture *sensu aperto*, and he thus suggests that the 'wondrous and great' things shown to them (and expressed in their writing) are greater than

---

[24] *Emendatio Vitae*, ed. by Spahl, pp. 230/65–232/70. Rolle evidently counts himself part of this select group.

[25] For a possible exception to this trend, see Rolle, *Melos*, 43, ed. by Arnould, p. 134: apparently referring to the 'secret' knowledge inspiring his interpretation of Scripture – that is, his ability to gloss verses as describing heat, sweetness and song – he writes, 'Siquidem ex superis secretum suscepi dum subii solicite pro solacio celesti in corpore sedere'.

[26] Rolle, *Contra Amatores Mundi*, 5, ed. by Theiner, p. 91.

whatever has been revealed to him.[27] In *Contra Amatores*, this positioning is presented quickly, but the same point is made at greater length in *Melos*, part of a defence of Rolle's authority following a long first-person account of his experiences of heat and celestial song:

> Nimirum misterium mitto modernis, etenim antiqui sublimia sciebant. Archanum absconditur ab omnibus avaris: vix unus hoc accipit dum est in hoc mundo. Claudit enim Conditor ianuam Scripture ut lateant legentibus que liquide lucescunt, sed amicis hanc aperit ardenter qui amant, ut aliis ostendant quod hii intellexerunt ...[28]

> While the ancients doubtless knew lofty things, I utter a mystery to modern people. This secret is hidden from all the greedy, and scarcely one person catches hold of it while he lives in this world. For the Creator closes the gate of Scripture so that things which are quite clear are hidden from readers, but he opens it to his friends who ardently love him, so that they may show to others what they have understood.

This prose is admittedly dense, but Rolle appears to be claiming that an inspired interpreter can find in Scripture the *arcanum* ('mystery', 'secret') of the ecstatic experiences he has discussed in the foregoing pages, and that such an interpreter is obliged to share this arcane knowledge with the uninspired multitudes, those who could read Holy Writ endlessly without ever reaching the same interpretive conclusions. It would be easy enough to make this point without referring to the *antiqui*, and the purpose of their invocation here is not immediately clear.[29] In light of the passage from *Contra Amatores*, however, the important distinction seems to be the number of different 'lofty things' (*sublimia*) that were revealed to them, as opposed to the singular *mysterium* or *arcanum* that is the focus of Rolle's writing.[30] This contrast thus appears to offer another gesture of humility, though, as *Melos* continues, the hermit insists that the greater number of

---

[27] Cf. the various claims for patristic inspiration in his Latin Psalter commentary: e.g., Lambeth MS 352, f. 140ᵛ: '... *columpnas*, id est sanctos doctores, misso ad eos Spiritu sancto, quorum doctrinis sustentamur et exemplis, qui gracia spirituali habent Spiritum sanctum', f. 153ᵛ: '*Quoniam dixisti* per inspiracionem internam loquens sanctis *in eternum*', and ff. 163ᵛ–165ʳ: '*Extendens celum*, id est aperiens Scripturas per doctores ... Sed tunc *emitte Spiritum tuum* in corda eorum per internam inspiracionem' (on Pss 74.4, 88.2 and 103.2 and 30).

[28] Rolle, *Melos*, 43, ed. by Arnould, p. 134 (corrected).

[29] I read Rolle's *etenim* as a conjunction introducing a clause that clarifies the preceding one: cf. *DMLBS* s.v. *etenim* (c).

[30] Albin, *Melody of Love*, p. 277, suggests that Rolle invokes the *antiqui* to claim that their revelations were 'more recondite', but this translation would require a comparative *sublimiora* rather than the text's *sublimia*.

their mystical insights does not make the ancients holier than him.[31] Regardless, just as the Fathers expressed their inspired understandings of Scripture, so too Rolle feels compelled to share his insights by writing commentaries, and, though his glosses offer considerably less variety, they still supplement patristic interpretations with something new.[32]

Throughout his writings, Rolle repeatedly advocates for his special status as a *modernus* whose authority is nevertheless comparable to the Fathers, and, more generally, for the existence of 'modern' saints – though the saints of today are relatively private people, without public miracles, and therefore harder to identify.[33] At the opening of *Melos*, for example, the hermit seeks to silence critics who claim that 'non dignatur Deus indulcorare homines in hoc mundo, nec magnificare modernos in melliphona multitudine, sicut solebat sanctos qui antiquitus ambulabant' ('God does not deign to refresh human beings in this world, nor to magnify moderns in the honey-voiced multitude as he did with the saints who ambled in antiquity').[34] On the contrary, he says, there have never been more devout (*devotior*) individuals than those living in his own lifetime, and, indeed, until the end of time, 'non finientur funditus hec fastigia a filiis fidelium' ('from the foundation, the peaks [of the Lord's house] will not be completed by the offspring of the faithful') – that is, the ranks of saints will continue to grow.[35] Of course, this is a general defence of 'modern' sanctity, but the same inscribed critique reappears, applied specifically to the creation of new glosses, in Rolle's final major work of exegesis, a commentary on passages from Job read in the Office of the Dead. Stressing the urgency of his writing, meant to save readers from the

---

[31] Rolle imagines someone arguing, 'Ergo sunt sanctissimi qui talia sciverunt, cum Deus hiis aperuit nosque nescimus' (Rolle, *Melos*, 43, ed. by Arnould, p. 134 [corrected]), i.e., that the ancients who knew such great things were holier, since God revealed things to them about which we have no knowledge. This argument is refuted on the basis of Rolle's experiences, since he has ascended higher in heaven than even seraphim.

[32] Cf. Rolle, *Incendium*, 32, ed. by Deanesly, p. 237: 'Ob hoc utique euenit huiusmodi amatori, quod nequaquam in aliquorum doctorum scriptis inueni aut reperi expressum', and Rolle, *Melos*, 5, ed. by Arnould, p. 16/19–20.

[33] See, e.g., Rolle, *Melos*, 38, ed. by Arnould, p. 118/2–11. For useful discussions of different uses of the *antiquus–modernus* trope across the Middle Ages, see the essays in Zimmermann (ed.), *Antiqui und Moderni*.

[34] Rolle, *Melos*, 1, ed. by Arnould, p. 3. Citing this passage, Albin, *Melody of Love*, pp. 123–24, suggests his claim of inspiration 'implicitly elevates [*Melos*] to the level of revealed Scripture', a reading which neglects Rolle's accounts of the place of inspiration in scriptural commentary.

[35] Rolle, *Melos*, 1, ed. by Arnould, p. 3. See, similarly, Rolle, *Incendium*, 14 and 33, ed. by Deanesly, pp. 185 and 240: 'Erratis enim, fratres, si putatis nunc nullos tam sanctos ut prophete uel apostoli fuerunt ... Si autem antiquitus Spiritus sanctus plures inspirauit, cur eciam non nunc assumeret amantes ad gloriam Domini speculandam, cum ipsis prioribus moderni approbati non sunt inequales?'

infernal torments which might otherwise await them after death, the hermit presents his critics as petty and misguided.

> Nec ego timeo hereticos aut inuidos qui forsitan insurgunt contra me dicentes aut me in exposicione errasse aut sacra verba congruenter non tractasse, non acceptantes me quia modernus sum, sed profecto qui bonos modernos reprobat hesternos non laudat. Non enim est Deus nunc minoris bonitatis quam fuit in primitiua Ecclesia, qui adhuc electos suos ad amorem eternitatis desiderandum preparat et quos vult celesti sciencia sapienciaque diuina inspirat. Verum sciatis quod episcopus non sum nec prelatus nec rector ecclesiarum, tamen solicitus sum pro Ecclesia Dei, si possem aliquo bono modo quicquam facere vel scribere quo Ecclesia Christi augmentum capiat in diuina dileccione.[36]

> I do not fear heretics or the envious who may rise up against me, saying either that I err in my exposition or that I do not treat the holy words properly. They do not accept me because I am modern, but, truly, he who reproaches good moderns does not praise the people of the past. Indeed, God is not now of lesser goodness than he was in the early Church, and he still prepares his elect to desire love of eternity and inspires whoever he wants with heavenly knowledge and divine wisdom. In truth, though you know that I am not a bishop or prelate or a rector of churches, I still care for the Church of God, and I seek in some way to do or write something that will make Christ's Church grow in divine love.

Rather than making any direct claims for inspiration, Rolle simply indicates that it would be foolish to rule out the possibility that *boni moderni* receive the same divine assistance in their exegesis as the ancients, and he implicitly offers his solicitude, the quasi-pastoral concern that motivates his writing, as evidence that he should be numbered among the inspired.[37] Intriguingly, the possibility of errant exposition, given here in the voice of his detractors, had been raised earlier in the commentary by Rolle himself, in another, more overt example of the hermit aligning his interpretive authority with that of the *antiqui*. As he turns to gloss what he considers especially enigmatic language, Rolle writes,

> O sancti seniores, orate pro me iuuene, vt non errem in hac exposicione, sed pocius digna et congrua valeam pronunciare. Alta enim

---

[36] Cambridge, University Library MS Ii.1.26, f. 157ᵛ (corrected against other copies); cf. Moyes, II, 195–96 (on Job 13.25).

[37] This passage therefore reflects what Watson, *Invention of Authority*, p. 198, identifies as Rolle's desire, throughout this late work, 'to be of spiritual benefit to his readers, and to address not only mystical specialists like himself'.

sentencia hic dominatur, et ideo conandum est vt non aliter quam bene exponantur.[38]

O holy elders, pray for me, a young man, so that I do not err in this exposition, but am instead able to make worthy and correct pronouncements. For a profound meaning is master here, and so one must strive to avoid expounding it wrongly.

As in *Contra Amatores*, Rolle presents himself as young or small in comparison to the Fathers of the Church, but now the *antiqui* are invoked not as authoritative antecedents but as fellow interpreters, holy men who were similarly inspired to cast light on biblical obscurities, and he is asking not for their guidance but for their prayers. A kind of exegetical Dante, the hermit is a humble junior member of this august company of interpreters, and yet, as he makes clear in *Melos*, he is confident that when he joins these saints in heaven he will discover, definitively, that his readings were as true as theirs.[39]

The specificity of Rolle's ideas about inspiration and authority, especially their focus on a single *mysterium* or *arcanum* related to his other mystical experiences, should make it clear that the hermit is not straightforwardly borrowing or reflecting some pre-existent scholastic theory. Instead, it seems more likely that his thinking on this subject grew out of his received understanding of one crucial topic – patristic inspiration – and his attempt to position himself in relation to the authoritative exegetes of late antiquity. The notion that the Fathers were inspired interpreters of Scripture is the clearest point of contact between the hermit's accounts of exegetical authority and those of his contemporaries in the schools, and glosses supporting such an understanding of patristic inspiration can readily be found in the sources for Rolle's early commentaries.[40] Of course, some of the major forms of scholastic literature, including commentary, were shaped by the observation that the Fathers often disagree (or, in some cases, appear to disagree), and it is, therefore, commonly acknowledged that their inspiration was intermittent and lesser in kind than that of biblical authors.[41] After praising Augustine and Jerome as harmoniously sounding

---

[38] Cambridge, University Library MS Ii.1.26, f. 149ᵛ (corrected); cf. Moyes, II, 169 (on Job 10.4).
[39] Rolle, *Melos*, ed. by Arnould, pp. 68/33–69/2.
[40] See, e.g., *PL* 162, 1580c and *PL* 191, 208b, 363d, 364d, etc. On the status of the Fathers in scholastic literature, see Backus (ed.), *Reception of the Church Fathers*, and Berndt and Fédou (eds), *Les réceptions des Pères*; on patristic exegesis specifically, see Dahan's essays, 'Tradition patristique', 'Tradition, progès, liberté' and 'Les Pères dans l'exégèse'.
[41] The variety of often contradictory interpretive opinions offered by patristic exegetes undergirds what Dahan has called 'un mitraillage herméneutique', essentially the accretion of differing interpretations, in many cases without any attempt being made to adjudicate between them or,

'reeds' (*fistula*) played by the Holy Ghost, for example, Robert Grosseteste (d. 1253) concedes, 'Spiritus sanctus non omnia et semper dictabat que isti duo sancti scribebant, sed eos reliquit aliquando propriis vocibus, ut ex discordia proveniret nobis aliquis utilis fructus' ('the Holy Ghost did not always dictate everything these two saints wrote but sometimes left them to their own words, so we might benefit from this discord').[42] In certain circumstances, however, scholastic exegetes could emphasise the Fathers' divine inspiration, even making them sound very much like the authors of Holy Writ. Seeking to praise Augustine at the start of his commentary on *De civitate Dei*, for example, John Ridewall OFM (d. *c.* 1340) argues that the text he is glossing has a double efficient cause: 'Licet enim Augustinus fuerit causa efficiens instrumentalis, tamen Dominus est efficiens principalis' ('Though Augustine was the instrumental efficient cause, yet the Lord is the principal efficient').[43] Ridewall's invocation of the *duplex causa efficiens* clearly follows from a thirteenth-century trend in Aristotelian prologues to biblical commentaries, where the division between principal and instrumental efficient causality allowed exegetes to acknowledge that 'the author of holy Scripture is God' even as they focused their interpretive efforts, with increasing sophistication, on the literary contributions of the human writer.[44] Ridewall, however, is working in the opposite direction, taking a text his two major sources, Thomas Waleys OP (d. *c.* 1349) and Nicholas Trevet OP (d. *c.* 1334), had attributed straightforwardly to Augustine and introducing the claim of God's principal efficient causality to emphasise the human writer's divinely inspired authority.[45] Taking this account in isolation, it would be hard to distinguish the inspired authority of Augustine from that of the biblical *auctores*.

When they attempt to clarify the relative positioning of biblical and patristic texts, however, or to distinguish between Scripture and its authoritative interpretation, scholastic theorists sometimes present the Fathers in

---

crucially, to parcel them out one or another of the senses of Scripture. See Dahan, *Lire la Bible*, pp. 17–18 and 223, and his *L'exégèse chrétienne*, pp. 140–41.

[42] Grosseteste, *De cessatione legalium*, IV.III.2–3, ed. by Dales and King, pp. 164–65; cf. Lewis, 'Grosseteste and the Fathers'.

[43] Oxford, Corpus Christi College MS 186, f. 1$^v$. See Smalley, 'Ridewall's Commentary', and *EFA*, pp. 121–32.

[44] Aquinas, *Summa Theologiae*, Ia 1, 10, resp. (Blackfriars edn, 1, 38–39). See *MTA*, pp. 75–84.

[45] Trevet writes, 'Causa efficiens ... beatus Augustinus fuit, qui de numero illorum fuit de quibus prophetando dicit Psalmista, 144[.11], *Gloriam regni tui dicent*' (Cambridge, Peterhouse MS 75, f. 1$^{ra}$), and Waleys agrees, writing, 'Circa vero causam effectiuam librorum de ciuitate Dei sciendum est quod beatus Augustinus, sicut colligi potest ex hiis que ipsemet dicit ...' (*Diui Aurelii Augustini ... de Ciuitate dei*, sig. a3$^{rb}$). For discussion of Waleys's work, see Smalley, 'Thomas Waleys', esp. pp. 86–98, and *EFA*, pp. 88–100. Trevet is discussed briefly in *EFA*, pp. 62–63.

ways that seem to foreclose the possibility of post-patristic interpretive inspiration. As part of his definition of the canon of Scripture, for example, Hugh of St Victor (d. 1141) identifies the works of the Fathers as forming a third part of the New Testament, after the gospels and the writings of the apostles, such that they mirror the position of 'hagiographical' books in the Old Testament, following the Pentateuch and prophets. This is surely a powerful statement of patristic authority, even after Hugh clarifies that the Fathers' writings are not actually part of the canon of Scripture, making them more aptly comparable to Old Testament apocrypha, books which 'non scribuntur in canone et tamen leguntur, ut Sapientia Salomonis' ('are not written in the canon and yet are read, like the Wisdom of Solomon').[46] A similar positioning of patristic writings at the periphery of Scripture is described vividly in the prologue to a *Sentences* commentary attributed to Peter Comestor (d. 1178). Invoking Moses's ascent of Mt Sinai in Exod. 19, Comestor identifies the mountain with Holy Writ, and he then claims that the writings of the Fathers are the limits (*termini*) which Moses is commanded to establish around it (cf. Exod. 19.12):

> Termini circa montem positi sunt agiograhi, id est sanctorum Patrum scripta, utriusque Testamenti intellectum nobis aperiencia. Hos autem terminos quidam, sicut Moyses, Domino vocante transierunt, uti primitivi Patres, qui solius Dei revelatione intelligenciam Scripture perceperunt.[47]

> The limits set around the mountain are holy writings, i.e., the writings of the holy Fathers, disclosing to us the understanding of both Testaments. Some have, like Moses, been able to venture beyond these limits when called by the Lord, e.g., the primitive Fathers [i.e., the apostles], who perceived the understanding of Scripture by the revelation of God alone.

According to Comestor, though inspired interpretation was available in the early Church, it is now only through the writings of the Fathers that the text of Scripture can be read and interpreted correctly: like the Israelites of Exod. 19, scholastic theologians may not ascend the mountain of Scripture

---

[46] Hugh of St Victor, *De scripturis et scriptoribus sacris*, 6, PL 175, 15d–16b; cf. idem, *Didascalicon*, IV.2, tr. by Taylor, p. 104. See further Dahan, 'Les Pères dans l'exégèse', pp. 111–13, and his 'Tradition, progrès, liberté', p. 24; Smith, 'What Was the Bible?', pp. 3–4; and FitzGerald, *Inspiration and Authority*, pp. 37–39. Similarly, at the start of his *Quaestiones de Epistolis Pauli*, Robert of Melun (d. 1167) identifies the parts of the New Testament as 'Evangelia, epistole, Actus Apostolorum, Apocalipsis, scripta patrum secundum quosdam' (Robert of Melun, *Œuvres*, ed. by Martin, II, 3). Dahan, *L'exégèse chrétienne*, p. 67, draws attention to similar statements made by Nicholas of Lyre in the fourteenth century. Likewise, the early fourteenth-century Parisian master John of Maroeuil notes that 'per sacram Scripturam aliquando intelligimus quod continetur in Biblia et in glossis sanctorum' (quoted in Leclercq, 'L'idéal du théologien', p. 125).

[47] Quoted in Martin, 'Notes sur Pierre le Mangeur', p. 61; cf. Saccenti, '*Materia*'.

for themselves, but they may behold it from the safe distance of the *termini*.⁴⁸ The Lombard's *Sentences* are therefore intended to map the dense forest of patristic verbiage (the mixed metaphors are Comestor's), so copious and confusing that some readers are terrified (*exterriti*) and give up theology altogether, fleeing to less challenging disciplines, 'ut ad phisicam, leges et huiusmodi' ('such as medicine, law and the like').⁴⁹

The critiques Rolle imagines levelled against his exegesis in *Melos* and his commentary on Job seem to be informed by these same ideas of patristic authority, with his would-be attackers, in the same way as Comestor, at once setting patristic exegesis apart from the writings of 'modern' commentators and suggesting that the inspiration enjoyed by the Fathers was distinct from the work of the Holy Ghost in the post-patristic Church.⁵⁰ As Gilbert Dahan observes, belief in patristic inspiration could thus foster a kind of exegetical fixity, creating a canon of commentaries to match the canon of Scripture, with the result that 'le travail de l'exégèse se limitant alors à la collation de commentaires autorisés'.⁵¹ Stephen of Tournai (d. 1203), for example, derides his contemporaries for their hubris and the trifling novelties of their commentaries, writing,

> Lapsa sunt apud nos in confusionis officinam sacrarum studia litterarum, dum et discipuli solis novitatibus applaudunt, et magistri gloriae potius invigilant quam doctrinae, novas recentesque summulas et commentaria firmantia super theologica passim conscribunt, quibus auditores suos demulceant, detineant, decipiant, quasi nondum suffcerint sanctorum opuscula patrum, quos eodem spiritu sacram Scripturam legimus exposuisse, quo eam composuisse credimus apostolos et prophetas.⁵²

> It seems to me that the study of sacred literature has become a workshop of confusion, seeing that students applaud only novelties and masters are kept awake by thoughts of glory rather than doctrine, everywhere writing new and modish little summas and commentaries relying on theological matters, with which they charm, transfix and deceive their audiences – as if the works of the holy Fathers were no longer sufficient, when we read that they

---

⁴⁸ The *primitivi patres* are identified overtly with the apostles in two *Sentences* commentaries drawing on Comestor's prologue: see Martin, 'Notes', p. 64; Saccenti, '*Materia*', p. 213, the former discussed by Colish, 'The Pseudo-Peter of Poitiers Gloss'.
⁴⁹ Martin, 'Notes', p. 61.
⁵⁰ For the variety of conflicting accounts of this vaguer kind of inspiration, see FitzGerald's useful study, *Inspiration and Authority*.
⁵¹ Dahan, *L'exégèse chrétienne*, p. 68, with further examples.
⁵² *PL* 211, 517ab; for further discussion, see Dahan, 'Les Pères dans l'exégèse', p. 113.

expounded holy Scripture with the help of the same Spirit with which, we believe, the apostles and prophets composed it.

As a canonist, Stephen was ready to limit the task of 'modern' biblical exegesis to the arrangement and explanation of inspired patristic glosses, but for anyone who devoted serious study to their exegetical writings, the insufficiency of the Fathers could quickly become apparent. Even Richard of St Victor (d. 1173), a fairly conservative commentator by the standards of his abbey, noted that patristic writers often failed to gloss the literal sense of some of the more difficult (*obscurior*) passages of Scripture, and he attacks the feigned piety of those who, like Stephen, 'quasi ob reverentiam Patrum nolunt ab illis omissa attentare, ... sed inertiae suae ejusmodi velamen habentes, otio torpent et aliorum industriam in veritatis investigatione et inventione' ('as though out of reverence for the Fathers, do not want to take on what was omitted by them, ... but holding this kind of veil for their laziness, they remain dull in their idleness and deride the zeal others have for the investigation and discovery of truth').[53] Similarly, if somewhat problematically, the prolific Dominican commentator Trevet begins his work on the Psalms by announcing that he will focus solely on that book's literal sense, since (he claims) 'omnes prisci temporis doctores circa allegoriarum misteria profunda perscrutanda totis studiis occupati' ('all the doctors of former times devoted their efforts wholly to studying the profound mysteries of allegories').[54] Here Trevet appears to be following the model of Thomas Aquinas OP (d. 1274), who, faced with the canonicity of Gregory's *Moralia* on Job, identified that work as fully treating the text's mystical senses, leaving him the task of glossing it *litteraliter*.[55] In all of these cases, it would seem that deference to the Fathers' authority is matched by a need to supplement or continue their work, to recover more fully the meaning of the biblical text.[56]

Unlike Rolle, however, the schoolmen did not need to invoke the idea of inspiration to establish their exegetical authority. As M.-D. Chenu indicates, the license to teach gave a *magister* all the authority he needed to offer glosses and theological opinions, and though this authority was

---

[53] PL 196, 527cd; cf. Dahan, *Lire la Bible*, p. 28; Chenu, *La théologie comme science*, pp. 387–88.
[54] Oxford, Bodleian Library MS Bodley 738, f. 1ʳᵇ; see further, Kraebel, *Experiments in Interpretation*, pp. 37–38.
[55] Parma edn, XIV, 2.
[56] Cf. Andrew of St Victor's description of biblical truth as buried ore, only recoverable with difficulty and bit by bit (*minutatim*), leaving moderns to continue the work of the Fathers: see Chenu, *La théologie comme science*, p. 388.

certainly lesser than that of the Fathers and could be dismissed easily by other writers as 'merely magisterial', it was clearly sufficient to support the continuing creation of commentaries.[57] Yet this does not mean that inspiration was altogether excluded from scholastic writers' understanding of new exegetical productions. In his *Summa quaestionum ordinarium*, for example, and specifically in his treatment of the 'perfection' or completeness of Scripture against Joachimite claims for an 'Eternal Evangel', the secular Parisian master Henry of Ghent (d. 1293) argues that, though Christ's promise that the Spirit will come to teach 'all truth' (John 16.13) could superficially be construed as supporting the eventual revelation of a third testament, this verse is more properly understood as describing further interpretations of the Old Testament and of Christ's own teaching.[58] This promised exposition comes in distinct stages, with the apostles first offering the rest of the New Testament as an interpretation of the gospels and Hebrew Scripture (in the latter case continuing the work of the gospels themselves), followed by the doctors and, in turn, post-patristic or 'modern' commentators. Each stage sees a diminution of authority, tied specifically to a decreasing certainty or consistency of inspiration, but Henry does not doubt that new biblical commentaries, with new interpretations, can still be inspired by the divine: 'Licet enim apostoli primitias Spiritus sancti receperint, virtutem tamen eius omnes posteri fideles recepturi vsque in finem mundi et per ipsam sacram Scripturam tractaturi' ('For although the apostles received the first-fruits of the Holy Ghost, its power will nevertheless continue to be received by all future generations of the faithful, even until the end of the world, and through it sacred Scripture will continue to be studied').[59] Henry urges each commentator to offer what he can to build up the exegetical edifice of Holy Writ, such that, until the end of time, 'continue augmentatur sacre Scripture intellectus et expositio' ('the understanding and exposition of sacred Scripture is

---

[57] Chenu, *Introduction*, pp. 113–16, and cf. his *La théologie comme science*, pp. 358–60.
[58] *Summa quaestionum*, art. 8 q. 6, sigs i4ᵛ–i5ʳ: 'Non enim promisit [Christus] Spiritum docturum aliquam aliam veritatem aut perfectorem quam ipse docuerat, sed potius explanaturum illam quam in Veteri Testamento et in sua doctrina euangelica inexpositam reliquit'. Dahan draws attention to this passage in several studies, see: *Lire la Bible*, pp. 28–33, 'Les Pères dans l'exégèse', pp. 109–111, 'Tradition patristique', pp. 349 and 355, 'Tradition, progrès, liberté', pp. 25–26. In *Interpréter la Bible*, pp. 117–42, he provides a French translation of the entire *quaestio*.
[59] Art. 8 q. 6, sig. i5ᵛ. Regarding the uncertainty on which of the doctors were inspired in their exegesis and the resulting diminution in patristic compared to apostolic writings, Henry claims, 'Non aequale pondus auctoritatis obtineat, quia non constat Ecclesiae doctores *aliquos* catholicos in Spiritu sancto fuisse loquutos sicut constat ipsi Apostolos in eo fuisse locutos' (sig. i5ᵛ, emphasis added). He does not identify which, if any, specific doctors he has in mind.

continuously increased').⁶⁰ The clear implication is that, though modern masters can never be certain when the more diffuse inspiration of the present age will strike, and though the authority of their *magisterium* means that, in any event, they need not worry about their own inspiration, they are nevertheless contributing to a larger interpretive enterprise that is guided and, as a whole, inspired by the Holy Ghost.

The crucial difference, therefore, between Rolle's approach to 'modern' commentary and that of scholastic writers like Henry seems to involve the concepts of 'magisterial' opinion and authority, concepts which are simply absent from Rolle's writings. This is not just to say that, as someone who studied briefly at Oxford, the hermit is unable to use these terms to describe his own glosses, but also that he does not engage with exegetical sources that he would consider straightforwardly classifiable in those terms, and that he does not, more generally, seem to be aware of 'magisterial' commentaries as a category of texts to which he might compare his own.⁶¹ His writings, including his commentaries, do not give us any examples of 'modern' exegetes other than himself, and this silence seems more likely to reflect, by and large, Rolle's unfamiliarity with scholastic commentaries than his hostility to the project of scholastic exegesis or his belief that university masters were unable to gloss the Bible with the same inspiration as he enjoyed. Indeed, while the emphasis on inspiration in the passages discussed above may seem to set Rolle's approach to exegesis apart from that commonly found in the schools, it is worth recalling the various instances in which the hermit pairs this inspiration with a call to rigorous study of the text, and the suggestion that, without the academic training needed to undertake such study, attempts at biblical interpretation imperil the soul.⁶² Further, though he may have been largely unfamiliar with their

---

[60] Ibid., sig. i5v–i6r: '. . . dignum est vt quandoque ad complendum sacre Scripture aedificium quilibet aliquid de suo offerat'.

[61] On routinely short stints at university, generally focused on the arts, see Logan, *University Education*. Frustration with the mandated arts course is reflected in the biographical Office lessons composed in anticipation of the hermit's canonisation, where it is said that Rolle 'desiderauit plenius et profundius imbui theologicis sacre Scripture doctrinis quam phisicis aut secularis sciencie disciplinis'. Woolley (ed.), *Officium and Miracula*, p. 23. On the prescribed length of arts study before advancing to higher disciplines, see Fletcher, 'Faculty of Arts', esp. pp. 374, 381–82 and 391–92; Courtenay, *Schools and Scholars*, pp. 30–36.

[62] Cf., e.g., Rolle, *Emendatio Vitae*, 9, ed. by Spahl, p. 208/5–6, suggesting that devout readers leave difficult passages of Scripture to 'disputatious and clever men', and *Super Canticum*, 2, in Rolle, *Unprinted Latin*, ed. by Hanna, p. 66/11–13, contrasting his readers with the uneducated laity; see too his attack on the wickedness of uninspired and uneducated would-be interpreters, 'qui docere volunt alios quod ipsi nesciunt, cum a Deo nec sint inspirati nec ab hominibus docti' (Lambeth MS 352, f. 175ʳ, on Ps. 118.2).

commentaries, Rolle certainly aspired to have his prose read by professional theologians, first claiming, for example, that *Incendium* was not written for 'magnis theologicis infinitis quescionibus implicatis' ('great theologians enwrapped in [or impeded by] infinite questions'), only to reverse course and say that, if they put away worldly concerns and are focused on divine love, these theologians are his ideal readers, for 'scienciores sunt eo de iure apciores sint ad amandum' ('of necessity, the more learned they are, the better suited they are for love').[63] This is not a rejection of academic theology (or exegesis) so much as a call for this work to be directed along proper caritative lines, and its blurring of the academic and mystical, its promotion of a studied devotion or devout study, is characteristic of the hermit's writing more broadly.[64]

The complexly intersecting ideas and influences informing Rolle's writings on inspired exegesis are perhaps captured most succinctly in the arrangement of books like Lincoln Cathedral Library MS 139, a copy of the *Magna glosatura* already in Lincoln in Rolle's lifetime (see Figure 5.1).[65] The major source for his interpretations of the Psalms, the *Magna glosatura* was a foundational work of scholastic biblical studies, but as he indicates in the prologue to his English Psalter commentary, Rolle appears to have considered it, like his other early scholastic sources, a *compilatio*, a convenient way of accessing the opinions of 'haly doctours', with the compiler adding few if any of his own readings.[66] Rolle's work with the *Magna glosatura* thus depends on the citational apparatus preserved in copies like Lincoln 139, in which patristic and early medieval sources are identified by means of a series of *signes de renvoi* positioned over phrases in the commentary, corresponding to abbreviated names repeated at the top of each page (e.g., 'AV' for Augustine, corresponding to two horizontally aligned points copied over glosses in Figure 5.1 beginning 'tanquam inherentem' and 'non meis meritis').[67]

---

[63] Rolle, *Incendium*, pr., ed. by Deanesly, p. 147; cf. Watson, *Invention of Authority*, p. 116.
[64] On Rolle specifically, see Kraebel, *Experiments in Interpretation*, ch. 3; generally, on this discursive mix, see, Johnson, *Life of Christ*.
[65] For the provenance of Lincoln 139, see Thomson, *Catalogue of the Manuscripts of Lincoln*, p. 107.
[66] Only twice in the *English Psalter* does Rolle cite 'þe glose' or what 'þe maistere sayes in his glose' (Huntington HM 148, ff. 56$^{vb}$ and 89$^{ra}$, on Pss 26.11 and 41.5; cf. Rolle, *Psalms of David*, ed. by Bramley, pp. 96 and 154).
[67] In addition to the Augustine, Jerome and Remigius, whose names are visible in Figure 5.1, the scribe writes abbreviations for Hrabanus Maurus ('RAB') and Cassiodorus ('CAS') over the right column of each page. It is almost certain that Rolle worked with a copy of the *Magna glosatura* containing at least some of these citations, allowing him to name patristic sources even as his phrasing indicates that he is quoting from the Lombard. See Kraebel, *Experiments in Interpretation*, pp. 112–13. Of course, his copy could also have made use of citations in the outer rather than upper margins, for examples of which see De Hamel, *Glossed Books*, pl. 9–12 and p. 23.

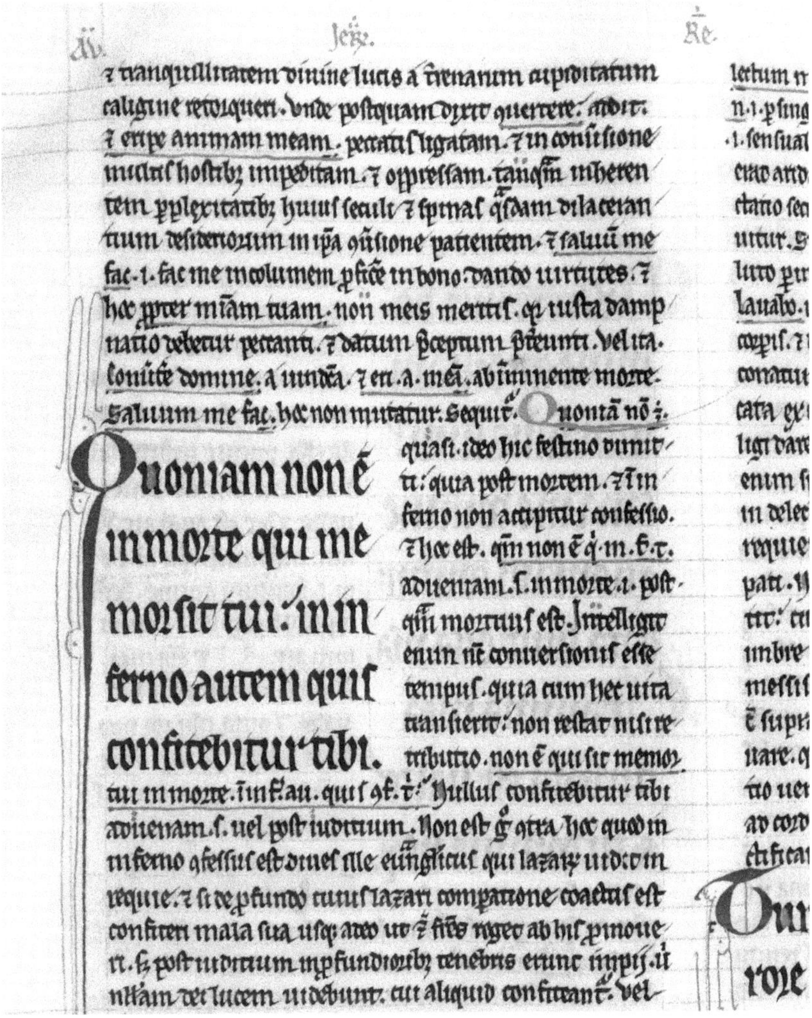

Figure 5.1   Lincoln, Cathedral Library MS 139, f. 12ᵛ (selection).
From the *Magna glosatura* on Ps. 5. 9-10, with citational symbols in the upper margin.
Reproduced by kind permission of the Dean and Chapter of Lincoln Cathedral.

The commentary's standard arrangement on this manuscript page, with its compiled interpretations arrayed around biblical verses written in a larger script, presents something of a visual analogue to Comestor's description of the scriptural mountain bordered by a forest of the

Fathers.[68] Faced with such pages, Rolle's ambition was to add some of his own interpretations to their collection of patristic opinions, contributing new readings of specific verses in a limited number of books (in particular the Psalter and Canticle), with the bulk of these glosses focused on religious experiences not otherwise mentioned in the received corpus of patristic commentary. As an avowed compiler, to return to the passage with which this chapter began, that is precisely what Rolle did, with his commentary on the Psalter, for example, generally preserving and abridging the patristic material he found in the *Glosatura*, supplemented by the occasional novel interpretation – and in the case of these glosses, the hermit moves from being a compiler to an inspired commentator. In his lemmatised commentaries, in other words, Rolle writes himself into what he sees as an ongoing interpretive undertaking, and in this respect his efforts are wholly consistent with contemporary university exegesis.

McGinn's account of Rollean inspiration therefore requires revision on a number of points. Certainly, the hermit's claims to exegetical inspiration were especially important to the commentaries written early in his career, but, rather than being a particular feature of these early works, we have seen that his interest in this inspiration continued across his later writings, prompting new and ever more elaborate discussions of his interpretive authority. Likewise, there is nothing in his writings to suggest that Rolle associated his inspired interpretations in particular with the 'mystical' sense of Scripture. Though he seems to have been generally uninterested in parsing the senses, the invocations of this paradigm that do appear in his writings make it clear that Rolle considered himself just as able (and inspired) an interpreter of the literal sense as he was of Scripture's spiritual registers.[69] Finally, nothing in his discussions of inspiration, or in his glosses more generally, suggests that the hermit thought his commentaries to be categorically opposed to university exegesis, that his inspiration set him apart from 'the academic theologians of the schools'.[70] In its binarism,

---

[68] Smith, 'What was the Bible?', p. 4, makes a similar observation about Hugh of St Victor's description of the canon and the visual aspect of the *Glossa ordinaria*.

[69] Cf. Rolle's explicit signalling of an allegorical reading in *Super Canticum*, 3, in Rolle, *Unprinted Latin*, ed. by Hanna, p. 80/11–14. In *Super Lecciones Mortuorum*, 4, Cambridge, University Library MS Ii.1.26, f. 158ʳ (on Job 13.26), he writes, 'Quod autem spiritualiter intelligenda non litteraliter predicta verba eciam per hoc quod sequitur manifestatur', referring back to glosses on the previous verse and indicating that the literalistic reading that follows continues from this spiritual reading (cf. Moyes, II, 197). He likewise identifies a novel gloss on Job 10.11 as literalistic (f. 154ʳ; cf. Moyes, II, 184). Finally, his commentaries on the Psalter include novel interpretations in both literal and spiritual registers: see Kraebel, *Experiments in Interpretation*, pp. 95–114. On the fraught critical history of the senses of Scripture, see Minnis, 'Figuring the Letter' (2016).

[70] McGinn, *Varieties of Vernacular Mysticism*, p. 342.

McGinn's claim that the fourteenth century saw a 'split between sterile academic theology and the lived theology of contemplatives' is generally exaggerated and unhelpful, and it is certainly too simplistic to account for the writings and influence of the Hermit of Hampole.[71] Quite clearly, Rolle was not an academic exegete, and his approach to building up the edifice of scriptural interpretation (to adapt Henry of Ghent's phrase) differed significantly from those adopted by contemporary commentators in Oxford or Cambridge. Yet Rolle shared basic sources, methods and theoretical underpinnings with these academics and, insofar as the hermit's texts were widely copied and read, in English as well as Latin, his commentaries may ultimately have done more than most university exegetes' to disseminate the ideas and forms of scholastic hermeneutics, under however quirky or eccentric a guise.

[71] Ibid., p. 337.

CHAPTER 6

# Guitar Lessons at Blackfriars
## Vernacular Medicine and Preacher's Style in Henry Daniel's *Liber Uricrisiarum*

*Joe Stadolnik*

According to the advice of English Dominican John Bromyard (d. *c.* 1352), preachers could stand to learn a good deal from guitarists.[1] His *Summa praedicantium* (*Treatise on Preaching*) advises preachers to take their cues from musicians, who know how to capture an audience's attention and keep it:

> Predica, inquit, longa themata vitando, quia sicut tediosum est quod citharedus in aula diu citharam preparat, ita et cetera. Et statim ad quiditatem descendendo inuectiones contra vitia in speciali faciendo, quia qui cithare omnes chordas simul tangit, confusam et ineptam facit melodiam, et quasi ludum videtur facere puerorum. Sic in predicatione. Intente mentes auditorum sunt quasi quedam tentiones chordarum stricte in cithara, quas tangit artifex cum plectro ut reddant consonans modulationem, licet non uno impulso feriantur.[2]

> Avoid long themes in your preaching, for just as it is tedious for a guitar-player in a hall to take a long time tuning his guitar, so it is [for preaching]. One should get to the essence of the matter straightaway, launching attacks specifically against the vices. For someone who plucks all the strings at the same time makes his melody confused and inept, seeming to play, as it were, some childish game, and so too in preaching: the minds of listeners are intent, rather like the tightness of the strings on the guitar, which the expert plays with his pick to render the appropriate modulation, but they are not struck at one go.

Bromyard's ideal guitar-player – or more properly his ideal lutist or harpist – avoids tinkering too long with his tuning or overdoing it with a lot of strumming ('plucking all strings at once'). This expert player knows how to entertain any music-hall crowd with a well-composed, melodic

---

[1] See Peter Binkley's *ODNB* entry on Bromyard, as well as his 'Bromyard and the Hereford Dominicans'.
[2] Bromyard, *Summa praedicantium*, art. VIII, §25, tr. adapted from Walls, *Bromyard on Church and State*, p. 145.

riff.³ And, just as a good guitarist arrives on stage with a tuned instrument, the expert preacher will avoid meandering introductions, knowing that it is better to excite an audience with immediate, uncompromising 'attacks upon the vices'. Neither the guitarist nor the homilist should waste any time before getting down to business, whether picking out a pleasing melody or inveighing against sin. Underwriting Bromyard's comparison is the assumption that both preaching and guitar-playing require a sense of each art's peculiarities and purposes. Like the artful musician, the artful preacher is an *artifex*, crafting each sermon to accomplish his particular ends, playing expertly upon the tautly intent, impressionable minds in the audience.

Unlike guitar-playing, however, preaching had purposes altogether more serious than mere entertainment. For Bromyard and his fellows, a sermon should guide the laity along a path towards salvation and away from sinful living. Such serious business called for a more sober professional than the touring guitarist as a model of conduct. Bromyard looks instead to the speaking habits of physicians. He admires their no-nonsense directness. Doctors – as he imagines them – teach patients just enough about their illness to get by:

> Et sicut medicus ad infirmi sanationem non in generali docet qualiter curari potest, sed in speciali, quo periculum illud incurrit et quomodo sanari potest, ita in speciali conditiones peccati et pericula sunt recitanda, et speciales inuectiones et doctrine sunt contra illas infirmitates adhibende per plana verba et laicis intelligibilia, non per curiositates et declarationes et rationes philosophorum et dubias naturas animalium, quae omnia litteratorum aures demulcent vel predicatium gloriam querunt, et infirmorum non curant sed cecant.⁴

---

³ Talents for guitar-playing and teaching sometimes coincide in a person. A teenaged Alastair Minnis laid down his share of riffs as a member of a gigging showband in Northern Ireland in the mid-1960s. Minnis mostly played rhythm guitar (with apologies to the strumming-averse Bromyard) and took frequent turns on organ, bass and lead guitar. His band covered songs of all kinds: rock and roll, R&B, folk, country and western, classics of the Irish songbook. They envied the extraordinary collection of American records over at Van Morrison's (with whom, he says, he would only 'occasionally hang out'). He is typically modest about his guitar-playing capabilities, instead prouder of the *aulae* where he played. Touring the Northern Irish countryside, his five-piece performed in both Protestant and Catholic church halls alike. This was before their rhythm guitarist went up to Belfast to study English, and before such ecumenical music-making seemed an unjustifiable risk in the face of the violence of 'the Troubles' (a euphemism, in Minnis's judgement).
⁴ Bromyard, *Summa predicantium*, art. VIII, §25; tr. again adapted from Walls, *Bromyard on Church and State*, pp. 145–46.

> And just as the doctor does not teach the sick about how he may be healed in general terms, but rather in specific ones – what danger they are in, and how it may be cured – likewise the conditions and dangers of sin should be spelled out specifically, and specific denunciations and teachings should be applied to counter those frailties in plain words, intelligible by the laity, not by way of far-fetched oddities and declarations and philosophical reasonings and the dubious natures of animals, all of which caress the ears of the learned, or have as their goal the reputation of the preachers, yet fail to heal the wounds of the sick, instead blinding them.

At the bedside, physicians need not – and, ideally, do not – provide patients with a ranging, general overview of medical knowledge. Rather, they educate them about their specific infirmities, passing on only enough knowledge to be immediately applied in treatment. Such targeted instruction about a sickness, or against a sin, entails a direct style appropriate to direct teaching. This style favours 'plain words, intelligible to the laity'; it avoids sophistry, unnecessary philosophising and allegorical illustration. The latter may be common preaching tactics, but in Bromyard's book they only serve frivolous purposes, such as literary pleasure or vain self-aggrandisement. His *Summa* lays out a theory of proper preaching style explicitly hostile to stylistic diversion, decoration or invention. Instruction delivered in a plainer mode – stripped of superfluous doctrine and conspicuous flourishes – will best serve the purposes of the discreet doctor and the Dominican alike.

Taken as a pair, Bromyard's examples of guitar-player and physician appear to present the preacher with competing models for their own practice. One would have preachers be dynamic performers in the pulpit, so as best to exploit the attention and interest of the audience in the service of moral instruction. The other expects them to communicate Christian doctrine bluntly, without any embellishments. Bromyard expresses both of these principles in an inflexible, prescriptive idiom, leaving to the would-be preacher the difficult task of reconciling their competing claims of dynamism and directness. His advice relies on preachers' sensibilities to balance these priorities, a process Bromyard figures musically, with the dynamic preacher finding a 'consonant rhythm' or 'key' for the sermon (*modulationem consonans*). Good teachers strike the right note.

Bromyard lays out his theory of good preaching in Latin, but the practice of preaching in later medieval England was, in large part, a vernacular enterprise. How else were readers of the *Summa* to reach audiences with plain words, intelligible to the laity, other than by preaching in a language they could understand? Arts of preaching thus comprised a genre of medieval literary theory written in the Latin of learned textual communities but persistently oriented towards vernacular practice out in the world. As such, the ideas of the vernacular cultivated in *artes praedicandi* found broad expression in medieval sermons composed according to the protocols of its Latinate theorising.[5] Whether by reading *artes praedicandi* themselves or by listening to sermons written in the styles they prescribed, medieval vernacular writers who studied preachers' conventions might easily put those Latinate lessons in clarity or eloquence into practice in other spheres of vernacular literate activity. This was the case in fourteenth-century England, across genres of Middle English textual making. Preachers' habits of locution and exposition escaped their original generic situations to be implicated in vernacular drama, prose for lay devotional reading and Ricardian poetry.[6]

Among the many writers who benefited from these preaching lessons in later fourteenth-century England, Henry Daniel OP stands out as an especially keen and insightful student, putting predicatorial theory to creative ends in order to convey, specifically, an abstruse body of medical knowledge in his Middle English prose. Though he has received some critical notice as an early pioneer of Ricardian technical writing, the details of Daniel's innovative contribution, and especially the sources of and priorities motivating his novel style, remain to be explored.[7] Here I take up the question of how his professional life and training as a Dominican, an order devoted to the ideas and practices of preaching, contributed to the shaping of his vernacular medical writing. After introducing Daniel and his text, I explore some of the major elements of his expository prose style, reading them against the rhetorical and preaching manuals that were the common fare of Dominican *studia* in his lifetime, and I thereby seek to illustrate what it means for this prose to be 'preacherly'. Finally, I consider the ways in which this Dominican style (and its concomitant rhetorical attitude) set Daniel apart from other medical authorities in later medieval England – at least, that is, in Daniel's own estimation. As we will see, Daniel wrote with a cultivated clarity that explicitly invoked the good

---

[5] For reservations about Latinate theorising and its remove from situations of vernacular writing, see Wogan-Browne et al. (eds), *Idea of the Vernacular*, p. 316.

[6] Studies of preaching in later medieval England have richly described its interaction with other literary modes: see Owst, *Literature and Pulpit*; Fletcher, *Preaching, Politics and Poetry*; Wenzel, *Preachers, Poets and the Early English Lyric*; and Spencer's learned and witty general study, *English Preaching*.

[7] See, for example, Hanna, 'Henry Daniel's *Liber Uricrisiarum* (Excerpt)'. Sarah Star's illuminating account of Daniel's contribution to a Ricardian vernacularising project appeared as this chapter was under revision; see Star, 'Textual Worlds'.

preacher's eloquence coached in *artes praedicandi*, an eloquence which, even in its plainness, might 'play upon the mind' of his readers. He inhabits that professional register of the preacher – somewhere between a guitarist and physician – to strike the right note in rendering rather technical medical matter into an accessible idiom.

Daniel's lengthy Middle English treatise, the *Liber Uricrisiarum* (c. 1379), presents a comprehensive guide to the unsavoury art of diagnosis by inspection of urine – hence the title, meaning 'the book of the judgement of urine'. He followed the *Liber* with his *Herbal*, a compendium on the medicinal qualities of plants (many of which he could grow in his garden in Stepney, outside of London).[8] While the *Herbal* survives today in only two manuscript copies, the *Liber Uricrisiarium* found a much wider audience, as witnessed by the thirty-seven manuscripts recording it in some form.[9] In the first of three books, the *Liber* offers a general introduction to the art of uroscopy, emphasising that the medieval medical practitioner's ability to draw the proper conclusions from a patient's urine was crucial to arriving at a correct diagnosis. The second book identifies the many colours of urine the physician is liable to encounter, along with their correspondent diagnoses, and the third describes the kinds of substances sometimes found in urine. In some manuscripts, these three books are followed by an English translation of Latin proverbs on uroscopy. The *Liber Uricrisiarum* is full of learned references to Latin source material, with wisdom marshalled from such venerated authorities as Galen, Constantine the African, Gilbert the Englishman and Avicenna. Throughout, Daniel finds every excuse to wander beyond his uroscopic subject-matter narrowly defined, to instruct his readers in, for example, anatomy, humoral theory, physiognomy and astronomy. Reading the *Liber Uricrisiarum* therefore requires endurance: Daniel writes expansively and indulges his digressive instincts, including deftly deployed proverbs and intriguing illustrative tales drawn from his life. This is no soggy storehouse of medieval medical knowledge. Daniel's artfulness as a writer and teacher animates the *Liber* and, therefore, despite its length and unseemly subject-matter, the result is a true masterpiece of Middle English prose.

Yet the text does not, in fact, begin in English. Addressing himself to a 'brother in Christ', presumably a fellow Dominican, Daniel first offers a

---

[8] On Daniel's *Herbal*, see Keiser, 'Through a Fourteenth-Century Gardener's Eyes'.
[9] On the complicated manuscript tradition of the *Liber*, see Tavormina, 'Uroscopy in Middle English', pp. 87–92.

substantial prologue in Latin, the language which – he admits – is especially dear to his heart.[10] Here he explains that he undertook this daunting vernacular project only in the spare time afforded to him among his other duties:

> Presens opus multorum auctorum ex libris eorumque commentatorum dictis multis laboribus prout potui per annos excolegi, non solum ordinis mei obedire laboribus diversis quod infirmitatibus et quandoque fere ad mortem frequenter interceptus.[11]

> With great labour over the years, I have compiled the present work as I could out of the books of many authors and of commentators upon them, frequently interrupted not only by the various preoccupations of my order, but at times brought close to death by infirmities.

This assertion of the humbly derivative quality of the *Liber* matches well with a self-effacing pose typically struck by late medieval vernacular writers, who, as Alastair Minnis has shown, would conventionally present themselves as just such workaday *compilatores*.[12] Daniel's contemporary John Gower, for instance, uses very similar terms to lament how sickness impeded the long, hard work of compiling his *Confessio Amantis*.[13] But Daniel's modesty accords, too, with Bromyard's advice in the *Summa*: good preachers and good doctors do not care for literary reputation – or, at least, they should seem unconcerned about it. This vernacular writer cowers before the prospect of criticism (or merely pretends to), and he deprecates himself as the 'smallest and lowest of Christ's servants' ('ego quidem tantillus ut puta minimus servorum Christi').

Such self-deprecation notwithstanding, Daniel shows himself to be a stylish writer of expository English prose, as he translates uroscopy's key terms or describes physiological processes in the *Liber Uricrisiarum*. Consider, for example, this passage, in which he explains why a knowledge of uroscopy is so useful in diagnosis:

---

[10] The Latin prologue is unedited, surviving in three different versions in twelve manuscripts. A later English translation survives in two further manuscripts. I quote from the text of Oxford, Bodleian Library MS Ashmole 1404, ff. 3$^v$–4$^r$, unless otherwise noted. The quoted comments ('lingua ... michi cara') are on f. 4$^r$. For a discussion of the English translation of the prologue, see Getz, 'Language of Medical Learning', pp. 12–16.

[11] Ashmole 1404, f. 3$^v$.

[12] *MTA*, pp. 190–99. For another example, see Chapter 5 by Kraebel, pp. 119–20.

[13] *Confessio Amantis*, pr. 61–62, in Gower, *English Works*, ed. by Macaulay, I, 4: 'Thogh I seknesse have upon honde / And longe have had ...'. In a related Latin gloss, Gower cites his 'labores' in compiling the *Confessio* despite his sickness (ed. by Macaulay, I, 3).

> Also uryn is sayde of þis worde of Grece, 'uryth', *id est* a demonstracioun, a schewynge, for mare certnely and mare verraly uryn schewes & telles þe state & þe dispocioun of mannis body, & namely of þe reynes, þan ony thynge ellys þat commys fra man. And þerfore when we wyll wet & knaw þe state & þe disposicion of mannes body within, & namely of þe ryenes, we take rede & counsell & wyte at þe uryne.[14]

Daniel delivers this little lesson in etymology in plain speech, and the hardest word, 'demonstration', is defined in apposition as 'a schewynge'. His foray into Greco-Latin jargon is not a gratuitous show of his own learning, but the basis for a simple and sensible argument for uroscopy's importance for diagnosis. He writes as Bromyard's good doctor is meant to talk. But there is some artfulness here, too, in Daniel's effusive use of doublets and triplets ('schewes & telles', 'take rede & counsell & wyte at'), and in his subtle shift in voice, from the impersonal constructions of the etymology to the first-person plural constructions of the conclusions to be drawn ('þerfore when we wyll wet & knaw ...'). This is plain English prose written with an ear for rhythm and in dynamic grammar, a straightforward style to engage an audience.[15]

More will be said below about the details of these expository techniques, but first one should note the general affinities between this emphasis on plain style and the notions of preaching articulated, again and again, across the principal texts of the medieval preacher's curriculum. Dominicans, from the very beginnings of their order, devoted themselves to 'study, preaching, and the profit of souls' ('studium vel predicationem vel animarum fructum').[16] All of their intellectual pursuits were to be undertaken with this mission in mind, as Robert Kilwardby (d. 1279), Dominican prior provincial, exhorted the English rank-and-file: 'All our chapters and discussions and debates and all the order's study aim at nothing else than to prepare people and make them fit for the salvation of souls'.[17] Friars preacher convened for such 'discussion and debate and study' at their local conventual *schola* or the more academically advanced *studia*. M. Michèle Mulchahey describes regular attendance of lectures and exercises at a

---

[14] London, Wellcome Collection MS 225, f. 4ᵛ. At the time of writing, no critical edition of the English text of the *Liber* is available, though a reading edition is forthcoming under the general editorship of Ruth Harvey, M. Teresa Tavormina and Sarah Star, to whom I am indebted for fielding my many questions about the *Liber* and its textual tradition. Jasin's 1983 thesis, a transcription of MS 225, has been an invaluable aid in navigating the text.
[15] On the stylistic features of Daniel's prose, see Jasin, 'Compiler's Awareness', with this passage discussed at p. 514.
[16] Galbraith (ed.), *Constitution*, pp. 203–4.
[17] Quoted in Binkley, 'Hereford Dominicans', p. 255.

conventual school as the 'foundational experience for the Dominican friar' and 'the cornerstone of every day of his life in the order'.[18] Thomas Waleys, another English Dominican, reports that it was specifically at those Dominican institutions that he learned the 'art and theory of the manner (*modo*) and form (*forma*) of preaching' that informs his *De modo componendi sermones* (*On the Manner of Composing Sermons*, c. 1342). He writes *De modo* in a 'simple style' (*grosso stilo*), 'following those things which I, one nourished in the Order of Preachers since my youth and having spent time in various general and provincial *studia*, comprehend of this art'.[19] His *De modo* teaches sermon composition according to lessons in structure and style accumulated by living according to the Dominican rule, among Dominicans, in Dominican *studia*. Such a life produces a sensibility for a particular *forma* and *modus* of the sermon, shaped by long, regular experience listening to them at the order's houses. Waleys's *modus* is something of a house style, habituated in Dominican institutions and practised at the pulpit.[20]

Living on the outskirts of London, Daniel could have made the daily commute to its Dominican *studium* at Blackfriars for those required sermons, lectures and exercises.[21] His attendance would have schooled him in a theory and style of vernacular instruction, fit to educate the laity in Christian doctrine. (And, at Blackfriars, friars convening for study could also trade books and knowledge on other topics, medicine included.)[22] Many texts on the typical Dominican syllabus offer advice on sermon composition: the foresaid English Dominicans, Bromyard and Waleys, were two popular theorists of proper preacherly style widely read in the

---

[18] Mulcahey, *Dominican Education*, p. 133.
[19] Cited and tr. in ibid., p. 474: 'Secundum ea in Ordine Praedicatorum a pueritia enutritus et in diversis studiis generalibus ac provinciis conversatus de arte huiusmodi comprehendo, grosso stilo composui'.
[20] If the homiletic *modus operandi* of friars preacher could be called a *habitus*, it is more akin to Erwin Panofsky's concept of *habitus* as a mental habit, a method of procedure, a set of principles regulating the act, rather than the *habitus* of embodied practices Pierre Bourdieu derived from Panofsky. See Panofsky, *Gothic Architecture*, pp. 20–21, 27–28. On Bourdieu's postface to Panofsky's book and his elaborations on *habitus*, see Holsinger, *Premodern Condition*, pp. 94–113.
[21] On Daniel's biography, see Keiser, 'Gardener's Eyes', and Harvey, 'Scientific Gardener'.
[22] The medieval library at the London Blackfriars held a fourteenth-century copy of Avicenna's *Canon Medicinae*, now London, British Library MS Royal 12 G. VI, given to Blackfriars by a certain Friar Nicholas of Worcester. John Dille, another friar some years Daniel's junior, donated books in 1421 that reflected his own medical interests: a second copy of Avicenna's *Canon*, as well as a treatise and aphorisms ascribed to the physician Urso of Salerno. These are, respectively, Oxford, Bodleian Library MS Laud. misc. 728 and Cambridge, Trinity College MS O.2.50. In his *Herbal*, Daniel mentions a former student, 'þat was my disciple and now is my mayster'; this could well be Dille, who appears to have served as prior provincial for a time around 1404. See Little, 'Provincial Priors', p. 497.

fourteenth century. Dominicans on the Continent wrote popular *artes praedicandi*, too, including works by Humbert of Romans (d. 1277, master-general of the order, 1254–63) and Jacobus de Fusignano (d. 1333). Medieval preachers could also look back for rhetorical advice to the pseudo-Ciceronian tradition and Augustine of Hippo's *De doctrina Christiana*. These texts – some Dominican, but all part of a broader medieval intellectual reading list – formed a rich repository of stylistic principles and tactics.

Daniel, then, writes his medical prose in that *stilus grossus* – an unpolished style nurtured by his order – and he adapts a preaching style cultivated among friars preachers at their *schola* and *studia* for his new uroscopic purposes in the *Liber* (a suitably 'gross style' for its substance, as it were). Preachers' principles and tactics of expression proved especially useful to Daniel as he translated complex Latin medical concepts into English. Learned Dominicans themselves debated whether and how to translate the subtleties of high theology into their vernacular sermonising.[23] When Daniel wrote his *Liber*, he found himself in an analogous predicament: many technical terms of Latin medicine had no English equivalents. Daniel's solution reflects his Dominican training. In one version of his prologue, he announces his intention to import some Latin words to make his own English lexicon sufficient to communicate the tenets of uroscopy:

> Nec mireris, O lector, si inveneris me ponere terminos quandoque Latinos et quandoque prope Latinum, quod facio magis brevitatis causa. Quapropter et expositus semel termino uno per quanto michi occurrexit non iterum expono eundem.

> Do not wonder, reader, if you find that sometimes I use Latin terms and sometimes somewhat Latin ones, which I do largely for the sake of brevity. Hence, when a term has been explained once, as often as it seems proper to me, I do not then explain it over and over.[24]

Daniel worries that his occasional use of a Latin or 'Latinish' term will invite criticism, and he pre-empts his reader's possible confusion with assurances of his reluctance to use them at all. He defends his practice of 'proper exposition' of such Latinisms as judicious and efficient, apparently sensitive to the potential accusation of trafficking in oddities, like the pedantic preachers so reviled by Bromyard. Of course, there is an irony

---

[23] On this debate among Italian Dominicans, see Cornish, *Vernacular Translation*, pp. 109–14.
[24] I quote this version of the prologue from Gloucester, Cathedral Archives MS 19, f. 1ᵛ.

to this hand-wringing: his caveat about Latinisms is made in Latin, for precisely those readers who could handle a few Latinate neologisms. His apology, then, serves to index something about his own language as much as excuse it, drawing the Latinate reader's attention to an element of his good vernacular style.

Popular rhetorical treatises of the fourteenth century offered guidance on precisely how to handle difficult words, or concepts too heavy or strange for popular, lay audiences. The *Rhetorica ad Herennium* called this technique *explanatio*:

> Explanatio est quae reddit apertam et dilucidam orationem. Ea conparatur duabus rebus, usitatis verbis et propriis. Usitata sunt ea quae versantur in consuetudine cotidiana; propria, quae eius rei verba sunt aut esse possunt qua de loquemur.

> *Explanatio* renders language plain and intelligible. It is achieved by two means, the use of current terms and of proper terms. Current terms are such as are habitually used in everyday speech. Proper terms are such as are, or can be, the designations specially characteristic of the subject of our discourse.[25]

Augustine offers analogous preaching advice in his *De doctrina Christiana*:

> Quamuis in bonis doctoribus tanta docendi cura sit, uel esse debeat, ut uerbum quod nisi obscurum sit uel ambiguum, Latinum esse non potest, uulgi autem more sic dicitur ut ambiguitas obscuritasque uitetur, non sic dicatur ut a doctis, sed potius ut ab indoctis dici solet.

> Good teachers have – or ought to have – such care in teaching that a word which cannot be expressed in good Latin except obscurely and ambiguously, but which as given in the common idiom has neither ambiguity nor obscurity, should be expressed not as the cultured but rather as the uncultured are wont to express it.[26]

These two rhetorical authorities instruct readers to accommodate difficult words of some conceptual heft by providing explanations in plainer, lighter speech. In *Ad Herennium*, familiar 'current terms' (*verba usitata*) can explicate unfamiliar 'proper terms' specific to a discourse (*verba propria*). Augustine warns that 'good Latin' can be obscure and ambiguous where the common, uncultured idiom would be much clearer. Medieval manuals followed suit. Waleys' *De modo* recommends that the preacher structure

---

[25] Caplan (ed. and tr.), *Rhetorica ad C. Herennium de ratione dicendi*, pp. 270–71.
[26] Augustine, *De doctrina Christiana*, in Sullivan (ed. and tr.), *Rhetoric of Augustine*, pp. 81, 83.

his sermon around 'singularly weighty words' (*verba* ... *singulariter ponderanda*) principally as a mnemonic strategy, using keywords as *aides-mémoire*. But this mnemonic convenience grounds pedagogical procedure. The meanings of these keywords, Waleys says, should be 'set forth in other plain words (*verbis claris*), for when they are not understood by the listeners they lack all profit'.[27] Waleys reinforces those lessons in 'definition' and 'explanation' that preachers learned from their rhetorical exemplars: weighty words require a few more plain ones to understand.

Henry Daniel's stated practice of explaining the 'Latin or somewhat Latin terms' in his medical text, then, was a coached preacher's tactic, and how to do so effectively was already a preoccupation of preaching style. Throughout the *Liber* he defines a good number of 'proper terms', that specialist's Latin vocabulary necessary for readers of his uroscopy, directly and deliberately. Indeed, Daniel is so deliberate in his approach to definition that 'definition' (or, rather, 'discripcion') is among the first words he defines. This pedantic gloss appears early in his text, as he provides his Middle English readers with a technical 'discripcion' of what is arguably his art's most proper term, 'urine', as it is defined by his authorities: 'Als sayis all auctores o þis faculte, þis is þe discripcion of vryn ....'.[28] Before providing that promised 'discripcion', however, he offers another clarification: 'Þe dyscripcion of a thyng is þe discrying what a thyng is', and only then does he go on to explain that urine is 'a lete [i.e., slow] and a suptel meltyng and clensyng of þe blud and of þe humoures'. A bit further on in the same discussion, he notes that 'definition' is another term of art for this familiar practice: 'diffinicion and discripcion are all an to say' – an equivalence he reiterates later in the text: 'Þis maner of malady is callyd of Constantyn in his fyrst buk of medcyns, 20 capitulo, *heroes*, and þus he discryes and diffynyss it. *Dyscrim* and *diffrum* [*sic*] a thyng is for to tell and to tech what þe thyng is'.[29] These may seem like gratuitous explanations: could readers not assume description is describing? Or that these two words are synonyms, without being told twice? But coming so early in the text, these lessons may be meant less for the reader's information than as a means of signalling an authorial self-consciousness about the procedures of translation. They point, in other words, to a pedagogical tactic of the *Liber*. For Daniel, 'telling what things are' through this habit of

---

[27] Quoted and tr. in Carruthers, *Book of Memory*, p. 114.
[28] The discussion in its entirety, including the portions quoted, is taken from Wellcome MS 225, f. 5ᵛ.
[29] Ibid., f. 21ʳ. This particular section of the *Liber* is discussed at length by Walsh Morrissey, 'Anxious Love'.

deliberate description is how this text explains its proper terms using current ones, and how it sets forth the meaning of weighty words using lighter ones. These are techniques of instruction pulled from the preacher's script.

Daniel defines the 'proper terms' of uroscopy formulaically, but the variety of such formulae at his disposal is itself impressive – and here his artful particularising of the general preacherly style begins to emerge. He will sometimes expeditiously translate Latin into English: 'We call in Latin *epar* þe lyuer in Ynglyss'.[30] He glosses other terms with quick, efficient declaratives: '*canales pulmonis* are þe pipis o þe lungys'.[31] He attends to the differences between a technical term and popular English usage: '*dies usualis*, i.e., þe day usuall, i.e., as þe comon peple callys and usit þe day'.[32] Despite all his learning, he happily includes himself among the common speakers of English: the tissue known in Latin as *omentum*, he says, resembles 'a maner mete we call pudding'.[33] As promised in the Latin prologue, the English *Liber Uricrisiarum* moves along quickly thanks to these descriptions: when jargon is defined, it can be used as a shorthand later. This brevity is another ideal of the preacher's *modus componendi*. Augustine, for example, warns against too much clarification: 'For though one gives pleasure when he clears up matters that need to be made understood, he becomes wearisome when he keeps hammering at things which are already understood'.[34] Waleys, too, warns against longwindedness, and Jacobus de Fusignano discourages indiscriminate description (*indifferenter diffinire aut describere*) in favour of sparing and approachable definitions.[35] Daniel's homespun metaphors – a reference to pudding here, or to raven's feathers and church bells elsewhere – exemplify the concisely evocative style of definition advocated by medieval arts of preaching.

A similar personalising, as it were, of a general preacherly style comes out in Daniel's use of another common homiletic technique. That is, Daniel often uses the Latin tag 'Anglice' ('in English') to signal a vernacular translation of foregoing Latin. Hence, for example, his primer on the cardinal directions: 'Alsa þare are 4 partys of þe world: *oriens, auster, occidens* & *boria*: Anglice est, south, west and north'.[36] In his dense introduction to humoral principles, 'Anglice' functions similarly:

---

[30] Wellcome MS 225, f. 6ʳ.   [31] Ibid., f. 77ʳ.   [32] Ibid., f. 57ʳ.   [33] Ibid., ff. 78ᵛ–79ʳ.
[34] Sullivan (ed. and tr.), *Rhetoric of Augustine*, pp. 87, 89.
[35] For Waleys, see Charland, *Artes praedicandi*, p. 338: 'praedicator ne sermonis prolixitate auditores fatiget'. For Jacobus, see Wenzel (ed. and tr.), *Art of Preaching*, pp. 58–59.
[36] Wellcome MS 225, f. 16ᵛ. Voigts, 'What's the Word?', p. 820, discusses this particular deployment of 'Anglice', marking the juncture between Latin and English.

> Alsa þar are 4 humores, *vir sanguinis, colera, fleuma* and *malancholya*, Anglice blud, color, flemme and malancoly. Now is þar 4 qualiteis awnswerand to þe 4 elementys and to þe 4 humores as *caliditas, frigiditas, siccitas* and *humiditas*, Anglice hathede, dryhede, caldhede and mosthede. Now þis word aunswerand in þis mater is as mykyll for to say as acordande in kynde.[37]

This introduction to the four humours and four qualities permits Daniel to use these Latin terms in his subsequent discussions without glossing them each time. He defines an English word proper to humoral theory here, too – *aunswerand* (answering), which he will later use in this specialist, humoral sense.[38]

This 'Anglice' tag was a staple of the macaronic syntax of fourteenth-century preaching texts. The Latin sermons of the English Dominican Robert Holcot (d. 1349), for example, as preserved in Cambridge, Peterhouse MS 210, mark translations of some Latin terms and concepts into English with the same tag. Sometimes Holcot translates just a single term: 'pedagium ... Anglice tol'.[39] Elsewhere 'Anglice' introduces a more complicated translation of the preceding Latin. Consider, for example, his expansion of Luke 2.49 as the theme for a sermon ('In hiis que Patris mei sunt oportet me esse'):

> In quibus verbis tria includuntur, scilicet: ligamen obedencie, *oportet*, conamen diligencie et sedulitatis, *me esse*, solamen reverencie et magne dignitatis, quia *in hiis que patris mei sunt*. In hiis, inquam, etc. Anglice: bond of buxumnesse, life of bysynesse, stat of worthynesse.

> In which words [i.e., of the theme] are three things included, namely, the bond of obedience in *must*, the work of diligence and action in *I* [must] *be*, the reward of reverence and great worth in *about my Father's business*. In English: bond of buxomness, life of busyness, state of worthiness.[40]

Holcot's sermons, along with others like it, rehearsed for Daniel the tactics of translating difficult Latin into an accessible English. This Latin was not only difficult for its obscure words – like 'pelagium' – but for the particular forms it took: this threefold, intricately rhymed Latin gloss on a gospel verse (*ligamen obedencie, conamen diligencie, solamen reverencie*) is rendered

---

[37] Wellcome MS 225, f. 14ʳ.
[38] See, for instance, ibid., f. 81ᵛ: 'And þis maner of colre [*colera citrina*] is lest noyous and lest wykked of all colers, for it is mast temper in qualite and mast aunswerand to sanguis'.
[39] Cambridge, Peterhouse MS 210, f. 43ᵛ. Quoted in Wenzel, *Macaronic Sermons*, p. 15. On Holcot, see also Hanna's contribution to this volume, and *EFA*.
[40] Peterhouse MS 210, f. 33ʳ, quoted and tr. in Wenzel, *Macaronic Sermons*, p. 18.

as measured, tail-rhyming English (bond of buxomness, life of busyness, state of worthiness). Neither Daniel nor Holcot invent this 'Anglice' tag, of course, but its association with preaching is important. Daniel reprises this translation tactic practised in one domain – the purview of his professional order – while writing in a new one, as he assembles an English medical vocabulary in his *Liber Uricrisiarum*. It is borrowed, in other words, from one professional register to serve similar purposes in another, and 'Anglice' could thus have the ring of the preacher's voice even when implicated in medical prose.

And this is not the only 'pulpit idiom' found in the *Liber*.[41] Daniel commonly uses another Latinate preacher's tag, 'verbi gratia', to introduce an illustrative example, but tells his readers what he means by it ('*Verbi gratia, id est* exampyll ...').[42] And, as a preacher would, he calls such examples 'similitudes'.[43] In sum, then, Daniel writes his vernacular medical text in the voice of the friar preacher, with habitual recourse to sermon style in translating the proper terms of uroscopy into current ones, and weighty words into plainer ones. For Daniel, medical prose clearly had much to gain from the practice of preaching.

Writing with style entails more than competent adherence to prescribed principles. Style accommodates eccentricity. On this point, the Dominican master-general Humbert of Romans sent mixed messages to the members of his order looking for rhetorical guidance in his *De eruditione praedicantium*. He takes a hard line against stylistic embellishment: 'A sermon should be simple, and devoid of all the empty ornaments of rhetoric'.[44] Humbert then cites Seneca in preferring language that is 'simple and unaffected' over an 'ingenious style'. Ideal Dominican language should pattern itself upon the practical language of medicine: 'A sick man does not look for eloquence in his doctor, and a doctor who gives his prescriptions in flowery language is like a ruler who cares more for elegance than practicality'.[45] But a simple, unadorned, pragmatic style is a style nonetheless; it takes craft to write clearly without any impression of affectedness, eloquence or ingenuity. The preacher crafting such a

---

[41] I borrow this term from Spencer, *English Preaching*, p. 112.
[42] Wellcome MS 225, f. 53ᵛ; see also f. 14ᵛ: '*Verbi gratia*, I se be exampyll paraventour þis man is calidus & humidus ...'.
[43] Ibid., f. 5ᵛ: 'Item a noþer similitude *id est* exawmple of causyng and of genderyng of vryn ...'.
[44] Humbert of Romans, *De eruditione praedicantium*, published as *Treatise on Preaching*, ed. by Conlon, p. 43. Waters, *Angels and Earthly Creatures*, pp. 61–62, discusses Humbert's 'oblique' approach to the problem of translation in preaching.
[45] Humbert of Romans, *Treatise on Preaching*, ed. by Conlon, p. 44.

transparent style needs to be inconspicuous about it. In *De doctrina*, Augustine calls the ideal homiletic eloquence 'a kind of careful negligence' (*quadam diligens neglegentia*), a deliberate and thoughtful style that does not advertise itself as such.[46] The conscientious preacher must affect an unaffected way of speaking. And, despite his aversion to ornament, Humbert suggests that preachers have a 'graciousness and sweetness of speech'.[47] A sweet style makes the medicine go down; a sermon must be graceful to have a lasting effect, otherwise it has been composed and delivered in vain.

What kind of rhetorical eloquence, then, was proper to a preacher's graceful style? Robert of Basevorn, in his *Forma praedicandi*, recommends the devices of the *Rhetorica ad Herennium*, while Humbert of Romans directs readers to the rhetorical advice of Augustine: 'the bishop of Hippo describes in detail the metre, the length of syllables and the oratorical figures which may be properly used'.[48] Humbert also recognises that this gracefully unaffected preaching requires an unteachable gift for gab, a knowledge of the 'intricacies and the resources of language'. He proposes a number of disqualifying attributes for the preacher on that basis: 'a weak memory, or an ignorance of Latin, or an inability to express himself well in the vulgar tongue, or any fault of this kind'.[49] The preacher's fluency in Latin and the vernacular did not just facilitate explanation – only those with a talent for language could compose sermons with the required 'sweetness of speech', or that Augustinian quality of 'careful negligence'. These stylistic requirements introduce a new kind of difficulty to the task of the Ricardian prose translator. The related difficulty of expressing Latinate sense through vernacular words worried a number of Middle English writers (Daniel among them), and recent scholarship has carefully attended to the debates over the possibility of translation and its politics in the late-fourteenth century.[50] But for Dominican preachers, any such trepidations over the lexical or political difficulties of proper translation were accompanied by a corresponding anxiety over handling that language with proper graciousness and careful negligence, enjoined by Augustinian authority and professional codes alike. Finding the right words might be hard, and arranging them into a right order harder, but finding the right key – a register both plain and sweet – demanded that every vernacular

---

[46] Sullivan (ed. and tr.), *Rhetoric of Augustine*, p. 81.
[47] Humbert of Romans, *Treatise on Preaching*, ed. by Conlon, p. 44.   [48] Ibid., p. 43.
[49] Ibid., pp. 43 and 42, respectively.
[50] See Hanna, 'Difficulty', and Cole, 'Chaucer's English Lesson'.

preacher aspire to an unteachable eloquence over and above matters of word and sense.

Throughout his *Liber*, Daniel likewise finds creative ways to, as it were, honey the rim of the glass bearing his medicine. His translation at times proves to be quite inventive indeed, as he expresses the matter of uroscopy in accessible, delicately weighed English, no matter how indelicate the subject might seem to modern ears. For instance, he renders a pithy if crude Latin axiom on the digestive process into an English one:

> Egestion is in schytyng, ingestyon is etyng, and degestyon is defyyng, as says þe vers: *Qui bene degerit, ingerit, egerit, est homo sanus*. Ȝyf þu wyll ete, defy, and schyte, þu art hale whar þu gas or sittys.[51]

*Grossus stilus* indeed. Daniel preserves the proverbial feel of this unrhymed Latin 'vers' by rendering it as a rhyming couplet in English, a sort of verse that his vernacular readers would likely recognise.[52] So Daniel communicates the axiomatic quality of the Latin original; this pragmatic aspect of language requires proper vulgarisation as much as its technical terms do. He is considerate of this intricacy of language as he translates with a wit and wisdom worthy of the standards set by Humbert. He versifies this Latinate vocabulary into easily comprehended English.

Daniel has other ways to cushion the delivery of his medical concepts for English readers. Elsewhere, for example, he turns to a domestic vocabulary to describe the making of seed in the gonads of both sexes. The *semen* of men and women, he says, is 'traveld and swynkyn as buttur in þe kyrne, and swongyn and wroght and knodyn in þe ballok stanys of þam bath as past or dawgh in a vessell'.[53] Biological process is illustrated by a pair of images drawn from daily life: butter in the churn, dough in the kneading bin. Both images are expressed through doublets and triplets of synonyms: 'traveld and swynkyn', 'swongyn and wroght and knodyn'. Indeed, this sort of synonymous reiteration – reminiscent of ps.-Ciceronian *synonomia* so favoured by Latin writers and late-medieval translators alike – is a ubiquitous tactic of Daniel's vernacularising *modus*: he brings together English near-synonyms as if to refine his translation toward a proper sense of a Latin term.[54] Such a tactic befits a plain instructional style – it is both quick and precise in its way, and it relies

---

[51] Wellcome MS 225, f. 30ʳ.
[52] On the quotation and translation of Latin proverbs in Middle English texts, see Cannon, *Literacy to Literature*, pp. 183–89.
[53] Wellcome MS 225, f. 130ᵛ.
[54] On doubling in Middle English prose, see Mueller, *Native Tongue*, pp. 147–61.

on words that are current and clear, rather than swapping one specialist term for another. These English reduplications have a gracefulness to them in their verbal variety, too, as each new English rendition smooths the reader's approach to a more exact sense of the corresponding Latin. This seems to be Daniel's realisation of the 'careful negligence' so prized by Augustine and Humbert in good teachers. In the *Liber* he teaches with deliberation and thoughtfulness.

But such rhetorical embellishment can easily be taken too far, and arts of preaching scold those who do preach pretentiously or in too high a style. Bromyard, for example, condemns too-clever instruction through subtleties and animal allegories as pointless literary bloviation, crafted to glorify the preacher himself. Waleys complains of preachers who 'seek the display of their own knowledge and not the utility of the people'.[55] Precisely such concerns are reflected in Daniel's prologue, and specifically when he takes pains to have Latinate readers of the *Liber* believe he composed this vernacular medical text with its utility, rather than self-serving ostentation, in mind. He thought it was useful, for one, because it was to be the first uroscopy in English, as far as he knew.[56] After all his studies, he would not wish to be a 'lamp underneath a bushel', keeping all this knowledge of Latin uroscopy to himself.[57] We have already seen him introduce himself as a simple man barely up to the task of translating Latin uroscopy into a new vernacular. His commitment to that performance is total:

> Ego quidem tantillus, ut puta minimus servorum Christi articulus, et primus ut reor hanc facultatem in Anglica lingua docens, inproperia et obloquia quomodo evadere potero, qui invidia pleni sunt et, ut aliis sapientes esse videantur, solum linguacitate languentes sunt nequam homini modernorum?[58]

> Indeed, how will I – who am certainly the lowest and smallest of Christ's servants, and since, as I reckon, this is the first work teaching this faculty in the English language – how will I possibly avoid the mockery and naysaying of those who are full of envy, and who are so many mere blatherers blathering, in order to be seen as wise by worthless men of these modern times?

Daniel humbles himself 'as the lowest of Christ's servants' and trembles at the prospect of critical attacks from uncharitable quarters. From this pitiful

---

[55] *De modo componendi sermones*, in Charland, *Artes praedicandi*, p. 338: 'Ad ostentationem suae scientiae et non utilitatem populi quaerere'.
[56] Ashmole 1404, f. 3ʳ: 'Nec hanc scienciam in anglico traditam memini me legisse sed neque audisse'.
[57] Ibid., f. 3ᵛ: 'Idcirco ne lucernam sub modio'.   [58] Ibid., f. 3ʳ⁻ᵛ.

defensive crouch, he launches his (characteristically Dominican) counter-attack. Such envious critics make for bad readers and even worse speakers; their language is inordinate and unruly. (I have translated Daniel's Latin phrase 'linguacitate languentes' as 'blatherers blathering', and an early English translator of this prologue renders it the 'muche speche of spekyng men'.)[59] Even worse, their critique is all badly motivated, since, like bad preachers, Daniel's worst readers care little about knowledge and quite a bit more about the appearance of knowing. His *Liber*, he says, will provide a good training in uroscopy to those who would put that knowledge into practice with discretion and not live a 'pompous, chatty, mistaken life, as physicians nowadays habitually do' ('vita pomposa verbosa ac mendosa ut medici moderni solent'). Thus, Daniel takes issue with modern physicians' disordered lifestyles: a self-styling pomposity (*vita pomposa*) on the one hand and a profligate style of speech (*vita verbosa*) on the other. These modern physicians are hardly the figures of stylistic rectitude so admired by the Dominican preachers of prior generations. Bromyard had pointed to doctors' sparing bedside manner as a model for the good preacher's directness. For Humbert of Romans, their pragmatic manner of speech, stripped of flowers or the markers of eloquence, was what inspired patients' confidence. Daniel's low opinion of modern medical discourse – full of boasting, falsities and fables – cuts against his order's longstanding tendency to idealise doctor's professional manner as a model for preaching.

Daniel's performance of modesty as a medical writer in his Latin prologue is further belied by the rest of his English book. The *Liber* not only corrects bad translations of Latin terms, but its author renders its English uroscopy with a deft hand. His corrections are blunt and direct. Many people who think themselves wise doctors mix up kidney stones (*calculus*) and intestinal pains (*colica passio*); but such 'wys lechys' are discounted as no more than 'jangelers and smaterers', so easily 'dissayved' by a resemblance between the terms in Latin.[60] Similarly, he is exasperated by a common erroneous distinction between two respiratory conditions, *ptisica* and *ethica*. He insists these are one and the same. If only physicians would look back to their Latin authorities, with a better knowledge of the language, they might learn this, too, 'but Latyen hath many an unstedfaste k[n]okker at his gate'.[61] Daniel, judging by the *Liber*, has worn down his knuckles rapping at Latin's door, with all the treatise's technical clarification and dense reference to his old authorities. He kept knocking and, in

---

[59] Oxford, Bodleian Library MS e Mus. 187, f. 1$^r$.   [60] Wellcome MS 225, f. 50$^r$.
[61] Ashmole 1404, f. 51$^v$.

his prologue, he stands holding the door open to his English readers, letting them in on a long intellectual tradition. Yet – in keeping with his order's priorities for preachers – he presents himself modestly, as a paragon of perseverance rather than brilliance.

Daniel's low opinion of contemporary physicians surfaces throughout the *Liber*, and he is particularly disdainful of their pompous way of speaking. It would seem that their speech, earlier elevated to an ideal of plainspoken eloquence by Waleys and Bromyard, had by Daniel's day taken on the worst qualities of modern preachers' style. These bad doctors speak just like bad Dominicans. His conflated criticism of Dominicans' and doctors' speech comes attached to a minor point of uroscopic polemic, as he rails against the frequent confusion of whitishness ('whytished') with true whiteness ('verra whythede'), or sometimes with yellowishness ('ʒalowyshed').

> Bod oft-tym whytished in uryn or in ypostasi is taken for ʒalowyshed and for verra whythede amang þes dog lechys and emang þam þat has not verra undyrstandynge, þat seis lytill and spekis mykyll and wald be sene and may not for dulhed lere, as mony of myn awn ordor.[62]

Ignorant medical practitioners – 'these dog leeches' – misrecognise 'whitishness' in urine. For one, they lack true ('verray') understanding of these finer shades. They adjudge the evidence with little discernment but nevertheless they talk at length about what they see (they 'see little' though they 'speak much'). These practitioners are too stupid or slothful to learn proper doctrine (they 'may not for dullness learn'), yet they speak nevertheless for appearances (they 'would be seen'). Daniel's 'dog leech' exemplifies all those stylistic failures of ostentatious preaching deplored by Waleys and Bromyard, rather than that good, spare medical style of the physician they idealised. They cannot meaningfully explain difficult, proper terms (like whiteness and whitishness), never mind craft a definition balancing fulsomeness with a pleasing brevity. Indeed, these physicians have no interest in doing so. Instead these talkative types cultivate a vain, longwinded style (they clearly didn't read their Augustine). Daniel explicitly links the stylistic failures of bad medical and mendicant speech. Pompous physicians speak too much and study too little, just 'as many of myn awn ordor', he says. Indeed, Daniel's 'dog leeches' have much in common with his fellow *domini cani*, or 'dogs of God'.[63] So the model

---

[62] Ibid., f. 134ʳ. Jasin, 'Compiler's Awareness', p. 521, discusses this comment as a critique of other medical practitioners, but not other Dominican preachers.
[63] Friedman, 'Friar Portrait', p. 182.

profession of well-ordered, disciplined talk in Dominican preaching manuals is here discredited as a field of practice rife with the same profligate and useless speech so deplored by the same. Daniel, modest though he is, has little good to say about his contemporaries and peers, whether they be his fellow Dominicans or his fellow students of medicine.

Reading the *Liber Uricrisiarum* against the theories of the vernacular advanced in Dominican preaching texts reveals how Henry Daniel builds his treatise's English style of medical translation according to the principles and procedures of vernacular instruction cultivated over the course of his professional life as a friar preacher. Such principles outline a way of teaching in English which prizes plain expression of learned doctrine over ingenious high style. It is ever searching out a balance between brevity and clarification, and it is sharply critical of stylised, inflated language designed for self-promotion rather than the teaching of others. In this, the *Liber* might be an instructive case for scholars of a Ricardian vernacular culture soon to flourish after this text's original composition in the 1370s. Daniel transposes certain notions of vernacularity articulated in a precedent Latin discourse around preaching into his Middle English medical prose: notions like Augustine's careful negligence and Humbert's unadorned graciousness, appealing brevity and clarifying directness, found expression in the compositional style of his uroscopy. While he was among the first translators of Latinate medicine into the vernacular, Daniel could find models for making that knowledge accessible to a new English readership, as readily theorised in the mendicant curriculum and practised in mendicant life.

Ever the conscientious teacher, Henry Daniel knew that many English readers would have no need for a compendious, encyclopaedic uroscopy like the *Liber* (never mind the patience for it). For this reader, Daniel translates a number of aphoristic rules, which he found appended to the *De urinis* of Isaac Judaeus:

> Now sall I say þe rewles þat Ysaac gyfes in þe last end of hys *Buk of Uryns* sa þat wha may not con þe substaunce and þe pith of þe thyngys þat are said before, or ellys paraventour he may not report þam be hart, lat hym hald hym paed with comon reules shortly gyfen … Wha sa may not have o þe gavyls, lat hym glene after þe byndars.[64]

Daniel likens a complete reading of the *Liber* to a heavy harvest. These shorter rules, then, make provision for lighter minds. Such gleaners may

---

[64] Wellcome MS 225, f. 138ʳ.

gather up what kernels of insight they might find, coming along after better reapers have swept the fields. This agricultural metaphor evokes an Old Testament scene – when Ruth begs to gather up the remnants of the grain harvest in Boaz's fields (Ruth 2.7: 'ut spicas colligeret remanentes, sequens messorum vestigia'). It would also recall, for English readers of his own time and for centuries afterward, a regular seasonal practice allowed to certain of the poor, the gleaning of fields after harvest.[65] Chaucer, another modest Ricardian *compilator*, poses as a gleaner in his *Legend of Good Women*, and perhaps he best describes the feeling of learning from teachers who combine a compendious mind with generosity and thoughtfulness:

> And I come after, glenyng here and there,
> And am ful glad yf I may fynde an ere
> Of any goodly word that ye han left. (F.75–77)

---

[65] Ault, 'By-Laws of Gleaning'; Jordan, 'The Gleaners'.

CHAPTER 7

# The Re-cognition of Doctrinal Discourse and Scholastic Literary Theory
## Affordances of *Ordinatio* in Reginald Pecock's *Donet* and *Reule of Crysten Religioun*

### Ian Johnson

This essay concerns itself with creative but problematic dissonance and diversity in medieval scholastic literary theory and textual practice. It aims to show how one remarkable practitioner of vernacular scholastic literary theory, Reginald Pecock (d. c. 1459), Bishop of Chichester, deployed theoretically inflected discourses in order to service diverse orders of worth in his works.[1] This study therefore focuses on a repertoire of scholastic techniques used by Pecock, and most particularly *compilatio* and *ordinatio* – twin pragmatic principles with starring roles in the textual practice of scholastic literary theory in the later medieval period.

No modern scholar has done more to show how medieval literary culture exploited the recombinant powers of *compilatio* and *ordinatio* than Alastair Minnis, whose achievement in this area has its origins in his collaboration with his esteemed and much-loved mentor Malcolm

---

[1] On diverse orders of worth and related concepts, see Stark, *Sense of Dissonance*, esp. ch. 1. Though Stark's impressive and thought-provoking monograph is in the field of economic sociology and concerns itself with the behaviour of firms, its conceptualising of dissonance and heterarchy, and the contention that it 'is the friction at the interacting overlap of multiple performance criteria that generates productive recombinations' (p. 27), would seem to have an intriguing applicability to the study of interactively frictional discourses in Pecock, inasmuch as Reginald creates friction by introducing his own criteria to govern the traditional discourses that he recombines so inventively with his own words. This essay owes a considerable general debt to Stark, though I have naturally had to make fairly extensive adaptations of his approach in order to make it appropriate for textual studies. The ideas that Stark applies to firms I apply to discourses. Therefore, where Stark's object of analysis is the firm as a heterarchy, which is 'an organizational form of distributed intelligence in which units are laterally accountable according to diverse principles of evaluation' (p. 27), my object is the Pecockian œuvre, whose diverse parts are put into mutual relation with each other, at times contradictorily, in an *ordinatio* sometimes justified in perfectly traditional ecclesiastical terms but at other times (or even simultaneously) encoded in a subversively rationalistic, anti-scriptural fashion directly opposing settled institutional norms. Pecock thus attempts to refashion internal boundaries within his works and across religious culture, regrouping textual and cultural capital in so doing and inventing an *ordinatio* and a discourse anew, or as Stark puts it of the firm: 'the heterarchical firm is redrawing internal boundaries, re-grouping assets and perpetually reinventing itself' (p. 27).

Parkes. Minnis has not stopped revisiting and refining our understanding of the vital importance of *compilatio* and *ordinatio* in medieval literary thinking and textual practice since those early days (and long nights) spent haggling over texts and ideas in Parkes's pipe-smoke-filled lair above the porters' lodge at Keble College, Oxford.²

This chapter is, then, about what Reginald tried so ambitiously to do with *ordinatio*. In attempting to account for what Pecock was up to and for its significance, it builds on the well-established approaches of Minnis in this field. It investigates theoretical diversity in practice at the most perilous pressure points of discursive culture – in other words, those locations where the articulation and control of spiritual authority in this world and the tapping of divine authority from the next were both at stake. Before we do this, however, let us remind ourselves of some of the key terms and ideas attaching to *compilatio* and *ordinatio* that arose from the legendary collaboration with Parkes.

## *Ordinatio* and *Compilatio*

St Bonaventure's definition of the compiler in the prologue to his commentary on the *Sentences*, as introduced to academe by Parkes and Minnis, has become especially well-known over the last forty years or so: 'Someone else writes the materials of others, adding, but nothing of his own, and this person is said to be the compiler'.³ Typically, compilers do not originate anything, but they rather exercise considerable freedom in selecting, juxtaposing and ordering materials. The mode of the compiler is the mode of the excerptor (*modus excerptoris*).⁴ Hence, for example, Minnis's discussion of Chaucer as compiler has long been a standard reference point of *Canterbury Tales* criticism.⁵ In this essay, however, his definitions of *compilatio*'s sibling, *ordinatio*, provide the main jumping-off points.

In *Medieval Theory of Authorship*, Minnis begins defining *ordinatio* by observing how Robert Kilwardby (d. 1279) and his successors perceived and prioritised, in typically scholastic fashion, a vital consanguinity between a text's disciplinary method and its structure:

> The organisation of an author's material into books and chapters – how the text is divided up into its constituent parts, how the material is collected

---

² See Minnis's various works on the subject: 'Discussions of *Compilatio*' (1979); *MTA*, esp. pp. 190–210; 'Discourse of Compilation' (2006). Parkes's major contributions in this field include '*Ordinatio* and *Compilatio*' and 'Compilation of the Lectionary'.
³ Quoting from *MTA*, p. 94.   ⁴ *MTA*, pp. 192, 204.   ⁵ Ibid., pp. 190–210.

together – appears to be regarded as the physical manifestation and consequence of the mode of procedure relevant to the science in the text, the 'definitive, divisive and collective mode'.[6]

The 'form of the treatise' (*forma tractatus, ordinatio partium* or *divisio textus*) takes account not only of the parts of a text being 'mutually ordered to each other', but also of its end, 'the *finis* intended by its *auctor*'. In this scholastic textual system, hierarchy abounds, and works are conceived as consisting of 'superior and "subordinate" parts'.[7] *Ordinatio* is an active principle not only within but also beyond the individual text. As Andrew Kraebel aptly puts it:

> Key to all of these kinds of *ordinatio* is ... a sense of the human actor (author, commentator, scribe, librarian) constructing textual units by imposing an arrangement on a series of independent parts, arranging words to form sentences, sentences to form chapters, chapters to form texts, texts to form a volume, volumes to form a collection.[8]

Sometimes the scholastic compulsion to order the textual universe ran into dauntingly uncooperative materials: *ordinatio* could turn into a messy business when works, as they so often did, failed to line up nicely in organised parts and wholes. Minnis reports tellingly on how a variety of medieval exegetes found – or, rather, fabricated – a bewildering variety of different orders in the most profusely heterarchical work of all, the Psalter. That supremely sophisticated and most honest of biblical commentators, Nicholas of Lyre OFM (d. 1349), memorably concluded that the Psalter defied ordering by authors, chronology of composition, or materials. Nevertheless, as Minnis points out, 'the fact that these possibilities have been envisaged is a point of considerable substance. The concept of *ordinatio* has informed Lyre's analysis of his text'.[9]

It was not only exegetes attempting, like Nicholas, to find order in authoritative texts, but also compilers, in putting together their works, who tried to find and apply an *ordinatio* in defining, dividing and collecting materials. Articulating a justifiable principle or a logic on which to proceed was an occupational challenge, for which a choice of different *ordinationes* was available. For example, in Bartholomew the Englishman's (d. 1272) *De proprietatibus rerum*, 'the basic organisation of material follows the order and distinction of substances; further subdivision of material follows the order and distinction of things (which are subordinate to substances)'. And Brunetto Latini (d. 1294), in his *Livres dou trésor*,

---

[6] Ibid., p. 147.   [7] Ibid., pp. 147–48.   [8] Kraebel, '*Ordinatio*', p. 77.   [9] *MTA*, p. 153.

adopted an *ordinatio* 'in accordance with Aristotle's distinction between the three parts of philosophy, theory, practice and logic'.[10]

A corollary of good *ordinatio* is soundly contextualised referencing. Vincent of Beauvais (d. *c.* 1264) and John of Wales (d. 1285) habitually directed their readers back to the whole collected works, the so-called *originalia* of *auctores*.[11] Parts always had to be related to the wholes from which they derived. Labouring in the same tradition, Reginald Pecock, as we shall see, took immense pains to cross-refer amongst the individual works of his own œuvre, thereby laying claim to an impeccable *ordinatio* in the parts and the whole of his entire output, which, as far as he was concerned, transcended and outdid what he saw as the disorganised mishmash of traditional doctrinal discourses.

Pecock, in his own inimitable fashion, aggressively wielded these theoretically freighted practices of scholastic textuality – and especially some of the routines, rhetoric and ideology of *compilatio* and *ordinatio* – in dealing with authorised ecclesiastical discourses, including the Ten Commandments, the Apostles' Creed and orthodox definitions of God as creator or as infinite. These, by recourse to a range of scholastic techniques, he variously fragments, repeats, dislocates, generically re-scripts, deconstructs, reconstructs, outdoes, occludes, appropriates, subverts, cross-references, quotes, re-glosses, spurns, rescues and reconfirms in an idiosyncratic combination of *compilatio* and *ordinatio* mixed with a measure of self-commentary and outright authorial self-assertiveness. Despite the obvious friction between conventional articulations of doctrinal discourses and Pecock's own novel revisions of them, the perspective of each on the other results in an idiosyncratic hybrid of self-editorial dissonance and consonance of intriguing theoretical character and consequence. By analysing some examples, mainly from Pecock's *Donet*, we will see how not only his literary production, but also the potential reader experience constituted, as an outcome of his distinctive use of key elements of scholastic theory, an arena for co-existing rival doctrinal discourses and their redistributed recognition and re-cognition.[12]

---

[10] Ibid., p. 155.   [11] Ibid., pp. 157–58.

[12] Pecock, *Donet*, ed. by Hitchcock, cited henceforth parenthetically by page number. For general studies on Pecock, see Scase, *Reginald Pecock*; Green, *Bishop Reginald Pecock*; Brockwell, *Bishop Reginald Pecock*; Lahey, 'Reginald Pecock on the Authority of Reason'; and Campbell, *Call to Read*, esp. pp. 27–60 for discussion of the construction and likely capacities of Pecock's historical and implied audiences. For developments in the fifteenth-century English Church as a context for the religious literary culture of the time (including Pecock), see Gillespie, 'Chichele's Church'.

## Reassembling and Reordering Virtues

Pecock was clearly doing something different from other bishops of his time. While he organised his multi-textual programme, his episcopal colleagues were recuperating classical textuality and rhetorically bolstering each other through praise modelled on the practices of antiquity, as well as supporting the disciplines of penitential and affective piety which were so familiar to the fifteenth century.[13] Where Pecock, however, was in step with his episcopal contemporaries – though he took his own rather novel and idiosyncratic approach – was, in Vincent Gillespie's words, in his 'primary concern ... for the effective religious instruction of the laity, [and in] arguing that most engaged Christians managed complex concepts and abstract ideas in their own commercial and professional lives'.[14] It must be remembered that, in London in the mid-1400s, the prosperous and politically engaged bourgeoisie and gentry were increasingly capable of devotional and theological discrimination: hence the policy in the capital of only allowing graduates to preach to them. Such people (who, as sources of funding and practical support for various ecclesiastical institutions, had to be kept onside) could therefore reasonably be expected to be able to exercise a considerable degree of their own judgement on matters of Christian teaching.[15] This, after all, was the era of Whittington College, of the circulation of common-profit books, and of more informal circles of education and piety involving fraternities, guilds and households.[16] The implication of all this for Pecock was that he felt confident in presenting challenges to the reasoning faculties of his readership, whom he expected, as burgeoning lay scholastics (nevertheless subordinate to the clergy), to

---

[13] See Cole, 'Heresy and Humanism', for an illuminating discussion of changes in episcopal culture at this time.

[14] Gillespie, 'Fatherless Books', p. 177. For discussion of Pecock's recourse to theological syllogisms making use of professional skills and social customs, see Johnson, 'Goostly Chaffare'.

[15] For the broader cultural and ecclesiastical context of this, see Gillespie, 'Chichele's Church' and Lindenbaum, 'London after Arundel'. For a study of mainstream lay spiritual ambition in late medieval England, see Rice, *Lay Piety and Religious Discipline*.

[16] See Scase, 'Common-Profit Books'. For discussion of Pecock's approach to managing an independent-minded laity, see Westphall, 'Reconstructing the Mixed Life', esp. pp. 267–70, and Johnson, 'Goostly Chaffare'. See Campbell, *Call to Read*, pp. 148–80 and 198–216, for the place of reason and how it relates to Scripture in Pecock's theological and socio-educational scheme, and pp. 223–43 for discussion of Pecock's endeavour to cultivate social, educational and amicable relations between clergy and laity. For a fine anatomisation detailing Pecock's reworking of traditional doctrinal and catechetical discourses, see Smith, 'Reginald Pecock and Vernacular Theology', pp. 171–207.

manage and reconcile the rival discourses of his system and of traditional structures of doctrine.

In ranking reason higher than any other form of authority, including Scripture, Pecock risked offending mainstream institutions and Lollardy alike. The hyper-scholastic Reginald, however, was comfortable with being provocative because, in his eyes, God never transgressed against reason anyway – and neither did the Bible. For him, the same principle of reason was the identifying feature of humanity's creation in the image of God and was thus the very ground of truth, philosophy and ethics:

> Scripture is not ground to eny oon such seid vertu, gouernaunce, deede or trouthe, . . . but oonli doom of natural resoun, which is moral lawe of kinde and moral lawe of God, writun in the book of lawe of kinde in mennis soulis, prentid into the ymage of God, is ground to ech such vertu, gouernaunce, deede and trouthe.[17]

Throughout his works, and with especial vigour in his *Donet*, Pecock reclassified the entirety of Christian doctrine under 'Four Tables' of 'meenal' (instrumental) virtues (that is, virtues to do with 'means' leading to other virtues) and 'eendal' (ultimate) virtues (virtues which are an 'end' in themselves). In doing this, he claimed to render in better *ordinatio* the customary mainstays of the Church – the Ten Commandments, the Seven Deadly Sins, Works of Mercy and Cardinal Virtues. These Pecock decries as no better than 'loose giblets' (*Donet*, p. 146) for their lack of *ordinatio*. His Four Tables, so he repeatedly claims, are more comprehensive, concise and easier to remember. Pecock's goal was no less than to confer a reformed *ordinatio* – in effect a *disordinatio* or *re-ordinatio* of the universality of doctrinal discourse – on the entire religious sensibility and conduct of every individual Christian.

In the *meenal* and *eendal* tables of his *Donet*, Pecock takes the traditional order of virtues and splits them up, recategorising them, spreading them out and recombining them in ways that would surely have disorientated a contemporary readership. He redefines every single virtue, making each one of them, listed in a new *ordinatio* in the form of his own idiosyncratic catechetical cycle, obey the formula *to live + adverb + to oneself/God/ neighbour*. Under this formula, the action of virtuous human living is qualified through a defining adverb and applied to self or God or neighbour. For example, the first table, which consists of the eight 'meenal' (instrumental) moral virtues, is constituted thus: *to live learningly; to live*

---

[17] Pecock, *Repressor*, ed. by Babington, I, 18.

*praisingly; to live dispraisingly; to live prayingly; to live thankingly; to live worshippingly; to live disworshippingly; to live sacramentally*. The second table, consisting of the seven 'eendal' (perfective) virtues towards God, is constructed thus: *to live to God ghostly; to live to God obediently*, then *rightfully/justly, meekly, truly, benignly, largely*.

Virtues, for Reginald, are repeatable arcs of behaviour in due order, consisting in each instance of an assumed agent/subject, an action (which is always the all-encompassing and teleological action of *living*), a manner of action (expressed by an adverb) and one or more object(s) of action – God, oneself or one's neighbours. The apparent syntactically and ontologically transitive completeness of logistical process and tight order in each instance of the exercise of virtue therefore bespeaks a satisfactorily perfectible action servicing an appropriate object and objective through a fitting manner. It also makes for a satisfying rhetorical and psychological completeness. Pecockian virtues – unlike their counterparts in the Virtues and Vices tradition, which typically are grouped more statically in an inventory of noun-based concepts – are thus reschematised from the outset more dynamically in terms of an ordered repertoire of structured virtuous actions. In this repertoire, something defined and definitive is to be accomplished. In routine Virtues and Vices tradition (as in the *Summa virtutum de remediis anime*, the *Fasciculus morum* or Chaucer's *Parson's Tale*), each virtue has a name and definition.[18] Each is a noun, and each remedies particular vices. Pride, the all-begetting original sin, for example, is customarily countered by the prerequisite virtue of meekness/humility. As a mainstream churchman, Pecock would surely not have disapproved of this tradition, but he defines virtues and their operation very differently.

Let us take an example from his megalomanic *re-ordinatio* and re-compilation of the metadiscourse of Christian catechesis and moral doctrine. Where better to start in the *Donet*'s dialogue between the Father and the Son than the first virtue of the First Table? This is the virtue of *living learningly*, in which active diligence in the understanding and the remembering of all truths that should regulate our acts of will and reason are to be directed towards God, ourselves and others:

> Sone, it is forto wille, chese and be bisie forto knowe, leerne and kunne and þanne aftir forto remembre all þo trouþis, whos kunnyng and remembring

---

[18] Wenzel (ed.), *Summa virtutum*; Wenzel (ed. and tr.), *Fasciculus morum*; Chaucer, *The Riverside Chaucer*, ed. by Benson et al., pp. 288–327.

> schulen be meenys to vs forto governe vs in dedis of oure wil aftir resoun or feiþ, anentis god immediatly, anentis vs silf immediatly, and anentis oure neiȝboris immediatly. (p. 27)

No one, orthodox or Lollard, would have objected to such prioritising of attentive spiritual diligence in the knowing and remembering of all the truths that should regulate our acts of will and reason as a prerequisite for pious self-development. As the first virtue of the First Table, this is Pecock's starting point in his new *ordinatio* of Christian life. He is inaugurating a new spiritual *ductus* – that is, as Mary Carruthers defines the term, 'the con*duct* of a thinking, listening and feeling mind on its *way* through composition'.[19] In redistributing cognition, Pecock attempts to prompt in his readers a new *ductus* by which to order their moral and spiritual progress through the various parts of his œuvre. His original moral virtue to counter original sin, encompassing every detail and purpose of Christian living and salvifics, is, very significantly, a virtue of cognition and of the exercise of reasoning memory. In traditional treatises on virtues one would, at the beginning of the work, expect not a passage on cognition, learning and reasoning, but a distinctly less scholastically freighted message about humbling oneself and becoming properly aware of one's sinful state in order to be able to remedy it. Here, however, is no self-reviling abasement or self-meeking. Learning, reasoning and understanding are much more important to the logically re-ordinating Pecock.

In his exposition of this enabling virtue, opening his whole scheme of re-compilation, Pecock discusses the issue of whether living learningly is rightly categorised as a moral virtue. The Son initiates this discussion by asking the Father whether living learningly is not in fact a moral virtue, but only an intellectual or 'knowingal' one. The Father responds by confirming that it is a moral virtue because it is a business, an occupation and a disposition of the will to acquire knowledge and understanding of Pecock's Seven Matters, whether by scriptural revelation or through natural reason:

> And siþen such a bisynes and an occupacioun or disposicioun or habit is not ellis þan drawen oute of þe wil, or comaundid of þe wil to oþire powers to be doon, aftir þe doom of resoun, it folewiþ nedis þat þe first seid poynt of þe first table is a moral vertu or his moral vertuose dede. (p. 111)

---

[19] Carruthers, 'Concept of *Ductus*', p. 196. See too her definition in ibid., p. 200: 'So, *ductus* is the way(s) that a composition, realizing the plan(s) set within its arrangements, guides a person to its various goals, both in its parts and overall.'

Whether or not every contemporary academic would find this argument convincing, this passage nevertheless clearly signals that, for Pecock, the spiritual and the moral life are inextricably bound up with cognition and the exercise of reason. This conclusion valorises a perfectly decorous scholarly disposition which was foundational to an overall project – one that, ironically, attracted the considerable disapproval of contemporary academics. Not only is the knowledge of spiritual and divine truths brought about through exercising and following the 'doom of resoun', so too is the concomitant exercise of virtues. This inevitably involves willed actions – actions, it is hoped, that will become a matter of 'disposicioun or habit', that is, *habitus*.[20] As elsewhere in his remediation of customary ecclesiastical discourses, Pecock yokes together for his readership discourses or logics that the run of his contemporaries kept separate, and he thereby offers his readers an unsettling yet at times innovatively hybrid intellectual and religious experience.

Proceeding from his presentation of this opening intellectual yet nevertheless moral virtue, Pecock unfolds a scheme of virtues with its own continuingly idiosyncratic intellectual and moral order and agenda. Let us look now at how he defines another particular manifestation of virtue in his scheme, in this case a virtue that is more intuitively moral-looking than that of *living learningly* – that of *living toward our neighbour ghostly* (pp. 60–61). After reciting the eight moral virtues of the Fourth Table – living 'toward oure neiȝboris goostly, attendauntly, riȝtfully, mekeli, accordingli, treuli, benyngnely (or myldeli) and largeli' (p. 60), the first point of the Table, *living towards our neighbour ghostly*, is given a fuller definition:

> Sone, it is oure willing bi whiche we williþ to him goodis which, forto to him ȝeve, or forto to him sette, and forto fro him take, is not in a creaturis

---

[20] Medieval usage of the term *habitus* is narrower than Bourdieu's notion, being preoccupied with how the mind acquires a well-coached moral condition directively through repeated good actions. For example, Giles of Rome, in his commentary on the Canticle, citing Aristotle, announces that goodness depends on our actions, 'for, according to the Philosopher [i.e. Aristotle], we become good because we perform good actions, and like mental conditions (*habitus*) are begotten from like actions' (Minnis and Scott, p. 247). Nevertheless, a Bourdieusian understanding of the concept does have relevance to Pecock here, because it concerns itself with how imitation produces mental habits, the socialisation of individuals and thus the formative structures and functions of society. See also the useful discussion of *habitus* with reference to Middle English literature, in Breen, *English Reading Public*, and in particular the following definition: 'The habitual action is virtuous because it combines the stability of second nature within the order of right reason' (p. 48). Breen also makes a point which reveals illuminatingly how *habitus* was seen by no less than Thomas Aquinas as a matter of *ordinatio* at the spiritual level: 'because the *habitus* of original sin, which Aquinas likens to a physical illness, everyone is born out of alignment, with an "inordinatam dispositionem partium animae (disordered arrangement of the faculties of the soul)" (Q, 82, a. 1, res)' (p. 75).

> power: as ben his blisful rewardis to be had in hevene, and goddis gracis freely helping him þidirward, in þre maners tauȝt in þe ijᵉ parti of 'cristen religioun', þe iijᵉ trety. Þis goostlihode of a man anentis his neiȝbore is a spice, or a membre, of þe al hool general freendli love which a man ouȝte have to his neiȝbore. (p. 61)

This ghostly living towards one's neighbour may be exercised by praying to God for grace for that neighbour, or by treating him as a friend. Clearly, this virtue has affinities with Christ's familiar injunction to love one's neighbour as oneself, as does each of the virtues in this Table. Here, however, the point is that any ghostly goods willed on the neighbour's behalf are not in the neighbour's power to win for his neighbours. On the contrary, they are God's to give. Although the willing of one's neighbour's spiritual good and salvation is, for Pecock, foundational, we do not find mention or recommendation of the conventions of prayerful petitioning for the reduction of time in Purgatory or pleas for intercession for one's neighbours. Such discourse is strikingly absent and occluded (but may also potentially be quietly accommodated) by Reginald's conception of *living towards our neighbour ghostly* as expressed above. Here, his attitude towards traditional doctrinal discourses is one of non-indication rather than one of outright taunting. Some readers may have found his silence to be more deafening and defamiliarising than others would have done, however.

## Defamiliarisation and Refamiliarisation: *Disordinatio* and *Re-ordinatio* of the Apostles' Creed and the Ten Commandments

More spectacular examples of defamiliarisation have their impact on the most basic features of traditional doctrine and the catechism, which Pecock deliberately submerges and redistributes within his œuvre among his Four Tables. *Disordinatio* through *re-ordinatio*, as we shall see, goes hand-in-hand with a concomitant and perhaps-compensatory attempt at counter-defamiliarisation – *re-ordinatio* of *disordinatio*. Pecock nevertheless feels the need to reassure his readership that all apparently occluded or excluded points of the faith are still 'really there' throughout his overarching enterprise. This he shows at the beginning of the second part of the *Donet*, when the Son, quite understandably, asks the Father to tell him where, in the first part of the work, may be found the Twelve Articles of the Creed, the Seven Deadly Sins, the Five Wits, the Seven Works of

Mercy, the Three Theological Virtues, the Four Cardinal Virtues, the Seven Gifts of the Holy Ghost, the sacraments and the Ten Commandments. To this point in the work, as far as the Son can tell, of 'so famose soortis, distincciouns or particiouns, fadir, ʒe make not mensioun of oon' (p. 103). It is significant that the *ordinatio*-obsessed Reginald has the Son define these discourses as, above all, 'soortis, distincciouns or particiouns' rather than words or works of holy discipline. The Father then launches into a long disquisition, intending to show how all these seemingly ignored pillars of the faith can in fact be found after all, safely secured in the first part of the work. This assertion gives Pecock a golden opportunity to exercise his argumentative and hermeneutic powers on the set texts he most favours – his own works. The consequential unlocking of *sententia* from his own works, requiring an effort of scholastic exposition that would normally only be exercised upon works of some canonicity, valorises not only his powers as an exegete but also the authority of his texts.

Starting with the Apostles' Creed, he asserts that anyone looking at the first part of the *Donet* will find therein all Twelve Articles of the common Creed and 'manye mo articles which ben moche to be bileeued as þi xij ben' (p. 103). The most likely response by contemporary readers to this assertion, however, may well have been one of puzzlement, simply because the Twelve Articles of the Apostles' Creed in no way leap self-evidently out of the first part of the *Donet*. Reginald has made them unrecognisable by ignoring, mutating, veiling and/or dispersing them deliberately in his very different rival system. For all his claims of recognisability and equivalence in this work, he has gone to great lengths to make the traditional unrecognisable as a matter of policy. Or, rather, in starting from the ground up with his own rationalistic system, he simply does not recognise or accommodate the traditional in the first place.

The *Donet* would appear, then, to be simultaneously powered and hindered by competing logics. Pecock nevertheless claims – observing and advertising impeccably scholastic due process in scrupulous referencing – that the First Article of the Creed is in fact located in the fourteenth and fifteenth chapters of the first part of the *Donet*:

> Þe first article of þe commune crede, which article is þis, 'y bileeue into god þe fadir, maker of heuene and of erþe,' þou schalt fynde in þe xiiij$^e$ and xv chapitris of þe first parti afore going. (p. 103)

In chapter 14, true enough, we see that God the creator and his relationship to his creation are indeed declared: 'He is aloone maker of alle othire þingis out of nouȝt, keper and reuler of hem which ben clepid creaturis' (p. 85). This statement, however, forms part of the treatment of Pecock's First Matter, 'what is god' (p. 84), in which the Trinity is discussed. Belief in God the creator, however, is not the main focus of the discussion at this point. If we look where we are told to in chapter 15, we also find a mention of God as creator, 'his making of aungels and of men, of heuenes elementis and of alle her contentis in so manye diuers kyndis' (p. 86). This passage, however, falls under the discussion of God's so-called undergracious benefits, that is, those benefits which are lower than the so-called *benefits of grace*. The first 'undergracious' benefit is the one that Pecock clearly has in mind at this point. His reporting of this benefit certainly acknowledges God as maker of heaven and earth, but it scarcely rings out like an Article of the Creed. There is no familiar communal voicing of belief that one would normally find whenever the Creed was articulated. Instead, in typical Pecockian style, we are presented with a more analytic and comprehensive definition of God's actions as creator, itemising the properties of the heavens not only for their contents but also for their different kinds – their categories, natures and modes. An awareness of – or anxieties about – the incommensurability, or, at the very least, the striking lack of resemblance of Pecock's approach to that of the Creed (and other central doctrinal discourses of the Church) conceivably encouraged Pecock to compensate overtly in the second half of the *Donet*. Or it could also (or instead) have been a deliberate and thoroughly planned pedagogical ploy to familiarise: for after making his new system somewhat familiar (or at least accessible) in Part One through rational explanation driven home by the common pedagogical technique of repetition, he then endeavours in Part Two of his work to make things still more comfortably familiar by creating a multiplicity of connective tissue to discourses and concepts well-known yet now strategically sidelined. Despite his claim that he had already completely covered the first Article of the Creed as an 'undergracious' benefit, he nevertheless cites soon afterwards – somewhat aggressively, triumphantly and overgoingly, yet at the same time defensively and self-justifyingly – the rest of the whole text of the Apostles' Creed in the vernacular (pp. 103–4), pointing out the chapters in Part One where he has already dealt with its Articles adequately – and, for sure, better than any of the Creed's Articles manage to make sense by themselves. The connective tissue created by Reginald between his own articulation of the Creed and its traditional manifestation represents more than a mere mechanism of coordination – it is a site in which Pecock initiates, develops and asserts his own practice of justifying worth.²¹

Rather more vaguely, though, Pecock states that however many Articles of the Creed may be found 'in þese same now seid xiiij, xv and xvi chapitris, and in oþire chapitres of þe first party afore going, y committe to þe jugement of þin owen [that is, the reader's] wijsdom' (p. 104). In other words, *work it out for yourself; judge for yourself if you see it*. Here, we see at work, in combination with the typical compiler's disavowal of personal authority and respect for the free judgement of the reader (*lectoris arbitrium*), Pecock's pedagogical philosophy raised to the status of readerly method.²² His readers are exhorted to work out the connections themselves and to come to authoritative readings by exercising their own God-given reason in discovering and generating truths via the decorously cited cross-references. Mishtooni Bose, who convincingly finds in Pecock's approach the influence of Thomas Aquinas, describes this mode of 'reason discoursing' (*ratio discurrens*):

> The whole operation of teaching consists of this 'causing' of knowledge in another individual, which is brought about by the prompting of that person's natural reason. We should not, he argues, attribute the title of 'teacher' principally to men, but should reserve first place always for God. However, the element nearest to knowledge itself is 'the reason discoursing (*discurrens*) from principles to conclusions.' The image of the *ratio discurrens* is central to our arguments being pursued here, in that it depicts knowledge as a dynamic activity that is fully achieved in mental exercise.²³

Pecock can be confident about readers reasoning their way through connectivities thematically sufficient for the task, since Part One of his work covers such a broad generality of topics that they are bound to be able to find a good range of things in various places connecting to individual Articles of the Apostles' Creed.

Pecock further undermines the authority of the Apostles' Creed to his own advantage by drawing attention to the issue of whether or not the Apostles actually wrote it. This issue he does not discuss here, but, having successfully raised doubts, he refers his readers to his own *Book of Faith* for

---

²¹ Stark is suggestive here: 'Organizations can be seen as patterns of ties, but they should also be seen as sites in which actors engage in practices of justifying worth. Network ties are mechanisms of coordination but always alongside performance criteria and the evaluative principles on which they are based.' (Stark, *Sense of Dissonance*, p. 24).
²² For discussion of *lectoris arbitrium*, see *MTA*, p. 201.
²³ Bose, 'Two Phases of Scholastic Self-Consciousness', pp. 100–1.

further exploration of the matter (thereby citing an authority in the best scholastic fashion, only that authority happens to be himself, and is out of reach in another one of his works and thereby somewhat deferred).[24] The potential divestment of apostolic authorship from the Apostles' Creed implies even greater potential for the comparative authority of the *materia* and the *sententia* of the *Donet*, as articulated and commented upon by Pecock, whose recourse to reason is, in his own eyes, more powerful at outreasoning the Creed than the authority of apostolic authorship could offer anyway, even if its authenticity could be confirmed.

Pecock then takes a further swipe at the authority of the text of the Apostles' Creed. He declares that its most authentic and complete form is not the familiar text recited in Church but is, more credibly, all those articles of belief arising from the entirety of the New Testament:

> But þis y dare wel seie and avowe: þe crede of þe apostlis ben þe al hool noumbre of alle þo articlis to be bileeuid which ben conteynyd wiþynne þe writing of þe new testament, fro þe begynnyng of the newe testament into the eende of þe newe testament. And þerfore þe ful and hool crede of þe apostlis is moche lengir þan ben þe xiiij, xv and xvj chapitris of þe first party of þis present book. (p. 104)

In a remarkable rhetorical move, Pecock declares the New Testament to be a better, longer and fuller version of the Creed. He has of course already bumptiously advertised that in his Four Tables his treatment of what the Creed treats is shorter and better and more codified than the Creed (and presumably therefore also better than the New Testament's full text). So, on the one hand, Pecock anxiously quotes the Creed as if to prove that he is following it, yet, on the other hand, he denies its absolute completeness and authority by over-writing it with all the teachings of the New Testament, upon which he of course considers that he can improve too, thanks to his belief in the precedence of reason over Scripture. Still, it is rather startling at this point that the self-vauntingly non-scriptural rationalist Reginald, seemingly trying to have it both ways, invokes the New Testament rather than reason to help him out-Creed the Creed.

A further instance of readers being invited to dislocate and relocate familiar discourse and experience occurs with the Ten Commandments. Pecock pores over the Decalogue's alleged moral, intellectual and theological inadequacy and its incompleteness at great length and in painstaking detail. One of his many complaints is that the Ten Commandments are

---

[24] Pecock, *Book of Faith*, ed. by Morison.

formally inadequate for the purposes of being digested and rearticulated by the human mind and human discourse. Moreover, they fail to accommodate the totality of God's commandments, unlike Reginald's *Donet*, which is designed to give its readers 'general confuse [i.e., integrated] knowing' (p. 1) of the universal scope of Christian teaching:[25]

> Wherfore nedis folewiþ þat þe seid comoun foorme of þe x comaundementis is not such foorme þat þerbi and þerynne we mowe se, recorde, remembre and reporte sufficiently to vs silf and to oþire, as nede or oure profite askiþ, þe hool summe of goddis comaundementis.
>
> And who so wole, who so nyle, at þe ferþest it folewiþ þat nouȝwhere nyȝe þe seid foorme availith to þe seid purpos as þe vj seid chapitres doon of þe first party of þis book. (p. 145)

Here, in a staggeringly brash bid for *translatio auctoritatis* (to recycle Minnis's own medieval scholastic neologism),[26] Pecock endeavours, even more than he does with the Apostles' Creed, to show that each Commandment has already been fully accommodated in six of his earlier chapters – as, for example, with the Second Commandment against taking the Lord's name in vain:

> 'Þou schalt not take þe name of þi lord god in veyn, ffor þe lord þi god wole not haue him vnpunyschid which takiþ his name in ydel'. This comaundement þou schalt fynde afore in þe iiij$^e$ chapitre of þe afore going first party, where it is tauȝt þat þou schalt reuerence, preise and worschip oure lorde god. (p. 126)

True enough, the familiar commandment is, as Reginald says, to be found (albeit in unfamiliar guise) in Part One, chapter 4. Thus, we find, under consideration of the virtue of *living praisingly toward God*:

> ffadir, what is it forto lyue anentis god preisingly, as it is þe secunde poynt of þe first table?
>
> Sone, it is forto, at sum whilis, whanne oþire grettir seruicis of god, þat is to seie, fynal seruicis of god, schulen not þerbi be lettid, and whanne a man in his semyng haþ nede forto be kyndeled and quykened into goostly freendful loue toward god or toward him silf, a man forto preise god in him silf, or in

---

[25] For Pecock's concern to give his readers an overall sense of the big picture, extending to an overarching discipline of interiority in which his works are interlinked, see Johnson, 'Mediating Voices and Texts', pp. 137–46. See also Campbell, *Call to Read*, pp. 68–69 and 175–76, for Pecock's criticism of the Decalogue, and ibid., pp. 250–53, for discussion of his correction, amplification and improvements of traditional liturgical discourses.

[26] Minnis, *Valuing the Vernacular* (2009), p. x.

> his seyntis, or in his benefetis, and in his oþire werkis; þat is to seie, forto declare or witnesse, bi inward or outward speche, sum excellence or worþines or goodness of god in him silf, or in his worchingis, or in his seintis, or in enye of hise creaturis. (pp. 28–29)

It is by no means obvious here that the prohibition of the Second Commandment is being tackled. Instead, some virtuous opposites to taking the Lord's name in vain are highlighted. As in his treatment of *living worshippingly or honouringly* in the same chapter (p. 32), Pecock is clearly more interested in inculcating good habits, and such good habits are not merely to be directed towards God, but towards everything in creation made by him. If one were to practise the virtues recommended here, then one would presumably avoid taking the Lord's name in vain and therefore find that one was complying with the Second Commandment. When the Son then asks the Father to what avail such praising is, the Father tells him that it preserves loving and good will towards God and neighbour, and keeps the mind and affections on God so that they do not descend to worldly and fleshly concerns. There is not anything directly here on taking the Lord's name in vain, let alone on not going 'vnpunyschid' for doing so. Positive practice and positive attitude define and obliquely refract this re-glossed virtue, as with the virtues discussed earlier with regard to *ghostly living towards the neighbour*.

The somewhat moveable and dispersible Second Commandment is also accommodated, so Reginald tells us, 'vndir anoþir skile in þe iij$^e$ and v poynt of the ij$^e$ table, and in þe iij and vj$^e$ poynt of þe iiij$^e$ table' (p. 127). Here, the accommodating is accomplished more recognisably than many of his other accommodations of familiar to unfamiliar. This we see in the third and fifth points of the Second Table – respectively the virtues of *living rightfully or justly towards God* (in other words, performing promises made to the Almighty) and *living truly towards God* (that is, being truthful in affirming, denying and performing deeds before God) – and also in the third and sixth points of the Fourth Table, which are to do, respectively, with *living righteously or justly towards our neighbour* (performing promises made to our neighbour) and *living truly towards our neighbour* (being truthful in affirming, denying and performing deeds towards our neighbour).

The textual belabouring and heavy cross-referential traffic servicing the Second Commandment in the best scholarly manner, as with the rest of the Decalogue, is so extensive and intensive that, for all Pecock's refrain of disapproval at its lack of system, digestibility and comprehensiveness, and for all his deconstruction and repackaging of it, the Decalogue not only survives in the *Donet*, but thrives awkwardly but productively as an insuperable metatext, a recessive but resolutely unpalimpsestuous source and textual *auctoritas* that simply cannot be displaced but will continue to be followed and displayed. In the first part of the *Donet*, then, Pecock seems initially to ignore the Decalogue in such a manner that makes it difficult to see where and how it is being replaced, but it nevertheless comes, in the second part of the work, to be re-recognised to the point of its vernacularised *ipsissima verba* being brandished in hopeful connectivity with the many loci of its earlier ostensible ignoring, deconstruction, supersession, denial and displacement. Yet again, Reginald is trying to have his cake and eat it.

### Re-glossing and Re-citing God's Infinity: Remediating Prayer Scholastically

So far we have seen Pecock endeavouring to produce his own distinctive new *ordinationes*, openly challenging familiar public discourses of Holy Church by refracting them through generically alien forms. Reginald was capable, however, of being equally innovative in recombining logics and genres without being so overtly subversive. We shall see next how Pecock energised his text by the novel conjoining of scholastic and devotional elements that did not normally keep each other's company: here prayer and praise meet cross-reference, argumentation, definition, analysis and exposition. Different in kind from employing the familiar procedures of theological or devotional treatises, the next case for discussion, drawn from the *Reule of Crysten Religioun*, is innovative in its scholastically characterful generic hybridity.

We arrive, however, at this example from the *Reule* intertextually via a cross-referential departure point – the following definition of the infinity of God in the *Donet*:

> Neverþelees, in such maner as creaturis mowen him discryue, God is oon being, oon substaunce infinite, þat is to seie, vnmesurable greet in goostly greetnes, infinite good, infinite maiestful, infinite fair, myri and swete, infinite myȝty, wijs and louyng, infinite mercyful, piteful and desirose, infinite large, fre and gentil, infinite trew and infinite trowþe. (p. 85)

This definition, for all its affective stateliness, is a fairly routine description of God, expressed, as definitions tend to be, in the third person. But Pecock connects it with a more unusual treatment of the infinity of God, to which he directs his readers when, shortly after this definition, he refers the Son to the first treatise of the *Reule of Crysten Religioun* for 'more of þis mater' (p. 86). Amidst this teaching in the *Reule* is a scholastic – and very long – exposition of the infinity of God, but one which is scripted, intriguingly, in the shareable voice of prayer.[27] This prayerful passage is of an inventively scholastic nature, interweaving discourses of prayer, argumentation and analysis, and therefore achieving a distinctively Pecockian blend of heaven-bound intimacy and relentless rationalism. Here, Pecock fuses his – and by extension his reader's – reasoning and imagining of divine infinity with a concomitant praising of the Almighty, in an astonishing ventriloquial hybrid of scholastic definition and prayer:

> Lord, þou3 al þou be knowun for preisable and loueable for þat þou art a greet worþi being, a goodnes, a majeste, my3te, wisdom and love, wiþ oþere more noble condiciouns rehercid, 3itt þou art not knowun for ouer wonderfully and ouer excellently preisable and loueable but if it be knowun þat ech of þese condicions is vnmesurable and infinite.[28]

The Almighty is addressed in a rather academic manner: some of his praiseworthy qualities remain unreferenced, being cited alongside named positive qualities 'wiþ oþere more noble condiciouns rehercid', as if God can reasonably be expected to check in other parts of Reginald's œuvre (such as the fuller definition in the *Donet* perhaps?) for which other qualities he can be praised. It is a strange sort of praise indeed that withholds terms of praise and replaces them with such vague self-referencing – but this is entirely typical of Pecock, whose habits of destinerrance would have made even Jacques Derrida blush.[29]

The ability to know about God's infinity is premised by Pecock on what he presents, in scholarly fashion, as something of a logical argument, duly arranged around the dialectical pivots of 'þou3 al ... for þat ..., 3itt ... but if'. In this prayer referring to cognition, the illimitable (i.e., 'ouer') lovability and praisability of God are predicated on the human ability to know that the conditions of the Almighty are infinite. Note here the combination of implied praise with a formally delicate and precise

---

[27] Pecock, *Reule of Crysten Religioun*, ed. by Greet, pp. 44–70.
[28] Ibid., p. 49. For discussion of this passage as a rehearsal of doctrine in a prayerful 'corporate voice', see Campbell, *Call to Read*, pp. 57–59. See ibid., pp. 110–47, for discussion of Pecock's shaping of prayer as a rational argument-centred discipline for layfolk.
[29] *Destinerrance*, a term playfully coined by Jacques Derrida, concerns itself with his own habitual referral of his readers to elsewhere in his œuvre for meanings and definitions of key terms and ideas. For interesting discussion of this, see Miller, 'Derrida's *Destinerrance*'. In his jest about the origins of the term, Miller provides quite a useful definition of it: 'Perhaps no such origin for the word exists. Perhaps the word itself is the consequence of a *destinerrance*, a wandering from locus to locus that to some degree takes for granted its meaning as something always already established somewhere else' (p. 895). Such a definition would also appear to apply to Pecock.

laying-out of seemingly logical conditions and categorical qualifications marshalled to drive forward what is implied. This praise is presented as stemming from a scholarly appreciation of God's infinity: Pecock attempts to bestow upon his readership such an appreciation by demonstrating God's infinity through a suitably mind-boggling syllogism based upon repeatedly doubling the distance from London to Rome – a distance which, however many times one doubles it, will always remain finite, unlike God. As a consequence, argues Pecock, the idea of divine infinity must pain and astonish the imagination and the only intellectually respectable and appropriately pious response is one of excessive wonder.[30] Indeed, Pecock is perfectly happy to give a place in his discursive economy to wonder. Because wonder up-ends the routines of rational interpretation, it renders normal cognition useless, pushing the believer into a state of pious marvelling affectively receptive to the grace of God and to the teachings of the Church. In this moment of transcendent sincerity, Reginald's scholasticism embraces its limitations, albeit that such transcendence is syllogistically achieved.

A little later, developing his exposition of God's infinity with intensified analytic adoration, Pecock provides a re-glossing that also remediates the rhythm and cadence of prayer and praise with argumentative self-referencing:

> Out of þe iij$^e$ trouþe, þe iiij$^e$ and þe v$^e$ to gidere, comeþ forþ þis xiij$^e$ trouþe, þat not oonly þou hast alle þese perfecciouns and nobiltees afore named actualy in þi silf, but also þou art alle hem and ech of hem, fforwhi al þing þat is, or it is þi creature or it is þi silf. (p. 69)

The conclusion here, the thirteenth truth ('þis xiij$^e$ trouþe'), is that because God – who is laudatorily addressed in piously totalising formulas, suitable in a prayer like this one – possesses and is all perfections and noble qualities, then anything that exists is either one of God's creatures or God Himself. Feeding into this conclusion are the passage's third, fourth and fifth truths ('þe iij$^e$ trouþe, þe iiij$^e$ and þe v$^e$ to gidere').[31] The third truth is that this maker unmade, and this keeper unkept, is infinite in being; the fourth, that this maker unmade, this keeper unkept, is not but one, and there may be no more such save him alone; and the fifth, that this maker unmade, this keeper unkept, is maker and keeper of all creatures.[32] These three truths duly lead up to Reginald's delivery of the conclusion of

---

[30] Pecock, *Reule of Crysten Religioun*, ed. by Greet, pp. 51–52. [31] Ibid., p. 69.
[32] Ibid., respectively, pp. 58, 60, 61.

this passage, which takes the form of the thirteenth truth. The chapter accordingly ends with a prayerful summation, which, in the act of addressing God as infinite, also incrementally calibrates a series of increasingly exalted academic discourses through which his creatures substantiate and corroborate that same infiniteness. Thus, Pecock combines his own address to, and his own naming of the qualities of, the Almighty with the very processes of asserting and demonstrating God's infiniteness that he would like his readers to learn, practise and internalise from taking on board and reasoning their way through his textual œuvre – and, one must assume, also to share with him in praying to the Almighty in such terms themselves:

> Lo, lord, þis maker unmaad and þis keper vnkept, infinite in being aloone, maker and keper of alle creaturis, art þou, lord god, whom alle creaturis witnessen to be, alle creaturis proclamen and crien to be, and whom alle creaturis arguen and proven to be, as it is schewid.[33]

Once more, Pecock takes the lead in mixing direct address to the Almighty in his own shareable voice with self-valorising cross-referencing, also in his own voice. In this passage he confirms the unique qualities of God in a *gradatio* of discursive actions practised, so he claims, by all of God's creatures. Attestation through witnessing ('witnessen') is succeeded by a somewhat more emphatic proclaiming and crying out ('proclamen and crien'), whose mere assertiveness is in turn upgraded to arguing ('arguen'), which finally results in the triumphant conclusiveness of proving ('proven') leading to the manifestness of God's infinity being 'schewid' openly. Reginald demonstratively envelopes this escalating sequence of more and more prestigious academic discursive actions in a cross-referential reassurance that in his writings all of this has indeed been textually 'schewid' ('schewid' in Middle English can mean 'expounded' as well as, more simply, 'shown'). In this moment of argumentative prayer, the cognitive yet spiritual first virtue of Pecock's First Table, that of *living learningly*, is realised, exercised and expounded par excellence.

## Conclusion: Authorising the Order of the Pecockian Unfamiliar

Pecock's novel and astoundingly ambitious reconfiguration of Christian knowledge and doctrine was a gargantuan programme, endeavouring to efface and outdo traditional discourses of the Church whilst at the same

---
[33] Ibid., p. 61.

time taking pains palpably, even anxiously, to be equivalent or answerable to that which it would displace. Time and time again, Reginald rejects a full range of authoritative discourses and practices of the Church, doing so in a fittingly scholastic manner. In this chapter we have seen him not writing about pride, the first Vice, and how to remedy it, but about *living learningly* instead. We have also seen him avoiding the self-meeking that usually commences spiritual treatises, and not only taking no account of the desirability of prayerfully petitioning heaven for those in Purgatory, but also indulging himself in the occlusion and deconstruction, in Part One of the *Donet*, of the Decalogue and the Apostles' Creed to the point of rendering them absent or unrecognisable. He also takes a swipe at the authenticity and the authorship of the Apostles' Creed and reprehends the Decalogue for being, in his eyes at least, inadequate, incomplete and unfit for human consumption or memorialisation. Additionally, the prohibition of the Second Commandment against taking the Lord's name in vain becomes somewhat hidden in Pecock's preoccupation with *living praisingly*.

Yet he attempts, in Part Two of the *Donet*, to remediate his earlier aggressively self-vaunting moves with a medley of compensatory reassurances that the traditional discourses are, in fact, still alive and well in his œuvre. It is important that we take note of how, in both his rejection of standard doctrinal discourses and his (re)accommodation of them in his own new system, Reginald deploys a full repertoire of scholastic terms, practices and attitudes: *ordinatio*, *compilatio*, *ratio discurrens*, analytical definition, counterargument, quotation of *ipsissima verba*, referral to *lectoris arbitrium*, citations of *auctoritas*, properly labelled cross-referencing and textual citation, self-commentary, glossing, re-glossing, and even (in the case of the marginalising of the Apostles' Creed against the New Testament and also against his own work) a double appeal to the canonical hierarchy of the texts within the Bible and the authority of reason within his own corpus of works. It is also typical of Pecock's scholastic piety that he has no difficulty with mixing argumentative cross-references with praise and prayer.

At times, Pecock presents his readers with strangely paradoxical textual mixes and layers: the familiar made unfamiliar and then made familiar again, albeit under the remit of the Pecockian unfamiliar. In some of the examples discussed, for instance the Creed and the Ten Commandments, there is a doubleness – a cognitive and cultural dissonance – in which, on the one hand, readers would have experienced doctrine in new, perhaps unrecognisable, forms and would have had to accommodate existing knowledge to the new context of Pecock's overall design, and yet, on the other hand, they would then have found themselves encountering Pecock belatedly citing traditional discourse, which they would subsequently have to superimpose on their all-too-recent accommodation of old to new, as with his treatment of the Apostles' Creed and the Decalogue. Readers would have had to negotiate the accountability of the new elements to the old and vice versa. Such readers would likewise have found themselves labouring to accommodate a recognisable definition of the infinity of God to the subsequent treatment of the same topic couched in a novel discourse-mix blending prayerful praise, cross-referencing and expository analysis. The challenge to exercise *ratio discurrens* necessitated by such textual combinations and recombinations, at the heart of which lie the attitudes and practices of *ordinatio* and *compilatio*, aligned with the standard scholastic conception of the 'definitive, divisive and collective mode' (as cited from Minnis's treatment of Kilwardby at the beginning of this chapter), must have occasioned in Reginald's readership, if not new knowledge, then new understandings and perspectives on doctrine and theology generated through the different discursive logics and authorities brought into dialectical play with each other. The mutual accountability of elements situated at times ambiguously between the old and new is both a lateral relation, in that a formal equivalence and status is posited between both instances, but paradoxically at the same time a hierarchical one, inasmuch as one textual item would ostensibly have been in a position of originary authority and greater prestige in relation to the other.

Despite some obvious friction between Pecock's own new discourses and traditional ones, the perspective of each on the other results in an intriguingly self-intermediating hybrid of resources and possibilities. The necessary accommodation of each to the other in an 'organizing dissonance' would have begotten a 'pragmatic organizational reflexivity' in writer and user alike.[34] Their dissonance is both organising and organised, and it invites the modern academic to rethink – just as much as medieval users would have been invited to rethink – their understandings of religious knowledge and their routines of pious practice that might otherwise have been taken for granted.[35] Pecock, in attempting re-cognition of the familiar, ended up recognising it dissonantly within his own unfamiliar discourse.[36]

---

[34] Stark, *Sense of Dissonance*, p. 27.   [35] Ibid., pp. 27, 32.
[36] I would like to acknowledge with gratitude the helpful and illuminating comments of my fellow editors on earlier drafts of this chapter.

CHAPTER 8

# *Arts of Love and Justice*
## Property, Women and Golden Age Politics in *Le Roman de la Rose*

### Jessica Rosenfeld

In the middle of Book II of the *Ars Amatoria*, Ovid offers a variation on the origin myth of civilisation, an early version in miniature of the narrative of creation that opens the *Metamorphoses*. All was chaos, confused and without order, until the earth and sky were separated, birds filled the sky and fish the seas. Humans walked the earth, but alone, until a man and woman chanced to find each other:

> Tum genus humanum solis errabat in agris,
>   Idque merae vires et rude corpus erat;
> Silva domus fuerat, cibus herba, cubilia frondes,
>   Iamque diu nulli cognitus alter erat.
> Blanda truces animos fertur mollisse voluptas:
>   Constiterant uno femina virque loco;
> Quid facerent, ipsi nullo didicere magistro:
>   Arte Venus nulla dulce peregit opus.

> Then mankind wandered in the lonely fields; brute strength was theirs and forms uncouth; woodland was their home, their food grass, their bedding leaves; and for long none knew his fellow. Beguiling pleasure is said to have softened those fierce spirits: a man and a woman had tarried together in one spot; what were they to do, they learnt themselves with none to teach them: artlessly did Venus accomplish the sweet act.[1]

Unlike Lucretius, his most direct source in this passage, Ovid attributes civilising power to sexual desire and pleasure. People lived rough, solitary lives until, by chance it seems, a man and a woman found themselves in

---

[1] Ovid, *Ars Amatoria*, II.473–480, in *The Art of Love and Other Poems*, ed. and tr. by Mozley, pp. 98–99. The relevant intertext is Lucretius, *De rerum natura*, V.1014–8, ed. and tr. by Rouse, pp. 456–57; in the longer passage, Ovid also nods to Virgil, *Georgics*, II.266, ed. and tr. by Fairclough, pp. 154–55; on the effect of allusions to Lucretius and Virgil in this passage, see Watson, 'Love as Civilizer'; also Leach, 'Georgic Imagery', pp. 145–46. Huot, 'Bodily Peril', pp. 53–54, reads this passage in light of the topos of male sexual dominance of unruly women. See esp. Fyler, *Language and the Declining World*, pp. 62–65.

the same place. Without need of instruction, they were guided by Venus to perform the acts of love and were thus mollified. The context of this miniature history is, unsurprisingly, ironic, as Ovid's narrator has paused in the midst of explaining how to soothe the rage of a woman who believes she has been betrayed. The 'strong medicines' (*medicamina fortia*, II.489) necessary in this case are the softening remedies of physical love; such activities have civilised humans (and provided pleasure to animals, in the extended passage) since their first primitive encounter.

Such irony should not prevent us from taking seriously the claim that Ovid implicitly makes in this passage – that sexual desire is a political force, in the most foundational of terms. It brings a couple together and provokes the end of a wild life of mere subsistence. In Lucretius, human beings are 'softened' by compassion for their offspring and ultimately civilised by participation in family life, which precipitates comity with neighbours (V.1019–20). And, in another tale of civilisation's origins, this contained in Cicero's *De Inventione*, people scattered about in fields and woods are assembled by a single great and wise man, speaking with reason and eloquence about virtuous and useful occupations.[2] Ovid uniquely and wittily imagines the first human assembly brought about by chance, then sex – a pointed and literal example of the intersection of *eros* and politics that resides at the heart of much of his poetry. It is my aim in this chapter to elucidate some of the implications of Ovidian erotic politics for medieval literary texts composed under Ovid's sign. Explicating 'political context' is a familiar aim of literary criticism, and one might immediately consider patronage, or literary treatments of marriage, as obvious intersections among the erotic, poetic and political. Yet Ovid's mini-history should encourage us to consider the possibility that medieval erotic poetry is engaged in political thinking at an even more fundamental level – dissecting the nature and origins of human association. If we have become used to seeing 'the *materia* of love in a moral perspective' in vernacular medieval literature, especially in the wake of Alastair Minnis's *Medieval Theory of Authorship*, a political perspective also shapes the frame.[3] For, as Minnis reminds us, medieval authors would learn from Aristotle – if sometimes in mediated ways – that politics 'embraces' ethics and ethics embraces politics.[4] At the end of Aristotle's *Nicomachean Ethics*, the philosopher turns to the science of laws – the framework necessary for

---

[2] See Fyler, *Language and the Declining World*, pp. 62–63, reading Ovid's passage as allusion to and parody of Cicero.
[3] *MTA*, p. 183.   [4] Ibid.

individuals to pursue a happy life of virtue, thus linking, as Aquinas notes in his commentary, the *Ethics* to the *Politics*. And in the *Politics* we are reminded that a given regime is only successful if it is judged as fostering the ethical lives of its citizens, with the happiness of the whole depending upon the happiness of each part.[5]

What would it mean, then, to understand erotic poetry as 'pertaining to politics', understanding politics as one of the categories of knowledge that comprehends this literature? Late medieval vernacular literature participated in the project of the reception of Aristotelian philosophy, responding to the rapid assimilation of translations of the philosopher's treatises on natural science, logic, ethics, politics and psychology into university and broader intellectual discourse.[6] For love poetry, the newly available works of Aristotelian practical philosophy were one terrain for working out the relationship between individual and social desire. And for the avowedly intellectual and enormously influential *Roman de la Rose*, which claims to 'enclose' 'l'art d'Amors' (l. 38),[7] this meant – among many other things – a playful yet incisive exegesis of the erotics of ownership contained in Aristotle's *Politics*, an analysis of the origins of human association that reveals the necessarily gendered and unavoidably economic dynamics of sociality.

Jean de Meun's section of the *Rose* returns repeatedly and variously to the narration of political origins, most often to the idea of a Golden Age – an origin story that does not narrate the human shift from solitude to assembly, but instead imagines an idyllic communal past before it was shattered by vice and conflict, specifically conflict over wealth and women. Erotic desire emerges in these stories of early political community as part of a constellation of relationships to the law and to possession. In each telling, the *Rose* emphasises different aspects of these communities, yet they all exist prior to positive law and private property. Jonathan Morton has recently, and aptly, characterised the *Rose* as 'particularly preoccupied by

---

[5] Aristotle, *Politics*, II.5. For convenient translations of Aristotle's work, see *Politics*, tr. by Saunders, and *Aristotle's Politics*, tr. by Lord.
[6] See Karnes, *Imagination, Meditation and Cognition*; Rosenfeld, *Ethics and Enjoyment*; Robertson, *Nature Speaks*; and Morton, *Philosophical Context*. On Jean de Meun's location in Paris and demonstrated knowledge of university intellectual debates and culture, see Minnis, *Magister Amoris* (2001), pp. 2–8. On Jean's continuation of the *Rose* as a 'summa or encyclopedia of university learning', see Wei, *Intellectual Culture*, p. 363. Morton and Nievergelt (eds), *Thirteenth-Century Thought*, was published after this essay was composed; in what follows, I have noted the essays that are especially relevant to my argument (esp. Knox, 'Human Nature', and Toivanen, 'Personal and the Political'), and I hope my chapter is in keeping with the larger aims of that valuable project.
[7] The *Roman de la Rose* is cited parenthetically from Lecoy's edition and Dahlberg's translation.

what is lost and what is gained in the passage from a primitive, animalistic, natural state to a more human, civilised way of living'.[8] Yet while the Golden Age narratives produced by Raison, Ami and Genius all posit a 'fall' into civilisation as it was known in the thirteenth century – with princes, courts, war and the pilfering of the earth – there is no real questioning of the naturalness of human community *per se*, though 'natural' is not a self-evident concept and may be conceived of in terms of prelapsarian creation, postlapsarian compensatory human nature or Aristotelian telos.[9] In the imagination of the *Rose*, humans did not wander alone prior to civilisation, but lived in social harmony. What distinguishes the Golden Age from the ages that follow is the intervention of positive law – the courts and rulers necessary to adjudicate competing claims over goods that have become private instead of common.

Property and possession thus emerge in the *Rose* as the nexus between *eros* and politics. The lover-protagonist, Amant, exhibits a desire for the rosebud that is not merely a private desire, in terms of individual and personal *eros*, but a *privatising* desire, in that it expresses a desire for possession – private property – thus placing his quest in a political framework. In the *Rose*, it is via the question of property that individual erotic desire – in this case the heterosexual possession of another – becomes a matter of public concern.[10] The problem of possession – what should be held in common and what should be held privately – is one of the first questions of political philosophy, beginning with Socrates' argument for common ownership of property, women and children in Plato's *Republic* and Aristotle's critique of this idea in the *Politics*. The question of what Amant can possess, and whether he can possess the rose, animates the poem.

The links between love and property in the *Rose* are thus not accidents of language, as one might imagine that Amant's wish for the rose to 'belong' to him or to be 'his' signals his general desire for romantic faithfulness (the equivalent of a modern drugstore-bought Valentine's Day card or candy with the commanding request, 'be mine'). More specifically, Jean de Meun links Amant's possessive desires to politics via repeated excursions into Golden Age mythology with its accompanying

---

[8] Morton, *Philosophical Context*, p. 87.
[9] On medieval ideas about 'the naturalness of human association', see Luscombe, 'State of Nature'; Nederman, 'Origins of Society'; and especially Toste, 'Naturalness of Human Association'. On medieval theories of ownership in prelapsarian and postlapsarian contexts, see Minnis, *From Eden to Eternity* (2016), pp. 117–34, and Garnsey, *Thinking about Property*.
[10] On possession as a subject of Middle English romance, see Smith, *Arts of Possession*.

notions of communal property. The fall from the Golden Age is typically linked to a fall into private property – establishing ownership as a mark of fallen modernity.[11] In the thirteenth century, however, ownership was not necessarily accepted as an inevitable feature of contemporary life, and the *Rose* was written in the midst of vigorous scholastic debates about property, natural law and positive law. As Janet Coleman explains, economic developments in the twelfth and thirteenth centuries, along with the role of the mendicant orders as major voices in scholasticism, meant that 'the moral and intellectual problem of the legitimacy of private property' was raised in ways it had not been since the patristic period.[12] Jean's continuation of the *Rose* comprehended debates about positive and natural law, particularly with respect to property and possession.[13] Canon law left open numerous questions regarding property, and university quodlibets and commentaries discussed a number of pressing topics: the meaning of legal terms such as *dominium* (lordship), property, possession and use of material goods, and questions of jurisdiction over ecclesiastical and lay goods.[14] Thus, when Aquinas articulates a theory of private property in his *Summa*, he is not only examining the question from a theoretical perspective, but speaking to the decades of debate between the mendicant and secular orders about property, possession and law.[15]

In addressing possession in the context of erotic poetry, the *Rose* registers the gendered nature of questions about property, present in scholastic political philosophy, but elided in more specific legal contexts. Amant's erotic pursuit highlights the gendered differences concealed in the concept of 'human association'. While collective ownership of women and children was not a live political possibility in medieval Europe, the *Rose* raises questions about the 'naturalness' of singular affection, the unremarked gendering of communal life as imagined in Golden Age narratives and the link between the politics of ownership and erotic desire.[16] If a

---

[11] Milan, 'Golden Age', argues against understanding Jean de Meun as advocating a 'radical' program of return to common property.
[12] Coleman, 'Property and Poverty,' p. 611.
[13] On Jean's *Rose* as focused on contradictions in discussions of natural law (*ius naturale*) with respect to property and more broadly, see Knox, 'Human Nature'.
[14] Coleman, 'Property and Poverty', p. 638. On the ambiguity of Gratian's *Decretum* on the relationship between natural law and private property, see ibid., p. 617. Kuttner, 'Gratian and Plato', p. 93, observes that Distinction 8 of the *Decretum* 'partly serves to illustrate the words "*communis omnium possessio*" in Isidore's description of the *ius naturale*' (see Isidore, *Etymologies*, V. IV.1, ed. by Lindsay).
[15] Coleman, 'Property and Poverty', p. 622.
[16] Kuttner, 'Gratian and Plato', discusses the way Gratian and medieval commentators on Plato addressed the problem of Plato's prescription of common wives and offspring.

foundational question of politics, raised in Plato's *Republic*, is whether to hold women in common, and the Golden Age posits a paradise of shared property, what does this mean for men and women? It is left to the female speakers in the poem, Raison and La Vieille, to bring the role of women in politics to our attention. Raison's discourse suggests that the drive to possess a feminine object is both part of the civilising process and a sign of the inevitable corruption of that process. With La Vieille, Jean introduces a discord between the allegorical truths sought by classical mythography and the literal truth sought in Aristotelian practical philosophy.[17] This discord is registered most clearly in La Vieille's insistence that we consider women – as objects and as obscured subjects of politics. Recent scholarship on the *Rose* has argued against readings of the poem itself as feminist, dismissing the possibility of 'bodytalk' or other forms of subversion of the patriarchy, and I am not here to disagree.[18] But even a non-feminist or anti-feminist *Rose* can bring our attention to the gendered aspects of ethical and political discourse that are otherwise elided by certain kinds of abstract or allegorical thought. In making this argument I am modifying Morton's persuasive reading of Jean de Meun's preoccupation with the Golden Age as a commitment to a 'poetic mode which promises allegorical rather than literal truth', as I show in what follows how the *Rose* uses that myth to stage the conflict between mythical, allegorical and historical, literal knowledge.[19] Minnis has shown the way that Jean as medieval Ovidian 'magister amoris' made not only allegory but also literalistic satire function powerfully in their turns, with satirical theory providing a means for unveiled attacks on human folly.[20] The literal commitments of the *Rose* might also be seen in its engagements with scholastic philosophy, which deploys its forms to seek literal, comprehensive truths, a comprehension that can pry into the occlusions of the fabulists and poets.

## A Rose of One's Own

The poem's first narration of a Golden Age myth – Raison's account of the castration of Saturn – follows a long exchange between Raison and Amant

---

[17] See Wetherbee, 'Literal and Allegorical', p. 278, on La Vieille as voice of experience, 'profound humanity', contingency and the natural.
[18] See Guynn, 'Authorship and Sexual Violence', and Morton, 'Where are the Bodies?' On feminist readings of male-authored medieval texts, see Burns, *Bodytalk*.
[19] Morton, *Philosophical Context*, p. 89.
[20] Minnis, *Magister Amoris* (2001), pp. 21, 87 and 82–118, *passim*.

on the question of possession, establishing property as a central concern and setting up a conflict between allegorical and literal pursuits of truth. Raison explains that she wants lovers to be free of the covetousness (*couvoitise*, l. 4565; p. 99) that incites grasping, whether for material objects or bodily pleasure. She first speaks specifically in the context of women who exchange their bodies for money and gifts; in turning to address Amant's desire directly she speaks about covetous desire for the love object itself. Raison suggests that Amant is fully captured by his desire for pleasure, 'Por ce velz tu la rose avoir, / tu n'i songes nul autre avoir' (ll. 4573–4; p. 99: 'Your intention runs nowhere but upon wishing to have the rose; you dream of no other possession'). In this bifurcated address to the problem of covetousness in love – women covet the goods of men and men covet women – Raison introduces a gendered logic to possession that ramifies throughout the poem. She explains the way that possessions enslave the possessors, and laments that fraud (*Baraz*, l. 5125; p. 107) has caused previously common goods to be appropriated (*aproprié*, l. 5127; p. 107) by people who have thereby lost their natural freedom (*naturel franchise*, l. 5129; p. 107). She attributes this state of affairs to a false faith that Fortune can conquer Nature, can in fact confer possession of objects that Nature has made inherently foreign to them (*les fet estranges*, l. 5289; p. 109).

If Raison articulates general Boethian truths, Amant hews to a personal, literal, non-universalising stance. He responds to Raison by praying to be taught what things of the world are indeed available for him to possess, wishing to know 'quels choses peuent estre moies / et se du mien puis riens avoir' (ll. 5292–93; p. 109: 'what things can be mine, and if I can have things of my own'). Raison shares the unsatisfying information that 'toutes vos choses / Son en vos meïsmes encloses' (ll. 5311–12; p. 110: 'all your possessions are enclosed within yourself'). In this statement, Raison may subtly echo and undermine the poem's opening claim that 'l'art d'Amors' is 'tote enclose' (l. 38) in its lines, for she evacuates the necessity for a learned technique to gain external objects of desire. Instead, she says, one must learn that one already possesses all necessary things. Amant's resistance to Raison's arguments on behalf of virtuous friendship, and against a love ruled by Fortune, begets an outburst that precipitates the poem's engagement with the origins of the fallen world. Amant rejects Raison's advice to seek 'quele amor sauvage' (l. 5347; p. 110: 'some primitive love'), a love that has not existed on earth, he says, since the days before the giants rebelled against the gods. Amant's introduction of the notion of a 'former age' into the poem portrays it as savage, pre-civilised, with the intention of dismissing any idea that he should pursue a virtue non-existent on the earth he inhabits. Indeed, he avers, Cicero may have searched history for the existence of the pure love recommended by Raison, but he did not find it 'de cels qui a son tens vivoient, / qui si ami de boiche estoient' (ll. 5383–4; p. 111: 'among those who lived at his time and were his dinner-mates'). Amant remains committed to a notion of the possible, the literal, the individual and the contemporary.

Raison, then, tries another tack, suggesting that Amant pursue a general love of all humankind and the golden rule. The neglect of both, she says, has necessitated earthly judges. She explains, 'Tu peuz amer generaumant / touz ceus du monde leaumant. / Aime les touz autant conme un, / au mains de l'amor dou conmun' (ll. 5417–20; p. 111: 'You can lawfully love all those of the world in a general way: love them all as much as one, at least with the love of what is common to all'). To love 'generally' in Raison's terms is not to love a large collection of people, but entirely to abandon the love of particular, singular people in favour of loving what is common among them. Morton observes that the 'astonishing *rime riche*' of 'conme un' and 'conmun' formally performs the blurring of the individual with the general.[21] For Raison, this love is equivalent to the golden rule, and its abandonment has necessitated earthly judges to punish the evil that results.

Raison's arguments prompt an abstract question from Amant about the relative worth of Love and Justice.[22] He requests that Raison 'me faciez un jugemant / d'Amor et de Joutice emsenble, / li quels vaut mieuz, si con vos senble' (ll. 5450–52; p. 112: 'make a reasoned statement about love and justice and their relationship. Which is worth more, as it seems to you?'). Amant's question comes in quodlibetal form, a question that might be answered in the abstract terms of practical philosophy. Raison, instead, offers a mythical history supporting the overwhelming value of love. She elaborates that, in the wake of Jupiter's castration of Saturn – who reigned along with Justice – lordship and positive law became necessary. Without love, human-invented forms of justice must enter. And yet, without love, as Raison contends, justice is inevitably corrupt and grasping – as criminal as the evil it was created to punish.

Raison explains that if people, now, lived as peacefully and lovingly as they did in Saturn's age, 'Ja mes roi ne prince n'avroient, / ne seroit bailliz

---

[21] Morton, *Philosophical Context*, p. 93.
[22] On the political and social roles of love and justice in the poem, see Toivanen, 'Personal and the Political', pp. 120–29.

ne prevoz' (ll. 5528–9; p. 113: 'They would never have a king or a prince. There would be neither bailiff nor provost'). Her logic echoes *Metamorphoses*, I.91–93, where Ovid speaks of a world in which humans did not need written law, for they followed the internal rule of reason and thus no courts had been built, no judges installed.[23] Any hope for the return of justice evaporates with her example of Appius, who infamously attempted to use his juridical power to possess Virginia, daughter of Virginius. The corrupt Appius arranged for his sergeant to appear in court and declare that Virginia belonged to him, as a slave. The sergeant states plainly, 'la pucele est moie' (l. 5571; p. 114: 'the girl is mine'). With this illustrative story, we find the poem's first specific example of human political corruption, one that significantly revolves around the question of which man – father or purported slave-owner – has the rights to possession of a woman.

In opening the question of erotic desire and property, the discourse of Raison and Amant posits a divide between an idealised pre-political age of general love and a fallen politics driven by erotic possession. Early scribal revisions of the *Rose* suggest that Amant's quarrel with Raison was understood as a debate about whether one should seek a common or a private love. The *B* group of manuscripts elaborates on Amant's desire for private possession of the rose, in opposition to common love.[24] Nine of these manuscripts contain an interpolation in which Amant tells Raison that he cannot love her because he knows that she will have loves other than his.[25] All civilised men, 'a bourc ne a vile' ('in city or in town'), are her potential lovers, and Amant does not wish to share his beloved. He states his wishes quite plainly: 'Je ne voil pas, ne vous poist mie, / Approprier commune amie. / J'en voil une avoir moie quite' ('I do not wish, nor can you make me appropriate a common love. I wish to have a love entirely my own').[26] Amant's use of the verb *approprier* is noteworthy, as it appears not only by Raison to describe the fraudulent privatisation of common goods, but also

---

[23] Ovid, *Metamorphoses*, ed. and tr. by Miller, pp. 8–9.
[24] See Huot on the *B* remaniement, which in its long versions demonstrates 'a greater interest in the integration of diverse literary and intellectual traditions, and a greater appreciation for the transformation of the erotic allegory into a vehicle for moral, satirical, and philosophical material' (Huot, *Romance of the Rose*, p. 132).
[25] See Huot's discussion, in *Romance of the Rose*, p. 150, and her appendix with these lines, pp. 360–61. Huot sees Amant's desire to possess the Rose privately as owing to his 'courtly ethos' (p. 150).
[26] Huot, *Romance of the Rose*, p. 360, ll. 275–77.

in Ami's discussion of the original privatisation after the fall from the Golden Age. He explains that in the wake of corrupt government, people covetously appropriated (*par covoitise aproprierent*) what had previously been common (*ce qui conmun iert devant*), like the sun and the wind (ll. 9629 and 9631; p. 173). Amant, by contrast, does not speak against such privatisation, but uses *approprier* to mean taking ownership of a common love object. Huot observes that Amant seems to have difficulty distinguishing between Raison and La Vieille – between desire for an unlimited abstract human capacity and the 'common love' advocated by the bawd.[27] That confusion is surely the source of some of the humour in this revised scene – Amant speaks to Raison as though she were a prostitute. But because Amant's mistake is one of literal reading, it also reinforces Amant's role as a pursuer of private property in literal terms. The debate between Amant and Raison revolves around their different understandings of what it means to move from the individual to the general. For Raison, to love commonly is to love an extracted quality inherent in all individual versions of a species; for Amant, to love commonly is to bestow love on a large and indeterminate number of individual objects.

This conflict between allegorical and literal readings legible in Raison's conversation with Amant points us to Aristotle's *Politics* as an unacknowledged literal referent that troubles the allegorical treatment of Golden Age politics. Amant rejects Raison based on principles recognisable as the justification of private property found in the *Politics*, a text translated *c.* 1265 by William of Moerbeke, just prior to Jean's composition of the *Rose*. The *Politics* was immediately taken up in university curricula, with commentaries by Albertus Magnus and Thomas Aquinas written within the first decade of its circulation.[28] While Jean does not cite the text of the *Politics*, he engages directly with its questions and understandings of why private property is preferable. Aristotle's work argues against the idealising of a political regime in which all land and other wealth, women and children are held in common. In refuting the claims for the desirability of common property in Plato's *Republic*, Aristotle casts common ownership as itself political – one option for constructing the state – rather than pre-political. Moreover, he argues that the terms 'common' and 'property' are mutually exclusive – the very nature of belonging is private.

---

[27] Ibid., p. 151.
[28] Dunbabin, 'Reception and Interpretation'; Martin, 'Some Medieval Commentaries'.

## (Masculine) Political Animals

The translation of Aristotle's *Politics*, with its definition of the human as a 'political animal' (*civile animal*, I.2, 1253a), did not introduce a radically new idea into medieval thought, but its academic reception nevertheless inaugurated an endeavour to elaborate, methodically, the nature of human sociality.[29] In the commentaries, this elaboration meant – among other things – squaring the 'naturalness' of human political association with understandings of the Fall as a fall into politics, often equated with princely rule and private property. The notion of an idealised 'golden' pre-political age is unthinkable for Aristotle, since humans who are separated from law and justice (*separatum a lege et iustitia*) are the worst of all animals, just as humankind at its most virtuous and perfect is the best animal (I.2, 1253a).[30] After defining the components of political community – slaves, family, property and money – in the first book of the *Politics*, Aristotle turns to understanding the best way for a society to be ruled, the first question being what is to be shared. A given society might share everything, nothing or some things (II.1, 1260b). Aristotle agrees with the Socrates of Plato's *Republic* that communities should be as united as possible, but disagrees with the sharing of wives, children and property that Socrates recommended towards that goal.[31] He argues, ultimately, that sharing ownership of objects is not a means toward unity.

A major objection to the common holding of wives, children and property takes the form of a lesson in grammar and logic, a lesson resonant with Raison and Amant's debate. Whereas Socrates argued that the unified voice of everyone (*omnes*) proclaiming things 'mine' or 'not mine' signified political unity, Aristotle counters that the double meaning of 'all' (*omnes*) speaks against such an idea (II.3, 1261b). As Aquinas explains in his commentary, the statement 'this is mine' (*hoc est meum*) can be understood collectively (*collective*) – as referring to property communally held – or distributively (*distributive*) – as referring to individually held property

---

[29] See Toste, 'Naturalness of Human Association', pp. 120–21. For the Latin, see Aristotle, *Aristotelis Politicorum Libri Octo*, ed. by Susemihl, cited by book/chapter and Bekker numbers.

[30] Toste, 'Naturalness of Human Association', p. 118, discusses the fact that scholastic commentaries on the *Politics* had to address the question of the associability of the speculative religious life.

[31] Garnsey, *Thinking about Property*, argues that Aristotle intentionally simplified *The Republic*'s vision of the ideal city as recommending full sharing of wives, children and property throughout the entire city (pp. 26–27 and 6–30, *passim*), with the aim of 'sharpening the dialectic he was conducting with him' (p. 27).

(II.ii.185; II.ii.1).³² Against the argument of *The Republic* that communal ownership will universalise the strong attachments that people have to their private belongings, Aristotle argues that communal ownership evacuates the sense of individual attachment and affection. Belonging, by its nature, is exclusive. As Aquinas glosses, 'Ex hoc enim ipso quod est proprium huius, non est alterius' (II.ii.185; II.ii.1: 'For by the very fact that it belongs to this person, it does not belong to another') – the very idea of collective ownership is revealed to be a paradox.

This argument about the grammar and logic of possession is linked to assumptions about human psychology and emotion. Aristotle observes that people take better care of their own property than of common property, an argument restated by Aquinas that 'propria magis homines amant et procurant quam communia' (II.ii.187; II.ii.3: 'human beings love more, and take better care of, their own things than they do common things').³³ Friendship itself diminishes in a political community in which wives and children are common, and in such a society 'mimime dicere "meum" aut filium patrem aut patrem filium' (II.iii.193; II.iii.4: 'fathers and sons rarely call sons or fathers "mine"'). Aquinas attributes the intimacy to the words themselves, with feeling arising from language, explaining further,

> Unde familiaritas, quae ex istis nominibus provenit in civitate, qua unus dicit, hic est meus pater vel filius aut frater, parum curabitur si quilibet antiquior de quolibet iuniore dicat eum esse suum filium, et e converso, quilibet iunior dicat quemlibet antiquiorem esse suum patrem, et omnes coaetanei dicant se esse fratres.

> Intimacy arises in the political community from the words one uses when one calls a particular person one's father, son, or brother. And so people will care little about such intimacy if anyone older should call anyone younger his son, or, conversely, anyone younger should call anyone older his father, or all of the same age should call themselves brothers. (II.iii.4; II.iii.193)

The sweetness of vocabularies of attachment are thus diluted if wives and children are common. Aristotle uses the analogy of the imperceptibility of a little sweetness (*dulce*) mixed into a great quantity of water (II.5; 1262b).³⁴ It is, Aristotle says, 'indescribably pleasurable' (*delectationem*

---

³² Citations to Thomas's commentary give the book, lecture and comment numbers first in Spiazzi's edition, then in Regan's translation.

³³ On Aquinas's attitude toward private property, see Minnis, *From Eden to Eternity* (2016), pp. 117, 130.

³⁴ Carruthers, *Experience of Beauty*, pp. 80–107, discusses the sweetness of style recommended in ancient rhetoric in connection with medieval medical, religious and aesthetic discourses.

*inenarrabile*) to think about something as one's own (*putare aliquid proprium*, II.5; 1263a).

Aristotle makes the case, therefore, for the benefits of private ownership, with the additional argument that private property will be and should be publicly shared – a distinction between ownership and use. Virtue in fact depends upon this distinction enabled by private property. Aristotle gives the examples of generosity, in that one must have property to give or share, and restraint, in that another must have claim to his own wife for one to exercise sexual restraint in her presence (II.5; 1263b). As if overhearing nostalgic praise for a golden age of common property, the philosopher criticises those who would blame current evils on the fact that property is not common. He specifies that he speaks of 'disceptationes ... circa contractuum et falsorum testimoniorum iudicia, et divitum adulationes' ('disputes over contracts and judgments based on false testimony, and fawning over the rich'). But in these cases, he avers, 'nihil fit propter incommunicationem, sed propter malitiam' (II.5; 1263b: 'these things arise out of wickedness, not from the lack of sharing'). For Aristotle, political unity actually arises from education, emerging out of shared customs, philosophy and laws (*consuetudinibus, et philosophia, et legibus*, II.5; 1264a). Moreover, unity demands some level of division, for one cannot speak about the harmony of a single note (II.5; 1263b).

In the commentaries on the *Politics* that take *quaestio* form, one sees the question of common ownership of women, children and property being raised for discussion.[35] Peter of Auvergne (d. 1304) includes treatments of questions that would seem to have settled answers (e.g., whether incest is sinful according to nature and in itself), and yet nevertheless raise problems concerning the differences between animals and humans and how to understand 'nature' when raised in the context of social formations. On Book II, Peter discusses 'whether the property of a political community should be common' ('utrum possessiones civitatis debent esse communes') and 'whether it is advantageous for the women and children of the political community to be common, as Plato explains' ('utrum expediens sit ciuitati mulieres et pueros esse communes, sicut soluit Plato').[36] Peter typically resolves these discussions by following Aristotle's arguments, stating for example that common ownership of wives and children diminishes

---

[35] For a listing of questions in some commentaries on the *Politics*, see Flüeler, *Rezeption*, II, 101–68.
[36] Peter of Auvergne, *Questiones super libros Politicorum*, Book II, qq. 4, 6. I am grateful to Marco Toste for sharing a portion of his forthcoming edition of the *Questiones* in draft form, as well as for his extraordinarily helpful comments on this essay. See also the partial edition and list of questions in Flüeler, *Rezeption*, I, 169–227 and II, 101–12.

friendship, and thus the appropriation (*appropriatio*) of wives and children is inexpedient. Yet he also elaborates on the relevance of broader questions, such as the relationship between the pleasure of ownership and Aristotle's definition of happiness in Book X of the *Nicomachean Ethics*. Peter distinguishes between contemplative and practical or political ways of life, as Aristotle does, and argues that, since pleasure increases happiness (*delectatio adauget operationem felicem*) and as wise politics (*prudentiam politicam*) guides the action essential for the achievement of happiness, then private property should be promoted (though its use should be communal).[37]

Giles of Rome's *De regimine principum* treats these questions in the beginning of Book III, where he discusses the community of the city and argues against Socrates's and Plato's recommendations for communal ownership.[38] Contrary to the idea that common property would minimise strife, Giles argues that it would increase strife, as men are typically self-deceived about their own proper good, believing they should possess more than they in fact need (III.1.9). He follows Aristotle in explaining that the love of a few children known certainly to belong to oneself is greater than the love of many children of uncertain parentage. Taking up the metaphor of honey and water, he explains that the love of two or three children will not make innumerable children pleasing and beloved (*non posset reddere placibilem et dilectam*, III.1.10); and, further, when love is diminished, care is diminished accordingly. Again citing Book II of the *Politics*, Giles notes that Aristotle acknowledges the seeming wisdom of Socrates's ideas, and the attractiveness of the idea of a city organised for maximum unity, but actual experience shows that such an organisation does not lead to the greatest peace and prosperity (III.1.11).

As these examples indicate, the philosophical reception of Aristotle's *Politics* makes explicit and concrete what the *Rose* engages with more implicitly – the language and concepts offered by political philosophy for exploring human sociality in terms of pleasure, desire and practical happiness. In the *Rose* and in contemporary commentaries, the *Politics* inspires an investigation of the desire for possession, the relationship between language and the world and how the pleasure of one's relationship to the world is legible in language use. While explicitly countering any

---

[37] Peter of Auvergne, *Questiones super libros Politicorum*, II.6.
[38] Kempshall, *Common Good*, p. 145, discusses Giles's interpretation of Plato's community of wives as having a 'spiritual, not material, sense'. For the Latin text cited in what follows, see the Rome, 1607 edition, beginning at sig. Dd3ᵛ.

Arts of Love and Justice: Le Roman de la Rose    173

idealisation of primitive humanity, the *Politics* addresses the same questions as Golden Age mythology: What is an ideal political community? How does community relate to the division of property? Yet where fables of Golden Age societies typically speak in unmarked terms about human comity and common possessions, Aristotelian political philosophy speaks in terms of gendered power dynamics, masculine ownership and the fate of women as property. Even as Jean's *Rose* is repeatedly compelled by narratives of the loss of an idyllic political scene, it is also interested in exposing the logical and historical fallacies of these tales and in bringing to bear the gendered realities and psychological insights of Aristotelian political theory.

### 'Sanz rapine': Literalising the Golden Age

Raison's directive to 'aime les touz' may thus be read as one response in the *Rose* to the larger intellectual questions raised by Aristotle's *Politics*, a response that inaugurates a series of poetic disputes about the potentials and drawbacks of the pursuit of collective ownership. Her recommendation of love for all, communally, establishes virtuous love as pre-political, an understanding reinforced by her claim that such love precedes and supersedes Justice. Amant, for his part, places his experience of possessive love outside politics, telling Raison that he does not wish to submit his version of love to judgement against Justice (ll. 5455–6; p. 112). Ami, however, takes Amant's erotic, possessive love for an individual object and places it back in a political framework. Material possessions structure the conversation between Ami and Amant from the very moment of Ami's entry into the world of the poem. He fulfils the role of friend in a time of need, in this case Amant's material impoverishment, a condition that is impeding Amant's ability to woo the rosebud with gifts. Ami's turn to the Golden Age is inspired by his critique of feminine acquisitiveness. In the midst of advice to Amant about moderate gift-giving, Ami oscillates between condemnations of the universal avarice of women, exchanging themselves for material goods, and positing the possibility of a love object who might be 'leaus de queur' ('loyal of heart', l. 8278; p. 153). As he once again swings toward descriptions of women madly running after 'borsees' ('purses', l. 8322; p. 154), he turns to a nostalgic vision of a former age when love affairs were 'sanz covoitise et sanz rapines' ('without greed or rapine', l. 8330; p. 154) and when 'sanz rapine et sanz covoitise / s'entracoloient et besoient' (ll. 8402–3; p. 155: 'without rapine or covetousness, they would embrace and kiss each other'). In Ami's version of paradise, possessive, erotic love somehow coexists with communal property, and law is present, yet uncorrupted, allowing people to live 'par leaus amiabletez' ('in lawful companionship', l. 8414; p. 155).

The negative language used to describe this paradisal state raises logical problems for understanding the place of politics in Ami's Golden Age. Ami declares, intriguingly, 'N'encor n'avoit fet roi ne prince / Meffez, qui l'autrui tost et pince. / Trestuit pareill estre soloient / ne riens propre avoir ne voloient' (ll. 8415–18; pp. 155–56: 'No king or prince had yet committed any crime by robbery or seizure. All were accustomed to being equal, and no one wanted any possessions of his own'). These are ambiguous statements: Are the kings and princes present, but behaving well? Or do they not exist yet? If they are present, how are we to imagine a society in which all are equal and without property, and yet kings and princes have their roles to play? It is possible that the lines are meant to suggest that, in Ami's Golden Age, law is instinctive, and thus law and rule are present as internal, uncorrupted principles and the as-yet non-stealing princes are not there. On the other hand, as Minnis observes, Aquinas imagined that even in Eden dominion and hierarchy existed in the form of a 'managerial elite' who worked toward the common good rather than for profit.[39] Depending on how one interprets Ami's words, they may suggest the possibility of the compatibility of Aristotelian politics and paradise, or the opposing cynical notion that positive political structures are identical with corruption and lawlessness. If the latter sense is taken, then it is impossible to imagine a king without criminality. By expressing the absence of robbery alongside an absence of desire for possession *tout court*, Ami's discourse points up not only the difficulty of imagining ideals of equality and communalism, but the way these concepts lose their integrity without the contrasting framework of princely rule, private property and rapine.[40]

Ami's return to his discussion of political origins after the excursion of the *mari jaloux* reinforces this critique. After the emergence of poverty and vice, he explains, people had 'la grant ardeur d'avoir aquerre' (l. 9547; p. 172: 'burning desire to acquire possessions'). With this ardour inflamed, property-holding and structures of governance emerge simultaneously: 'Aus proprietez lors se tindrent, / la terre meïsmes partirent' (ll. 9562–3; p. 172: 'Then they held properties, and they even divided up the earth'). After electing 'un grant vilain' ('a great scoundrel', l. 9579; p. 172) to rule them, the ruler was robbed, and – at the urging of the people – a policing

---

[39] Minnis, *From Eden to Eternity* (2016), pp. 116–17.
[40] On the apophatic character of Ami's discourse, see Morton, *Philosophical Context*, p. 100.

force and taxation emerge. Such, Ami explains, is the origin of princely rule. Political structures themselves arise to remedy vice, but are simultaneously – as in the speech of Raison – vehicles of further conflict and corruption.

The same ironic, negative logic applies to Ami's representation of Golden Age lovers, 'sanz' rapine and greed. These lovers do not commit injurious acts of theft – *rapine* – and they do not harbour desires aimed at the belongings of another – *covetise*. Ami thus describes a community in which erotic love could be experienced without sinful desire for or appropriation of property, an eroticisation of Raison's paradise in which the reign of love obviates the need for justice. Yet the gendered terms in which Ami has already discussed the failures of women raise questions about the scene that he has here constructed. If men as well as women love *sanz rapine* – without robbery or rape – we are already imagining that a woman 'belongs' properly to a particular man. In his attempt to illuminate a paradise in which erotic pleasure can coincide with an idealised, pre-political space, Ami cannot help but suggest that erotic pleasure is inextricably tied to possession, and thus to politics. 'Leaus amiabletez' carries with it an impossible ideal of pleasurable property without possession. Ami's evocation of an idyllic Golden Age reveals that all of its supposed pleasures depend precisely upon the corrupt features of the fallen world – the drives toward acquisition, of material goods and women.

Ami's paradoxical ideal is not, however, an inevitable outcome of attempts to imagine political origins. Genius also speaks of an age of Jupiter marked by the parcelling out of land, though the pre-agricultural period is not linked to any notion of idealised love, suggesting that the Golden Age myth does not demand a link between common property and non-acquisitive love to be legible. With La Vieille, furthermore, we discover that it is possible to address a time before the law without positing a 'golden' former age. Her discourse instead exposes the false fantasy of a previously existing natural paradise in which property and women are held without conflict. In her pessimistic view of the primitive world prior to the law, human sociality is threatened by unbridled masculine rapaciousness.[41]

---

[41] The subversive possibility of La Vieille's speech has long been a question in criticism on the *Rose*. Kay, 'Body of Knowledge', p. 218, observes that, unlike other feminine speakers in the poem (e.g., Raison), 'the Vieille identifies herself *as* a woman' and that she both embodies and subverts misogynistic discourse. Morton, 'Where are the Bodies?', p. 137, argues that the poem signals the masculine origins of La Vieille's speech via allusions to Ovid and Aristotle that could not believably be voiced by an uneducated former prostitute, thus undercutting any subversive potential.

La Vieille's refusal of mythology and allegorical truth places her in the realm of experimental, empirical truth – aligned with both her autobiographical experience and the literal truths of the university arts curriculum. She is an arts master, though she did not attend a school of love where students are instructed in theory (*l'en leüst la theorique*) and she knows everything by practice (*par la practique*, ll. 12773 and 12774; p. 222).[42] She here makes a distinction between theory and practice, authority and experience, but also lays ironic claim to the faculty of arts and the domain of practical philosophy – she can lecture from a chair (*en chaiere*) with her endless knowledge (l. 12787; p. 222). Her language of practical experimentation – *experimenz* have made her wise (l. 12775; p. 222) – aligns her with the knowledge claims of the poem's *apologia*, which begs forgiveness for its denigration of women, meant only to educate men about women and women about themselves.[43] The narrator claims that he merely follows the learning of worthy men, who knew the ways of women 'car touz esprovez les avoient, / et tex es fames les troverent / que par divers tans esproverent' (ll. 15200–2; p. 259: 'because they had tested them all and had found such ways in women by testing at various times'). La Vieille has conducted her own tests and discovered differently. As Wetherbee observes, La Vieille 'is able to deduce empirically from the experience of a full life in a fallen world the vestiges of that responsiveness to Nature which Raison had taken for granted'.[44] And yet, like one of her most famous progeny, Chaucer's Wife of Bath, La Vieille engages 'not just with male authority but with male methods of argument', allowing her forms of knowledge that exceed feminine experience.[45]

La Vieille's discourse not only competes with the allegorical 'truths' articulated elsewhere in the poem, but also reveals the ironies of the unstated assumptions of scholastic philosophy. In her speech, a feminine voice speaks both as unrealised potential subject of politics and as the personified object of that politics as it exists – in both theory and practice. In her role as master, she speaks from experiential authority, and is thus motivated simultaneously to teach and to accomplish revenge against the

---

[42] Kay, 'Body of Knowledge', p. 218, notes that she is the only figure in the poem who speaks in the form of a university lecture.
[43] Guynn, 'Authorship and Sexual Violence,' p. 653, argues that the apologia excludes women as epistemological subjects, making this passage part of a 'larger attempt to exclude women from public speech and to universalise a male subject'.
[44] Wetherbee, 'Literal and Allegorical', p. 278.
[45] Minnis, *Fallible Authors* (2008), p. 253. Although, as Minnis notes, La Vieille sticks to the topic of love (the 'olde daunce'), his reading of the Wife of Bath as (occasional) *doctrix* can open up readings of Jean de Meun's old bawd as well (p. 259).

men who abandoned her once she lost her beauty – authority and passionate emotion are here brilliantly and impossibly intertwined. Her only vengeance, she explains, is to teach her doctrine (*par aprendre ma doctrine*, l. 12849; p. 223), and part of her teaching has directly to do with an acknowledgement of the erotic drive to private possession and the link between pleasure and private property. La Vieille advises Bel Acueil that he should promise every potential lover – even if there are a thousand suitors – that he alone will have the rose, swearing to the rose's indivisibility. At the same time, she reveals that this drive is gendered masculine, for she advises women never to place their hearts in one man alone – such a singular love will lead necessarily to her unfreedom and enslavement, as men inevitably abandon women when they are bored. La Vieille is pleased with her student, whom she judges to be writing down her teaching 'ou livre du queur' ('in the book of [his] heart', l. 13471; p. 232). She is confident that he will continue his studies and 'seraiz mestres con gié' ('become a master like me', l. 13475; p. 233), with a license to teach. She continues with advice about how to effectively 'pluck' men of their wealth. It is a consistent irony that she speaks as an Aristotelian arts master, yet uses that mode of discourse to produce truths outside its purview. She shows the mistakes of not recognising women as subjects, but then proves her inability to inhabit the position of an Aristotelian political subject.

La Vieille's version of a discourse of 'former' times involves a disquisition on the natural inclinations of men and women that were bridled by the imposition of law and governance. She explains that 'women are born free' and that law takes away their natural freedom. Nature 'nous a fez . . . / toutes por touz et touz por toutes, / chascune por chascun conmune / et chascun conmun a chascune' (ll. 13855–58; p. 238: 'has made all us women for all men and all men for all women, each woman common to every man and every man common to each woman'). Her gendered rhyming and wordplay here – the chiasmic structure of the lines enclosing the masculine 'all' and 'each man' by 'all women' and 'each woman', respectively – serves as a riposte to Raison's unmarked (but masculine) 'conme un / conmun'. In La Vieille's description of primitive humankind, the men and women of former times are equally erotic subjects and potential subjects of politics. Yet they enter into political life – here equated with marriage – asymmetrically. In La Vieille's telling, marriage is necessary because the rapacious and capricious character of men harms women: 'car quant chascun jadis vaiet / la fame qui mieuz li saiet, / maintenant ravir la vosist, / se plus fort ne la li tosist, / et la lessast, s'il li pleüst / quant son voloir fete en eüst' (ll. 13877–82; p. 238: 'In former times, when a man saw the woman who suited him, he wanted to carry her off immediately, if someone stronger did not take her away from him; / and he left her, if he pleased, when he had done his will with her'). Women are only 'par loi prises et mariees' ('captured by law and married', l. 13860; p. 238) so as to prevent masculine contention and murder and to help in the rearing of children. Marriage, as conventional human law, usefully restricts men, discouraging them from murder and the abandonment of offspring, but it restricts the freedom of women, who chafe at its bonds.

Rape, considered in generalised, mythographic terms, as in Ami's discourse, may be left unspecified – a vicious act belonging to a fallen contemporary world, but not to an idealised past. But La Vieille demonstrates the way that the methodical literalism of scholastic philosophy demands that genders, if not individual faces, be placed on the consideration of ethical and political acts. Aquinas's treatment of robbery (*rapina*) and theft (*furtum*) as distinct property crimes in the *Summa* similarly illustrates the way that scholastic method can bring gendered perspectives into view. In his third proposed objection to the notion that robbery and theft are different crimes – one performed openly, one secretly – Aquinas notes that rape is not differentiated by whether it is done secretly or not – it is rape in either case (IIaIIae, q. 66, art. 4, obj. 3). His reply counters, however, that 'raptus mulieris non potest esse occultus ex parte mulieris quae rapitur' (rep. 3: 'the robbery of a woman cannot be secret on the part of the woman who is taken') and thus the specific nature of the injury suffered may be different for the woman than for those from whom she was stolen. Aquinas's logic here suggests that the understanding of certain acts with respect to property are obscured when women are seen only as property, any crime committed as against her guardian, and she is not seen as a human subject with her own access to reality.

La Vieille addresses both logical and empirical contradictions and elisions in the discourse of Ami, acknowledging that any Golden Age in which property was held in common must also posit an erotic world in which women are held in common. Her Golden Age makes both women and men into political and erotic subjects, but instead of a primitive ideal it is rather a telos installed by Nature that has never in fact been experienced. Any notion of a primitive, paradisal state is obviated by masculine tendencies toward rapine – not of goods, but of women defined as goods, belonging to other men. La Vieille's voice is disruptive precisely because she offers a 'realistic' portrayal of human nature rooted in the discourse of the thirteenth-century arts faculty – she speaks of actual human political subjects rather than an obscured fantasy of prelapsarian common love. In

La Vieille's teaching, the Golden Age is not to be contrasted with narratives of primitive human violence, but primitive masculine violence, specifically. Claims about an originary unmarked 'human' condition cannot survive contact with the teaching of the old bawd.

In La Vieille's terms, 'justice' comes to be defined not as a system of laws and governance, but a natural teleology. She concludes her discussion of human struggle against the bonds of chastity with the claim that 'Ainsinc Nature nos joutise, / qui noz queurs a deliz attise' (ll. 14127–8; p. 242: 'Thus Nature regulates us [makes us just] by inciting our hearts to pleasure'). Justice, for La Vieille, is not a political principle, but a telos installed by nature, oriented toward pleasure.[46] From one perspective, this animal, bodily pleasure is not grammatical – not the pleasure of saying 'this is mine' – and thus seems distant from the political pleasure of claiming a possession in distinction from another. And yet, the *Rose* has already constructed for us a world in which Amant's drive to possess the rose – his mode of natural regulation or 'joutice' – is linked to questions of common versus private ownership at the human political origin. We might then reconsider the actual distance between Aristotle's indescribable pleasure in thinking about one's own things and Ovid's evocation of sexual contact as the beginnings of human sociality.

Jean de Meun's *Rose* offers an exploration of the gaps between the allegorical and the literal, gaps exposed by the erotic drive narrativised in the poem. The poem's turn with La Vieille from the fabular mode to the purportedly historical does not expose a 'true' representation of man's primitive state, but resolves allegorical truths about the 'human' condition into a gendered – if still generalised – reality. In a political sphere in which women are to be considered in the same category as property, the heterosexual desire for erotic possession will always be political, and will inevitably be an asymmetrically gendered desire.[47] What the *Rose* provokes us to consider is whether the political, in turn, is always erotic, inevitably refracted through the pleasures of possession.

---

[46] On La Vieille's 'determinism', see Robertson, *Nature Speaks*, p. 129.

[47] Beyond the scope of this essay is the relevance of Rubin's 'Traffic in Women', which informs my thoughts here. Her classic essay questions the fiction that 'the exchange of women' founds all culture, examining this myth as justification for women's lesser social status. See Parvulescu, 'European Kinship', for a reflection on the continued significance of Rubin's argument.

CHAPTER 9

# The Many Sides of Personification
## Rhetorical Theory and *Piers Plowman*

### Nicolette Zeeman

One working definition of allegorical narrative is that it is a text that comes into being at the confluence of two or more mutually glossing or interpreting discourses, one of which has some kind of narrative or ecphrastic element. As a result, allegorical narrative inevitably encourages several dimensions of interpretation. Given that multiplicity of this sort is present in all language, of course, what we call allegorical narrative (or just 'allegory') merely foregrounds or exaggerates a fundamental feature of all language. The identification of a text as allegorical may therefore be a matter of emphasis and orientation rather than an absolute distinction. Nevertheless, it is also true that, in its more extreme forms, allegorical narrative is characteristically multi-dimensional, episodic and contrastive; it is also often oppositional, argumentative and formally disruptive. There are few fixed rules about how it is put together. Viewed across time and in terms of genre, allegorical narrative is eclectic and flexible about the forms and discourses it uses, its modes of figuration and the degree to which it includes explicitly analytical or preceptive language – as the diverse examples of the *Aeneid*, the *Cosmographia*, the *Roman de la Rose*, the *Pelerinage de vie humaine*, *Piers Plowman*, the *House of Fame*, *Mankynde*, the *Faerie Queene*, *The Castle*, *Bleak House*, *Ulysses* and *Mother Courage* make clear.[1]

In the Middle Ages and early modernity, allegorical narrative often uses highly developed forms of *prosopopoeia* and personification – linked and overlapping figures that were in antique and medieval rhetorical theory often identified with each other. Although *prosopopoeia* and personification are by no means identical with allegory,[2] they are like allegory more generally in that they involve a substantial degree of discursive multi-

---

[1] See Fletcher, *Allegory*; Quilligan, *Language of Allegory*; Whitman, *Allegory*; Teskey, *Allegory and Violence*; Copeland and Struck (eds), *The Cambridge Companion to Allegory*; Crawford, *Allegory and Enchantment*; Silk, 'Invoking the Other'; Zeeman, *Arts of Disruption*.
[2] Paxson, *Poetics of Personification*, p. 1; arguing for the connection, however, see Breen, 'Introduction'.

dimensionality. Nevertheless, this chapter is primarily about *prosopopoeia* and personification, and about allegory only by wider association.

In their most easily recognisable forms, the figures of *prosopopoeia* and personification denote a speaker (in the case of *prosopopoeia*, at any rate), animate being or 'person' with potentially genericising features, a characterising historical or personal story, or a name that is a noun or concept. Within the figure of *prosopopoeia*/personification any number of elements or structures can comment on and interpret each other: 'character', name, history, category, concept, body, gender, face, feature, clothing, action, speech or rhetorical dilation. The figure achieves new heights of inventiveness in the vernacular literature of the later Middle Ages. However, sometime in the later seventeenth to eighteenth centuries writers seem to lose the sense that elaborate forms of *prosopopoeia*/personification, especially those that foreground their own discursive multi-dimensionality, are an engaging tool for organising complex meaning. This is usually associated with moves toward some kind of narrative naturalism. Where personifications survive, it is often in more overtly poetic or figurative genres, but even when they do, they tend to take a somewhat schematic and depleted form; as a result, in this later period personifications are often subject both to the criticism that they are too poetical, intellectual or 'unnatural' (surely they were always unnatural?) and the criticism that they are facilely simplistic and reductive.[3] Of course, many modern texts do still contain what are in effect personifications, and many of them are just as strange and non-naturalistic as medieval or early modern ones; nevertheless, these figures tend to be superficially naturalised within fictional or dramatic forms, and as a result usually not acknowledged as such. Kafka's Klamm and the assistants, Dickens's Harold Skimpole and Mr Krook, the dead son of Bloom in Joyce and Brecht's Mother Courage are all personifications of a sort.

Perhaps as a result of this later historical shift to different styles of allegory and personification, I think it is sometimes still hard for modern readers to recognise the wit and dynamism of medieval and early modern personification, with its boldly 'compound' or multi-dimensional forms (sometimes partly naturalising, but always partly not).[4] It seems clear that what made *prosopopoeia*/personification a thought-provoking thing in the Middle Ages was precisely its many-sidedness – one version of which is its

---

[3] See Silk, 'Invoking the Other'.
[4] Paxson, *Poetics of Personification*, pp. 39–40; see also Griffiths, *Personification*; Mann, *Langland and Allegory*; Raskolnikov, *Body against Soul*.

endlessly inventive exploitation of the potentially contradictory polarities of person/body/speaker and term/concept/generic dimension/discursive exploration. A recent essay collection on personification in the *Yearbook of Langland Studies* emphasises the work of embodiment, metonymy, person and animacy in the personifications of *Piers Plowman*.[5] While anthropomorphic forms, bodies, speech and even the appearance of inner psychological life can be glossed and nuanced by words, ideas, precepts and their dilation, it is also the case that words, ideas, precepts and dilations can be glossed and nuanced by anthropomorphic forms, bodies, speech or imagined inner life. In this chapter, however, I will be emphasising a different tendency in some of the recurring or long-sustained personifications of *Piers Plowman*. I will be investigating the extreme ways that the conceptual, and often seemingly 'naturalistic', continuities of these anthropomorphic, speaking personifications are complicated and disrupted by the addition of dimensions that can only be described as contrastive, contradictory and most definitely non-naturalistic. Figures such as Piers Plowman, Conscience, Pacience and Haukyn, whom we might have been tempted to read as Langland's more recognisable and coherent 'characters', in fact change radically and – for a modern reader with residually naturalising expectations about narrative, person and personification – counterintuitively in meaning. In *Piers Plowman*, the art of personification achieves a highpoint of mimetic and colloquial immediacy and yet, paradoxically and surprisingly, also of multi-valency and non-naturalness.

In the last part of the chapter, I will revisit these four personifications, asking of each of them the perhaps surprising question, 'lay or ordained?' To a modern reader it may seem bizarre to be unclear about whether a protagonist is a priest or not, but I will argue that Langland does indeed cultivate this ambiguity. If he does, this illustrates once again the many-sidedness of his personifications. But it may also have implications for reading the poem: it might reveal some of Langland's reservations about the role of the institutional church, and it might also tell us what he thinks is important about a given 'person'. It may, in other words, say something about the broader cast of Langland's spiritual thought. Whether or not someone is ordained may matter less to Langland than the much more difficult question of what kind of moral or spiritual place they seem to occupy or be seeking.

---

[5] See Breen, 'Introduction'; Orlemanski, 'Langland's Poetics of Animation'; Waters, 'Voice of the Sluggard'; Bude, 'Wet Shoes'; Flannery, 'Response'; in the previous issue of the journal, see also Calabrese, 'Posthuman *Piers*?'.

Before I get to *Piers Plowman*, however, I will first revisit the Latin rhetorical theory of personification inherited from antiquity by the Middle Ages and its continued life through the period. As we will see, the structural contradictions – the hybridities – of medieval *prosopopoeial* personification are in many ways already laid out in these Latin rhetorical texts.

It is a great pleasure to write this essay for Alastair Minnis, without whose groundbreaking and endlessly generous work on medieval scholastic theories of literary form, the rhetoric of affect and the classification of the arts, so much recent medieval scholarship, including my first book, could not have been written. The later part of this essay may also recall Alastair's work explaining the late medieval indulgence and embedding 'Piers's protean pardon' in the scholastic theology of Langland's day. If in this essay Alastair illustrates the very non-scholastic and non-technical ways that Langland talks about the institutional practices of the church, here I too will develop some ideas about the way that Langland's personifications reveal his ambivalence about the institution of ordination and the status of the priesthood.[6]

What we call personification classical and medieval theorists named (amongst other things) *traductio, immutatio, prosopopoeia, conformatio* or *ethopoeia*. Long associated with *enargeia*, the 'enlivening' of the text, this figure of thought takes many forms in the Middle Ages, and definitions of it oscillate between those that emphasise its substitutive nature (as an anthropomorphic figure that 'stands in for' or 'animates' something)[7] and those that emphasise its speakerly nature (most recognisable to modern readers as *prosopopoeia*).[8] We might not only say that the figure shares in the multiple discursivity that characterises allegorical narrative more generally, but also that the figure's dynamism is a result of its own particular versions of structural hybridity.

---

[6] On Piers's pardon, see Minnis, *Valuing the Vernacular* (2009), ch. 3.
[7] Several twentieth-century works on personification emphasise animate abstraction: see Frank, 'Art of Reading'; Griffiths, *Personification*; Bloomfield, 'Grammatical Approach'.
[8] For readers who emphasise the speakerly aspect of personification, see Paxson, *Poetics of Personification*; Alexander, 'Prosopopeia'; Zeeman, *Arts of Disruption*, pp. 19–33. This speakerly aspect has been occluded by the post-medieval term 'personification', primarily defined as the animation of inanimate phenomena, perhaps due to the term's seeming association with making a 'person' (from a thing?); though its formulation is in fact analogous to *prosopopoeia*, which also alludes to masks and actors, as does the Classical Latin *persona*. The first *OED* citation for 'personification' is 1728 (s.v. 'personification', 1a). On the later critical history of the figure, see Silk, 'Invoking the Other'.

In *De oratore* Cicero describes the figure as a form of metonymy, the substitution of one term for another 'for the sake of ornament', and his examples include gods' names employed to refer to the phenomenon over which the god has jurisdiction ('Ceres' for corn), but also place names that refer to the people that are in them ('Rome' for its people, 'the curia' for the senate) or objects that refer synecdochically to a related state of being ('the toga' for peace, 'arms' for war); Cicero also cites 'the use of the names of the virtues and vices to stand for the people who possess them ... "where avarice has found its way", or "loyalty has prevailed"'.[9] The *Ad Herennium*, misattributed to Cicero but much more widely disseminated in the Middle Ages than Cicero's later rhetorical writings, says similarly that the figure 'may be applied to a variety of things, mute and inanimate', and cites a city as an example. A related, if implicit, description of personification as animating substitution can be seen in Donatus's fourth-century *Ars grammatica*, which divides metaphor into four types depending on how it combines categories of the inanimate and animate.[10] In the twelfth century, Conrad of Hirsau explains that personification is a kind of metonymy, 'where a container appears in place of that which is contained, that is faith for the faithful person, idolatry for the idolator, and in the same way with the rest, so that the virtuous man is shown by a virtue, and the vicious man by a vice'.[11]

However, some of the other antique and medieval terms that are often used for this figure – *prosopopoeia*, *conformatio*, *ethopoeia* and *adlocutio* – give more weight to the idea that this is a speaking figure.[12] These terms and their associated definitions do not map neatly onto those mentioned above because, although they might denote the substitutive, animating type of personification (somebody standing for something), they tend to refer primarily to historical or mythological individuals. Still, these definitions always associate some kind of generic or conceptual attributes with the historical or mythological individual, thus attributing a generic or

---

[9] Cicero, *De oratore*, III.XLII.167–8, tr. by Rackham, II, 130–33; Cicero does not use the term *prosopopoeia* here, though he does mention 'personarum ficta inductio' at III.LIII.204 (II, 162–63); see Paxson, *Poetics of Personification*, pp. 15–16.

[10] Caplan (ed. and tr.), *Rhetorica ad Herennium*, IV.LIII.66, pp. 400–1; Donatus, *Ars grammatica*, III.6, in Keil (ed.), *Grammatici Latini*, IV, 399; for English see Copeland and Sluiter (eds), *Medieval Grammar and Rhetoric*, p. 97.

[11] Conrad of Hirsau, *Dialogus super auctores*, in Huygens (ed.), *Accessus ad Auctores*, pp. 99–100.

[12] See Paxson, *Poetics of Personification*, pp. 11–22; Specht, '"Ethopoeia" or Impersonation', pp. 1–8; Alexander, 'Prosopopeia', pp. 97–102; James-Raoul, 'La Personnification dans les arts poétiques', pp. 36–47. The originally Greek *prosopopoeia* alludes etymologically to 'face' or 'mask' and also to dramatic *persona*, and so brings with it strongly performative connotations: see Paxson, *Poetics of Personification*, p. 13.

conceptual character to the speaking person. In this second cluster of definitions, however, what is primarily at issue is the attribution of character and speech:

> Another figure of thought which may be used to produce force is the figure called *prosopopoeia*, for example, 'Imagine that your ancestors are rebuking you and speak such words, or imagine Greece or your country in the form of a woman ...'.[13]

Here Demetrius (*On Style*, possibly second-century BC) makes clear that *prosopopoeia* can have a substitutive dimension ('your country in the form of a woman'), but he simultaneously emphasises that this is a figure capable of speech, engaging the attention, interest and feelings of the reader or hearer through the use of words. It is an amplificatory and discursive figure. In *Orator*, as in *De oratore*, Cicero does not use the term *prosopopoeia* (he does not here name it at all); but he nevertheless insists on the speaking nature of this stylistically elevated figure of thought, which may represent the state as speaking, call up the dead or make 'mute objects speak'.[14] Here, in other words, although continuing to emphasise the substitutive or animating aspect of these figures, Cicero gives equal emphasis to their speaking nature – the opportunity for rhetorical dilation and conceptual investigation that they afford. We might note too the huge range of people and things that the figure allows to speak. *Conformatio* is the term of choice in the *Ad Herennium*, where the figure can be either 'a mute thing or one lacking form' made articulate or an 'absent person' made present (the text's second example is 'great Lucius Brutus'). The *Ad Herennium* makes clear that, for the rhetoricians at least, the crucial feature of this figure is speech. If this speech is supposed to be 'in character', that is, in some way clarifying and descriptive of the speaker, this also means amplification, exploration, development; this in turn means that the figure not only has a generic or conceptual dimension, but also that it might reflect on and complicate that dimension:

> [*Conformatio*] consists in representing an absent person as present, or in making a mute thing or one lacking form articulate, and attributing to it a definite form and a language or behaviour appropriate to its character. ... It is most useful in the divisions under 'amplification' and in 'appeal to pity'.[15]

---

[13] Demetrius, *On Style*, 265, tr. by Innes, in Aristotle, *Poetics*, pp. 502–3.
[14] Cicero, *Orator*, XXV.85, XL.138, tr. by Hubbell, in *Brutus*, pp. 368–69, 412–13.
[15] Caplan (ed. and tr.), *Rhetorica ad Herennium*, IV.LIII.66, pp. 398–401; see Paxson, *Poetics of Personification*, pp. 14–15.

This figure is, in other words, a heuristic tool for investigating terms, phenomena, categories or qualities; it performs this investigation by means of anthropomorphised and dramatised verbalisation and ventriloquisation.

The huge variety of forms taken by this figure could be well illustrated from Quintilian, although the *Institutio Oratoria* was not read in its complete form before the fifteenth century.[16] The *Praeexercitamina* of Priscian (*c*. 500), variously available in the Middle Ages, gathers the different forms of this figure and the rhetorical exercises associated with it under the term *adlocutio*, 'the imitation of speech accommodated to imaginary situations and persons': the category is variously subdivided, and it includes *eidolopoiia* – 'when words are put in the mouths of the dead' – and *prosopopoeia*, understood as a substitutive, animating figure, 'as when Cicero gives speech to the fatherland and to the republic'. Priscian also notes that this speech can be part of a dialogue or an internal conversation: 'there are unmixed forms of [*adlocutio*], as when it is posited that someone is speaking to himself; and there are double ones, when he speaks to others'.[17] In Geoffrey of Vinsauf's early thirteenth-century *Poetria nova*, the term used is *prosopopoeia*, and the definition is again substitutive or animating but also associated with speech and amplification: 'Personification, come forth. ... Give power of speech to that which has in itself no such power – let poetic license confer a tongue. So the earth, feeling Phaeton's heat, complained to Jove; so Rome, with dishevelled hair, bewailed in tearful voice the death of Caesar'; Geoffrey's personally composed illustrations include the laments of the cross and nature at the crucifixion.[18] A fourteenth-century German commentary on the *Poetria nova* comments: 'Here he teaches the fifth method of prolonging material, namely through prosopopoeia, which is a kind of speaking attributed to something not possessing the ability to speak'.[19] Vincent of Beauvais puts it even more briefly: 'Prosopopoeia est cum inanimalium et

---

[16] Quintilian, *Orator's Education*, IX.II.29–36 and XI.1.41, ed. and tr. by Russell, IV, 50–53 and V, 30–31. On the medieval reception of the *Institutio*, see Copeland and Sluiter (eds), *Medieval Grammar and Rhetoric*, p. 66.

[17] Priscian, *Praeexercitamina ex Hermogene versa*, in Halm (ed.), *Rhetores Latini Minores*, pp. 557–58; tr. in Miller et al. (eds), *Readings in Medieval Rhetoric*, pp. 64–65 (substantially altered); see Specht, '"Ethopoeia" or Impersonation', p. 5.

[18] Geoffrey of Vinsauf, *Poetria nova*, ll. 462–507, in *Poetria nova and its Sources*, ed. by Gallo; for the English, see *Poetria nova*, tr. by Nims, pp. 33–34; see also ll. 1414–24 (Nims, p. 56). On the influence of the *Ad Herennium* on this text, see Martin Camargo's introduction to Nims's translation, p. 12.

[19] This is the Dominican Reiner von Cappel (d. 1384), cited from Wolfenbüttel, Herzog August Bibliothek MS Guelf. 286 Gud. lat., f. 8ᵛ, by Woods, *Classroom Commentaries*, p. 80 (see also p. 55).

persona et sermo fingitur [*sic*]' ('*Prosopopoiea* is when both person and speech are invented for inanimate things').[20] The general observation to be made here, then, is that *prosopopoeia*/personification participates in the narrative discontinuities that are a feature of much allegorical narrative, with its often 'markedly episodic and hypotactic' nature.[21] But these Latin theorists also point to the way that the figure is structured round constellations of polarities that are always potentially contradictory or at odds with each other. We could describe these polarities as term/concept/discursive exploration versus person/body/speaker; but we might also describe them as seemingly coherent person versus multi-faceted conceptualisation and dilatory speech.

The consequences of such tensions can be seen in many vernacular allegories. To take some well-known examples, in the *Roman de la Rose* personified terms and concepts are repeatedly compromised, complicated and even thrown into question by being made into persons, actants and speakers. I am not just thinking of Danger (the 'resistance' of the rose) falling asleep, or Bel Acueil (the rose's 'fair welcome') being imprisoned; I also have in mind Bel Acueil represented and courted in the form of a man, Raison arguing against erotic love while offering to be Amant's lover, or Nature framing her 'philosophical' discourse on the universe with the acknowledgement that because she is a woman she cannot stop talking. But equally often in the *Rose* both the 'person' and the 'concept' of personification are stretched and subverted to near-breaking point by extreme forms of semantic multi-valency and discursive dilation. The speech of Faux Semblant, for example, segues across many different dimensions of 'false seeming', undermining any single reading of his imagined 'person' or name; Nature's disquisition on the nature of the cosmos is a chiasmus of contradiction and self-subversion; while, in an access of internally conflicted 'philosophy', Genius exhorts his followers to fornicate in order both to save the world and be saved in heaven. We might compare the contradictory effects of many other well-known medieval personifications: the way that the Natura of Alan of Lille's *De Planctu Naturae* talks herself into acknowledging that she is responsible for the abuses of nature about which she complains; the way that Esperance (Hope) in Guillaume de Machaut's *Remede de Fortune* plays the role of Boethius's Lady Philosophy while taking a name and speaking an ideology that entirely contradict Boethian 'philosophy'; the way that in Chaucer's

---

[20] Vincent of Beauvais, *Speculum Doctrinale*, 4.130, cited from the 1494 edition, f. 50$^r$.
[21] Madsen, *Rereading Allegory*, pp. 72–73.

*House of Fame* Fame represents not only a misogynistically 'feminine', fortune-like fickleness, and a personified lie and a truth trying to get out of a spinning twig house, but also the works of Virgil and Ovid. Texts such as these make clear that structural contrast and contradiction are fundamental to the imaginative and conceptual work of much *prosopopoeia*/personification.

This is also true of the figure of *prosopopoeia*/personification in *Piers Plowman*. All-pervasive in the poem, the figure has long been recognised to exemplify its labile and dynamic diegesis, dominating both the detailed workings of the poem's thought and language and also its larger narrative structures. At a local level, Langland's inanimate words are constantly becoming animate ('Sleep and sory sleuþe seweþ hem evere', 'hire moneie and marchaundiȝe marchen togidere', 'siþ charite haþ ben chapman').[22] Michael Calabrese has recently analysed this phenomenon in the poem through the lens of posthumanism, claiming that '"human" agency no longer resides in the single self but is dispersed' across the text.[23] But, as Lavinia Griffiths and Jill Mann showed long ago, the fact that Langland's terms are constantly on the brink of animacy, personification and speech also derives from 'his deep imaginative engagement with the nature of language'.[24] This verbal formulation of the issue also reflects the complex interplay of word, concept, discursivity, animacy and person that underlie the figure of *prosopopoeia*/personification. Echoing Maureen Quilligan's seminal formulations of 'allegory as pun', Mann recognises the fundamental connection between Langland's wordplay and his personifications:

> Language ... not only names the objects that make up our physical life, it also names the invisible qualities which animate the physical world and constitute its hidden dynamics ... Its generative capacities, its transformational powers are the index of the world's multiplicity, multiplicity of dimensions, relationships, potentialities.[25]

Many of Langland's personifications also dilate on themselves and what they represent; as Griffiths says of his confessing vices, 'he gives them their own voice and allows them to create themselves ... through speech'.[26] It is precisely these dilatory personifications who appear over extended passages

---

[22] *Piers Plowman*, B.Prol.45, 63, 64. All citations of *Piers Plowman* refer to Schmidt's parallel text edition, with 'i', 'j', 'u' and 'v' regularised.
[23] Calabrese, 'Posthuman *Piers*?', p. 11 (later he goes on to associate these effects with the poem's incarnational thought: pp. 22–25); see also Bude, 'Wet Shoes'.
[24] Griffiths, *Personification*; Mann, *Langland and Allegory* (citation p. 19).
[25] Mann, *Langland and Allegory*, p. 23; see Quilligan, *Language of Allegory*.
[26] Griffiths, *Personification*, p. 57.

of narrative – several of them also making multiple appearances – that will be my focus here. Despite their informal and lively conversationalism, many of them shift counter-intuitively over the course of their appearances, manifesting themselves as different versions of the term, concept, phenomenon or person that they represent, sometimes simultaneously, but usually sequentially. I am not sure that the provocative disruptiveness of these personifications has been fully appreciated.[27]

It is true that critics such as Griffiths and Mann have recognised aspects of this phenomenon, particularly as it operates at a local level; Griffiths, for example, documents how personification sits at the confluence of many different discourses, and towards the end of her book claims that 'personification is ... the vehicle for the multiple displacements of Langland's allegory'.[28] Edwin Craun has gone so far as to say of Langland's personifications that 'because they are named with polysemous words, they cannot be sustained actants within a narrative', though he does not develop this suggestive claim.[29] Calabrese signals the textual implications of his observations by drawing on the work of David Lawton and A. C. Spearing on textual subjectivity, arguing that 'subjectivity is not only divided among different discourses but dispersed and collective at all levels of the narrative, composition and transmission of the text, provisionally assigned to one name or body but always subject to reattribution and recompilation'.[30] The argument that Langland recognises the complex and compromised nature of human volition and agency is one that I would in many ways endorse even more strongly than Calabrese, who finally pulls back from some of its most radical implications.[31] But Langland's multiple and metamorphic personifications are not just indicators of the shifting nature of subjectivity. They are also being used to explore a whole range of linked but multi-dimensional phenomena that cannot be summed up in single terms, definitions or figures – even as they also highlight for us precisely this fact.

---

[27] For Ralph Hanna, writing recently, personification is 'always static'; Hanna accommodates variation in the speech of Pacience, for example, with the summary observation that Pacience 'remains governed by the rules of personification' and speaks only what it is 'appropriate for [him] to enunciate' (Hanna, *Patient Reading*, pp. 321, 319).
[28] Griffiths, *Personification*, p. 104 and *passim*; Mann, *Langland and Allegory*.
[29] Craun, *Lies, Slander and Obscenity*, p. 158.
[30] Calabrese, 'Posthuman *Piers*?', p. 18 (see also p. 12); see Lawton, 'Subject of *Piers*'; Spearing, *Medieval Autographies*.
[31] Calabrese, 'Posthuman *Piers*?', pp. 29–34; see Zeeman, *Piers Plowman*, ch. 2, and Zeeman, 'Willing'.

It is in my view still hard for modern readers to comprehend the many-sidedness of some of the figures who reappear in *Piers Plowman* or are present for long stretches of it. While readers have recognised the mutating forms of Piers Plowman and the narrator, for example, there have been limits on how much of this mutation they have been prepared to acknowledge in personifications such as Conscience, Pacience or even Haukyn. I believe it is difficult to resist the residually sense-making or naturalising impulse whereby personifications who become familiar over the course of the poem come to feel like recognisable quantities or 'known' persons; it remains tempting to feel that they have some kind of core meaning or identity.[32]

At a small scale, of course, readers have had few such problems. They have noticed how Langland's personifications can take different social roles or even genders, be at one moment aspirational and at another dubious, and oscillate between expressing a conceptual version of their name and a more institutional one. The metamorphic manifestations of Wraþe, 'som tyme a frere', but also implicitly identified with the priestly *possessioners* who attack the friars, and whom they attack in return, have long been observed; Wraþe is also a nunnery and monastery cook, whose 'joutes of janglyng' ensure that spiteful anger is found among both nuns and monks (B.5.135–79).[33] Coveitise segues similarly across the genders and the trades, explaining that he, along with his corrupt ways, has been apprentice to the merchant Symme-atte-Style, but that he is also a cloth seller; 'he' is implicitly also his wife, both a weaver and a brewer; Coveitise has also learned to pare coins, and practises money lending, usury, financial brokerage and theft.[34] Nor have readers had problems with the series of Langlandian personifications that go under the same name as another, apparently distinct, personification: the two personifications named Truþe, the two named Anima, and the three called Pees, all of whom look very different from each other.[35] Readers have also explored other, more thought-provoking forms of many-sidedness in the poem's personifications:

---

[32] In this essay I hope to do for personification in *Piers Plowman* what David Aers did so brilliantly for allegorical ecphrasis long ago, by showing how the meaning of the tree of *charite* mutates over the course of its appearance; see Aers, *Christian Allegory*, pp. 89–109; also Griffiths, *Personification*, pp. 81–89.

[33] On Wraþe, see Griffiths, *Personification*, p. 62; Langland, *Piers Plowman*, ed. by Pearsall, p. 39; Hanna, *Penn Commentary*, pp. 101–2; see similarly on Sleuþe, Calabrese, 'Posthuman *Piers*?', pp. 12–14.

[34] B.5.196–255. See Griffiths, *Personification*, ch. 3, esp. pp. 59–63.

[35] See the personifications that appear at B.1.148–54 and B.18.121–65; B.9.1–59 and B.15.12–36; B.4.47–103, B.18.166–228 and B.20.331–54.

the discovery that the term *mede*, the name of a personification primarily connected with the unscrupulous use of and desire for goods, can also denote the spiritual rewards that 'God of his grace graunteþ in his blisse / To þo þat wel werchen while þei ben here';³⁶ or the revelation that Studie, primarily associated with a spiritually oriented pursuit of understanding and desire (Latin *studium*) and also the source of virtuous disciplines such as scriptural studies, theology, music, logic and grammar, also includes more dubious and deceiving arts: *astronomye, geomesie, sorcerie* and *alkenamye*.³⁷ The most egregious example of this kind of personification slippage, and one often noted by readers, is Contricion, who under the blandishments of comforting friars has become his own inversion: by the last lines of the poem he has 'clene foryeten to crye and to wepe'.³⁸

Another interesting example is Langland's Clergie. In my view, in his main manifestation Clergie personifies a capacious version of Latin *doctrina*, 'Christian teaching', and encompasses the full range of revealed understanding available to Christians, whether elementary, lay or learned.³⁹ Nevertheless, at points the term *clergie* seems to refer to 'the clergy', and at the end of the B.13 'feast of Pacience', Clergie the personification seems briefly and without warning to turn into a trivial and debased version of the Christian understanding that he had represented:

> ... Are ye coveitous nouþe
> After yeresȝeves or ȝiftes, or yernen to rede redels?
> I shall bryng yow a Bible, a book of þe olde lawe,
> And lere yow, if yow like, þe leeste point to knowe.⁴⁰

A number of readers have attempted to naturalise or smooth over this moment. Traugott Lawler, for example, reads it as a simple foible of Clergie's imagined character, as a 'friendly dig' at the expense of

---

³⁶ B.3.232–33; see, for example, Griffiths, *Personification*, ch. 2; Simpson, *Piers Plowman*, pp. 41–44. For the huge bibliography on the term and personification *mede*, see Galloway, *Penn Commentary*, pp. 217–24 and *passim*. On paradiastole and the 'hypocritical figure' that underlie this and other forms of ethical slippage in the poem, see Zeeman, *Arts of Disruption*, ch. 1–2.

³⁷ B.10.170–217. See Zeeman, *Piers Plowman*, ch. 3 (esp. pp. 127–31).

³⁸ B.20.370. This has been noticed by many readers, but for a powerful recent reading of it, see Aers, *Beyond Reformation?*, esp. pp. 136–37.

³⁹ See Zeeman, *Piers Plowman*, ch. 4; some recent readers have continued to take the different view that Langland's *clergie* denotes learned theological understanding (see, for example, Langland, *Piers Plowman*, ed. by Pearsall, n. to C.11.78–80).

⁴⁰ B.13.184–87. On *clergie* as 'the clergy', see Zeeman, *Piers Plowman*, p. 143; on the corruption of the personification Clergie at the feast of Pacience, see pp. 261–62; but also Zeeman, *Arts of Disruption*, ch. 2, where I treat Clergie as an example of the 'Hypocritical Figure'.

Pacience's idealism.[41] But to normalise Clergie's altered perspective, that is, to read him as if he is just a colourful person (or a fluid subjectivity), is to miss the structural recurrence of such moments in the poem as a whole;[42] even more important, it is to ignore the fact that Clergie is a personification – and a Langlandian one at that – along with the complex and multiple conceptual work that personification can do. Langland is not just being entertaining here. He is also asking the reader to think about the very different things that the phenomenon of *clergie* can be when used and abused by fallible humans. This brief scene exemplifies vividly Langland's capacity to dramatise within the action of his poem the dangerously different dimensions of *clergie* and the spiritual risks that it entails: just as *studie* (term and personification) can denote both spiritual desire and some very problematic arts, so *clergie* (term and personification) can denote both Christian teaching and pointlessly learned pedantry. To neutralise this moment of its conceptual complexity is to deprive it of much of its challenge.

With Clergie, we have arrived at one of the more sustained or recurrent personifications of Langland's poem. Although a number of readers have indeed seen something of the fluidity of these repeatedly appearing or familiar personifications, I propose that there is still a critical reluctance to acknowledge the degree of their multi-dimensionality and the thinkerly work that it can do.[43] In these figures, just as in those that appear more briefly, Langland uses the figure of personification to collect, circle round and work over a constellation of aspects, phenomena and issues, which can be verbal or conceptual, material or institutional, aspirational or corrupt. In personifications of longer duration, different elements of the term 'personified' are placed in conversation with each other in exactly the same way as in those who only appear more briefly. Indeed, these personifications of longer duration may also share something with those personifications who share a name with another very different one: the two Truþes, the two Animas and the three personifications named Pees. In the case of Pees, Langland surely means us to pause over the relation of these separate personifications to each other (what is it about *pees* that means it can be all these things?) and he may also mean us to observe that several different words can be used to describe aspects of a single phenomenon (what

---

[41] Lawler, *Penn Commentary*, p. 55.
[42] Compare Studie, discussed above; also Zeeman, *Arts of Disruption*, ch. 2.
[43] Exemplified recently by Hanna's tart remark that the speech of Pacience 'remains governed by the rules of personification' (Hanna, *Patient Reading*, p. 318).

exactly is the relation between Pees and Hende Speche at B.20.349–56, for example?). In the case of Anima, Langland again plays this game of separate personifications; but he also introduces perhaps the poem's most extreme version of the one personification with many names/sides:

> 'The whiles I quykke the cors,' quod he, 'called am I *Anima*;
> And whan I wilne and wolde, *Animus* ich hatte;
> And for þat I kan and knowe, called am I *Mens*, "þouȝt";
> And whan I make mone to God, *Memoria* is my name;
> And whan I deme domes and do as [Truþe] techeþ,
> Thanne is *Racio* my riȝte name, "Reson" on Englissh;
> And whan I feele þat folk telleþ, my first name is *Sensus* –
> And þat is wit and wisdom, þe welle of alle craftes.'[44]

Although Langland's Isidorean list of Anima's names is unusual in the poem, I doubt that the thinking that underlies it is. Neither is this catalogue a commentary on Anima alone. It also offers different names for, and perspectives on, many other terms and personifications in the poem: the narrator under his name Wil ('whan I wilne and wolde, *Animus* ich hatte'), Thouȝt or Wit ('for þat I kan and knowe, called am I *Mens*'), Imaginatyf ('whan I make mone to God, *Memoria* is my name') and Reson ('whan I deme domes and do as [T]ruþe techeþ, / Thanne is *Racio* my riȝte name, "Reson" on Englissh'). As for the line 'whan I feele þat folk telleþ, my first name is *Sensus* – / And þat is wit and wisdom, þe welle of alle craftes', could we hypothesise that Langland is here thinking of the processes that he elsewhere calls 'kynde wit' (or even 'kynde knowing')?[45] In the end, the important point is that Langland is interested in putting terms to work and using their many meanings to find out what they can tell us about the various phenomena to which they refer, but which they can never sum up.

Personification is one of the primary methods with which he does this, and Piers Plowman, the narrator/Wil, Conscience, Pacience and Haukyn constitute some of the most ambitious and surprising examples of this kind of work in the poem.

Perhaps because Piers Plowman's name is a proper name, rather than a concept noun, readers seem to have been more at ease with his changing and escalating status over the poem.[46] As he shifts from the role of overseer (albeit a strongly ethical one) in the fields (B.6) to gardener in the spiritual

---

[44] B.15.23–30, emended; Langland is here citing Isidore, *Etymologies*, XI.1.13, ed. by Lindsay.
[45] Davlin, 'Kynde Knowyng'; Zeeman, *Piers Plowman*, pp. 6–7, 102, 105, 161, 235–42 and 255–56.
[46] See, for example, Griffiths, *Personification*, pp. 90–91.

orchard of the human *herte* where the tree of *charite* grows (B.16), to coworker with Grace and Conscience in the founding of the church, the barn of *unite* (B.19), Piers's mutating roles have been seen to reflect the changing and escalating preoccupations of the poem, as it homes in on the life of doing well, the redemptive work of Christ and the foundation of the church. Piers's disappearance at the end of the poem is again an index of where the poem has got itself to. Much ink has been spilt on Piers's many meanings and his associations with both the ordinary working man and Christ himself, with both a vernacular layman called Piers and the apostle Peter on whom the Church was founded.[47] One of the ways in which Piers's multi-dimensionality has long been understood is through the paradigms of typology, whereby scriptural, historical and ordinary human beings are all understood to be part of a divinely established and mutually referential system of historical instantiations through time. Typologically, Piers the spiritual man can be all these things or, rather, all these different spiritual realities can be seen through him.[48] At the same time, these very associations also mean that Piers is also a form of *prosopopoeia* or personification, a figure with identifiable and to some degree genericising characteristics – he is at various levels of practicality, pastoralia and spirituality, a worker, a maker and gatherer of food, one who cares for and feeds others, Langland's idea of the good man. Piers is not just a type, in other words; he is also one of Langland's counterintuitively multi-dimensional personifications.

The poem's narrative 'I', often called Wil, is another such figure. A highly influential articulation of this view is that of Lawton, who in 1987 read this narrative 'subject' in multiple ways that reflected the plethora of possible critical approaches to the poem available at the time.[49] Equally influentially, Anne Middleton read the poem's narrative voice as a complex instantiation of 'experience' put together out of a series of troubled but rebellious authorial self-descriptions, some of them emblematic and spiritual, and some derived from the social circumstances and historical moment of his own life.[50] Calabrese charts the many features of this 'I' and his overlaps with other protagonists, both within a particular version of the poem and across different ones: overlaps that have the

---

[47] See Hanna, *Penn Commentary*, pp. 185–89; Zeeman, *Arts of Disruption*, ch. 9 and 10; also Zeeman, 'Not Peter or Perkyn', pp. 298–99.
[48] Carruthers, *Search for St Truth*, ch. 5 and 6; also Salter, *English and International*, pp. 125–31; and Griffiths, *Personification*, pp. 65–75.
[49] Lawton, 'Subject of *Piers*'.
[50] Middleton, 'Narration and the Invention', and her 'Acts of Vagrancy'.

potential to characterise him as a *wil*, an observer, a vice, an active life or as *recheles*.[51] In my own work, I have claimed that this 'I' may only be named Wil in the parts of the poem where he is in dialogue with his cognitive powers: these cognitive powers bring the willing aspect of the 'I' into focus, but only for as long as the poet looks at him in terms of the division of the subject into its desiring and knowing parts (it may be a mistake to call him 'Wil' elsewhere). I also claim that Langland's term *wil* is multi-valent: as with so many of his central terms, *wil* encompasses very different versions of 'willing' – both the rational and moral 'volition' of the moral and upright self, and also the problematic forms of desire that can be characterised as 'wilful'.[52] It may be important that we cannot at any given moment be sure which of these Wil is. All this means that the pastoral problem of knowing the Christian subject (the ultimately impossible task set for all priests and confessors) is fundamental to the poem's whole diegesis. If the mysterious, only ever glimpsed, multi-valency of Piers Plowman is one of the inspirational mechanisms of the poem, the dubious multi-valency of the narrator is one of the mechanisms by which it reminds the reader of how difficult it is to be a human being – and how difficult it is to know or read another one.

At several points, the poem contrives to make us feel that Conscience is something of an old friend of the narrator, the 'same person', in other words: 'And as Crist wolde þer com Conscience to conforte me þat tyme, / And bad me come to his court …', 'And þanne called I Conscience to kenne me þe soþe …' (B.13.22–3; B.19.9). However, Sarah Wood has recently made the case that Conscience looks different at different points in the poem, claiming – surely rightly – that these various orientations relate less to some kind of psychological development than to the issues at stake as the poem progresses (in this respect he is also like Piers Plowman).[53] Wood claims that Conscience begins in B.3–4 as 'a layman, a "courtly" character', developing in B.13–14 into 'an embodiment of the virtuous layman' or 'the virtuous (lay) penitent imagined in vernacular penitential literature'; by the time he reappears in B.19 it is as 'a knight,

---

[51] Calabrese, 'Posthuman *Piers*?', pp. 14–18. For another approach to the narrator and his relation to the community, see Simpson, 'Power of Impropriety'.

[52] Zeeman, *Piers Plowman*, pp. 68–78 and 102–3. In the C text this 'I' is also addressed as 'Wil' by Holichurch (C.1.5); but I think this too can be subsumed into the idea that it is only in teacherly situations, where Langland is thinking about the relation of understanding to the desiring and willing subject, that the poet identifies his narrator as *wil*.

[53] Wood, *Conscience and Composition*, pp. 13–19 and *passim*; Wood also claims that Conscience evolves over the various versions of the poem.

although now characterised as a herald' and in B.20 he is 'apparently ... a lord and certainly all too susceptible to lordly Hende Speche'.[54] There is undoubtedly a broadly recognisable trajectory to his appearances, which reflects the gradually more pastoral and spiritual nature of the poem's themes, ending with the ecclesiastical concerns, but also the apocalyptic reversals, of the final passus. However, at the same time, there is still a naturalising continuity to Wood's readings. This can also be seen in her reading of Conscience's final B.20 corruption and inversion of himself (even as she acknowledges that there is in fact something to be 'smoothed over'): 'like too many of his peers ... lordly Conscience welcomes the friar right into the household. Conscience's allegorical role as accuser of sins is fatally compromised by the literal level of his presentation as a knightly figure easily seduced by a friar'.[55] It will be clear that in my view what happens to Conscience in B.20 is akin to what we have seen in Studie and Clergie, and that to naturalise it is once again to miss the provocative multi-valency of Langlandian personification.

Pacience has excited hugely variant responses in readers. For Anna Baldwin and Vincent Gillespie, Pacience represents a version of the words of the Paternoster, 'fiat voluntas tua' ('thy will be done'), but also the 'willed selflessness' and lack of egotism that make all the virtues and love of the neighbour possible: 'Patience ... makes men poor in heart and so more charitable'.[56] Wood and Hanna have both stressed the penitential dimensions of Pacience, especially in the scene with Haukyn and Conscience.[57] For David Aers, however, Pacience represents, among other things, an arrogant indifference to human need combined with an overweening belief in human powers for meritorious action – in particular a Franciscan overconfidence in the work of poverty; for Nicholas Watson, Pacience is a 'spiritual elitist' with an entirely uncompromising sense of the pastoral enterprise, unable to take into account the limitations of an ordinary sinner such as Haukyn.[58] In my view this great discrepancy of views of Pacience is the result of reading as an homogenous or naturalistic 'whole' a figure who is in fact a composite of different aspects: in Pacience Langland once again uses personification as a heuristic tool for looking at the many different things that can be gathered under the rubric of *pacience*.

---

[54] Ibid., pp. 46–47, 59, 71 and 104.   [55] Ibid., p. 104 and n. 78.
[56] Baldwin, 'Patient Politics', p. 99, and her 'Triumph of Patience', pp. 74, 76 and 82; Gillespie, 'Thy Will be Done', pp. 106 and 112–19.
[57] Wood, *Conscience and Composition*, ch. 2; Hanna, *Patient Reading*, pp. 269–351.
[58] Aers, *Sanctifying Signs*, pp. 122–33; Watson, 'Pastoral Theology', pp. 85 and 108; see also Hanna, 'Langland's Patience'.

At the feast of Pacience, this personification certainly advocates accepting forms of material denial as part of a fundamentally spiritual outlook; again, in the following scene with Haukyn and Conscience, it seems clear that Pacience represents a spiritually driven and even penitential acceptance of lack that is one counterpart to Haukyn, with his trust in the active life of bread making and feeding people. But this is not the sum of Pacience's meanings. In *Arts of Disruption* I have argued that the pastoral connotations of Pacience mean that he does not just represent the self-denial of the one confessing; he also represents the patience, love, humility and self-denial that are required of the pastoral carer. But I also believe that in the last part of Pacience's appearance something even stranger happens: Pacience turns into an extreme and problematic (in)version of his pastoral self. The bullish and confident version of patient poverty that Pacience espouses in this last part of his appearance (so effective that it supposedly makes the sins impossible) is both an exaggeration of spiritual poverty to the point of distortion and a dangerous exaggeration of the kinds of supportive pastoral things that the clergy might say to console the poor.[59] It is not possible to document this argument in detail here, but suffice to say that much of Aers's concern about Pacience's 'pelagian' overconfidence may look different once we see that Langland is actually exploring this problematic possibility – not in the portrait of Pacience as a whole, but in its last section. Similarly, Watson's concern about Pacience's pastoral indifference to the ordinary sinner also requires reassessment in this context. Not only has Pacience in fact represented several gentle forms of pastoral care, but in this last section Pacience takes the notion of supportive pastoral care to a new and dangerous extreme, arguing that material poverty itself can make you good; the figure whom Watson has read as deeply uncompromising in fact turns into a bizarre compromiser.[60] Once again, Langland is experimenting by using his personification Pacience to push a version of 'patient' pastoral care for the poor so far out of shape that much of it is no longer really recognisable as Christian pastoralia at all. It is hard to think of a comparably experimental and multi-dimensional use of the figure of *prosopopoeia*/personification.

---

[59] Zeeman, *Arts of Disruption*, pp. 87–100, 170–77.
[60] In this respect Pacience's position on the salvific power of poverty has come remarkably to resemble that of the priest whose mechanistic method of teaching the ploughman his Pasternoster (any method will do as long as it works) Watson so engagingly praises at the beginning of his essay (Watson, 'Pastoral Theology', pp. 85–87).

And what, finally, of the question 'lay or ordained'? Although Piers Plowman, Conscience and Pacience are at some points presented as lay figures, at other points the poem seems to imply that they occupy something like a pastoral or priestly role.[61] Many readers have been reluctant to acknowledge this possibility, presumably either due to a sense that in the Middle Ages the lay/ordained distinction was a hard one, or due to a residual sense that the personified 'person' must still be one or the other. Nevertheless, none of these personifications is in fact organised round a categorical separation of the lay and the ordained. The human beings and spiritual states referred to at various points in the poem under the terms 'Piers Plowman', *conscience* and *pacience*, could after all occur both in the laity and in the clergy. Once again, what is at issue here may be the many-sidedness of *prosopopoeia*/personification.

The possibility that Piers Plowman, Conscience and Pacience might have a priestly dimension has in fact been partly recognised by a small number of scholars. Craun, for example, has asked if Study and Conscience are clerical or lay;[62] Fiona Somerset and Nicole Rice have also claimed that some of the poem's personifications have a kind of lay/clerical 'hybridity'.[63] The issue has been recently revisited by Aers in his important *Beyond Reformation?*. Here Aers argues that Langland is to a remarkable degree prepared to look beyond the current endowed ('Constantinian') institution of the Church; emphasising how, throughout *Piers Plowman*, the established structures and offices of the Church are shown to be deeply compromised, Aers claims that the vision of the true Church that emerges in B.20 is best described as a 'congregation' of spiritual and Pauline *fooles*: 'totally independent of papal church and lay elites ... these "fools" escape classification in terms of the modern church's ... hierocratic division between clergy and laity'.[64] I want here to foreground Aers's last words

---

[61] The argument I will pursue here bears a relation to claims made in Zeeman, *Piers Plowman*, where I argued that, in writing about human powers of understanding and their objects, Langland purposely chose terms that could refer to institutional roles and activities – the Church, the schools and their learning – but also allowed him to be much more inclusive: *wit, studie, clergie, scripture* and *kynde*. Langland's personification Clergie, for example, is not narrowly equivalent to the usual Middle English meanings of *clergie* ('learning' but also 'the clergy'), but stands for the many forms of revealed understanding and teaching handed down via revelation, Scripture, Church tradition and the priesthood; Clergie represents both the most learned version of these teachings and the most elementary or lay version of them. See Zeeman, *Piers Plowman*, ch. 4 and *passim*.

[62] Craun, *Lies, Slander and Obscenity*, p. 158.

[63] Somerset, *Clerical Discourse*, p. 33; Rice, *Lay Piety and Religious Discipline*, p. 99.

[64] On Langland's *fooles* (B.20.61–63, 74–79), see Aers, *Beyond Reformation?*, p. 151, as well as pp. 105, 125–28, 158–60 and 170–72. For a reading of the end of the poem perhaps in

about Langland's relative indifference to the laity/clergy distinction. Elsewhere in the book, Aers also notices how at certain points Langland seems to treat the work of 'prechours and preestes' simply as a job, comparable to that of any virtuous working person; and he also returns several times to the poem's ambiguity about whether or not Conscience is ordained.[65] What I think Aers points to at the very least is a Langland remarkably indifferent to the distinction between these two states, a Langland focused only transitionally on the institutional and material practices of the church, including the office of the priesthood. This emphasis is reinforced by the essentially 'imaginative' ways in which Langland describes church ritual in the poem as a whole: his language at these points is invariably non-technical, but also contextually and materially undetailed; it is built up, almost dialectically, out of a series of circumstantial propositions and elements.[66] Langland's impressionistic depictions of ritual practice reflect the fact that his real concern is with the moral motives, spiritual desires and gifts of grace for which the ritual is ultimately just the channel.

The clearest example of this ambiguity about ordination is Piers Plowman. Early on in the poem he is a representative of the ordinary working life, but by B.15 Piers Plowman manifests what Rice calls 'lay-clerical hybridity', a capacity to see love in a person that is associated with, but transcends, that of clerics:

> Therfore by colour ne by clergie knowe shaltow hym nevere,
> Neiþer þoruȝ wordes ne werkes, but þoruȝ wil oone,
> And þat knoweþ no clerk ne creature on erþe
> But Piers þe Plowman ... (B.15.209–12)

Rice comments: 'in order to stand for the apostolic life and function ... as a "lens through which Charity's 'persone' is finally disclosed", Piers must transcend earthly "clerks" while somehow embodying the best of clerical authority and lay industry'.[67] By B.19, moreover, Piers is explicitly identified with Peter, the apostle upon whom the Church and the priesthood, with its power to give absolution, are founded:

---

sympathy with that of Aers, see Simpson, *Piers Plowman*, pp. 213–15 and 218; arguing against such radical reformist readings, see Barney, *Penn Commentary*, pp. 246–48.

[65] On the 'prechours and preestes' (B.19.230–34), see Aers, *Beyond Reformation?*, p. 18; for Conscience, see the discussion below.

[66] This has been illustrated in different ways by a number of major essays: see Lawler, 'Pardon Formula'; Aers, *Sanctifying Signs*, ch. 2; Minnis, *Valuing the Vernacular* (2009), ch. 3.

[67] Rice, *Lay Piety and Religious Discipline*, p. 99, citing Aers, *Christian Allegory*, p. 88.

> And whan þis dede was doon, Dobest he [Christ] þou3te,
> And yaf Piers power, and pardon he grauntede:
> To alle maner men, mercy and for3ifnesse;
> To hym, myght men to assoille of alle manere synnes,
> In covenaunt þat þei come and kneweliche to paye
> To Piers pardon þe Plowman – *Redde quod debes*.
> Thus haþ Piers power, be his pardon paied,
> To bynde and unbynde ... (B.19.183–90)

Here Langland explicitly refers to the sacramental power of the priesthood to 'bind and loose', that is, to absolve the sins of those who repent. Nevertheless, he feels no need specifically to mention the priesthood or the ritual of ordination; his description remains materially non-specific and institutionally uncontextualised. The same is true as the forces of vice and Antichrist gather and we hear how Grace has also given Piers the power to consecrate the eucharist at the mass (here simply and non-specifically formulated as 'My3t to maken it') and give it to those who have paid their spiritual dues:

> Grace, þoru3 Goddes word, gaf Piers power,
> My3t to maken it, and men to ete it after
> In helpe of hir heele ones in a monþe,
> Or as ofte as þei hadde nede, þo þat hadde ypaied
> To Piers pardon þe Plowman, *Redde quod debes*. (B.19.390–94)

Langland's description of these scenes signals the priestly dimension of what Piers is doing but without specifying it technically or explicitly.

However, in this second passage the figure who actually speaks to the community, publicly offering them the eucharist, is Conscience. In his first appearance in the poem, Conscience does indeed seem to be, just like Piers Plowman, a lay figure. But he too has escalating ecclesiastical connotations. As we have noted, Wood has associated his B.13–14 scene with Pacience and Haukyn with the vernacular discourses of penitence, though she still insists that everything he says could have been said by a layman;[68] Aers too is categorical that 'Langland never represents Conscience as a priest'.[69] While what Wood and Aers say is technically true, however, it seems perverse not to acknowledge that the work in which Conscience and Pacience are engaged in B.13–14 is pastoral and priestly. Indeed, the confessional dimensions of the scene are confirmed by the fact that much

---

[68] Wood, *Conscience and Composition*, ch. 2.   [69] Aers, *Beyond Reformation?*, pp. 61 and 168.

of Haukyn's B Text confession ends up back in the C Text in the 'confessions' of the sins. But we can also see these confessional and pastoral dimensions in the detail of the scene. Throughout, Conscience and Pacience's approach to Haukyn is sharp-tongued and humorous, but 'consistently "in a curteis manere"', as was required of the good pastoral carer; the narrator even poses the technical pastoral question, 'Ac whiche ben þe braunches þat bryngen a man to sleuþe?'[70] At the end of B.13 Conscience treats Haukyn in the approved confessorial manner, 'accusing' him, but not so aggressively as to put him off confession and reform:

> Thus Haukyn þe actif man hadde ysoiled his cote,
> Til Conscience acouped hym therof in a curteis manere,
> Why he ne hadde wasshen it or wiped it with a brusshe. (B.13.458–60)

Conscience goes on to speak in an explicitly pastoral manner, instructing Haukyn on contrition, confession and satisfaction, finally encouraging him to have hope, providing he does by Conscience's *techyng*: 'Shal noon heraud ne harpour have a fairer garnement / Than Haukyn þe Actif man, and þow do by my techyng'. Pacience too describes penance as a *sheltrom* ('defense') and source of hope, and in the following lines he runs through the practical penitential theology of contrition, confession and satisfaction (B.14.25–26; 81–96). It seems clear that Conscience and Pacience are pastoral carers participating in an informal (and thus characteristically Langlandian) version of the ritual of confession, with Conscience and Pacience performing a priestly role, but once again without being technically identified as priests.

The same is true in B.19–20. Here Conscience has already participated with Grace and Piers Plowman in the allegorical establishment of the Church: the priestly work of building the barn of *unitee*. We should scarcely be surprised to find that it is Conscience who is in charge of the ritual and pastoral work of confession and penance.[71] It is Conscience who worries about the friars and finally agrees to let them into the barn of *unitee* (B.20.242–45), and it is Conscience who organises a confessor for the people in the barn,

---

[70] B.13.410. On benevolent pastoralia, see Simpson, *Piers Plowman*, p. 143, citing B.13.459; and Zeeman, *Arts of Disruption*, pp. 88–100, 113–17, 171–77.
[71] Aers continues to ask about the nature of sacerdotal presence in these last sections; see, for example, Aers, *Beyond Reformation?*, p. 127.

> ... a leche, þat koude wel shryve,
> Go salve þo þat sike were and þoruȝ synne ywounded.
> Shrift shoop sharp salve, and made men do penaunce
> For hire mysdedes þat þei wroȝt hadde,
> And þat Piers pardon were ypayed, *redde quod debes*. (B.20.305–9)

When the community finds this priestly 'spiritual doctor' too harsh and calls for another, it is again Conscience who has to deal with the renewed offers of the friars; this time the community receives an altogether more lenient fraternal confessor, 'a surgien ... þat softe kan handle, / And moore of phisik bi fer, and fairer he plastreþ / Oon Frere Flaterer ...' (B.20.314–16). In short, it seems perfectly clear that Langland here sees Conscience as part of the ordained organisational structure of the church. As the vices and the hordes of Antichrist assemble, it is Conscience who gathers his community within the barn, offering them the eucharist (engagingly but non-technically described as 'breed yblessed, and Goddes body therunder'), ministered by Piers Plowman:

> 'Comeþ,' quod Conscience, 'ye Cristene, and dyneþ,
> That han laboured lelly al þis Lenten tyme.
> Here is breed yblessed, and Goddes body therunder.
> Grace, þoruȝ Goddes word, gaf Piers power,
> Myȝt to maken it ...' (B.19.387–90)

How can Conscience here not be performing a version of the mass?

The possibility of lay/priestly cross-over can be seen in one more personification. This is Haukyn, also named *Activa vita*, whose work is always precisely referred to as the making of *wafres*.

> For alle trewe travaillours and tilers of þe erþe,
> Fro Mighelmesse to Mighelmesse I fynde hem wiþ wafres.
> Beggeris and bidderis of my breed craven,
> Faitours and freres and folk with brode crounes.[72]

Although the term *wafre* refers more generally to crisp cakes baked in irons, Pearsall and Schmidt state that Haukyn's *wafres* may also denote eucharistic wafers; despite this, they deny that Haukyn's 'active life' could

---

[72] B.13.240–43; see also B.13.225–27, 273. On Haukyn, see Calabrese, 'Posthuman *Piers*?', pp. 16–18.

include the work of the priesthood.⁷³ But, given what I have already said about Langland's imaginative and non-technical ways of alluding to the work of the priesthood, can we be so sure? It is true that Haukyn's *wafres* can be ordinary bread such as will satisfy the hungry (B.13.266–69, 271). But elsewhere Haukyn speaks more ambiguously; he speaks of finding food for the pope, and, wishing in return for *provendre*, a *personage* or just a pardon, he goes on:

> And þanne wolde I be prest to þe peple, paast for to make,
> And buxom and busy aboute breed and drynke
> For hym and for alle hise, founde I þat his pardoun
> Miȝte lechen a man – as I bileve it sholde. (B.13.251–54)

Haukyn's overt logic here is that if the pope recognised and rewarded his work, he would make bread for the ordinary people with alacrity ('þanne wolde I be prest to þe peple, paast for to make'). But, as so often in Langland, Haukyn's language throws up other possibilities. What he would like from the pope in return for his work, after all, is *provendre* (both 'provender' and 'prebend') or a *personage* (benefice), while his 'prest to the peple' seems at the very least to pun on 'priest'.⁷⁴ Haukyn's implied parallel between the pope's gifts or powers and his own bread certainly raises a question about their relation, especially as he goes on to ruminate on the fact that all ecclesiastical powers to channel grace – including those of the mass and thus the *wafre* – depend on the repentance of the people:

> For may no blessynge doon us boote but if we wile amende,
> Ne mannes masse make pees among Cristene peple,
> Til pride be pureliche fordo, and þat þoruȝ payn defaute.⁷⁵

---

⁷³ Langland, *Piers Plowman*, ed. by Pearsall, nn. to C.15.194 and 198; Langland, *Piers Plowman*, ed. by Schmidt, nn. to C.15.200–33. Lawler claims that the first citation of the term 'wafer' with clear eucharistic connotations is 1559 (see *OED*, s.v. 'wafer', n.), but he misses the 1371 and 1375 instances in Raine (ed.), *Fabric Rolls*, pp. 124 and 127, cited in *MED*, s.v. 'wafer', n. 1; Lawler also observes that making *wafres* does not necessarily make Haukyn a priest; see Lawler, *Penn Commentary*, pp. 66–67.

⁷⁴ Schmidt also comments that this is an 'idle jest', adding that Haukyn 'could never be entitled to a clerical living'; Langland, *Piers Plowman*, ed. by Schmidt, n. to B.13.244 and 246; likewise, Lawler, *Penn Commentary*, p. 69, naturalises these remarks as Haukyn's fantasy of being a 'quack cleric'. Both seem to miss the kinds of allusive work that Langland performs referentially and by wordplay. (I have similar objections to Lawler's categorical remarks on Haukyn's Latin at *Penn Commentary*, p. 71.)

⁷⁵ B.13.258–60; even as Haukyn opens up this ambiguity, however, he complicates it by claiming in his characteristically worldly and materialistic manner that it is through lack of real bread ('þoruȝ payn defaute') that this repentance might come about.

My purpose here is not to prove that Haukyn is also a priest: it is rather to show that Langland actively invokes the possibility that 'he' (the active life) appears both in the lay and the ordained. As Gregory the Great made clear, *activa vita* is every bit as much part of the priesthood as it is of the laity: 'For the active life is to give bread to the hungry, to teach the ignorant with the word of wisdom, to correct those going wrong, to call the proud neighbour back to the way of humility ....'.[76] With Haukyn as with other figures in the poem, then, Langland's language reveals a striking openness about the distinction between the lay and the ordained.[77]

The fact that Langland's personifications are sometimes lay and sometimes ordained is just one of the many forms of personification multivalency in the poem. Langland's remarkably fluid attitude towards persons and institutions means that he constantly asks us to pay attention to what lies 'behind' or 'within' them – just as he repeatedly demands that we look through his personifications to the spiritual processes towards which they can only ever gesture. This undoubtedly tells us something about his attitude to the institution of the Church. But it also tells us about his attitudes to the phenomena of language, allegory and personification: Langland's personifications are famous for coming and going in a manner that is often remarkably obscure, sudden or mysterious.[78] At one minute they can be vividly and naturalistically present, and at the next they are mutating and transforming before our very eyes.

Langland almost certainly represents an extreme version of a more general medieval recognition of the imaginative and conceptual possibilities of *prosopopoeia*/personification. Latin rhetorical texts going back to antiquity make it clear that theorists recognised that the figure operated dynamically across potentially contradictory dimensions, in particular the polarities of term/concept/generic dimension/discursive exploration and person/body/speaker. Unlike the readers and theorists of later centuries, medieval readers and theorists did not seem to worry about the complexity or the unnaturalness of the figure. The same goes for those who used it. In the Latin literature of the Middle Ages, but above all perhaps in writings in

---

[76] Gregory the Great, *Homiliae in Hiezechielem*, II.II.8, ed. by Adriaen, p. 230; also citing this passage, see Lawler, *Penn Commentary*, p. 63.

[77] Has light been cast on Langland's striking disengagement from the institutional Church by Robert Adams's recent identification of Langland with an ordained member of the Rokele family? The fact that by the B Text the poet seems to represent himself as married (B.18.428–30) means that, if the historical Langland had been ordained, then he no longer lived in accord with his vows of ordination. See Adams, *Langland and the Rokele Family*.

[78] Salter, *English and International*, ch. 5; Aers, *Beyond Reformation?*, pp. 98–99 and 149–51.

the vernacular, the figure took on a life that we may not yet quite have got the measure of. It seems clear that the authors of much medieval narrative allegory – not to mention the authors of many more dialogue texts that also make use *prosopopoeia*/personification[79] – revelled in the inventive possibilities that the figure offered for exploring subjects, but also categories, concepts, perspectives, postures, social roles and even the institution of the Church.

---

[79] See Zeeman, *Arts of Disruption*, pp. 26–33. Here I discuss the kinds of dialogue text in which *prosopopoeia*/personification occurs: sometimes, but not often, in scholastic or university-derived dialogues, but very frequently in more elementary pedagogical writings and in debates directed at wider audiences. I argue that, unsurprisingly, the figure often appears in texts that are particularly concerned with issues of accessibility, enlivenment and perspective.

CHAPTER 10

# *Encountering Vision*
## Dislocation, Disquiet, Perplexity

### Mary Carruthers

At the opening of his influential treatise on *The Mind's Way to God* (*Itinerarium mentis in Deum*), Bonaventure (d. 1274) describes how such a mental journey begins, using as his example St Francis's visionary encounter with a six-winged seraph, in whose bosom appears an image of Christ crucified. This is how Bonaventure describes his own experience:

> Cum igitur exemplo beatissimi patris Francisci hanc pacem anhelo spiritu quaererem, ego peccator, qui loco ipsius patris beatissimi post eius transitum septimus in generali fratrum ministerio per omnia indignus succedo, contigit ut nutu divino circa Beati ipsius transitum, anno trigesimo tertio [i.e., 1259] ad montem Alvernae tanquam ad locum quietum amore quaerendi pacem spiritus declinarem, ibique existens, dum mente tractarem aliquas mentales ascensiones in Deum, inter alia occurrit illud miraculum, quod in praedicto loco contigit ipsi beato Francisco, de visione scilicet Seraph alati ad instar Crucifixi. In cuius consideratione statim visum est mihi, quod visio illa praetenderet ipsius patris suspensionem in contemplando et viam, per quam pervenitur ad eam.

> Around the thirty-third anniversary of the saint's death, by God's will, it happened that I – a sinner, and altogether unworthy to succeed as seventh Minister General of the Friars after that same most blessed father's passing – went away to Mount La Verna, as to a quiet place, in my distressed state seeking peace of spirit, and staying there, while I was composing in my mind various mindful ways of ascending to God, among the rest there occurred [in my thoughts] that miracle which in the very place had happened to blessed Francis, that is the vision of a winged Seraph with the likeness of the Crucified. In considering which, it immediately seemed to me, that an envisioning [of a Seraph] could show this father's state during his contemplating and the path through which one arrives at it.[1]

---

[1] Bonaventure, *Itinerarium mentis in Deum*, prol.2, in Bonaventure, *Opera Omnia*, v, 295. My translation, after consulting that of Ewert Cousins, p. 54. Francis died in 1226; thirty-three is of course the span of Jesus's life.

Bonaventure, in some turmoil of mind occasioned near the anniversary of Francis's death, seeks out a quiet place where he can be alone. He seeks out a mountain that is not at all on his habitual, daily routes. That it is also the very spot of Francis's miraculous vision is of course integral to his task, but it is his dis-location and his dis-quieted anxiety of mind and spirit that are emphasised in this account, as well as his being all alone. He is *anhelus*, literally 'distressed in his breathing' – and seeking peace of spirit: *spiritus* should be understood here both physically as 'breath' and emotionally as his 'spirits', his feelings. He goes to that solitary place in order to remember 'mindfully' (as we now would say) and, through such considered remembering, to compose – 'dum mente tractarem'. *Tractare* is the common verb in medieval Latin for invention, the ordinary process of what we now call 'getting our ideas'. It also includes the procedure of 'composition', disposition and organisation, the need to identify a structure within which one can organise one's 'ideas' and 'proofs' (*argumenta*) as one invents them and draws them into 'place' (*tractare*) in one's composition. Bonaventure is 'tracting' a composition about contemplation, how a human mind can ascend toward God using a method, a structured itinerary, for his thinking (which is what a 'method', from the Greek word for 'path', basically is). It is significant also that he does not speak of 'intellect' in this passage but of 'mind' (*mens*), understood at this time as the type of perception-based cognition derived from our human experiences through our *anima sensitiva*.[2] There is no suggestion here of any miracle for him. Francis's divine revelation was a miracle (*miraculum*), but Bonaventure claims no such experience for himself and promises no direct Pauline *raptus* to his audience.

What he does 'discover' by recalling Francis's experience is both his materials ('arguments') and a dispositive organisation for his own composition concerning the stages of contemplation, the *itinerarium mentis* that can lead the mind steadily upward. Others can *use* Francis's vision (the six wings, centrally located about the likeness of Christ crucified) as the basic

---

[2] A helpful discussion of this medieval psychological commonplace is in the widely disseminated Cistercian treatise *De spiritu et anima*, long attributed to Augustine but actually in great part the work of Alcher of Clairvaux, in the early thirteenth century. Chapter 34 of this work discusses the differences between *mens* and *anima/spiritus* at some length. See 'Treatise on the Spirit and the Soul', tr. by Leiva and Ward, in McGinn (ed.), *Three Treatises on Man*, pp. 232–33. Katherine Tachau has wisely observed that, while medieval psychologies located cognitive functions in both the sensitive and intellectual aspects of the soul, philosophers from Descartes often confused and conflated the two, with the result that historians now had best keep in mind that 'when one has described a late medieval scholar's views on either sensitive cognition or intellectual cognition, one has not yet treated that scholar's entire account of natural cognition': Tachau, *Vision and Certitude*, p. 10, n. 19.

compositional outline for subsequent meditations, seeking understanding of the divine (*in Deum*) through their own human *mens*. Bonaventure translates Francis's individual gift into a shared, communitarian instrument. He clearly found such ordering devices useful – perhaps even essential – for his own composing, as well as helpful tools for his audiences' reception, for, when delivering an oration, he regularly asks his auditors to imagine such a device, in order to keep in mind the themes and arguments he is making. As another example, at the start of his *Lignum vitae*, one of his most popular sermons, Bonaventure advises his audience:

> Et quoniam imaginatio Arbori iuvat intelligentiam, ideo quae ex multis pauca collegi in imaginaria quadam arbore sic ordinavi atque disposui, ut in prima et infima ramorum ipsius expansione Salvatoris origo describatur et vita, in media passio, et glorificatio in suprema. Et in prima quidem ramorum serie quatuor altrinsecus secundum alphabeti ordinem ponentur versiculi, similiter in secunda et tertia, ex quorum quolibet instar fructus unica pullulatio pendet, ut sic sint quasi duodecim rami afferentes duodecim fructus iuxta mysterium ligni vitae. Describe igitur in spiritu mentis tuae arborem quandam, cuius radix irrigetur fonte scaturitionis perpetuae. ... Porro ex huius arboris stipite duodecim rami frondibus, floribus et fructibus adornati consurgant.

> Since making a mental image aids understanding, I have arranged mentally in the shape of a tree a few matters that I have collected from among many, and have ordered and disposed them in such a way that in the first or lower branches are described the Saviour's birth and life, in the middle his passion and at the top his glorification. In the first group of branches there are four versicles placed opposite one another in alphabetical order; likewise in the second and third groups of branches. From each of these branches hangs a single fruit. So there are, in effect, twelve branches bearing twelve fruits, as with the sacred Tree of Life (Apoc. 22.1). Draw in spirit a particular tree in your mind, whose root is irrigated by an ever-flowing fountain (Apoc. 22.1). ... Next, from its trunk rise together twelve branches adorned with leaves, flowers and fruits.[3]

Bonaventure was deeply indebted to traditions of monastic meditation that were revivified and adapted by the Victorines and other twelfth century contemplative orders, the Carthusians, Norbertines and Cistercians in particular.[4] They all shared a common complex practice,

---

[3] Bonaventure, *Lignum vitae*, prol.2–3, in Bonaventure, *Opera Omnia*, VIII, 68–70. My translation, after consulting that of Cousins, p. 120.

[4] In his twenty-third sermon on the Canticle, Bernard of Clairvaux suggests imagining the bedroom of the King as having three chambers, construing it as a device for remembering and organising one's meditation (discussed further below). Among the Victorines, the Ark of Noah and the Ark of the

an art or *techne* in Aristotle's term, for reading, meditation and contemplation – what, in this chapter, I will discuss as an art of invention and composition. It is perhaps useful to reflect on the lexical fact that Latin *oratio* derives from *orare*, 'to pray'. A common monastic term for contemplation is *pia memoria*, translating a Greek term, *mneme theou*. Most often they just called the exercise *memoria*.[5]

Uncommon, often solitary, locations and disquiet of mind – anxiety[6] – are part of its preparation procedure. This feature was not initiated by the desert monks, but in fact is characteristic of Roman rhetoric. In Book X of his *Fundamentals of Rhetoric*, Quintilian describes those in the throes of inventive meditation as 'lying back looking at the ceiling, mumbling to ourselves to stimulate thought', or walking about in their bed-chambers and making 'those gestures that accompany our stronger feelings, and themselves help to stimulate thought – waving the hand, contorting the face, goading and sometimes striking ourselves' or the table, biting our nails – and talking aloud with ourselves.[7] This is, he says, the method (the word he uses is *ratio*) that he recommends, along with, of course, continuous practice (*exercitatio*). At this preliminary stage, he advises, it is best not to work with a secretary, not only because dictation will slow down your thoughts as you wait for the amanuensis to write what you say, but also because the presence of another may inhibit the strong gestures and passionate subvocalised inner conversation that stimulate your composing. He also recommends working in a small, familiar room (such as a bed-chamber) and in solitude: Demosthenes 'used to hide away in a place

---

Tabernacle were popular, as is apparent in meditations on monastic life by both Hugh (d. 1141) and Richard of St Victor (d. 1173) which use the biblical plans of these structures as mental devices for invention; similarly, Peter of Celle (Benedictine, d. 1183) and Adam of Dryburgh (Carthusian, d. 1212?) composed meditations using the Ark of the Tabernacle as their mental organising tool. See Carruthers, *Craft of Thought*, esp. pp. 171–276.

[5] Two essential discussions of this exercise, and of the cultural values that supported the exercise of monastic *memoria*, are Hadot, *Philosophy as a Way of Life*, and Leclercq, *Otia Monastica*. An important general study is Leclercq, *Love of Learning*.

[6] In his Latin-French dictionary of *c.* 1490, Guillaume Le Talleur, *Dictionarius familiaris*, ed. by Edwards and Merrilees, p. 17b, gives *anxius* as the meaning of *anhelus*, synonymous with French *angoisseux*. Middle English *angwisshous* derives from and shares meaning with the French word (see *MED*, s.v. 'angwisshous', adj., citing uses from the thirteenth century on).

[7] Quintilian, *Orator's Education*, X.III.15–27, tr. by Russell, IV, 343–49. Quintilian gives practical advice here about composition methods and habits, from initial invention in secluded meditation, to the use of wax tablets and the importance of erasing, and on through the best preparation for improvising during oral delivery, in X.III–VII. This material was included in the *mutilis* Quintilian redactions known in the Middle Ages: see the preface to Winterbottom's edition of the *Institutionis Oratoriae*, pp. vii–viii. These practices, taught commonly in ancient education, became an integral part of monastic teaching and practice also, the chief means of their transmission in the Middle Ages: see Carruthers, *Craft of Thought*, passim, and also Ward, 'Quintilian and the Rhetorical Revolution'.

where no sound could be heard and no prospect seen, for fear that his eye might force his mind to wander'. So, Quintilian continues, 'let the silence of night, an enclosed chamber (*clusum cubiculum*) and a single lamp keep us sharp', for 'working by lamplight ... gives the best kind of privacy'.[8] Latin even has a word for it: *lucubratio*, work done at night by lamp-light, a word used regularly in medieval meditation practice as well.

The twelfth-century Benedictine abbot Peter of Celle characterises his cell as the antithesis to the burdens of his regular offices, the room of silence in which 'I draw deeply from the quiet which has now been granted me. The mind has a more extensive and expansive leisure within the six surfaces of a room than it could gain outside. In fact, the smaller the place the more extended the mind, for when the body is constrained the mind takes flight'.[9] This play of leisure (*otium*) against daily busy-ness (*negotium*), expressed in the inverse relationship of physical constraint and mental expansion, is a common theme in twelfth-century writing on meditation. The pagan philosophers, Peter says elsewhere, 'sought quiet, hidden places, where they could cultivate the mind', and in this respect, he says, the claustral and philosophical disciplines 'embrace in each other's arms and kiss away from the crowds'. The smallest, physically most constrained of such places within the *cubiculum*, the bed-chamber, was the bed, *lectulus*, itself. Undoubtedly impelled by its role in the Canticle of Canticles – the favourite of some memorable twelfth-century contemplation – the bedroom is the innermost sanctuary, in which leisure works the hardest. This can be done in the daytime, Peter says, when minds 'removed from earthly activities ... graze among the lilies' of reading. But it is even better when done in 'the silence of the middle of the night'.[10] Paradoxically, the constrained enclosure liberates his meditating mind. This too is a pervasive theme in monastic rhetoric. And it is indeed his mental 'cell' that he is celebrating, for Benedictines of Peter's time had no actual bedroom of their own – the monks all slept in a common dormitory.

In his 23rd sermon on the Canticle, Bernard of Clairvaux also characterises the inventive 'bedroom', *cubiculum*.[11] For him, it is clearly a mental, not a physical place. Like Peter of Celle, Bernard required it to

---

[8] Quintilian, *Institutiones Oratoriae*, ed. by Winterbottom, X.III.25–6. See also Lewis and Short, *A Latin Dictionary*, s.v. 'lucubratio'.
[9] Peter of Celle, 'On Affliction and Reading', in *Selected Works*, tr. by Feiss, p. 139.
[10] Peter of Celle, 'The Discipline of the Cloister', VIII and XV, in *Selected Works*, tr. by Feiss, pp. 86–87, 94. See further, Carruthers, 'The Desert'.
[11] Bernard of Clairvaux, *Sermons on the Song of Songs*, tr. by Walsh, II, 25–41.

be his way of 'dis-locating' himself from the daily concerns of his abbatial and other duties. (Like so many twelfth-century abbots, including Peter of Celle, Bernard was *un homme d'affairs*, very much engaged with the events of his day, and 'in the world' rather more than he was 'in the desert'.) Bernard constructs his *cubiculum* – which is that described as the King's bedchamber in the Canticle – as an architecture plan, the *ratio* for the composition he is conceiving. It is a place that comes with many chambers, for, Bernard says (citing Isaiah), the King has more than one queen, his concubines are many, his maids beyond counting, and each one has her own secret rendezvous place with the Bridegroom. And this self-dis-locating location is also a place of great dis-quiet. The first chamber within it is the special place from which the Bridegroom governs the cosmos. 'This is a remote and secret place', Bernard says, 'but it is not a place of repose'. For the seeker who contemplates God in the universe 'is not allowed to rest and be quiet'; the contemplative is 'awe-struck', 'delighted' but also restless, and Bernard quotes the Bride: 'Although I sleep, my heart is awake'. The second chamber of the *cubiculum* is where God exercises justice; it is the place of 'the fear of the Lord' and the beginning of Wisdom (unlike the first, in which Wisdom is a teacher but is not yet 'within us' – in this second chamber of judgement, Wisdom is received within us). But neither is this second a place of quiet – 'neither here nor there [in the first chamber] does the contemplative find rest, because there he discovers a busy God, here an angry God'. The second chamber is 'a place of horror' – but it is also where the contemplative, appearing at the bar of divine justice, hears God say, 'Your sins are forgiven you', and at that point he is 'suddenly inspired with so great a confidence (*fides*)' and delight that he can now (if he should be so invited) enter the inmost chamber, the bedroom of the loving King, of Christ as God's Wisdom, and that – finally – is the place of quiet, 'the only place where peace reigns'. But the sole way even to try to discover it is by going through the two prior chambers of cognitive and emotional un-quiet, awe-struck wonder (in the first) and horrid fear (in the second).

The wonder and awe that Bernard speaks of as the contemplative gazes on the cosmos are the first ingredient of the composing process which his triple chambered *cubiculum* organises. Bernard places this moment at the start, correctly, for it always initiates some change of direction, either at the very start of or within a narrative. It is the moment when a person walks into some large, very decorated space, or sees a complicated highly-wrought artefact and comments that 'the eye does not know where to look first'. There are many parallels to this moment in medieval vernacular literature as well, such as in some romance descriptions where one is asked to visualise in one's imagination some ornamented surface in complicated, ever-burgeoning detail (two examples are the description of Dido's Carthage in the *Roman d'Eneas*, or, in *Sir Gawain and the Green Knight*, that of the Green Knight and his horse decked out in their holiday gear). And there are also parallels in musical experiences, for instance, the complications of motet singing, especially those employing not only different melodies for each voice but different languages. They present a similarly complex and perplexing experience for the ear, as the ear does not know where first to listen.

This is an essential principle, one that specifically employs a viewpoint that is polyfocal and multiple, neither fixed nor single focused – as is later, linear 'Renaissance' perspective. The resulting 'confusion', 'perplexity' and 'bewilderment' are markers of learned appreciation, not boorishness or ignorance, for this initial perplexity is neither belittling nor exclusionary, but draws one's eye and ear, one's searching, associating and constructing mind (what was known among scholastics as an *investigatio rememorativa*) – first towards and then into and through a work, asking 'What is this?' and 'How is this done?' with pleasure and admiration both for the display of surpassing skill that created the work and for the puzzle of how it is made. It focuses attention on the supreme human artistry – the 'wizardry' – apparent through the material craft. But it is not only a principle of aesthetic admiration, but at the same time of new composition. 'I wonder what that is?' and 'Who are you?' and 'How do you do that?' are the basic questions that structure not only literary works but all the other arts as well.

And 'wonder' begotten in 'perplexity' is not only a composition tool, but a philosophical principle. Indeed, for Aristotle, it is the first principle of philosophy. Early on in the *Metaphysics*, Aristotle defines various kinds of human knowing. He distinguishes sense perceptions (*aisthesis*) from truthful knowing, for sense perceptions are the basis of our knowing, but they are not in themselves knowledge – they cannot alone distinguish what is real from what is illusory. They become our experiences only after being processed into concepts and retained as such in a mental form that our minds can later use for making new thoughts. Humans begin to know by means of their particular experiences (*empeiria*), as other animals do, and from many such experiences they are able to devise teachable principles for their arts (*techne*) and for reasoning (*logismos*). As Aristotle says, 'In general the sign of knowledge or ignorance is the ability to teach, and for this reason we hold that art rather than experience is scientific knowledge (*episteme*); for artists can teach, but the others cannot'. But there is still another kind of human knowing, and that is wisdom, philosophy, which knows the causes of things. And 'it is through wonder that men now begin and originally began to philosophise. ... Now he who wonders and is perplexed feels that he is ignorant' and thus starts asking questions about the causes of things.[12]

It is said that the Middle Ages produced no theoretical accounts of art, but only technical manuals. That is superficially true, but only because their *techne* already embodies principles deriving from monastic exercises that themselves are also profoundly 'philosophical' and meditative, for example those in the best-known treatise on manual crafts from the Middle Ages, *De diversis artibus* of 'Theophilus', written around 1120. This Theophilus has been identified as a north German Benedictine monk – therefore learned, as his prose indicates – and a master metalworker, associated with a number of fine objects made for churches and liturgical service. His work is in the form of advice to a novice, who is also both a monk and a craftsman; he gives him both moral and practical counsel:

> His uirtutum astipulationibus animatus, karissime fili, domum Dei fiducialiter aggressus tanto lepore decorasti; et laquearia seu parietes diuerso opere diuersisque coloribus distinguens paradysi Dei speciem floribus uariis uerantem, gramine foliisque uirentem ... quodammodo aspicientibus ostendisti ... Nec enim perpendere ualet humanus oculus, cui operi primum aciem infigat: si respicit laquearia, uernant quasi pallia; si consideret parietes, est paradysi species; si luminis abundantiam ex fenestris intuetur, inestimabilem uitri decorem et operis pretiosissimi uarietatem miratur.

> Animated, dearest son, by these supporting virtues [of wise judgement, which Theophilus has just taught him], you have approached the House of God with confidence, and have adorned it with so much beauty; you have embellished the ceilings and walls with varied work in different colours and have, in some measure, shown to beholders the paradise of God, glowing with various flowers, verdant with herbs and foliage. ... For the human eye is not able to consider on what work first to fix its gaze: if it beholds the ceilings they glow like brocades; if it considers the walls they are a kind of paradise; if it regards the profusion of light from the windows, it marvels at the inestimable beauty of the glass and the infinitely rich and various workmanship.[13]

---

[12] Aristotle, *Metaphysics*, I.1–2., ed. and tr. by Tredennick, 1, 7 and 13.
[13] Dodwell (ed. and tr.), *De diversis artibus*, III. pref., p. 63.

Notice that the beauty of this building is all in its plenteous surface details – decorated ceilings, walls, windows – and in its colours, gold and many others, glowing like Paradise itself. And also note that 'the human eye is not able to consider on what work first to fix its gaze'. This is how the audience is fully drawn into the work, beginning from a sense of overwhelming, magnificent amplitude but then finding its way through the multiple sensory invitations which the ornaments make. The viewer is as much a 'maker' of the whole experience as the original artisan. She must look and look, and look again. This perplexing scene draws you into the work through constant questioning – you cannot just stand back and admire the view, for you are given no certain place from which to stand. 'Question' after all is from the same Latin root as 'quest' – a search, an investigation, a 'going-into' – *in-venire*, an invention.

In *Piers Plowman*, the narrator, identified at various points as (the) Will, is in a continual state of dis-location ('wandering' is his life's condition), dis-quiet (his restless anxiety punctuated with anger) and perplexity as he encounters the series of strange creatures who populate the world that had seemed so normal from his katascopic view atop the Malvern Hills of 'alle manere of men, þe mene and þe riche, / Werchynge and wandrynge as the world askeþ' (B.Prol.18–19).[14] It is worth noting also that here at the beginning he is looking east (B.Prol.13), the orientation of *mappaemundi*. But he soon loses that detached perspective. From the poem's beginning, he is dis-located, in a place 'wist I nevere where', in strange garb ('in habite as an eremite vnholy of werkes'), and within a wonder ('a merveillouse swevene'). After that first view from Malvern Hills, Will's dis-orientation never varies in this very long dream poem. Similarly in *The Divine Comedy*, the pilgrim Dante begins his complex set of visions in a state of complete disorientation, dislocated and disquieted, perplexed and frightened by strange creatures, whom he questions even after he finds his inadequate guide in the weak-voiced, often puzzled Virgil. The disoriented, anxious narrators immediately begin to ask questions, and they continue to do so until the end. At the end of *Paradiso*, Dante merges with the ultimate 'strange' sight ('quella vista nova'),[15] but Will, through the figure of Conscience, sets out on his quest again, still questioning.

A related moment in romance literature (and there are many to choose from) comes in Chaucer's *Squire's Tale*, often presented as merely parodying an adolescent taste for sci-fi adventure – a pure oriental fantasy, to be

---

[14] Langland, *Piers Plowman*, citing Schmidt's edition of the B Text by passus and line.
[15] Dante Alighieri, *Paradiso*, XXXIII.136, ed. by Petrocchi, IV, 557.

contrasted with the sober, classical philosophising of his wiser father. And it is certainly oriental, so by definition 'strange'. At the court of 'Cambyuskan', during a high feast, an uninvited, foreign knight rides suddenly into the hall and up to the high table; he is mounted on a brazen horse and carrying a sword, a ring and a mirror. The court falls silent: 'In al the halle ne was ther spoken a word / For merveille of this knyght; hym to biholde / Ful bisily they wayten, yonge and olde' (V.86–88). The knight names the powers of the various toys he has brought: in the mirror one can see adversities and learn who is friend or foe, with the ring understand the languages of birds, with the sword cut through and then repair one's foes, and with the horse travel anywhere one wants to go. 'He that it wroghte', the knight says, 'koude full many a gyn' (V.128), many tricks of his art. And the knight rides out of the hall and goes off to dress more appropriately for the feasting, leaving his now-immobile horse parked in the main courtyard, attracting onlookers.

What is most interesting to me in this long scene, the first part of the *Squire's Tale*, is the emphasis placed on crafting and craft mastery. The 'strange' provenance of these gifts excites the court as much and in the same ways, I think, as the perplexing, ingenious encounters in *Piers* and *The Divine Comedy*. The strange knight's presents are products of wizardry – but of human wizardry, *techne* not miracle. As artefacts, they may seem entirely different from the strange personified fictions of dream vision, but they share an essential quality. They are figures of wonder, and require questioning. The items brought by the knight in the *Squire's Tale* do not excite fear or terror in the court, but rather curiosity, admiration, wonder and speculation: How are they made? How do they work? Above all, they occasion general scientific discussion and dispute. The brass steed seems almost alive:

> Greet was the prees that swarmeth to and fro
> To gauren on this hors that stondeth so;
> For it so heigh was, and so brood and long,
> So wel proporcioned for to been strong,
> Right as it were a steede of Lumbardye;
> Therwith so horsly, and so quyk of ye,
> As it a gentil Poilleys courser were. (V.189–95)

A few remarks are made among the assembly about Pegasus, and some raise the cautionary example of Sinon's gift horse to Troy. But because 'they kan nat the craft' (V.185), even the engineers among them can't figure out how to make it move out of the yard, where it inertly stands.

The mirror's qualities occupy the optical physicists among the group, citing Alhazen and Witelo (the two main authors on the academic subject of *perspectiva*, showing how very current the Squire's scientific interests are), and saying that by means of 'composiciouns / Of anglis and of slye reflexiouns' one could 'naturelly' (V.229–30) make a mirror that is able to show such things. And the sword excites the metallurgists and alchemists, who speculate about what procedures might have been used to harden the metal and what chemicals ('medicynes', V.244) might be used to produce such a result. There is no talk of magic in these explanations – all are natural, all invoking craft knowledge and principles of natural philosophy. The only technical gadget that the group gives up trying to figure out is the ring that allows the wearer to understand birds – but only because, they admit, they lack any knowledge concerning a craft of rings (although Solomon, wisest of men, is said to have possessed such knowledge).

Another such moment – this time not in a romance tale (a genre that, after all, is comprised of many such moments) – occurs in the Middle English poem *Pearl*. This is a dream-vision, a genre designed for philosophising. It opens with a man, identifying himself as a jeweller who has 'lost' a pearl. So far so ordinary. But, he says, he lost it as it fell down away from him in a garden, the garden he is now in himself. This is curious – what is a jeweller doing in a garden? Surely this is not his usual place of business. Moreover, he is in an acutely anxious state, desolate from the loss that so grievously oppresses his heart. It immediately turns out that he is mourning the loss of his two-year-old baby daughter, who is buried in a plot, clad in earth (as he says), within the garden. So, at the start of this visionary poem, our narrator is both dis-located and dis-quieted. He also wants urgently to discover something, to 'invent' (in the Latin sense) that which is now lost to him, for she is literally 'covered over' – *oblita* in Latin, which is also the word for 'forgotten' – and he greatly desires to uncover her, to dis-cover and to remember her. In his great grief and distress of spirit, the jeweller lies down upon his baby daughter's grave:

> Bifore that spot my honde I spennd
> For care ful cold that to me caght;
> A deuely dele in my hert denned,
> Thagh resoun sette myseluen saght,
> I playned my perle that there was penned,
> Wyth fyrce skyllez that faste faght.
> Thagh kynde of Kryst me comfort kenned,
> My wreched wylle in wo ay wraghte.
> I felle vpon that floury flaght;

> Suche odour to my hernes schot
> I slode vpon a slepyng-slaghte
> On that precios perle withouten spot. (49–60)[16]

In his dislocated, anguished and anxious state, the dreamer experiences a sudden onslaught of sleep, a 'slepyng-slaught' – not a biological sleep, but that state that expands the mind via its visionary powers:

> Fro spot my spyryt ther sprang in space –
> My body on balke ther bod in sweven.
> My goste is gon in Godes grace
> In aventure ther mervayles meven.
> I ne wyste in this worlde quere that hit wace. (61–65)

He has no idea where he is, but at least here instead of grief he feels pleasure and joy – pure delight – in a landscape that comprises a forest, with brilliant cliffs at the horizon, and a river flowing between him and them. It is a perplexing place, for the forest trees have indigo trunks and silver leaves, the gravel is made up of pearls and birds of flamboyant colours fly all about, harmoniously singing. The dreamer has certainly relocated to a pleasant visionary chamber, in which he walks about in a playful, blissful frame of mind, all grief forgotten (86), looking and listening without any particular direction. Indeed, his eye does not know where to look first.

Then a child standing at the base of the shining cliffs on the river bank opposite him catches his eye. As he focuses on her, she becomes familiar: 'I knew hyr wel, I hade sen hyr ere. / . . . / On lenghe I loked to hyr there – / The lenger, I knew hyr more and more' (164, 167–68). She is of course his baby girl, and his heart fills with 'gladdening glory' as he recognises her:

> The more I frayste hyr fayre face,
> Her fygure fyn quen I had fonte,
> Suche gladande glory con to me glace
> As lyttel byfore therto was wonte.
> To calle hyr lyste con me enchace
> Bot baysment gef myn hert a brunt.
> I sey hyr in so strange a place,
> Such a burre myght make myn herte blunt.
> Thenne veres ho up her fayre frount,
> Hyr vysayge whyt as playn yvore,

---

[16] Stanbury (ed.), *Pearl*, cited by line. On the theme of grief in the poem, see especially Bernau, 'Feeling Thinking'.

> That stonge myn hert ful stray astount –
> And ever the lenger the more and more.
>
> More then me lyste my drede aros;
> I stod ful stylle and dorste not calle.
> Wyth yyen open and mouth ful clos
> I stod as hende as hawk in halle. (169–84)

He has a strong desire to call out to her – but something is not right. What is she doing here, in this place so strange, so unfamiliar? *I saw her in so strange a place*, he says. The surprise sight stings his heart into a state of bewildered confusion, 'ful stray astount', and he becomes very afraid. Instead of rushing to her, his eyes open wide (in wonder and terror), he is afraid to speak, and standing as still as a hawk in a hall, he is paralysed by dread at what might come next – from his own little baby girl. This emotional passage, from joyous marvelling at the strange wonders to frightened, frozen bewilderment, comes about because something entirely familiar to him – his daughter – is in a confusing place. This is stressed in the poem. A hawk in a hall is a bewildered creature, subdued by a world deeply unfamiliar. What is this, that looks like his daughter but evidently is not really? The longer he looks, the stranger she seems. The familiar made strange and profoundly de-familiarised is just as bewildering, maybe even more so, as the marvellous itself. And all such cases produce wonder, questioning and philosophising. For of course, this scene is prelude to the whole rest of the poem, as the adult human jeweller is gradually instructed by his two-year-old – the first of many reversals of his familiar world. But heaven is like that.[17] Philosophy begins in acts of wondering. This poem's complex philosophising is conducted entirely as a dialogue touched off by this moment of wonder; dialogue is the literary form most associated at this time with doing philosophy, and indeed jeweller and maiden soon settle into their task. Her art in teaching him depends on stretching, distorting and de-familiarising the mundane meanings of the common words.[18]

*Pearl* demonstrates that the meditations invited by dislocation and perplexity are not only fructified by means of academic theological demonstration, but by the practices that make art. It has often been pointed

---

[17] Compare the strange heavenly geometry of Hildegard of Bingen's *Scivias* visions, analysed by Caviness, 'Hildegard as Designer'. An exemplary analysis of how *Pearl* stretches, twists and weaves language is Borroff, '*Pearl*'s "Maynful Mone"'.

[18] This exchange is well analysed by Minnis, 'Discourse Beyond Death' (2015).

out that the narrator's craft as a jeweller is reflected in the poem's intricate form, its key-words winding and twisting together like the metal wires that a jeweller uses to weave a pearl tiara fit for 'a maiden of menske' (162), or that the divine architect wove for human vision through the words of the apostle John describing the heavenly Jerusalem as a jewelled box. It is the practical art of the maiden as a teacher that clarifies and lessens the dreamer's initial anxiety by complicating it, making their dialogue more decorous, fruitful and truthful, and fit for purpose within the linguistic economy of heaven. Like all artists she also has to accommodate the natural composition of her material, and in the end her artful teaching is constrained by the limits of her human pupil. As Aristotle observed, art is able to teach — that is how we recognise art as true *techne*. But *techne* is not that same thing as *episteme*, the universal causal principles that philosophy defines. *Techne* requires particular materials with which to fashion a specific artefact according to the teachable methods particular to a craft. By that standard, the narrator's final human being, at rest with himself as both 'homely hyne' and 'precious perle', is as fitting a product of the maiden's practical craft as the poem reflects that of the jeweller.[19]

[19] I am very pleased to be able to honour Alastair Minnis, whom I have known for so many years. Our friendship has always suited the Horatian ideal of being at the same time delightful and beneficial. He has brought these same qualities to all his many contributions to the study of literature and language, through his publications, his collaborations with colleagues and his students. He is a proven master of the art of teaching, in the model of the Pearl maiden herself.

CHAPTER 11

# *George Colvile's Translation of the* Consolation of Philosophy

## Ian Cornelius

'A totally exceptional quantity of effort was spent in bringing this work nearer to general knowledge'.[1] So Max Manitius, surveying the medieval commentaries on and translations of Boethius's *De consolatione philosophiae* (*Consolation of Philosophy*). He estimated that only the grammatical treatises of Donatus and certain books of the Bible received more attention from medieval scholars. As a mixed-genre work read and studied over a long period and wide geographical area, the *Consolatio* affords especially rich testimony to dispensations of textuality and experiences of reading in premodern Europe. Modern understanding of the *Consolatio*'s medieval reception has advanced prodigiously in recent decades, and one of the salient research areas has concerned the techniques of medieval translators.[2] Whereas modern literary translation has been shaped by the norms of novelistic reading – in which the text is often presumed to stand on its own, its meaning accessible without recourse to an apparatus of other texts – 'late medieval academic translation', as it is termed, was modelled on the norms of the medieval schools, where meaning was normatively construed through and by means of glosses and commentaries. Modern translators may benefit from scholarly commentary on their texts, but they are not expected to intrude commentary-material into the text itself. Yet this is what one finds in many medieval translations. Much like reading itself, translation is an activity that differs in expression from one culture to

---

[1] Manitius, *Geschichte der lateinischen Literatur*, I, 34.
[2] Key studies of the medieval reception of the *Consolatio* are Gibson (ed.), *Boethius*; Minnis (ed.), *Medieval Boethius* (1987); Minnis (ed.), *Chaucer's 'Boece'* (1993); Hoenen and Nauta (eds), *Boethius in the Middle Ages*; Black and Pomaro, *Boethius's* Consolation of Philosophy; Glei et al. (eds), *Boethius Christianus?*; Kaylor and Phillips (eds), *Companion to Boethius*; Kaylor and Phillips (eds), *Vernacular Traditions*; and McMullen and Weaver (eds), *Legacy of Boethius*. The key statements on translation style are Minnis and Machan, '*Boece* as Late-Medieval Translation' (1993); and Copeland, *Rhetoric, Hermeneutics and Translation*, ch. 4 and 5.

another. Medieval translation was often conceived – and practised – as the extension of an ongoing exegetical endeavour into a new language.

Among the English translations of the *Consolatio*, Geoffrey Chaucer's *Boece* has served as a paradigmatic illustration of the late medieval academic style.[3] The Old English *Boethius*, though influenced at times by glosses, is a different kind of endeavour – less a translation of the *Consolatio* than an adaptation of it.[4] John Walton's versified *Boethius*, dated 1410, responds to the exigencies of verse form, but also exhibits characteristic features of the academic style, for Walton incorporates exegetical material via the *Boece* (his principal source) and independently, through direct consultation of Nicholas Trevet's commentary on Boethius's text.[5] Throughout the fifteenth century and well into the following one, the translations of Chaucer and Walton evidently satisfied demand,[6] for there were no new complete translations of the *Consolatio* into English until 1556, when John Cawoode printed a translation by an otherwise unknown George Colvile.

The 1556 print states on its title page that Colvile employed a 'prynte' of Boethius's text, not a manuscript (see Figure 11.1). In a prologue, Colvile dedicates his work to Queen Mary (r. 1553–58). These two features anchor Colvile's activity in a post-medieval world, yet the translation is in other respects a medieval throwback. There are marginal explanatory notes, the content of which is traceable to medieval commentaries, while Boethius's poems are intercalated with material likewise derived from a medieval commentary. Finally, Colvile's wording occasionally suggests that he knew Chaucer's *Boece*. Evidence for this last point is equivocal. What is clear is that Colvile's procedures are closer to those of Chaucer than to subsequent English translators of this text.[7] Whereas most subsequent translators adopt the principle of *sola scriptura*, separating text from commentary, Colvile permitted these categories to interpenetrate.

---

[3] See Minnis and Machan, '*Boece* as Late-Medieval Translation' (1993); Machan, *Techniques of Translation*, and Machan (ed.), with Minnis, *Sources of the 'Boece'* (2005). The text is edited in *Riverside Chaucer* and in *Chaucer's 'Boece'*, ed. by Machan.
[4] See Godden and Irvine (eds), *Old English Boethius*, I, 50–72.
[5] On Walton's sources and translation style see Minnis, 'Aspects of the Medieval Traditions' (1981), pp. 343–47, 350–51; Johnson, 'Walton's Sapient Orpheus'; and Cornelius, 'Boethius', pp. 285–86. Walton's dependence on the *Boece* was established by Cossack, *Über die altenglische metrische Bearbeitung*, and subsequently in Science (ed.), *Boethius*, pp. lii–lviii. Science's edition should be used with caution and in consultation with Schümmer, *John Waltons metrische Übersetzung*.
[6] On the manuscripts and early prints of the Middle English translations see Cornelius, 'Boethius', pp. 287–88, with references.
[7] Subsequent English translations of the *Consolatio* are listed by Donaghey, 'Post-Medieval Translation', pp. 316–17; and Phillips, 'English *Consolation*', pp. 102–5, 112.

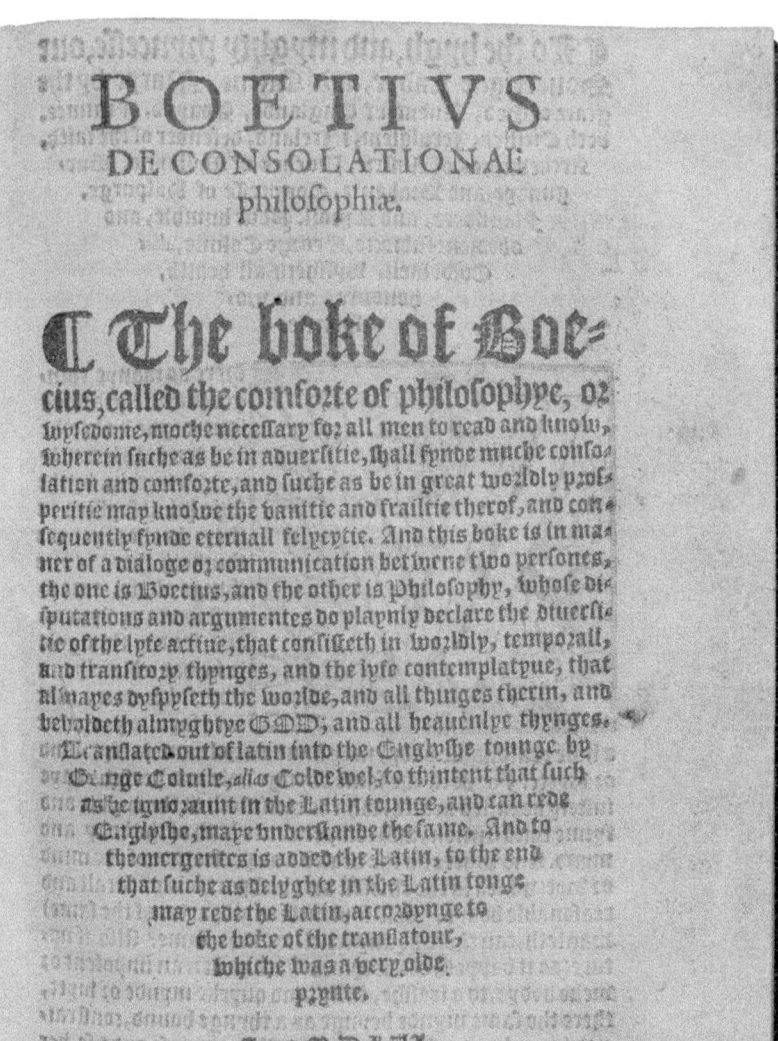

Figure 11.1 The title page of George Colvile's translation of Boethius's *De consolatione philosophiae*, printed by John Cawoode in 1556.
Newberry Library, Chicago, Case Y 672 .B204. Reproduced by kind permission.

He transmitted literary scholasticism into the vernacular language of the mid-sixteenth century.

## Author, Print and Reputation

The 'George Coluile, *alias* Coldewel' who produced this translation has not been identified.[8] The 1556 print is a quarto, quired in fours, unpaginated and signed B–Z, Aa–Ff after an unsigned quire of preliminaries.[9] Pages are divided vertically into three columns, with the translation printed in blackletter type in the widest, central column, and bordered on the inside by the Latin text of the *Consolatio*, printed in italic (see Figure 11.2). A narrow outer column is reserved for explanatory notes in English; these are printed in a blackletter type smaller than that used for the main text.[10] Preliminaries consist in the dedication to Queen Mary (sig. [A]1ᵛ–2ʳ), an 'argumente or summe of thys booke and whereof it treatyth' (sig. [A]2ᵛ–3ʳ) and 'The Prologe of George Coluile, Alias Coldewell to the reader' (sig. [A]3ᵛ–4ᵛ). The contents of the 'argument or summe' and 'prologe' will be discussed below. In the dedication Colvile recommends, as the supreme philosophical wisdom, the prayer 'that a hole reasonable body, may haue an hole and perfyt mind or wytte' (sig. [A]1ᵛ). This theme – *mens sana in corpore sano* – has been taken as slight support for identifying our author with a Cambridge physician of the same name.

Colvile's reputation has always been slight, and the 'state of knowledge' may be summarised briefly. In 1897 the Tudor Library series reprinted Colvile's English text, including the marginal notes.[11] In 1933 Henry Burrowes Lathrop offered a brief appreciation:[12]

> Colvile knew his Latin grammatically, and was able to follow unhesitatingly the scholastic subtleties of Boethius's reasoning. He can also express himself in English clearly and vigorously without apparent effort. He is free from affectation and pedantry of style, and makes no attempt to give a spurious

---

[8] See Botley's *ODNB* entry, s.v. 'Colvile [Coldewel], George', and references there.
[9] STC (2nd ed.) 3201. The online USTC (accessed January, 2019) lists fourteen copies but omits copies held by the Boston Athenaeum, Newberry Library and the libraries of Princeton University and the University of Minnesota (all recorded in Worldcat). Thomas Warton, Philip Bliss and other early scholars reported later editions of Colvile's text, dated 1561 and 1566, but their reports remain uncorroborated. See Warton, *History of English Poetry*, II, 35 n.; and Wood and Bliss, *Athenae Oxonienses*, I, col. 48. Bliss is presumably the source for subsequent references, by Bax and others, to a 1561 edition.
[10] Wakelin, 'Possibilities for Reading', places this page layout in the context of other bilingual printing in England in this period.
[11] Bax (ed.), *Boethius' Consolation*. [12] Lathrop, *Translations from the Classics*, pp. 54–56 (p. 54).

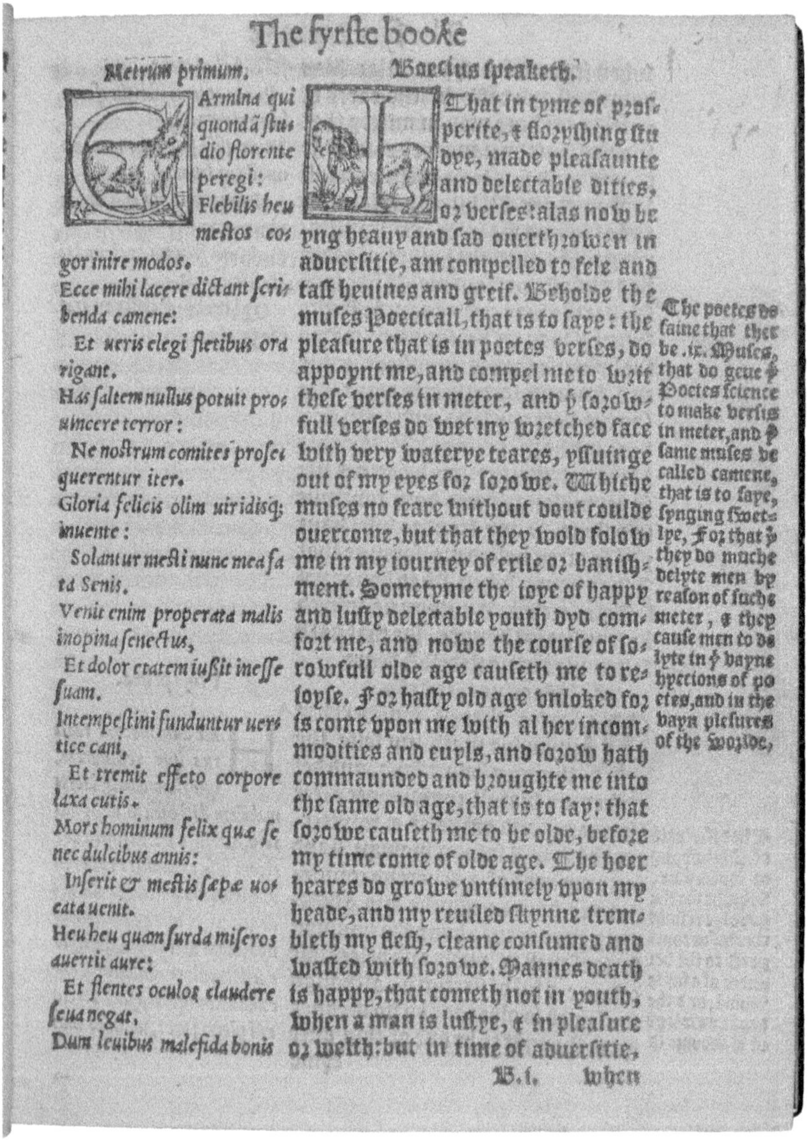

## The fyrste booke

*Metrum primum.*

Armina qui
quondā stu-
dio florente
peregi:
Flebilis heu
mestos co-
gor inire modos.
Ecce mihi lacere dictant scri-
benda camene:

Et ueris elegi fletibus ora
rigant.

Has saltem nullus potuit pro-
ss incere terror:

Ne nostrum comites profec
querentur iter.

Gloria felicis olim uiridisq;
inuente:

Solantur mesti nunc mea fa-
ta Senis.

Venit enim properata malis
inopina senectus.

Et dolor etatem iussit inesse
suam.

Intempestini funduntur uer-
tice cani.

Et tremit effeto corpore
laxa cutis.

Mors hominum felix quæ se
nec dulcibus annis:

Inserit & mestis sæpe uo-
cata uenit.

Heu heu quam surda miseros
auertit aure:

Et flentes oculos claudere
seua negat.

Dum leuibus malefida bonis

### Boetius speaketh.

That in tyme of pros-
perite, & floryshing stu-
dye, made pleasaunte
and delectable dities,
or verses: alas now be-
yng heauy and sad ouerthrowen in
aduersitie, am compelled to fele and
tast heuines and greif. Beholde the
muses Poeticall, that is to saye: the
pleasure that is in poetes verses, do
appoynt me, and compel me to writ
these verses in meter, and þ sorow-
full verses do wet my wretched face
with very waterye teares, pssuinge
out of my eyes for sorowe. Whiche
muses no feare without dout coulde
ouercome, but that they wold folow
me in my iourney of exile or banish-
ment. Sometyme the ioye of happy
and lusty delectable youth dyd comfort me, and nowe the course of so-
rowfull olde age causeth me to re-
ioyse. For hasty old age vnloked for
is come vpon me with al her incom-
modities and euyls, and sorow hath
commaunded and broughte me into
the same old age, that is to say: that
sorowe causeth me to be olde, before
my tyme come of olde age. The hoer
heares do growe vntimely vpon my
heade, and my reuiled skynne trem-
bleth my flesh, cleane consumed and
wasted with sorowe. Mannes death
is happy, that cometh not in youth,
when a man is lustye, & in pleasure
or welth: but in time of aduersitie,

B.i.         when

*The poetes do
fayne that ther
be .ix. Muses,
that do geue þ
Poetes science
to make versus
in meter, and þ
same muses be
called camene,
that is to saye,
synging swet-
lye, for that þ
they do muche
delyte men by
reason of suche
meter, & they
cause men to de
lyte in þ vayne
hyperions of po
etes, and in the
vayn plesures
of the worlde,*

Figure 11.2   The 1556 print, sig. B1ʳ, showing the opening of Boethius's *Consolatio* and Colvile's translation of it.
Newberry Library, Chicago, Case Y 672 .B204. Reproduced by kind permission.

interest to his writing by colloquialism or ingenuity. His version, therefore, gives a just and adequate view of Boethius's thought.

This commendation pertains to Colvile's rendering of the *prosae*. Lathrop also remarked on the *metra*, of which he held a lower opinion: 'Colvile', he wrote, 'feels it his duty to "open" the numerous metaphors, thus producing an incongruous mingling of the imaginative and the flatly prosaic, and destroying the emotional effect which simple accuracy would have communicated'.[13] Lathrop's characterisation remains unsurpassed in subsequent work by literary historians,[14] but the *Helsinki Corpus of English Texts* has brought welcome attention to Colvile from linguists.[15] In the course of lexical studies, Matti Rissanen and Päivi Koivisto-Alanko have observed that Colvile's text is often similar to that of Chaucer, and they accordingly raise the question of source dependency. Koivisto-Alanko holds that Colvile's 'translation is an independent work' but acknowledges that Colvile was probably 'familiar with Chaucer' and that his translation 'sometimes looks like a modernisation of Chaucer'.[16] By contrast, Rissanen affirms that 'Even a superficial comparison between Chaucer's translation [and] George Colville's (1556) clearly indicates Colville's dependence on his predecessor'.[17]

My own conclusions are nearer to those of Koivisto-Alanko than to Rissanen: consultation of the *Boece* is objectively probable, but Colvile's text derives from an independent engagement with Boethius's Latin. Agreements between the translations may sometimes be attributed to agreements in the Latin commentaries employed by the two translators. That Koivisto-Alanko and Rissanen did not notice Colvile's use of a Latin commentary is an oversight attributable to the limitations of the *Helsinki Corpus*, which lacks selections from the *metra*, where intrusions of commentary material are obvious and frequent. As I will show, Colvile's differentiated uses of commentary in the *metra* and *prosae* account for the differences in translation style observed by Lathrop. To appreciate Colvile's approach to his task and assess the historical significance of his text, we need a better understanding of the sources he used.

---

[13] Ibid., pp. 54–55.
[14] See Donaghey, 'Post-Medieval Translation', p. 316; Phillips, 'English *Consolation*', p. 103; and Cummings, 'Classical Moralists', p. 387.
[15] Rissanen et al., *Helsinki Corpus*. See Koivisto-Alanko, 'Vocabulary of Cognition'; and Rissanen, 'In Search of *Happiness*'.
[16] Koivisto-Alanko, 'Vocabulary of Cognition', p. 402.
[17] Rissanen, 'In Search of *Happiness*', p. 245.

## The *Consolatio* in Print

Source study must begin where Colvile evidently did, with the Latin *Consolatio* in print. The title page of the 1556 edition states that the Latin text printed therein was set from 'the boke of the translatour, whiche was a very olde prynte'. It ought to be possible to identify this source.

By 1556 the *Consolatio* had been in print for over 80 years. The standard enumerative bibliographies record some 126 editions of this text prior to 1556.[18] I have examined, *in situ* or in digital facsimile, 71 editions from this period, or slightly over half the total recorded in the bibliographies.[19] This search has failed in its primary objective of identifying the edition used by Colvile (I supply detail at the end of this chapter), yet the corpus of editions assembled in the service of variant-hunting has broader interest, for it permits some general remarks on the early print history of Boethius's text.[20] This history has direct implications for our assessment of Colvile's work.

Uncertainties in dating preclude identification of an *editio princeps* of the *Consolatio*, but one of the contenders for that designation is a folio printed by Anton Koberger in Nuremberg in 1473 (*GW* 4573).[21] The 1473 print presents the *Consolatio* itself, an anonymous all-prose translation of the *Consolatio* into German, and a Latin commentary falsely ascribed to Thomas Aquinas. The commentary (I shall refer to its author as 'ps.-Thomas'), will play an important role in my argument. Ps.-Thomas drew from the *Consolatio* commentary of Nicholas Trevet (*c*. 1300), and his commentary was evidently available in Italy in the third decade of the fifteenth century, yet the few surviving manuscript copies post-date the 1473 Nuremberg print.[22] The commentary by ps.-Thomas was the first

---

[18] These are nos 4513–74 in vol. IV of *GW*, and the editions of the *Consolatio* listed at *IA*, part 1, IV, 428–42. Future researchers will want to employ the online Incunabula Short Title Catalogue, Datenbank Gesamtkatalog der Wiegendrucke and USTC and can probably ignore Luca Obertello's *bibliografia boeziana*, for this bibliography omits items recorded in *GW* and *IA* and is not governed by standard disciplinary principles. See Obertello, *Severino Boezio*, II, 8, explaining idiosyncratic use of the terms *ristampa* and *nuova edizione*. For the standard bibliographic usage, defining an edition as 'those copies printed from a single setting of type', see Tanselle, 'Bibliographical Concepts', pp. 18–21, and references there.

[19] For source repositories and editions consulted, see the Appendix.

[20] Compare the sketch at Donaghey, 'Post-Medieval Translation', pp. 315–16.

[21] On this print, see Bastert, 'Boethius unter Druck', and Palmer, 'German Boethius Translation'.

[22] Glei, '*Quae philosophia fuit*', pp. 192–96, summarises what is known about ps.-Thomas. Zonta, 'Le origini letterarie', pp. 410–29, documents influence of ps.-Thomas in Bonafoux Astruc's translation of the *Consolatio* into Hebrew, produced in Italy in 1423. See also Palmer, 'German Boethius Translation', pp. 290–91, and Courcelle, *La Consolation*, pp. 322–23.

*Consolatio* commentary to appear in print and was printed more often than any other. My 71-edition sample includes 36 in which ps.-Thomas accompanies the *Consolatio* as the sole commentary. Publication was concentrated in the later 1480s and 1490s; the latest edition I have seen is dated 1502, printed in Cologne by Henry Quentell (*IA* *121.019).

In 1498 Jean de Vingle printed an edition of ps.-Thomas accompanied by a new commentary on the *Consolatio* by the humanist Jodocus Badius Ascensius (*GW* 4569).[23] Badius's commentary was designed as an update and supplement to ps.-Thomas, and this configuration of texts – *Commentum duplex in Boetium de Consolatione philosophie*, as it was styled – was printed frequently in Lyon and Rouen over a period of about two decades. Philippe Renouard records twenty-nine editions.[24] My study sample contains sixteen, of which only two post-date 1515: an edition from Venice in 1524 (*IA* *121.083) and one from Caen *c.* 1529 (*IA* *121.088).[25] The 1529 edition from Caen was evidently the last.

The print history of Badius's commentary mirrored that of the *Consolatio* itself, for, after several decades of robust growth, printing of Boethius's text fell off a cliff. Of the 126 pre-1556 editions recorded in standard bibliographies, just eighteen were printed after 1515. It seems that the market had become saturated or else that demand evaporated. Paul Gerhard Schmidt has suggested that Badius's commentaries on medieval school-texts may have hastened their removal from school curricula by exposing their non-classical Latinities.[26] Whatever the cause of decline in printing of the *Consolatio*, the humanist commentary of Johannis Murmellius was ill-timed. The first edition was printed in 1514 in Deventer (*IA* *121.056).[27] There were only two subsequent editions, printed in Cologne in 1516 (*IA* *121.066) and 1535 (*IA* *121.097).[28]

Murmellius's commentary was the first new autonomous commentary on the *Consolatio* in the print era: it was designed to replace, not

---

[23] The best study is Glei, '*Quae philosophia fuit*'. Glei (ed.), '*Iodoci Badii Ascensii*', is a critical edition of Book I. See also Courcelle, *La Consolation*, pp. 331–32; Schmidt, 'Jodocus Badius Ascensius'; Nauta, 'Magis sit Platonicus', pp. 195–99, and Nauta, 'The *Consolation*', pp. 271–72. Obertello reports a separate earlier printing of Badius's commentary (Obertello I.14.22) and a 1523 edition of ps.-Thomas without Badius (Obertello I.14.49 = *IA* *121.082?); these seem to be errors.

[24] Renouard, *Bibliographie des impressions*, I, 146; II, 196–216; III, 395–96.

[25] The Venetian edition, printed by Octavianus Scotus, is recorded by neither Renouard nor Obertello.

[26] Schmidt, 'Jodocus Badius Ascensius', pp. 70–71.

[27] On Murmellius see Nauta, 'Humanist Reading'. The commentary incorporates Rudolph Agricola's notes on a portion of Book I.

[28] The 1516 edition is not recorded by Obertello.

supplement, ps.-Thomas. At least two other commentaries and a variety of other adjuncts to the *Consolatio* appeared in print before 1556. In 1521 or earlier, Simon Vincent printed a *Boetius cum triplici commento* (*IA* *121.077).[29] Tranches of commentary by Raymundus Palasinus intervene between those of ps.-Thomas and Badius throughout the text. Among the other items printed in this complex book and attributed to or signed by Raymund are a life of Boethius, verse arguments to each of the five books and a collection of *quaestiones* on the problems of divine providence and free will in Book V. The arguments, life of Boethius and the *quaestiones*, but not the commentary, appear in another print by Simon Vincent, perhaps dateable to 1515 and evidently unrecorded in standard bibliographies.[30] In place of commentary, this edition has brief marginal notes contributed by Humbert de Montmoret. Some gloss hard words or identify proper names; most function as finding aids, picking out key phrases and important points from Boethius's text. In 1522 Thomas Wolff printed an independent life of Boethius at the head of an edition without commentary (Basil; *IA* *121.080). In 1540 the commentary of Denys the Carthusian (composed *c.* 1465) was printed in Cologne with other works by the same author.[31]

This hasty review of print history permits two general remarks in connection with Colvile's translation. First, the 1556 title page is likely correct in describing Colvile's Latin text as 'olde': very few new editions of the *Consolatio* were printed during the forty years prior to publication of the English translation. Second, Colvile's source text is likely to have included a commentary. My study sample of seventy-one editions contains just thirteen editions *sans commentaire*. Of the commentaries, the one by ps.-Thomas is the most frequent, and there can be no question that Colvile used ps.-Thomas, as the following sections will demonstrate.

## Colvile's Prologue and 'Argument'

Colvile's prologue is syncretic, freely mixing the philosophical language of the *Consolatio* with the language of pastoral Christianity. 'The gyftes of

---

[29] Obertello records an earlier print of the ps.-Thomas-Badius-Palasinus trifecta (I.14.39), dated '1510?'. This is not in *IA* but see USTC 143555 and 143904 (the later dated 1512 in USTC metadata).
[30] I refer to Newberry Library Case Y 672 .B066. See Appendix.
[31] On this commentary see Nauta, 'The *Consolation*', pp. 268–69, and Macken, *Denys the Carthusian*, pp. 41–69. The commentary appears in *D. Dionysii Carthusiani operum minorum tomus tertius* (Cologne, 1540). I do not find this book in *IA*, but see USTC 626378.

fortune, and chaunce' are recast as 'the worlde, the deuyll and the fleshe' then converted back to Boethian idiom, as 'ryches, possessions, honors, dignities, power, aucthoritie, fame & suche other' (sig. [A]3$^v$). Soon after, Colvile anticipates Philosophia's argument that 'euyll fortune is better then good fortune' (sig. [A]3$^v$). In Colvile's account, these arguments from Book II join Philosophia's identification, in Book III, of 'perfyt felicyte or sufferaygne good' (sig. [A]3$^v$) as Boethius's central message. The last two books withdraw into the background.

Disproportionate attention to *Consolatio*, II is consistent with medieval reading traditions, for which the dialogue of Fortune and subsequent analysis of false goods were among the most frequent and productive points of engagement with Boethius's work. Harmonisation of the moral teachings of philosophy, the poets and Christianity is no less conventional. Despite these general correspondences, the translator's prologue may well be Colvile's own composition, entirely derivative of the reading tradition, yet independent of any single source.

By contrast, the content of the 'argument or summe' strongly suggests a prior source. Each of its components – potted history, conflation of narrative setting and compositional circumstance, exposition of the title, observations on genre and form, book-by-book summary – is a standard offering in the exegetical tradition. The source was probably ps.-Thomas.[32] Colvile lacks ps.-Thomas's external prologue in praise of philosophy, and his English text is much shorter and simpler than ps.-Thomas's prologue, but it often reads as a free translation of the medieval commentator. Dependency may be illustrated by the first sentences of ps.-Thomas's internal prologue and Colvile's 'argument', respectively:

> Boetius uir eximius consul Romanus fide catholicus extitit. qui disputans de fide catholica contra duos hereticos scilicet contra Nestorium & Eutiten. cum nullus esset qui eis resisteret Boetius ipsos in communi concilio deuicit. sicut patet in libro suo de duabus naturis in christo.[33]

> There was a noble man, a consul of Rome named Boecius, this man was a catholike man and dysputed for the faith in the comon counsayle agaynste the herytykes Nestoryus and Euticen, and confuted them, as it appeareth by a booke that he made, wherein he proueth two natures in Chryste. (sig. [A]2$^v$)

---

[32] The prologues of Murmellius and Badius supply the right kind of material, but their content is not close. Nor does Colvile's brief life of Boethius resemble the essays on this subject by Raymundus Palasinus or Thomas Wolff.

[33] I quote from the 1473 Nuremberg edition. Citations are to the folio numbers entered in an early hand in Newberry Library oversize Inc. 1966, here ff. 94$^{vb}$–95$^{ra}$.

Verbal parallels must be evaluated with caution, given the tralatitious character of this genre. The phrase *communi consilio*, for example, (English *comon counsayle*) may go back to *Contra Eutychen* itself.[34] Yet the correspondences are persistent. Although Colvile employs neither ps.-Thomas's schema of Aristotelian causes, nor his interpretation of Boethius's names, he transmits little without a counterpart in ps.-Thomas's prologue and retains nearly the same order of materials. (Whereas ps.-Thomas treats the prosimetrical form of the *Consolatio* before its dialogic form, Colvile treats dialogue first.) Only at the end of the argument, in the book-by-book summary, does Colvile seem to be following another source. These book-summaries were widespread in the commentary tradition.

## The Commentary

The prefatory material in the 1556 print makes no mention of the notes printed in the outer margins. These are less frequent than the brief Latin marginalia of Humbert de Montmoret (printed in Simon Vincent's ?1515 edition) and do not resemble them in content. Most are undistinguished, yet some can be sourced with confidence. The most egregious is perhaps a note to III.p8.10, stating that Alcibiades was a very beautiful woman:

> Alcibiades was the fayrest woman, that coulde be seen, in Aristotelles tyme, in so moche that his scolers broughte her to Arystotell, to loke vpon, & beholde. (sig. O1ᵛ)

This exegetical blooper may be traced all the way back to the early medieval glosses associated with Remigius of Auxerre (d. 908). The note is recorded in one copy of William of Conches's (d. *c.* 1155?) commentary[35] and may have been in the copy employed by Nicholas Trevet, for Trevet reported the following at this location:

> Dicit autem commentator hic quod Alcibiades meretrix quedam pulcherrima erat, quam videntes discipuli quidam Aristotelis ut eam videret ad illum eam adduxerunt.[36]

---

[34] See Boethius's prologue to that work: *De consolatione*, ed. by Moreschini, pp. 206–8. Boethius writes of listening quietly to debate *in consilio*, not of refuting the heresies in that public setting.

[35] William of Conches, *Glosae super Boetium*, ed. by Nauta, p. 140 *var. lect.*

[36] I quote from the unfinished typescript edition of E. T. Silk, available online at www.trinity.edu/sites/akraebel/trevet-boethius (last accessed 11 November 2022). Citations are to page numbers in the upper margin of the typescript. This passage is at pp. 367–68. On Trevet's commentary see Minnis and Nauta, '*More Platonico loquitur*' (1993); and Nauta, 'Scholastic Context'.

*Commentator* is Trevet's usual way of referring to William of Conches in this work.[37] Completed about 1300, Trevet's commentary was employed as a source by several later practitioners, among them ps.-Thomas, who supplied the following note at the end of his treatment of III.p8:

> Nota quod Alcibiades mulier fuit pulcerrima, quam videntes quidam discipuli Arestotilis duxerunt eam ad Arestotilem vt ipsam videret. (f. 145$^{va}$)

The error was loudly corrected by Badius, as previous researchers have noted.[38] Johannis Murmellius also identifies Alcibiades correctly, citing works of Cornelius Nepos, Plutarch, Thucydides and Marsilio Ficino.[39]

Colvile's moralising gloss on I.m5 (sig. C2$^v$) and his historical gloss on *proscriptio* in I.p4 (sig. D2$^v$) similarly agree with ps.-Thomas against Badius and Murmellius. The 'olde prynte' from which Colvile translated surely contained the commentary of ps.-Thomas and perhaps lacked Badius. Such a selection would have been old-fashioned in the middle of the sixteenth century, neglecting the new humanist scholarship. Yet 'neglect' may not be the right word: as my bibliographical survey has shown, the new humanist scholarship remained in a marginal position in the middle of the sixteenth century. The book market was presumably still flooded with old copies of ps.-Thomas.

## The English Text

### *Metra*

Colvile's expansive translation of the *metra* (which so distressed Lathrop) likewise draws from the commentary of ps.-Thomas. I have examined four of Colvile's prosified *metra* in detail: I.m2, I.m3, III.m1 and III.m11. Exceptionally, Colvile appends an interpretative note to the end of III. m11, Philosophia's exposition of Platonic *anamnesis*. The note derives from ps.-Thomas and presents the sort of material more often disposed in the margins of the 1556 print. Elsewhere, Colvile retains the general shape and progress of the Latin poems, even as he expands.

---

[37] Minnis and Nauta, 'More Platonico loquitur' (1993), pp. 9–10.
[38] See Courcelle, *La Consolation*, p. 332; and Grafton, 'Boethius in the Renaissance', pp. 412–13. I cite the commentary of Badius from the 1498 Lyon edition, which I consult in a digital facsimile of Bayerishe Staatsbibliothek, 4 Inc.c.a. 1476 a. This passage is f. 88$^r$.
[39] I cite the 1514 Deventer edition, which I consult in a digital facsimile of Koninklijke Bibliotheek, 227 E 7. This passage is sig. P2$^{r-v}$.

To illustrate Colvile's translation style and source dependency, I present ten diagnostic agreements in I.m2. In this meter Badius and Palasinus offer only a few grammatical addenda to ps.-Thomas's commentary. Their brief remarks contain nothing that may profitably be compared with Colvile's translation. By contrast, ps.-Thomas, Murmellius and Denys the Carthusian each present full commentaries; their glosses may be arrayed in parallel with one another and with Colvile's text. The entries below have the following elements:

1. In bold, passages from Colvile's translation, identified in parentheses by page signature and page line.[40]
2. The corresponding reading of the *Consolatio*, quoted from the 1556 print and identified by line number.
3. Ps.-Thomas's gloss, quoted from the 1473 Nuremburg print and identified in parentheses by folio number in the Newberry Library copy.
4. Murmellius's gloss, quoted from the 1514 Deventer print and identified in parentheses by folio number in this print.
5. Denys the Carthusian's gloss, quoted from the 1540 Cologne print and identified in parentheses by folio number in that print.
6. Chaucer's translation, quoted from the *Riverside* edition, with notice of variants on one occasion where they are relevant.

**in the depe care of worldlye and transytorye thynges (B3$^r$ 3–4).**

DCP 1: *praecipiti ... profundo.*
PS.-THOMAS: *precipiti profundo .i. cura rerum temporalium que precipitat hominem* (f. 100$^{va}$).
MURMELLIUS: *precipiti profundo: profunditate perturbationum: vnde non sit facile emergere* (f. 5$^v$).
DENYS: *[profundo quam praecipiti] .i. valde celeri, impetuoso ac praecipitante in vndantia ac abundantia aduersitatum, afflictionum, dolorum* (f. 14$^v$).
CHAUCER: *in overthrowynge depnesse.*

**in outwarde darkenes of ignoraunce (B3$^r$ 6–7).**

DCP 3: *in externas ... tenebras.*
PS.-THOMAS: *in tenebras externas .i. in ignorantias exteriores* (f. 100$^{va}$).

---

[40] I treat the first line of this meter as line 1 and begin again at 1 at the top of each successive page of the print.

MURMELLIUS: *in res terrenas ac corporeas illecebras spiritum sua contagione obtenebrantes* (f. 5$^v$–6$^r$).
DENYS: *[in tenebras externas,] id est, in maximas ignorantiarum, errorum ac vitiorum caligines, nisi sapientialiter reuocetur* (f. 14$^v$).
CHAUCER: *foreyne dirknesses* (Caxton, Thynne and two manuscripts have the singular, *derknes*).

### The care of temporall thinges (B3$^r$ 8–9).

DCP 5: *cura.*
PS.-THOMAS: *cura .i. sollicitudo rerum temporalium* (f. 100$^{va}$).
MURMELLIUS: *cura: cupiditas rerum externarum* (f. 6$^r$).
DENYS: *[cura noxia] id est, solicitudo nociua superflua de talibus recuperandis* (f. 15$^r$).
CHAUCER: *bysynes.*

### fre from cure of worldlye thinges (B3$^v$ 1–2).

DCP 6: *liber.*
PS.-THOMAS: *liber .i. solutus a cura rerum temporalium* (f. 100$^{vb}$).
MURMELLIUS: *liber quondam: cum nondum passionibus animi seruiret* (f. 6$^r$).
DENYS: *[quondam liber] id est, olim ab exilio, curis, tristitijs, diffortunijsque immunis* (f. 15$^r$).
CHAUCER: *fre.*

### the sterres or constellacions (B3$^v$ 8–9).

DCP 9: *sydera.*
PS.-THOMAS: *sidera .i. constellationes* (f. 100$^{vb}$).
MURMELLIUS: *Sydera: lumina* (f. 6$^r$).
DENYS: *ponitur plurale pro singulari, videlicet sydera pro sydere, vt sit sensus: videbat sydus lunae intransitiue, hoc est lunam quae vocatur sydus ... Possunt item per sydera lunae intelligi stellae Pleiades, que cum luna communicant in humido, habentes dominium super aquas ...* (f. 15$^r$).
CHAUCER: *sterres.*

### a man that with scyence had ouercom ignoraunce (B3$^v$ 10–11).

DCP 12: *uictor.*
PS.-THOMAS: *ipse Boetius victor ignorantie* (f. 100$^{vb}$).
MURMELLIUS: *victor id est voti compos* (f. 6$^r$).

DENYS: *[victor] .i. praeualens in sua astronomica inquisitione, inueniendo quod quaerebat, habebat stellam huiusmodi compressam* ... (f. 15ʳ).
CHAUCER: *this man, overcomere.*

### the stedefaste and hole fyrmament (B3ᵛ 22–23).

DCP 15: *stabilem ... orbem.*
PS.-THOMAS: *stabilem orbem firmamenti* (f. 101ʳᵇ).
MURMELLIUS: *orbem mundem id est celum stabilem* (f. 7ʳ).
DENYS: *[stabilem orbem] id est, incorruptibilem spheram coelestem* (f. 15ʳ).
CHAUCER: *the stable hevene.*

### the secret causes of naturall thynges (B3ᵛ 34–35).

DCP 22–23: *latentis / Naturae varias ... causas.*
PS.-THOMAS: *varias causas latentis nature .i. rerum naturalium* (f. 101ʳᵇ); *Item Boetius consueuit reddere causas latentes rerum naturalium* (f. 101ᵛᵃ).
MURMELLIUS: no gloss
DENYS: *[varias causas naturae latentis,] .i. occultarum naturalium proprietatum ac virium, actionum atque affectuum* (f. 15ᵛ).
CHAUCER: *the diverse causes of nature that weren yhidd.*

### with heuye chaynes, that is to say: with passions and vexacyons of the mind (B4ʳ 1–3).

DCP 25: *grauibus ... catenis.*
PS.-THOMAS: *grauidis cathenis passionum que mentem grauant* (f. 101ᵛᵃ).
MURMELLIUS: *Grauibus catenis: rerum terrenarum cupiditatibus* (f. 7ʳ).
DENYS: *[catenis grauidis,] .i. grauantibus, quam moris est apud quosdam quod captis mittitur catena in collo, seu alia corporis parte* (f. 15ᵛ).
CHAUCER: *with hevy cheynes.*

### with great wayte or heuynes, for the losse of temporall goodes (B4ʳ 4–6).

DCP 26: *pondere.*
PS.-THOMAS: *pondere amissionis rerum temporalium* (f. 101ᵛᵃ).
MURMELLIUS: *Pondere. terrestri solicitudine* (f. 7ʳ).
DENYS: *pondere tristitiae, vel ex onere catenae* (f. 15ᵛ).
CHAUCER: *for the grete weyghte.*

Colvile's expansions consistently draw from the commentary of ps.-Thomas. Treatment of I.m2.6 *liber* ('free') may serve as an example: Colvile's gloss 'from cure of worldlye thinges' corresponds precisely to ps.-Thomas's 'a cura rerum temporalium', lacking reference to either passions, the soul and servitude (as in Murmellius) or exile and misfortune (as in Denys). Later in the meter, Colvile's moralisation of Boethius's chains (*catenae*, 25–26) agrees with ps.-Thomas against both Murmellius's alternative moralisation and Denys's literalism. Where Colvile offers a moralising or explanatory gloss, this gloss agrees with ps.-Thomas against the other two commentators. Chaucer, meanwhile, appears concise and literal by comparison.[41]

Moreover, though ps.-Thomas was dependent on Trevet (whose glosses I have not reported above), Colvile regularly agrees with ps.-Thomas where ps.-Thomas differs from his precursor. Ps.-Thomas's glosses on *uictor* (12) and *stabilem ... orbem* (15), both used by Colvile, are without parallel in Trevet's commentary, while his gloss on *sydera* (9) simplifies Trevet's more exact *mansiones sideribus consignatas* (p. 44). In each of these cases, Colvile agrees with ps.-Thomas not only in semantics and phrasing, but also in precise lexical choices: Colvile's *constellacions* (translating *sydera*, 9), *ignoraunce* (expanding *victor*, 12), *fyrmament* (translating *orbem*, 15) and *passions* (expanding *cathenis*, 25) are reflexes of Latin words found in ps.-Thomas's gloss but not in the corresponding glosses of Trevet. Colvile's surprising translation of I.m3.9 *vibratus* as *fortifyed* (sig. B4$^v$) should be explained in the same way, as a lexical import from ps.-Thomas's gloss: Trevet glossed *vibratus* as *crispatus uel splendidus* (p. 61); Murmellius glossed as *motus* and *agitatus* (f. 8$^r$); ps.-Thomas glossed as *fortificatus* (f. 102$^{vb}$).

On occasion, Colvile's translations show him reading somewhat more widely in ps.-Thomas's commentary, drawing from the prose paraphrases and discursive notes that precede and follow *ad litteram* glosses. In comments on I.m2, ps.-Thomas divides the poem into parts and states that Philosophia first commends Boethius 'ab astronomia' (f. 100$^{vb}$) then praises his achievement in other sciences. That remark may stand behind Colvile's translation of line 7, where he expands 'Suetus in aethereos ire meatus' to 'was wonte to goo into the heuenly wayes by science of astronomy' (B3$^v$). (There is no mention of astronomy in ps.-Thomas's glosses to line 7 itself.) Similar cases may be found in Colvile's III.m1.

---

[41] Minnis and Machan, '*Boece* as Late-Medieval Translation' (1993), p. 175, similarly remark that 'Chaucer's use of the commentary tradition is restrained' by comparison with some of the medieval French translations of Boethius's work. Cummings, 'Classical Moralists', p. 387, describes I.m2 (in fact he refers to III.m11) as 'overtranslated, perhaps following Chaucer'. The translations are not alike.

The implication is that Colvile read ps.-Thomas with some care; when an expansion does not correspond to ps.-Thomas's word glosses or running paraphrase, its source should be sought in introductory remarks on the meter in question, or in the more digressive notes that follow *ad litteram* glosses in ps.-Thomas's commentary.

This methodological directive bears on a few difficult cases in which one may be tempted to posit a second source. Colvile's gloss on spring as the season 'when all growyng thinges springeth forthe' (I.m2.18; B3$^v$) corresponds to nothing in ps.-Thomas's running glosses but agrees closely with Trevet's comment at this location: 'tunc omnia uegetabilia pululant et germinant' (p. 49). The correspondence is exact, yet Colvile's addition could derive from ps.-Thomas's subsequent discursive note, explaining why flowers are brought forth in springtime ('illo tempore producuntur flores'; f. 101$^{va}$). In the next meter, Colvile marks the beginning of Boethius's elaborate simile of the evening sunburst with a parenthetical addition 'by example thus' (sig. B4$^v$), in agreement with Chaucer ('And ryht by ensaumple') and Trevet ('Deinde subiungit similitudinem dicens...'; p. 60). Ps.-Thomas has no analogous comment at this location, but he lays the *similitudo* out in detail at the beginning of his commentary on this meter.

A few other translation choices in I.m2, I.m3, III.m1 and III.m11 require comment. In rendering *sonora / Flamina* as *greate wyndes* (I.m2.13–14; B3$^v$), Colvile takes noise as metonymy for magnitude. Several lines below, where Philosophia proclaims Boethius's former understanding of the rotation of the heavens –

> Vel cur hesperias sydus in undas
> Casurum rutilio surgat ab ortu (I.m2.16–17)

– Colvile translates *hesperias* twice: 'And whye the ster called hesperus risyth in the resplendent est, and goeth downe in the occydent sea' (B3$^v$). *Occydent sea* renders *hesperias ... undas* correctly, in agreement with the commentators. Yet, as ps.-Thomas subsequently remarks, the epithet *hesparius* derives from Hesperus, the star that follows the westering sun into the sea (f. 101$^{va}$). By juxtaposing an unnamed star or heavenly body (*sydus*) and waves named for a particular star, Boethius's line does invite confusion. That construction is perhaps sufficient to explain Colvile's 'ster called hesperus', a meaning nevertheless ruled out by grammatical concord. At III.m11.14 Chaucer and Colvile agree in rendering *fomes* ('kindling-wood') as *noryshynge(s)* (Colvile as *the noryshynge and grounde*; sig. R2$^r$), a mistranslation that evidently had some currency in English schools.[42] Finally, Colvile neglects to translate I.m3.2 *luminibus* 'lights [> eyes]' and I.m3.5 *nondum* 'not yet', words duly glossed by ps.-Thomas. There is no reason to doubt that they stood in Colvile's copy of the *Consolatio*.

Omission of *nondum* is a trivial error, but Chaucer omits this word too, and it may be instructive to compare the two translations of this passage, which presents the elaborate simile of an afternoon storm followed by sunburst – or, rather, the first half of this simile, before the dramatic re-appearance of the sun. Here is Boethius:

> ut cum praecipiti glomerantur sidera Coro
> nimbosisque polus stetit imbribus
> sol latet ac nondum caelo uenientibus astris
> desuper in terram nox funditur. (I.m3.3–6)

Here is Chaucer:

> And ryght by ensaumple as the sonne is hydd whan the sterres ben clustred (that is to seyn, whan sterres ben covered with cloudes) by a swyft wynd that hyghte Chorus, and that the firmament stant dirked with wete plowngy cloudes; and that the sterres nat apeeren upon hevene, so that the nyght semeth sprad upon erthe. (*Riverside*, p. 399)

And here is Colvile:

> euyn so as (by example thus) the sonne lyethe hydde when the sterres be couered wyth cloudes of the swyfte wynde named chorus, and the fyrmament standeth closyd and coueryd with thicke showers, so that the nyght spredeth from aboue ouer all the earthe when that the sterres cannot be seene in the firmament. (sig. B4ᵛ)

Colvile's vocabulary is more pedestrian than Chaucer's: note, for instance, Colvile's *closyd and coueryd* in place of Chaucer's *dirked*, and his *thicke showers* in place of Chaucer's *wete plowngy cloudes*. (*MED* records *plowngy* only from the *Boece*, s.v. 'ploungi', adj.) The translations also share several distinctive features, which is my reason for quoting them here: both mark Boethius's word-picture as an 'example', both fail to register the specific force of the phrase *nondum caelo uenientibus astris* (to wit, the meteorological event seems to bring night prematurely, before the stars appear in the sky), both re-order Boethius's sentence, promoting the first branch of

---

[42] As noted by Machan (ed.), with Minnis, *Sources of the 'Boece'* (2005), p. 291, *noryssyng* is listed as a translation of *fomes* in the *Medulla Grammatice*, a fifteenth-century Latin-English glossary.

the main clause (*sol latet*) to initial position, and both render *glomerantur* as 'ben covered with cloudes' (in *Boece* this appears within a doublet translation). These agreements may appear to have considerable weight.

The first two agreements have already been noted and may be explained without positing Chaucer as source. To reiterate, Colvile's 'example' may reflect ps.-Thomas's introductory exposition of the *similitudo*, while Colvile's omission of *nondum* finds precedent in small lapses elsewhere in the translation. The remaining agreements supply no stronger evidence of Chaucerian dependency. Colvile's re-ordering of sentence elements is guided by ps.-Thomas, whose prose paraphrase takes precisely the same path through Boethius's syntax; where Colvile and Chaucer diverge at the end of the passage, Colvile follows ps.-Thomas. Turning now to the final agreement, Colvile's *when the sterres be couered wyth cloudes* may appear as an intelligent improvement on Chaucer's *whan the sterres ben clustred (that is to seyn, whan sterres ben covered with cloudes)*, rendering Chaucer's gloss rather than his literal translation.[43] Yet what at first appears to be a borrowing from Chaucer probably derives instead from ps.-Thomas. That commentator glossed the difficult word *glomerantur* as *inuoluantur* (*sic*, f. $102^{vb}$), probably borrowing from Trevet, whose gloss *nubibus inuoluuntur* (p. 60) stands behind the parallel passage in Chaucer's translation. Colvile might have taken *be couered wyth cloudes* from Chaucer, but ps.-Thomas's gloss would have directed him to that same translation.

The relationship between these two translators is confounded by the relationship between their respective commentators. To give one more example, I thought that I could identify a sure borrowing from Chaucer in Colvile's rendering of the very first word of the entire work, *carmina*. This is rendered by Chaucer as 'delitable ditees' and by Colvile as 'pleasaunte and delectable dities, or verses' (sig. B1$^r$). Yet inspection of the surrounding text shows that Colvile is here translating ps.-Thomas's prose paraphrase, in which the prisoner's past *carmina* are qualified as *delectabilia & iocunda* (f. 96$^{rb}$). Chaucer's adjective derives from Trevet's gloss (*cantus delectabiles*; p. 15), while *MED* records numerous instances of *dite* translating Latin *carmen*. These instances include the *Medulla Grammatice*. Hence a juicy phrase — one that appeared initially as good evidence of filiation between the two English translations — turns out, on closer inspection, to have been programmed by the Latin texts and pedagogies that subtend both translations.

---

[43] Colvile would not have been alone in improving Chaucer's translation at this point. Two manuscript copies of *Boece* and the editions of Caxton and Thynne omit *clustred . . . ben*.

## Prosae

In Colvile's *prosae* there is less interference from ps.-Thomas, and this fact ought to simplify comparison with Chaucer. My study of the *prosae* is based in III.p9 and IV.p4, selected because these segments are available in digital form in the *Helsinki Corpus of English Texts*.[44] Colvile's independence is demonstrated in the first instance by passages in which his translation agrees with the *Consolatio* against Chaucer. Colvile is indebted to Boethius's lexis at points where Chaucer is not.[45] His translation reflects Latin grammatical gender where Chaucer does not.[46] He translates minor words omitted by Chaucer,[47] and he preserves the phrasal and clausal structure of Boethius's text at points where Chaucer departs from it.[48] At other points where Chaucer errs, follows Jean de Meun or offers an idiosyncratic translation, Colvile agrees with Boethius's Latin.[49]

Chaucer and Colvile may also translate different aspects of the same text. At IV.p4.16, Philosophia asks Boethius to imagine misery *pura ac solitaria*, unmixed with any goodness. Chaucer translates only the second

---

[44] Quotations in this section are from Rissanen et al., *Helsinki Corpus*, which in turn derives its text of Chaucer from the *Riverside Chaucer*, and of Colvile from Bax (ed.), *Boethius'* Consolation.

[45] I print the reading of the *Consolatio* before the bracket, followed after the bracket by the corresponding readings of Chaucer's and Colvile's translations. III.p1.3 *perfeci*] *hadde maked* Ch; *perfyted* Col. 3p9.1 *felicitatis*] *welefulnesse* Ch; *felicite or blessednes* Col. III.p9.8 *iudicemus*] *demen* Ch; *iudge* Col (also IV.p4.42). III.p9.8 *confiteri*] *graunten* Ch; *confesse* Col (also III.p9.11). III.p9.9 *obscurum*] *dirk* Ch; *obscure* Col. III.p9.10 *parte*] *side* Ch; *parte* Col. III.p9.24 *promisimus*] *have behyght* Ch; *haue promysed* Col. IV.p4.9 *extrema*] *owtreste* Ch; *extreme* Col. IV.p4.9 *aeternam*] *perdurable* Ch; *eternall or euer contynuyng* Col. IV.p4.11 *efficacem*] *spedful* Ch; *effectuall* Col. IV.p4.25 *consequens est*] *folweth* Ch; *is a consequence* Col. IV.p4.26 *iudicia*] *studies* Ch; *iudgementes* Col. IV.p4.27 *affectus*] *lustes and talentz* Ch; *affectes and desyres* Col. IV.p4.40 *defensorum*] *advocattz* Ch; *orators and defenders* Col.

[46] At the beginning of I.m2, Colvile's feminine pronoun *her* reflects the grammatical gender of Latin *mens*. Chaucer has the pronoun *his*, which should be construed as neuter (the antecedent is *thought*). Chaucer's pronoun is consistent with English usage; Colvile's is a reflex of the source language.

[47] Chaucer omits III.p9.9 *omni*, IV.p4.23 *nunc* and IV.p4.40 *totos*. Witnesses to the *Boece* likewise omit IV.p4.22 *consequentia sunt*. Colvile translates these words. For notice of Chaucer's errors and idiosyncrasies, reported in this note and the next two, I am indebted to the editions of *Boece* cited in n. 3.

[48] At III.p9.10 Chaucer misplaces *concessum est*. At IV.p4.20 Chaucer shifts the position of *iniquitatis merito*. Colvile retains the order of the Latin text.

[49] At III.p9.4 Chaucer follows Jean de Meun. Colvile's *remayne* is preferable to Chaucer's *ben* as a rendering of III.p9.14 *manebunt*. Colvile retains the superlative degree of IV.p4.24 *indignissima*, whereas Chaucer does not. In the same section of the Latin text, Chaucer construes the subjunctive *videres* as optative, whereas Colvile recognises that it pertains to a clause of result. Soon thereafter, Chaucer's translation of IV.p4.27 *ita est* reflects Jean de Meun's French; Colvile translates the Latin. At V.p6.33 Chaucer introduces a change of speakers without precedent in the Latin textual tradition; in Colvile's translation the speaker remains Philosophia. At V.p6.35 Chaucer read *de rerum natura*, whereas manuscripts of the Latin text have *de rerum necessitate*, the reading translated by Colvile.

adjective, Colvile only the first. Colvile also errs at points where Chaucer would have set him right.[50]

In each of the cases discussed thus far, the Latin text that accompanies Colvile's translation in the 1556 print is unexceptional. At several other points in III.p9 and IV.p4, the 1556 Latin text varies from the text printed in modern editions. In these instances, Colvile's English agrees with the Latin text printed beside it, while Chaucer's translation reflects the standard Latin reading, thus demonstrating again Colvile's independence from the earlier translator. These readings will receive full discussion later in this chapter.

Commentaries add another layer of differentiation between the two translations. Colvile occasionally follows ps.-Thomas at points where Chaucer follows the *Consolatio* or another source. An example is I.p2.3, where Philosophia tells Boethius that she endowed him with *arma* (Chaucer: *armures*) sufficient to preserve himself, had he not abandoned them. Colvile renders *arma* as *knowelege and instructions* (sig. B4$^r$), apparently reflecting ps.-Thomas's gloss *documenta* (f. 101$^{vb}$). As in his translations of the *metra*, though much more rarely, Colvile imports explanatory glosses from ps.-Thomas's commentary and follows ps.-Thomas's guidance in construing syntax (e.g., at IV.p4.40).

Where Chaucer and Colvile introduce similar expansions and glosses, their agreement can usually be attributed to their respective commentators, Trevet and ps.-Thomas. An example is supplied by Philosophia's praise of Boethius at III.p9.28: 'O te, alumne, hac opinione felicem, si quidem hoc, inquit, adieceris!' Chaucer expands *si quidem hoc . . . adieceris* to 'yif thow putte this therto that I schal seyn' and Colvile's translation is nearly identical. The explanatory clause 'that I schal seyn' agrees verbatim with Trevet and ps.-Thomas, both of whom add 'quod modo dicam' to emphasise continuity of argument. Agreements in expansion of III.p9.7 *huiusmodi* and *ne dubitari quidem potest*, III.p9.9 *hoc*, III.p9.30 *Haec*, IV.p4.12 *necessarium*, V.p6.7 *transacta* and V.p6.13 *arripuit* are likewise traceable to agreements between the commentators.[51] As we saw already in the *metra*, ps.-Thomas's dependence on Trevet is a confounding variable.

---

[50] Examples may be found in Colvile's renditions of III.p9.2 *nec celebritatem gloria*, IV.p4.2 *releuetur*, IV.p4.24 *miseriores esse improbos* and IV.p4.37–38. Colvile's translation of IV.p4.38 gets Boethius's point exactly backwards. For IV.p6.33 *Cathoni* Colvile's translation reads *Plato*. The error is difficult to explain and may have been introduced by the compositor. The Latin text of the 1556 print is correct in each of these cases.

[51] At III.p9.29 *nihil ut amplius desideretur* and at IV.p4.23 *alia*, Trevet glosses correctly while ps.-Thomas, Chaucer and Colvile err together. Colvile's translation presumably derives from ps.-Thomas.

Once one takes account of the relation between Trevet and ps.-Thomas, the case for Colvile's dependence on Chaucer becomes correspondingly weak. I find no reason to posit Chaucer as a source in III.p9. The evidence of IV.p4 is equivocal. In their explanatory glosses to IV.p4.39, Colvile and Chaucer are closer to one another than to their respective commentators. Translations of IV.p4.8 are instructive because they present a cluster of agreements:

> Quorum magna spes et excelsa facinorum machina repentino atque insperato saepe fine destruitur. Quod quidem illis miseriae modum statuit: nam si nequitia miseros facit, miserior sit necesse est diuturnior nequam.
>
> *Chaucer*: Of whiche schrewes the grete hope and the heye compassynges of schrewednesses is ofte destroyed by a sodeyn ende, or thei ben war; and that thing establisseth to schrewes the ende of hir schrewednesse. For yf that schrewednesse makith wrecches, than mot he nedes ben moost wrecchide that lengest is a schrewe. (*Riverside*, pp. 446–47)
>
> *Colvile*: Of whyche foresayde wycked the gret hope and the gret compassing power of wyckednes, is oft destroyed with sodayne ende, and er they beware thereof: which foresayde sodden destructyon, truelye hathe appoynted them an ende of theyr wretchednes. For yf wyckednes makethe wycked folke then must he nedes be most wycked that longest is wycked. (sig. V4$^v$–X1$^r$)

There are three notable points of convergence here. Chaucer renders *facinorum machina* ('scheme of crimes') as *compassynges of schrewednesses*, Colvile as *compassing power of wyckednes*,[52] the two translators both resolve the participle *insperato* into a new clause, and they agree in rendering the Latin comparatives (*miserior, diuturnior*) as superlatives. Agreements are not attributable to the commentators, yet each could be a chance convergence, and the passages are marked by differences that cannot be attributed to lexical and grammatical modernisation. If Colvile consulted Chaucer at this point, why did he not follow Chaucer's lead in differentiating *miseros* and *nequam*? By translating both as *wycked*, Colvile misses the point of Philosophia's argument.

Relations between Colvile and Chaucer deserve further study. What is clear is that Colvile's translation did not originate as a redaction or modernisation of the *Boece*, and he did not employ the *Boece* in any systematic or consistent way.

---

[52] The editions of Caxton and Thynne have the singular number, *compassyng of shrewednesse*, thus somewhat closer to Colvile. Colvile's *power* derives from ps.-Thomas, who glosses *machina* as *magna potentia* (f. 169$^{ra}$).

## Colvile's Latin Edition

Where the 1556 Latin text differs from modern critical editions, the variants may serve to identify the edition from which Colvile worked. My study has identified four Latin readings of diagnostic value. The variants do not permit Colvile's 'very olde prynte' to be identified with any of the seventy-one editions I have seen, but they do narrow the field.

At IV.p4.14 in the standard text, Philosophia reasons that the wicked are unhappier when they go unpunished: 'alio quodam modo infeliciores esse improbos arbitror impunitos'. The Latin text of the 1556 print here reads *felitiores* and *punitos* in place of the corresponding negative adjectives. Colvile follows this reading: 'wycked folke that be iustlye ponyshed be more blessed' (sig. X1ᵛ). Ps.-Thomas's paraphrase likewise replaces negative adjectives with their positive counterparts ('arbitror improbos esse felitiores punitos'; f. 169ᵛᵃ), which suggests that the variant reading may have originated in commentary, subsequently transmitted to the main text. Read in context, the negative adjectives at IV.p4.14 are an elegant variation on Philosophia's plainer statement just a few lines above: 'Feliciores, inquit, esse improbos supplicia luentes quam si eos nulla iustitiae poena coherceat' (4p4.13). Perhaps this passage induced the commentator to simplify IV.p4.14.

Whatever the source of the *feliciores/punitos* variant, it is distinctive of French prints. The earliest edition in which I have found this variant was printed in Lyon by Jean Du Pré, dated 1487/8 (*GW* 4541).[53] It was then transmitted to subsequent editions. All Lyon editions between 1487 and 1514 have the *feliciores/punitos* variant at this location. Beyond the Lyon products, I have encountered this variant only in a group of editions from Caen and Rouen, printed between 1503 and 1515, and in the edition printed by Thomas Wolff (Basil, 1522). The standard reading was restored in the Lyon editions with contributions by Raymundus Palasinus, and in the 1529 edition from Caen.

Wolff's 1522 edition lacks ps.-Thomas's commentary, so it is *prima facie* unlikely to have been Colvile's source, and this judgement receives support from a variant reading later in IVp4. Near the end of this prose section, Philosophia affirms that, if the wicked only saw how they will rid themselves of the pollution of their sins by undergoing the torments of punishments (*poenarum cruciatibus*), they would not consider those things

---

[53] See the analytic description at Scholderer and Sheppard, *Catalogue of Books Printed*, VIII, 282. *GW* records three earlier editions from Lyon: 4535 (dated 1484/5), 4536 and 4539. All three were printed by Guillaume Le Roy. I have seen only the first of these, *GW* 4535.

(*hos*) to be torments (IV.p4.40). The masculine plural *hos* is the minority reading in early prints, but it is the reading of Wolff's edition. Several editions from Cologne and Strasbourg have the feminine plural *has* (the 1501 Strasbourg edition names *poenarum* as the antecedent), but most early prints have the singular pronoun *hoc*. *Hoc* is the reading of the 1556 Latin text, and it is the reading translated by Colvile, who writes that the wicked 'woulde not esteme *thys* for ponyshments' (emphasis added; sig. X4ʳ). Among the French editions I have seen, *hos* appears only in the Lyon editions with contributions by Palasinus and in the Caen edition of 1529, the same two copies that restore the standard reading at IV.p4.14.

A reading in III.m1 may permit the field of possible source editions to be narrowed. The opening of this poem reads, in Colvile's translation, 'He that wyll sowe a goodly felde wyth corne, fyrst he must ryd the same felde of shrubes and thorns' (sig. L2ʳ). Colvile's 'shrubes and thorns' translates '*fruticibus*', the reading of the 1556 Latin text, the best manuscript witnesses and about two thirds of editions in my pre-1556 sample. Yet *fruticibus* was vulnerable to corruption: other editions read *fructibus*, *frutibus* or *fructicibus*. To judge from the distribution of variants, the word was a perennial frustration to compositors: it is corrupted and set right again within subsequent editions by the same printer.[54] Among the editions with the *feliciores/punitos* variant, only six have the correct reading at III.m1.[55]

Two considerations prevent us from identifying Colvile's source with any of these editions. First, the evidence supplied by *fruticibus* is weaker than that supplied by variants at IV.p4.14 and IV.p4.40. In those cases, Colvile translated a corrupt source text. In this case, he translated the correct reading, and corruptions could be put right. In his commentary on this passage, Badius affirmed *fruticibus* to be the correct reading, and several copies in my sample have been corrected by hand, perhaps guided by the commentator. A corruption of *fruticibus* may have been corrected by hand in Colvile's copy.

Second, a variant not yet considered in my argument indicates that Colvile's source text probably cannot be identified with any of the seventy-one editions I have seen. This final variant occurs near the end of Philosophia's analysis of false goods in III.p9. The passage reads as follows in Moreschini's critical edition (I place key words in bold):

---

[54] For example, successive editions printed in Deventer by Jacob de Breda (Obertello I.14.14) read *fruticibus* (1485), *fructibus* (1490) and *fruticibus* again (1491, 1497). Jean Du Pré's edition of 1487 reads *fruticibus*, but the editions of 1490 and 1493 read *frutibus*.
[55] These six are Jean Du Pré's 1487/8 edition, Jean de Vingle's first two editions of the *Commentum duplex* (*GW* 4569, 4570) and three sixteenth-century editions of the *Commentum duplex* (*IA* *121.021, *121.033 and *121.060).

> dum rei quae partibus caret partem conatur adipisci, nec portionem, **quae nulla est**, nec ipsam, quam **minime** affectat, assequitur. (III.p9.16)

The vulgate Latin text edited by Machan has no substantive variants in this passage, and Chaucer's translation is accurate enough:

> and whanne thei enforcen hem to gete partie of a thyng that ne hath no part, thei ne geten hem neyther thilke partie that nis noon, ne the thyng al hool that thei ne desire nat. (*Riverside*, p. 429)

The Latin text printed beside Colvile's translation reads as follows:

> dum rei, quae partibus caret, partem conatur adipisci, nec portionem ullam nec ipsam quam affectat assequitur. (sig. O3$^v$)

There are two variants: *portionem ullam* appears in place of *portionem quae nulla est* and *minime* has been dropped. Together these variants yield a grammatical sentence, though without the precision of Philosophia's statement. Colvile translates this corrupt text:

> and when they labour to get part of a thyng that hath no partes, they nether gette anye porcion of the thynge, nor yet the selfe same thynge that they desyre. (sig. O3$^v$)

Agreement between Colvile's translation and the 1556 Latin text suggests strongly that the variants stood in Colvile's 'very olde prynte', yet I have thus far found the variants only in ps.-Thomas's paraphrase, which reads 'dum homines conantur .i. laborant adipisci partem rei que partibus caret homo non assequitur vllam portionem .i. partem nec ipsam rem integram quam affectat & querit' (f. 146$^{vb}$). This paraphrase was surely the source of the variant reading translated by Colvile and transmitted in the 1556 Latin text. If the variant cannot be found in earlier editions of the *Consolatio*, one may have to suppose that Colvile's 'olde prynte' was corrected by hand to agree with ps.-Thomas's paraphrase.

Taken together, the evidence presented here suggests that Colvile's source text was printed in Lyon, Caen or Rouen, sometime between about 1486 and 1515.[56] If we assume that Colvile lacked Badius's commentary –

---

[56] A further variant, though distributed more widely than the others, is consistent with the placement deduced on the basis of them. At IV.p4.20, in the context of an archetypal dislocation (see ed. Moreschini *ad loc.*), *respondi* survives only in certain prints from Cologne, Deventer, Hagenau, Leipzig, Louvain and Strasbourg. Elsewhere – that is, in Nuremberg and in all French (Strasbourg excepted), Swiss and Italian prints in my corpus – the corresponding reading is '... quod iniustum est malum liquet esse. [B] Tum ego'. This reading is present already in some early manuscripts and it is the reading glossed by ps.-Thomas. It is also the reading of the 1556 Latin text, and the reading translated by Colvile (sig. X2$^r$).

*Colvile's Translation of the* Consolation of Philosophy        245

and I have found no evidence to the contrary – the search area may be restricted to editions printed in Lyon between about 1486 and 1498. Provenance notes in *A Catalogue of Books Printed in the Fifteenth Century Now in the Bodleian Library* include Lyon books in English ownership in the sixteenth century, including copies of the *Consolatio*.[57]

## Colvile at the End of the Middle Ages

The sources and working methods identified in this study were not unique to Colvile and may be paralleled in other sixteenth-century translations. Anselmo Tanzo and Benedetto Varchi each intercalated material from ps.-Thomas into their Italian versions of the *Consolatio*, first printed in 1520 and 1551, respectively.[58] Dario Brancato remarks that Tanzo's sources and procedures express a 'conceptual grid similar to that used almost two centuries earlier',[59] and this assessment may be applied with equal validity to Colvile. Though positive identification of Colvile's source text remains a task for future investigators, his place in literary history is clear even at the present state of knowledge. He was a medieval epigone, his translation a late fruit of literary scholasticism.

Another way of getting at Colvile's historical significance is to look ahead, to subsequent translations of Boethius's text into English. The most famous of these is certainly Queen Elizabeth I's hasty private exercise, undertaken in late 1593, but a more apt *comparandum* is to the translation printed in 1609 under the pseudonymous initials 'I.T.', for this was the first new English translation to appear in print after that of Colvile.[60] The translator was probably the English Jesuit Michael Walpole (d. 1625). His translation style differs sharply from that of Colvile, as may be seen from the opening lines of the entire work:

> I That with youthfull heate did verses write,
> Must now my woes in dolefull tunes enditc,
> My worke is fram'd by Muses torne and rude,
> And my sad cheeks are with true teares bedew'd, (f. 1ʳ)

Here, for comparison, is Colvile's version of the same passage (see Figure 11.2 for an image of the page):

---

[57] Coates et al., *Catalogue of Books Printed*, II. See, e.g., entries B-384, B-387.
[58] Brancato, 'Readers and Interpreters', pp. 392–93, 402–3.   [59] Ibid., p. 394
[60] See n. 7. On the 1609 translation, see Houghton, 'Michael Walpole'.

> I That in tyme of prosperite, & floryshing studye, made pleasaunte and delectable dities, or verses: alas now beyng heauy and sad ouerthrowen in aduersitie, am compelled to fele and tast heuines and greif. Beholde the muses Poecicall, that is to saye: the pleasure that is in poetes verses, do appoynt me, and compel me to writ these verses in meter, and yᵉ sorowfull verses do wet my wretched face with very waterye teares, yssuinge out of my eyes for sorowe. (sig. B1ʳ)

The translators' divergent formal decisions (I.T.'s translation retains Boethius's prosimetrical form) express a deeper, perhaps epistemic, shift in self-understanding and purpose. Colvile's doublet translations and incorporated glosses channel the school-room practice of construing Latin. Readers are persistently reminded that this English text is a translation – that is, a representation whose truth resides elsewhere. By his fractured voice, Colvile invites readers to turn (back) to the Latin original and see for themselves what it says. I.T.'s version, by contrast, holds the reader's attention on itself. The lines quoted from I.T.'s version contain just one doublet, and it is here *metri gratia*. The single word *torne* would have been sufficient to render the sense of Latin *lacerae*, but I.T. needed a rhyme; *Muses torne and rude* is a stylistic compromise justified because the devices of meter and rhyme bind the text into a self-referential literary artefact. The animating force in I.T.'s translation is no longer the medieval schools, but rather the new English-language poetry of the Elizabethan period. The diction is that of recent literary English (*bedew'd* is used by Spenser). The expression *with youthfull heate* (Lat. *studio florente*) and the notion of framing in l. 3 are fine inventions, untethered from the Latin and confident of their own power. Though the 1609 print retains some marginal notes, the rhetoric of I.T.'s translation is one of autonomy, not deferral to an exterior or anterior authority. The two translations are separated by a distance much greater than the fifty years that intervened between them. Colvile continues the medieval reading tradition. If I.T.'s translation appears modern by comparison, it is certifiably so, for his translation was still acceptable in 1918, when reprinted in the Loeb Classical Library.[61]

---

[61] Boethius, *Theological Tractates*, ed. by Stewart and Rand, with the translation revised by Stewart. In the 1973 edition a new translation by S. J. Tester replaces that of I.T.
   I thank members of the Midwest Middle English Reading Group for discussion of an earlier version of this essay and volume editors for helpful commentary and suggestions. I thank the Newberry Library and the libraries of the University of Illinois at Urbana-Champaign and the University of Chicago for access to their collections, and the library of Loyola University Chicago for arranging access to the ProQuest collection Early European Books.

# *Appendix*

My study sample of pre-1556 prints of the *Consolatio* contains the following editions, cited by the numbers assigned to them in *GW* (pre-1500) and *IA* (post-1500): *GW* 4511, 4512, 4516, 4520, 4526, 4527, 4529, 4530, 4533, 4534, 4535, 4537, 4538, 4540, 4541, 4544, 4545, 4546, 4548, 4549, 4550, 4551, 4552, 4555, 4556, 4557, 4559, 4560, 4561, 4562, 4563, 4565, 4566, 4567, 4568, 4569, 4570, 4571, 4573, *IA* 121.015, 121.016, 121.017, 121.019, 121.021, 121.022, 121.030, 121.033, 121.034, 121.036, 121.037, 121.039, 121.041, 121.044, 121.045, 121.049, 121.053, 121.055, 121.056, 121.057, 121.060, 121.062, 121.066, 121.076, 121.077, 121.080, 121.083, 121.088, 121.097, 121.112.

The study sample also contains two sixteenth-century prints that I do not find in *IA*: *D. Dionysii Carthusani operum minorum tomus tertius* (Cologne, 1540), recorded as 626378 in the Universal Short Title Catalogue (USTC); and Newberry Library Case Y 672 .B066, the title page of which reads as follows:

> Textus Boetij.| Anitij: Manlij: Torquati: Seuerini | Boetij Ordinarij viri exco[n]sulis co[n]| solatio philosophica: & disciplina | scolariu[m]: cum agrutissima doctissi| mi viri Raymu[n]di Palasini Albien| sis dicti Valderici difficiliu[m] locor[um]| nec prius a quopia[m] tactoru[m] expla=| natione: & eoru[m] quæ prius p[er] scri=| ptores deprauata fuera[n]t emenda=| tione: Eiusde[m]q[ue] In singulos libros | Argume[n]tis pręterea et Hystorijs | astrologica quęda[m] per eu[m] declara| ta ad oculu[m] pręmonstrantibus: vt studiosi & legant & videant : Ad| ditu[m] est insuper Sulpitij Verulani | carme[n] iuuenile de moribus in me[n]| sa seruandis: et Quintiliani pręce| ptu[m] de officio scolast coru[m] (sic for *scolasticorum*) erga p[re]=| ceptores: perutilisq[ue] Hu[m]berti Mo[n]=| tismoretani de i[n]genuis adolesce[n]tu[m] | morib[us] libell[us] q[ue] et hęc o[mn]ia accura=| tissime correxit: et distica in singu| las prosas: et metra co[n]scripsit: Do| ctasq[ue] annotatio[n]es marginib[us] inse| ruit q[ui]busvallatus text[us] lectoribus | apertior sit futurus.

The Munich DigitiZation Center, a huge online collection, is the single largest source of books in my study sample. Other sources are the Newberry Library and the libraries of the University of Illinois at Urbana-Champaign and the University of Chicago, and digital facsimiles available via Gallica, e-rara, Biblissima, HathiTrust, the Internet Archive and the ProQuest collection Early European Books. Online repositories were consulted between July 2018 and January 2019.

CHAPTER 12

# When Did the Emotions Become Political?
## Medieval Origins and Enlightenment Outcomes

### Rita Copeland

When did the emotions become political? It would be natural to view a formal political analysis of emotions as a classical phenomenon that was reprised under new and more decisive terms in late humanism and reimagined in the early eighteenth century. In this political history of emotion from the seventeenth to the eighteenth centuries we would expect to encounter the work of Thomas Hobbes and Giambattista Vico. It would also be natural to take Hobbes and Vico at their word and read this recovery of the political dimension of emotion as part of a rejection of medieval philosophy. Yet I will propose quite the opposite: the grounds for this political turn were in fact laid in late medieval scholasticism. The precedent for humanist and Enlightenment-era political thought about emotion lies with a repudiated scholasticism and its reinvention of classical Greek thought. It is the history of rhetoric that reveals this turn to the political. The thread that links these transformations together is the political reception and re-absorption of Aristotle's *Rhetoric*, and the modern assimilation of the *Rhetoric* began in earnest with the most influential statecraft treatise of the Middle Ages, *De regimine principum*, written about 1277 by the scholastic theologian Giles of Rome (or Aegidius Romanus, d. 1316).

The interests of Alastair Minnis, whose scholarship is celebrated in this volume, cross literary and intellectual history. But we can lay the emphasis on *history*, for he has always committed his work to the diachronic study of cultural formations manifested in philosophy and theology, in literature and poetics, institutions of learning, and in manuscript and book production. As he has long recognised and argued, intellectual and literary history are intimately allied: in the largest sense each one gives us the other. Intellectual history is a kind of literary history, a reading of textual exchanges and reappearances, even if many of the practitioners of intellectual history might not always recognise commonalities with literary study. Literary study, of course, has always been capacious in its compass, incorporating fields such as my concerns here, the related histories of rhetoric and emotions. Literary history is distinctive for its methods of close, questioning reading bringing sublimated affinities to the surface. No one has done more than Minnis to argue for the surprising modernity, the long-reaching impact on thought and letters, of the intellectual and literary watershed that was medieval scholasticism.[1]

The thought processes and aesthetic reflections that we now call 'literary theory' represent a broad collection of ideas extending beyond strictly literary modalities to include questions about communication, political receptivity and experiential impact. How emotion registers in a program of political thought is as essential to 'theory' as any verbal or structural aspect of argument. The study of affective or emotional communication is a bridge linking the literary and the political, revealing the necessary social knowledge that poetry and politics share. To understand the emotions politically is also to understand them as part of the fabric of political persuasion and thus necessary to any theory of verbal communication. Such considerations should figure in our attempts to construct a history of theory. Scholastic thought on emotions and persuasion anticipates, in ways perhaps surprising (though we should never be surprised by the longevity of scholastic insights on language), some of the most dynamic theoretical developments of the following centuries. The history of 'theory' that I present in this essay traces the paths of Aristotelian reception in which a medieval innovator, long forgotten by his humanist and Enlightenment successors, can be recovered as a kind of prescient tutelary of a cultural lineage.

I will not make a case here for the direct influence of Giles of Rome on early modern theorists of emotions and politics, although such influence is not impossible. Rather, I want to set forth what is radically distinctive about Giles's approach to emotions as a subject of political thought, and why it bears comparison with the approaches of Hobbes and Vico. The direct impact of Aristotle's *Rhetoric* is common to and traceable in all of these approaches. The role of formal rhetorical thought is critical to the thematic chain that I pursue here, and it determines my selection of texts.

Before I trace the entry of Aristotle's *Rhetoric* into post-classical western Europe, I want first to explain what is important, for our purposes, about that text. The remarkable analytic of the emotions in Book II, chapters

---

[1] Here the subtle argument adumbrated in the closing chapter of *MTA* can exemplify the rich totality of his arguments: 'Yet some ... [Renaissance] attitudes can, as it were, be regarded as imaginative extensions of ideas which had emerged in scholastic literary theory' (p. 214).

2–11 of the *Rhetoric* gives the first systematic and precise account of individual emotions in ancient philosophy. Here Aristotle gives a detailed psychology of seven pairs of emotions relevant to the task of persuading an audience: anger and calmness, friendship and enmity, fear and confidence, shame and shamelessness, kindliness and ingratitude, pity and indignation, and envy and emulation. It is not Aristotle's only treatment of the subject: the survey of the emotions in the *Rhetoric* needs to be understood in relation to the analyses of the *pathē* in the *Ethics* and, beyond that, across Aristotelian psychology. But even so, the account in the *Rhetoric* is unique among ancient texts, and arguably remains so almost two and a half millennia later. Among its distinctive qualities within the ancient context is its focus on emotions in relation to other people, not in relation to things – not, in other words, as merely appetitive.[2] As Aristotle describes them here, emotions come about through social behaviour, through responses to people. What is often said about the analysis of the emotions in the *Rhetoric*, but which bears repeating, is that it is pragmatic, phenomenological and non-normative. Compared with other ancient thought, Aristotle's approach here is surprisingly non-judgemental, stressing what beliefs, intentions and awarenesses actually cause emotions. In this context, Aristotle is not speaking about how we should strive for goodness and the mean (as in the *Ethics*), but rather about how the orator can understand what produces anger or shame or love so that he can recognise, evoke or modify those emotions in an audience. Like others, Aristotle sees emotion as potentially intelligent behaviour because it is open to reasoned persuasion. Emotions are caused by thought and belief, responses to appearances which may not always be correct, but can be altered by arguments. Thus, emotional appeals can be a source of invention of an argument. Aristotle analyses the movement of emotions from cause to effect, and the components of each emotion: cognition, psychic effect and behavioural character or impulse. It is crucial to underscore that the cause and effect studied in the *Rhetoric* are not related to the orator's speaking: these are the conditions that already and continually characterise social and psychic life. The emotions are not conjured at the moment of speaking through the orator's mastery of style; they are a resource to be tapped by a knowing orator, providing the grounds or topics of the arguments he will make.

Modern phenomenology, especially in Heidegger's thought, has appreciated Aristotle's *Rhetoric* because it places rhetorical competence at the heart of collective deliberation, and it gives an important role to the

---

[2] Striker, 'Emotions in Context', p. 289.

emotions in directing formal rhetorical reasoning.³ For Aristotle, emotions are not mere psychic phenomena, but rather the very conditions of speaking (for example, fear impels us to deliberate, often collectively). In Aristotle's *Rhetoric*, emotions understood socially are a form of proof, a legitimate source of argument.

To us as moderns it may seem remarkable that the *Rhetoric* had little influence in its own time.⁴ More predictably, it was unknown to the Latin Middle Ages before the thirteenth century. The work arrived on the western academic scene in its authoritative Latin translation by William of Moerbeke around 1269, and from there it was immediately absorbed into the dossier of Aristotelian studies. But its distinctive character was not always recognised or appreciated. In medieval classrooms it had almost no traction as a rhetorical treatise, because it did not look like anything that medieval readers had inherited from the technical Ciceronian tradition which dominated the lower schools. While the *Rhetoric* was copied and circulated widely, it was not typically transmitted with other rhetorics, but most often with the Latin translations of Aristotle's *Ethics* and *Politics*.⁵ In these contexts it was received as a contribution to political thought and moral philosophy.

The first scholar in the Latin West to seize the opportunity to engage directly with Aristotle's account of the emotions was also the first Latin commentator on the text, Giles of Rome. Within only a few years of Moerbeke's Latin translation, somewhere around 1271, Giles produced a massive commentary on the work.⁶ But it is not in his commentary that Giles marks a profound response to the treatise on the emotions. Quite the contrary, Giles's exposition of Book II is disappointingly dependent on earlier medieval philosophical frameworks. It is not surprising that, on his first reading, Giles would overlook the pragmatic, social dimension of emotions in Aristotle's account, since the philosophical tradition that he had inherited virtually militated against a phenomenology of emotion, and Giles processes the Aristotelian discussion through what had become the canonical teaching of Thomas Aquinas. As with this and the earlier

---

³ Heidegger, *Aristotelian Philosophy*, tr. by Metcalf and Tanzer, pp. 75–91, 119–31 and 162–76; Gross and Kemmann (eds), *Heidegger and Rhetoric*.

⁴ On the ancient reception of the *Rhetoric*, see, e.g., Wisse, *Ethos and Pathos*, pp. 152–58; Solmsen, 'Aristotelian Tradition'.

⁵ On these points see, further, Copeland, 'Pathos and Pastoralism'; Beullens and de Leemans, 'Aristote à Paris'. For the Latin text of the *Rhetoric*, see Aristotle, *Rhetorica*, ed. by Schneider.

⁶ On this commentary, see, among many recent studies, Marmo, 'Egidio Romano'; Staico, 'Rhetorica e politica'.

medieval traditions, Giles's treatment in his commentary was essentially taxonomic and morally corrective. Aristotle's remark at the opening of Book II (1378a19–24) – that it is necessary to classify the emotions in order to know how they determine judgements – apparently seems to have prompted Giles to supply further classifications, and he devotes four *declarationes* at the start of his commentary on Book II to a philosophical ordering of the emotions.[7] Incorporating the ideas of his teacher Aquinas, he places the passions in the sensitive parts of the soul, dividing them into six that correspond to the concupiscible appetite (love and hate, desire and detestation, delight and sadness) and six to the irascible appetite (hope, despair, fear, courage, anger, 'mansuetude').[8] His interests here are largely to clarify the logical basis of Aquinas's analysis in the *Summa*, IaIIae qq. 22–48. Thus, because a passion is a 'movement', a *motus animae*, it must correspond to various kinds of motion, whether to active movement or to being moved. The opposite pairs (love and hate, fear and courage) can be further classified according to the kind of moral choice each represents, what may be good or bad. This is speculative philosophy put to the service of moral teaching, but it remains at a level of high abstraction. Interestingly, even though Giles later comments closely and often sensitively on each one of Aristotle's pragmatic accounts of individual emotions (for example, the relation between anger and insult, or anger and social class, or the difference between anger and hatred), he seems not to have envisioned an integration of his own philosophical overview with the psychological realism of Aristotle's analytic.

At this early point of his engagement with Aristotle, Giles may simply have been slotting in familiar answers as a placeholder for something that he had not yet fully grasped. But in the course of the next six or so years he would figure it out. Around the year 1277, just as he had to leave Paris after the condemnations of philosophical teaching at the university issued by Bishop Étienne Tempier, Giles produced one of his major works, his political and ethical treatise *De regimine principum* (*On the Government of Rulers*), which became the most influential of all the medieval mirrors of princes. This work, dedicated to the young prince who would become France's Philip the Fair (r. 1285–1314), was transmitted across Europe, surviving in over 300 copies of the Latin text and in many vernacular

---

[7] Giles of Rome, *Rhetorica Aristotelis cum ... commentariis*, ff. 49$^r$–51$^r$.
[8] Giles adds *mansuetudo* as a passion to the eleven treated by Aquinas, thus correlating his list more closely with Aristotle's pair, 'anger' and 'becoming calm'.

translations as well. In its vernacular versions it penetrated aristocratic courts and elite households from Italy, France and Iberia to German regions, the Low Countries, England and Sweden.[9] Its English version was rendered by the indefatigable translator John Trevisa, who probably made it for Lord Berkeley (d. 1417).[10] Thus, it entered vernacular literary culture as a work of moral philosophy, the main vehicle for the diffusion of Aristotelian political thought to lay audiences and, amazingly, a conduit for a wide knowledge of Aristotle's *Rhetoric*.

It is in this treatise that Giles reflects on the largest political impact of Aristotle's rhetoric of the passions. Janet Coleman and others have commented on how Aristotle's rhetorical thought informs the *De regimine* as a whole.[11] But I want to consider here how Giles transforms the role of the passions, having – I believe – digested the teachings of the *Rhetoric* in the years since writing his commentary. His treatment in *De regimine* marks a radical shift from what was the standard philosophical training.

While Aristotle's *Ethics* and *Politics* take priority among Giles sources, the *Rhetoric* is also cited throughout *De regimine*, in total almost ninety times and most densely in Giles's treatment of the passions. But the section devoted to the passions does not simply rehearse the matter of the *Rhetoric*: here Giles turns contingent persuasion into a programme of contingent rule and self-rule for the prince. *De regimine* inverts Aristotle's analysis of passions in an audience which an orator must understand, turning this around to give an account of the passions that a ruler must understand in himself. Of course this makes an explicit link with the *Ethics* and its discourse on the virtues and self-management. But Giles signals that a normative approach to emotions, such as given in the *Ethics*, is not adequate to the practicalities of politics. In politics and governance, general conditions and supervening truths will interact with shifting circumstances. In *De regimine* Giles sees in the passions a pragmatic knowledge that the ruler will use on himself. Giles's political outlook is decisively monarchical, and there is no getting away from that. But he imagines the prince as an interesting mixture of authority and self-reflexiveness. The force of rhetorical thinking transforms Giles's hypothetical prince into a kind of other to himself, a second self with whom the prince engages as an

---

[9] On the circulation of the text, see Briggs, *Giles of Rome's* De regimine, ch. 1; Perret, *Les traductions françaises*, pp. 50–91.
[10] Hanna, 'Berkeley and His Patronage'; Briggs, 'Patronage of Trevisa's *De regimine*'.
[11] Coleman, 'Some Relations'; Kempshall, 'Rhetoric of Giles of Rome's *De regimine*'; Kempshall, *Writing of History*, pp. 464–68, 470–78.

interlocutor. The prince, knowing the nature of emotions in general and his own emotions in particular, persuades himself, mobilises his own nature so that he can act.

Giles inaugurates his overview of the emotions (Book I, Part 3) with a justification that seems to echo the *Ethics:* one cannot rule oneself unless one controls the passions, knowing which ones are good and which ones are detrimental (chapter 2).[12] Following the template of his commentary on the *Rhetoric*, he takes love and hate to be the primary passions; accordingly, it is necessary first to show how it is appropriate for kings and princes to love and to hate, and in what ways (chapter 3). The argument he advances takes us into the heart of his transformation of Aristotelian rhetoric. Since someone who hates seeks to destroy the object of his hatred (as claimed in the *Rhetoric*), the ruler should want to love justice and hate vice in himself and in others. People are not to be hated and eliminated, but rather their vices (chapter 3). Hatred in a ruler is more detestable than anger, but inordinate anger in a ruler is terrible, too (chapter 7).

We can see how this brings the discourse on virtue from the *Ethics* together with an assessment of the causes and effects of the passions derived from the *Rhetoric*. In Aristotle's text, enmity or hatred is defined against and in relation to anger: anger can produce enmity, but anger is curable whereas enmity may endure; anger is always particular in its objects, while hatred can be directed against classes of people, and this cannot be cured. Thus, while the angry person wants the particular object of his anger to suffer, the hating person wants to destroy the whole detested class (1382a15). Aristotle uses these relations and distinctions to suggest how the speaker can use this knowledge to marshal and manufacture emotions in others:

> Manifestum igitur ex hiis quod contingit inimicos et amicos et existentes demonstrare et non existentes facere et dicentes dissolvere, et aut propter iram aut propter inimicitiam vacillantes ad utrumcumque elegerit quis ducere. (1382a16–20)

> From these [distinctions] it is clear how it is possible to demonstrate that people are enemies and friends, and to make them so when they are not and to refute those who claim to be so; and lead those who are wavering because of anger or enmity over to whatever position one chooses.

---

[12] All quotations and references are taken from the Rome, 1607 edition.

In Giles's use of Aristotle's precept, by contrast, the ruler must know such causes and effects in order to marshal the appropriate responses in himself so that he may govern others effectively. Here, the shifting circumstances of an audience's emotions become a mirror for the ruler himself, the measure of his own emotional fitness to govern others. What Aristotle would have the speaker know about the feelings of an audience becomes, in the *De regimine*, a programme of action for a prince. Thus, the prince should avoid hatred because he can inflict damage on more people (I give Trevisa's translation):

> Sufficit enim irato, quod alter contra patiatur, donec fiat condigna ultio. Sed odium exterminat, et vult non esse: non enim sufficit odienti, quod alter contra patiatur, sed vult eum interimi et non esse. Cum ergo conditiones odii sint multo peiores quam conditiones irae, magis cavendum est odium quam ira, immo iram transire in odium ... Est ergo huiusmodi odium cavendum a quolibet. Magis tamen cavendum est regibus et principibus, quia inferre possunt pluribus nocumentum.[13]

> For it is inow to hym þat is wrooth þat þe oþer haue harme and be ponysched forto he haue fol wreche. But hate destroieþ and wol vndo hym þat hateþ, for it is not inow to hym þat hateþ þat þe oþer haue harme but he wol þat þe oþer be destroyed and vndo. Þanne for þe condicions of hate ben moche worse þanne þe condicions of wrethe, it nedeth more to be war of hate þanne of wrethe and to be war þat wrathe passe not in to hate ... Þanne al men schulde be war of hate, and nameliche kynges and princes, for þei mowe greue and noye manye men.[14]

Citing *Rhetoric*, Book II, Giles rehearses all the differences between hate and anger which the orator needs to know. But he has turned these precepts into a princely self-help programme: Giles has used the contingent assessments of emotion found in the *Rhetoric*, making them into precepts for governance. One way that we might look at Giles's transformation of ancient precept is that here a ruler needs to govern a state as if the state were his argument and he were both producer and audience of that persuasion. The rhetorical control he would exert over his people will be predicated on the rhetorical power he exerts over himself. In Aristotelian terms: if the emotions are the ground of discursive invention, the dynamic motivation that leads to logos, here the emotions of the prince are a site of the invention of the state and the very content of the proof which is the state.

---

[13] *De regimine principum*, I.III.7 (p. 173).   [14] Trevisa, *Governance of Kings*, p. 128.

Giles seems to have had little knowledge of (or patience with) classical Ciceronian rhetoric when he began his career and produced his commentary on the new translation of Aristotle's *Rhetoric*.[15] But once he had incorporated the *Rhetoric* into his thought, he achieved his most dynamic and original perspective on the emotions. Giles begins with the social dimension of emotions in the *Rhetoric* and from there moves back to the subjective experience of feeling in the individual, here the ruler. The ruler has to manage his emotions, not because he is exceptional but because he embodies the social field on which emotions are played out. In doing this he has to recognise and mobilise his emotions, not simply extirpate them.

In Giles of Rome I believe that we see the kind of self-reflexive political thought about emotions that will develop further in Thomas Hobbes, who at the point of writing *Leviathan* had come to see the passions as necessary to, and constitutive of, political agency.[16] By the seventeenth century, engagement with Aristotle's conception of emotion was hardly unusual. Even the famous chapters in Machiavelli's *Il Principe* (1513/32) on fear, hatred, love and contempt could be said to convert dicta about how the orator should harness public passions into rhetorical strategies for managing a powerful persona. Renaissance teachers of Aristotle's *Rhetoric*, from George Trebizond (*Rhetoricorum libri quinque*, 1433–34) to Juan Luis Vives (*De ratione dicendi*, 1533) and John Rainolds (lectures on the *Rhetoric*), had assimilated the text into the disciplinary course of the *ars rhetorica* and had contended with its distinctive treatment of emotion. Let us pause for a moment over Rainolds, who was lecturing on Book I of the *Rhetoric* at Oxford in the 1570s, providing the earliest critical study on the text in England, and indeed the only rhetoric lectures to survive from the Tudor university classroom.[17] Rainolds treats the passions as moral instruments of social behaviour and determines that they are necessarily paired with eloquence. With this background it is not surprising that, in the following generation, Francis Bacon (1561–1626) was to praise Aristotle's *Rhetoric* as a textbook of morals.[18]

Hobbes, of course, was no teacher of rhetoric – indeed, early in his career he showed little patience with the art. Rather, like Giles of Rome almost 300 years earlier, Hobbes turned to rhetoric as a resource for political philosophy, as he recognised the necessity of eloquence as a tool

---

[15] This is suggested in Giles's treatise written at some point after his *Rhetoric* commentary, for which see Bruni (ed.), *De differentia rhetoricae, ethicae et politicae*.
[16] Gross, *Secret History*, p. 45; cf. Struever, 'Hobbes and Vico on Law', p. 69.
[17] Rainolds, *Oxford Lectures*, ed. and tr. by Green, p. 9.
[18] Bacon, *Of the Advancement of Learning*, Book II, ed. by Spedding and Ellis, pp. 437–38.

of civil science. This change in his understanding of the role of rhetoric has been seen by students of Hobbes – including Leo Strauss in the 1930s and, much more recently, Quentin Skinner – as a radical return to the humanist training of his youth, a revisionist embracing of the classical and humanist association of eloquence and wisdom. It has also been seen as continuous with his mid-career 'break' with Aristotelian 'scholasticism'.[19] But that break in the 1630s was also the point at which Hobbes first grappled with Aristotle's *Rhetoric* and produced his digest of the work, *A Brief of the Art of Rhetorick* of 1637, the first translation of Aristotle's *Rhetoric* into English. As Strauss has shown, the language of the *Rhetoric*, especially Book II on the emotions, is imprinted on Hobbes's writings from 1640 onwards: on his early *Elements of Law* (1640) and his later *De homine* (1658), as well as on *Leviathan* (1651). Looking at the arc of his career in this way, it is not surprising that in 1651 he would reserve an early chapter of *Leviathan* for an almost Aristotelian analytic of the emotions (see below). In this, Hobbes is seen as affirming the value of a 'humanist' Aristotle of the *Rhetoric*, where the emotions ground social life and political reasoning. But that political context for the emotions was already a rediscovery of late medieval scholasticism: it is what we find in Giles of Rome's incorporation of Aristotle's *Rhetoric* into his theory of statecraft. A scholasticism stridently repudiated by humanists had in fact contributed the very building blocks of what most defined humanist political thought.

It is tempting to think that Hobbes encountered Giles's *De regimine principum*. I know no certain proof of this, although the circumstantial evidence turns out to be promising. On the one hand, it is less likely that Hobbes would have read it in England. Despite its continuing popularity on the Continent through the seventeenth century, *De regimine principum* seems to have lost its footing in England after the earlier fifteenth century: 'One searches in vain for copies of the early *De regimine* editions in the libraries of English scholars of the later fifteenth and sixteenth centuries', laments Charles Briggs.[20] On the other hand, Hobbes spent a long continental exile in Paris from 1640 to 1651, where he wrote *Leviathan*. The *De regimine* had gone through several continental printings over the sixteenth and early seventeenth centuries, and it appeared again in Leiden in 1643 from the press of the influential printer Johannes Maire, who

---

[19] Strauss, *Political Philosophy of Hobbes*, pp. 33 and 35–43; Skinner, *Reason and Rhetoric*, pp. 346–47 and 356–75.
[20] Briggs, *Giles of Rome's* De regimine, p. 149.

apparently confused it with Thomas Aquinas's tract *De regno ad regem Cypri* (Figure 12.1).²¹ Maire had earlier brought out Descartes's *Discours de la méthode*, and was known for his editions of Erasmus. The conditions were certainly ripe for Hobbes to take note of his scholastic precursor in political theory. Perhaps the attribution of the 1643 edition to Aquinas would have given the work greater visibility or even prestige – although of course it could still be dismissed as merely scholastic. But without more direct evidence, what remains traceable for comparison is the path that leads from each back to Aristotle's analytic of the emotions.

The emotions claim an early and conceptually foundational chapter in *Leviathan*; here the understanding of emotion depends upon the common ground of language. Thus, we have to use language carefully to put emotion to work in politics. Emotions are not to be extirpated as sinful, nor are they to be written about normatively in a simple way. Because they drive us socially, they are to be mobilised towards constructive purposes. Hobbes uses Aristotle's theoretical framework: life is motion, not tranquillity, and emotions are part of the mutability of human life.²² While Hobbes is not unique among his contemporaries in giving the emotions an important role in practical reasoning, we must also recognise the distinctive importance of rhetoric to his political thought.²³

As Hobbes was famously to declare at the end of *Leviathan*, persuasive discourse is the only efficacious form of a civil science: he writes, 'For where[soever] there is place for adorning and preferring of Errour, there is much more place for adorning and preferring of Truth' (p. 390). His conception of eloquence is moral, and it includes understanding the habits of the soul, that is, what Aristotle presented as proof by *pathos*. In his *Brief* of the *Rhetoric* about fifteen years before, Hobbes had translated Aristotle's term *pistis* quite literally as 'belief', and had registered the Aristotelian division of three grounds of proof as three sources of 'belief':

> The belief that proceeds from our Invention, comes partly from the *behaviour* of the speaker, partly from the *passions* of the hearer; but especially from the *proofs* of what we allege.²⁴

The behaviour of the speaker corresponds to Aristotle's *ethos*, the passions of the hearer to *pathos*, and proofs of what we allege to *logos*. In *Leviathan*, the passions come in early in the work, in chapter 6, as elements of

---

[21] Potthast, *Geschichtswerke des europäischen Mittelalters*, I, 17.   [22] See Gross, *Secret History*, p. 44.
[23] See the overview by Schmitter, 'Theories of Emotion', esp. p. 14.
[24] Hobbes, *Brief of the Art of Rhetorick*, in *English Works*, ed. by Molesworth, VI, 424–25.

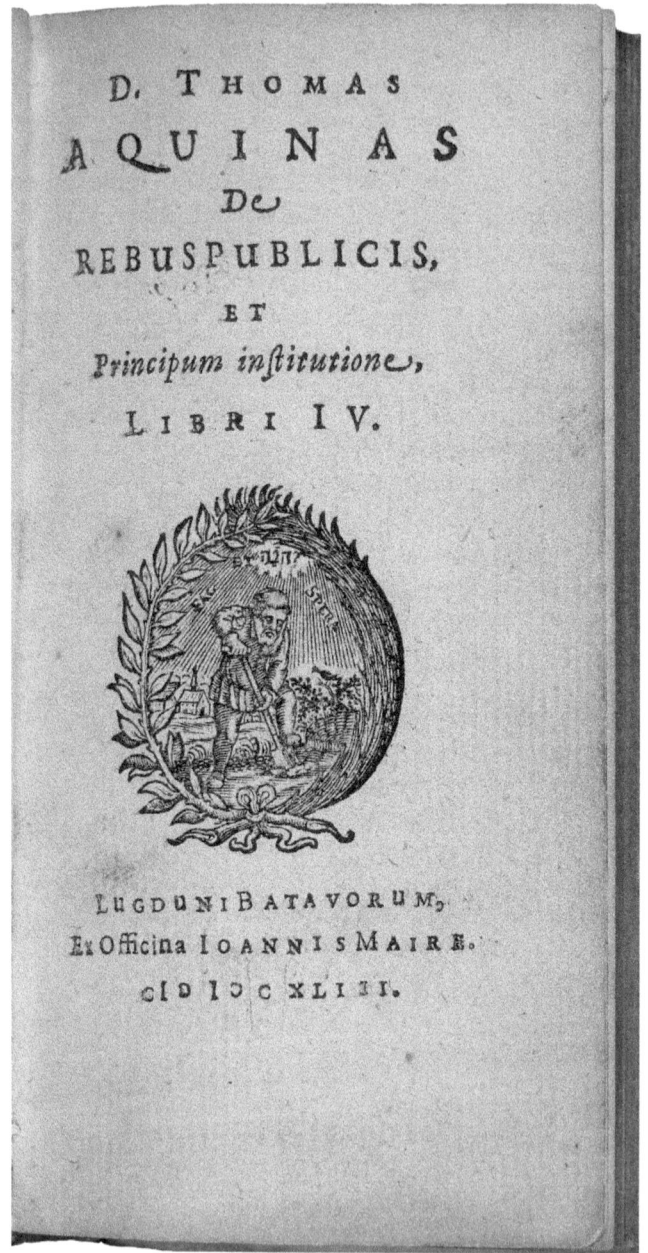

Figure 12.1  Giles's *De regimine principum*, misattributed to Aquinas. Published in Leiden by Johannes Maire, 1643.
Philadelphia, Henry Charles Lea Library, Kislak Center for Special Collections, Rare Books and Manuscripts, University of Pennsylvania. Reproduced by kind permission.

character and behaviour under the general aegis of 'mankind': 'Of the Interiour Beginnings of Voluntary Motions; commonly called the PASSIONS. And the Speeches by which they are expressed'. But his treatment of the passions is also intimately bound up with his analysis of language, as we can only agree on what the emotions are and what determines them if we can agree on how to name them and their causes:

> The formes of Speech by which the Passions are expressed, are partly the same, and partly different from those, by which wee express our Thoughts. And first, generally all Passions may be expressed *Indicatively*; as *I love, I feare, I joy, I deliberate, I will, I command* ... Deliberation is expressed *Subjunctively*; which is a speech proper to signifie suppositions, with their consequences; as, *If this be done, then this will follow* ... The language of Desire, and Aversion, is *Imperative*; as *Do this, forbeare that* ... The language of Vain-Glory, of Indignation, Pitty and Revengefulness, *Optative* ... These formes of Speech, I say, are expressions, or voluntary significations of our Passions: but certain signes they be not; because they may be used arbitrarily, whether they that use them, have such Passions or not. The best signes of Passions present are in the countenance, motions of the body, actions, and ends, or aimes, which we otherwise know the man to have.[25]

Thus, Hobbes extends Aristotle's thought about emotion as a source of argument to seeing emotion as the building block for a narrative about society. His account of the passions in chapter 6 begins with the individual subject and subjective interests, especially as these affect naming the emotions; the account culminates an analysis of social interaction. The passions are about power and cognition, ultimately about how we relate to others.[26]

Part of that interaction is 'deliberation': emotions are the motive for deliberation. Animals too deliberate, but humans deliberate through speech. Thus, what he calls the 'forms of speech' in deliberation are 'expressions, or voluntary significations of our Passions': these are not objective, conditioned as they are by subjective appetites and desires. The common expressions that we use are thus anchored to shifting and subjective opinion, and the corrective for this, to lead social passions towards adequate civil obedience, is the very civil science that *Leviathan* is intended to provide. Rhetoric, and a rhetorical conception of the passions, has to be incorporated into that science in order to know the audiences one seeks to teach.

In formal rhetorical treatises it is easy to see the centrality of emotion to invention or to the formation of argument. But the inventional role of the emotions – emotion as the ground and material of persuasive argument in

---

[25] Hobbes, *Leviathan*, ed. by Malcolm, II, p. 94.
[26] See Tuck, 'Hobbes's Moral Philosophy', p. 184.

a formal setting – can also be transposed from the precincts of rhetorical treatises and mapped onto other kinds of persuasive beginnings: historiographical, philosophical, literary. Thus, as we see, Hobbes gives the emotions a critical 'inventional' place in *Leviathan*.

This is the beginning to which Giambattista Vico turns in his 'discovery' of the origin of language and thus the beginning of human culture in the final version of his *New Science*, published in 1744. Vico had a career as a professor of rhetoric at the University of Naples, and this is the foundation of his contributions to rhetorical thought and teaching. The archaeology of culture that he performs in his *New Science* has been read – by scholars including Nancy Struever, Michael Mooney and David Marshall – in deeply rhetorical terms.[27] Here I will stress the evolution of Vico's rhetorical thought. I want to put particular pressure on how he uses Aristotelian thought about the emotions as a form of proof. For Vico, the emotions are a point of departure in human history and consciousness.

In several contexts before he completed the final version of his *New Science*, Vico gives the emotions a generative role in rhetoric. In his celebrated oration for the opening of the school year at the University in 1708, *De nostri temporis studiorum ratione* (*On the Study Method of our Time*, published the following year), he mounts a strong attack on the rationalism of his contemporaries – that is, the 'modern' method of study – for its prejudice against passionate persuasion and its insistence on reasoning divorced from emotion. According to Vico's argument, the passions are the foundation of eloquence and persuasive reasoning because they are where social engagement begins:

> Si non cum mente, sed cum animo tota eloquentiae. ... Eloquentia enim est officii persuadendi facultas. Is autem persuadet, qui talem in auditore animum, qualem velit, inducat. ... Itaque per corporeas imagines est alliciendus ut amet: nam ubi semel amat, facile docetur, ut credat: et ubi credit, et amat, est inflammandus, ut sua solita impotentia velit: quae tria nisi qui fecerit, haud persuasionis opus effecerit. ... Sed in hiis ipsis Rebuspublicis Oratores amplo, verso inflammato dicendi genere eximii, cum in Foro, tum in Senatu, et in factis concionibus cum summa Reip. utilitate, et maxima linguae gloria clauerunt.[28]

> Eloquence does not address itself to the rational part of our nature, but almost entirely to our passions. ... The role of eloquence is to persuade; an

---

[27] Among Struever's works, see 'Rhetoric and Philosophy' and 'Rhetorical Theory and Practice'. See also Mooney, *Vico in the Tradition of Rhetoric*; Marshall, *Vico and the Transformation of Rhetoric*.

[28] Quoting from the Naples, 1709 edition, here cols. 53–55, reproduced in Vico, *De Nostri Temporis Studiorum Ratione*, ed. by Veneziani.

orator is persuasive when he calls forth in his hearers the mood which he desires. ... The soul must be enticed by corporeal images and impelled to love; for once it loves, it is easily taught to believe; once it believes and loves, the fire of passion must be infused into it so as to break its inertia and force it to will. Unless the speaker can compass these three things, he has not achieved the effect of persuasion; he has been powerless to convince. ... Even under the republican form of government, orators have gained distinction by their fluent, broad, impassioned style of delivery in the law courts, the assemblies, and the religious convocations, to the greatest advantage of the state, and to the signal enrichment of our language.[29]

The idea here is that rhetoric should reclaim its function as persuasive speech, not merely ornamental and pleasing style. Eloquence is not for showing off or for other kinds of appearances, but for being in tune with the opinions of audiences. This reflects Vico's profound assimilation of Aristotelian thought – and indeed classical rhetorical thought as a whole – as against the more contemporary Ramistic evisceration of rhetoric's functions.[30]

It is Aristotle whom Vico invokes when he wants to foreground the passions as grounds of invention. His early *Institutiones oratoriae*, published in 1711, belies its appearance as a bloodless outline of doctrine by taking us to the heart of what Vico thought about emotional knowledge and rhetorical reasoning. In his discourse on topical invention, 'the common places of orators and dialecticians', he presents a synthesis of traditional thought on 'the art of finding arguments with respect to any given problem' (chapters 13–16) and follows with a gloss on Aristotle:

> Argumenta autem conciliantia et permoventia sunt oratorum propria; quia eorum propria est persuasio. ... Ex locis denique commoventibus desumuntur argumenta, quae in excitandis aut sedandis animorum affectibus versantur. Affectuum autem omnium princeps et scaturigo amor, quo persequimur bonum; primigenius autem eius filius odium, quo malum aversamur. Hos porro reliqua omnis affectuum familia sequitur studium, aversio, spes, metus, alacritas, languor animi, gaudium dolor, laetitia, moeror, exultatio, stupor, lenitas, ira, benevolentia, invidia, gratia, despicatus, indignatio, misericordia, aemulatio, gloria, pudor et verecundia. Optimi autem erit oratoris nosse et qui et erga quos et quibus de causis hoc vel illlo affectu homines soleant commoveri vel sedari: quam doctrinam recte explicat Aristoteles in *Rhetoricis* et multo rectius in *Moralibus*; ...

---

[29] Vico, *On the Study Methods of Our Time*, tr. by Gianturco, pp. 38–39.
[30] Mooney, *Vico in the Tradition of Rhetoric*, pp. 70–71.

> tamen mores et affectus cum rebus ipsis sunt commiscendi, et uti per corpus sanguis, ita per universam orationem diffundantur.[31]
>
> Arguments of conciliation and arousal are the province of orators. Persuasion is indeed their purpose. ... From the loci of arousal (*commoventibus*) are derived the arguments which are directed to the exciting or soothing of the emotions of the spirit. The first and fount (*princeps et scaturigo*) of all the emotions is love by which we pursue the good; its firstborn son is hate by which we avoid the evil. From these follow the remaining family of all the emotions – zeal and aversion, hope and despair, alacrity and faintness of spirit (*languor animi*), gladness and anguish, unrestrained joy and lamentation, exultation and dullness, mildness and rage, good will and ill will, grace and contempt, indignation and compassion, emulation and ambition, modesty and shyness. The best of orators will be he who knows which men are ordinarily led either to this or that emotion of arousal or calmness, toward whom, and for what reasons they are thus led. Aristotle explained this teaching best in the *Rhetoric* and even more in the *Ethics*; ... manners and emotions must be commingled with the issues themselves (*res ipsae*) and, as blood throughout the body, they are thus diffused throughout the entire oration.[32]

The emotions are cognitive mechanisms of social and moral relations so that in the hands of the orator they do not individuate us but bring us together towards a common purpose; and they work at the heart (or in the bloodstream) of discourse, not at its ornamental fringes. In this early work he lays out the foundation for his transformation of emotional topicality in the cultural archaeology of the *New Science*. The emotions have as important and generative a place in Vico's formal thought about persuasive discourse in the *Institutes* as they had in Hobbes's formal thought about society in *Leviathan*. In both authors the emotions claim early and conceptually foundational chapters. Later in *Leviathan* (chapters 27 and 28), Hobbes had given fear primacy among the emotions as the driving force behind submission to law. Vico too was to give fear primacy among the emotions, but he saw it as the generative impulse behind language itself.[33]

Rhetorical thought is so embedded in the *New Science* that it works at the very core of the historiographical enterprise and provides a fundamental conceptual system for rendering visible the cultural memory that Vico sought to recover. In his superb book on Vico, David Marshall calls this a process of rhetoric's progressive 'sublimation' in Vico's late work. Thus,

---

[31] Vico, *Institutiones oratoriae*, ed. by Crifò, chapters 17–18, pp. 86–92.
[32] Vico, *Art of Rhetoric*, tr. by Pinton and Shippee, p. 43.
[33] Cf. Marshall, *Vico and the Transformation of Rhetoric*, p. 102; Struever, 'Hobbes and Vico on Law', p. 72.

invention or discovery is not just a competence of orators, but a rhetorical capacity of all people to find arguments.³⁴ And this is where we come to Vico's account of the origins of language, in which emotion is the cause and rhetoric the result.

To modern readers, especially in literary and cultural history, the best-known passages in Vico's *New Science*, thanks in part to the influence of the late Hayden White and many rhetorical readers of Vico before and after him, are the chapters from Part 2 on 'Poetic Wisdom'.³⁵ It is to these passages that I also want to turn, to consider how Vico's theoretical model of rhetoric, worked out throughout his career, takes on profound historiographical implications. In this context poetry and rhetoric can be seen as proxies for one another.

Human language, Vico famously posited, began in tropes – first metaphor, then metonymy and synecdoche, and joined later, at a more cerebral stage, by irony. The tropes and figures of speech are the primary field shared by the systems of rhetoric and poetics, as Vico well knew. Thus, his key axiom:

> §409. Per tutto ciò si è dimostro he tutti it tropi (che tutti si riducano a questi quattro), i quali si sono finora creduti ingegnosi rituovati degli scrittori, sono stati necessari modi di spiegarsi [di] tutte le prime nazioni poetiche, e nella lor origine aver avuto tutta la loro natia propietà. ... E quindi s'incomincian a convellere queue'due comuni errori de' gramatici: che'l parlare de' prosatori è propio, impropio quel de' poeti; e che prima fu il parlare da prosa, dopoi del verso.³⁶

> §409. All [tropes] may be reduced to these four types [i.e. metaphor, metonymy, synecdoche, irony] which were previously thought to be the ingenious inventions of writers. But my discussion of them proves that they were in fact necessary modes of expression in all the early poetic nations, and originally had natural and proper meanings (*tutta la loro natia propietà*). ... Knowing this, we may begin to demolish two common errors of the grammarians: that prose is the proper form of speech, and poetic speech improper; and that men spoke first in prose and later in verse.³⁷

Vico has made non-proper speech the heart, the foundation, of discourse structure, the first manifestation of reasoning that will eventuate in politics. In other words, the tropes occupy an inventional position in his theory of discourse. Only later, he goes on to say, did humans develop

---

[34] Marshall, *Vico and the Transformation of Rhetoric*, pp. 3–8, 86 and 88.
[35] Notably, White, 'Tropics of History'.
[36] Vico, *Scienza nuova*, in *Opere*, ed. by Nicolini, pp. 521–22.
[37] Vico, *New Science*, tr. by Marsh, p. 162 (altered).

conceptual distance which enabled them to signify things as abstractions, what philosophy believes to be proper, literal speech.

The motivation of the first language, Vico points out repeatedly, was sensation and violent emotion. The early race of giants was frightened of the thunder and lightning, and they expressed their most violent passions by shouting and grunting, picturing the sky as an animated body which they called Jove (§377); we can scarcely enter into the imagination of the first people, whose minds were not abstract, who were immersed in the senses, and numbed or buffeted (*rintuzzate*) by the passions (§378); they embodied their fear of lightning in the figure of Jove (§379); through the fear born in their own minds they invented and named the gods:

> §382 ... la prima gente, semplice e rozza, si finse gli dèi *ob terrore praesentis potentiae*. Così il timore fu quello che finse gli dèi nel mondo ... non fatto da altri ad altri uomini, ma da essi a se stessi.[38]

> §382 ... the earliest people, being simple and uncouth, invented gods 'in terror of their manifest power'. Thus it was fear that invented gods in the world ... and not fear inspired by other people, but fear born within their own minds.[39]

Here we see that the social and civil causes of emotion that Aristotle describes have been moved further back into consciousness itself: inborn fear motivates language, which in turn – ultimately – gives birth to community, if we follow the inner logic of Vico's thought about rhetoric. Their fear may be inborn, but it emerges into the collective thought that is rhetoric.[40] The people attributed senses and emotions to physical bodies, so that their language was not one of analogy but of identity (§402); all languages employ metaphors derived from the human body or from human senses and emotions (§405); human words, formed first from onomatopoeia, next took shape as interjections articulated under the impetus of violent passions (§448). Fear is the dominant emotion charged with generating language. If Aristotle had provided a schema of the causes of emotions for use in discourse, Vico gives us emotions as the causes of discourse itself. In Vico's substructure of rhetoric, emotion is the topos, the topic or place, for the very invention of discourse. The next step is that, through deliberation and legislation, humans express their free will to turn their motivating passions into virtues (§135–36).[41]

---

[38] Vico, *Scienza nuova*, in *Opere*, ed. by Nicolini, p. 507.
[39] Vico, *New Science*, tr. by Marsh, p. 149   [40] Battistini, 'Three Essays on Vico', p. 7.
[41] Cf. Marshall, *Vico and the Transformation of Rhetoric*, p. 102; Struever, 'Hobbes and Vico on Law', p. 72.

Did Vico know Giles's *De regimine principum*? There is no evidence to argue in favour or against. There were prints of the text made in Rome and Venice in the early seventeenth century (1607 and 1617, respectively), and one of these might have passed through Vico's hands under various possible conditions – academic libraries, his father's bookshop, the book trade in Naples. Whether this work produced under the scholastic auspices of the Augustinian Hermits would have impressed him is even harder to determine. But that Vico might have read Giles of Rome's *De regimine* is less important to me here than the fact that Giles laid significant ground for an understanding of Aristotle's rhetorical evaluation of emotions on something like its own terms. This assessment brought emotions under the aegis of the dynamic or practical knowledge of politics, of which rhetoric is both a division and a tool.

In Giles of Rome, Hobbes and Vico we see a continuum of related responses to the Aristotelian legacy of pathos. For Giles, the emotions are the ground of a form of princely self-persuasion through which the ruler can embody a well-disciplined state. For the late-humanist Hobbes, a rhetorical understanding of the passions underwrites the common purpose of political deliberation. And Vico erects his political anthropology and philosophy of history on a foundation of rhetorical knowledge, the belief that the history of human consciousness is traceable through the sediments of rhetorical effects. What these relations suggest is that humanist and Enlightenment thinkers did not have to effect a radical break from scholasticism to discover that the emotions are political.

The 'history of emotions', which is transforming critical outlooks in literary studies, intellectual history and across arts and social sciences, still has an awkward relationship with 'history'. It is not simply the age-old question of 'do emotions have a history?' – whether evolutionary or anthropological or social. If we assume that they do, what kind of history would we write of them? Do we resurrect the periodisation debates of literary theory in the 1990s to observe or challenge the idea that modernity has a distinctive claim on subjectivity, that emotions have a different experiential valence before or after the Renaissance or the Enlightenment? And in what forms do we construct such histories? It seems to me least satisfactory to assemble case studies of emotion in artistic representations or historical records. Such approaches yield mosaic-like pictures of the past. But moving between the Middle Ages and early modernity to trace responses to Aristotle's powerful theory of communication reveals a remarkable continuity in the political conception of emotion. Here the Middle Ages becomes a crucial part of a long history of rhetoric and emotion, the beginning of the post-classical political analysis of the passions. The implications of this rhetorical turn for literary theory and fields such as social history and the arts, with which it shares so much common ground, are as wide and profound as we have the patience to make them.

# Bibliography of the Works of Alastair Minnis

## Gina Marie Hurley and Clara Wild

The following offers an account of the prodigious publications of Alastair Minnis, stretching from 1970 to the time the present volume has gone to press. (And he is still at work, so what is assembled here is necessarily open-ended and will quickly be in need of supplementing by the reader.) Like the scholastic texts of which Minnis is the *expositor eximius*, this chapter has a rather technical and precise *ordinatio*. Entries are arranged by year, and, for each year, monographs are listed first, followed by edited collections, articles and chapters, and finally reviews (titled and then untitled, the latter organised by author's surname).

### 1970

'An Aspect of Edna O'Brien', *The Honest Ulsterman*, 21, 27–31

### 1973

'Stiffs of Both Kinds', review of J. P. Donleavy, *A Fairy Tale of New York*, in *Fortnight*, 74, 22

### 1974

'Scandalously Good', review of Edna O'Brien, *A Scandalous Woman*, in *Fortnight*, 94, 14–15

'Twee and Crumpet', review of Julia O'Faolain, *Man in the Cellar*, in *Fortnight*, 86, 15

'Writing about Writing', review of John Braine, *Writing a Novel*, in *Fortnight*, 91, 14

### 1975

'"Authorial Intention" and "Literal Sense" in the Exegetical Theories of Richard FitzRalph and John Wyclif: An Essay in the Medieval History of Biblical Hermeneutics', *Proceedings of the Royal Irish Academy*, 75, section C, 1–31

'Louis MacNeice: The Pattern and the Poem', *Yearbook of English Studies*, 5, 225–42

'Force of Habit', review of Julia O'Faolain, *Women in the Wall*, in *Fortnight*, 105, 14

'Philosopher Poet', review of Terence Brown, *Louis MacNeice: Sceptical Vision*, in *Fortnight*, 101, 14–15

Review of Terence Brown, *Northern Voices: Poets from Ulster*, in *Fortnight*, 115, 15–16

Review of J. I. M. Stewart, *Young Pattullo*, in *Fortnight*, 109, 15–16

## 1977

'Discussions of "Authorial Role" and "Literary Form" in Late-Medieval Scriptural Exegesis', *Beiträge zur Geschichte der deutschen Sprache und Literatur*, 99, 37–65

## 1978

'Deliberate Delinquency', review of Francis Stuart, *A Hole in the Head*, in *The Honest Ulsterman*, 58, 81–84

Review of Masayoshi Itô, *John Gower, The Medieval Poet*, in *MÆ*, 47, 162–65

## 1979

'Late-Medieval Discussions of *Compilatio* and the Role of the *Compilator*', *Beiträge zur Geschichte der deutschen Sprache und Literatur*, 101, 385–421

'Literary Theory in Discussions of *Formae Tractandi* by Medieval Theologians', *New Literary History*, 11, 133–45

'A Note on Chaucer and the *Ovide Moralisé*', *MÆ*, 48, 254–57

## 1980

'John Gower, *Sapiens* in Ethics and Politics', *MÆ*, 49, 207–29

Review of Robert B. Burlin, *Chaucerian Fiction*, in *MÆ*, 49, 145–49

## 1981

'Aspects of the Medieval French and English Traditions of the *De Consolatione Philosophiae*', in *Boethius: His Life, Thought and Influence*, ed. by Margaret Gibson (Oxford: Blackwell), pp. 312–61

'Chaucer and Comparative Literary Theory', in *New Perspectives in Chaucer Criticism: Proceedings of the Second International Congress of the New Chaucer Society, at New Orleans, April 10–12, 1980*, ed. by Donald M. Rose (Norman, OK: Pilgrim Books), pp. 53–69

'The Influence of Academic Prologues on the Prologues and Literary Attitudes of Late-Medieval English Writers', *Mediaeval Studies*, 43, 342–83

'Langland's *Ymaginatif* and Late-Medieval Theories of Imagination', *Comparative Criticism*, 3, 71–103

## 1982

*Chaucer and Pagan Antiquity*, Chaucer Studies 8 (Cambridge: D. S. Brewer)

'The Sources of *The Cloud of Unknowing*: A Reconsideration', in *The Medieval Mystical Tradition in England: Papers Read at Dartington Hall, July 1982*, ed. by Marion Glasscoe (Exeter: University of Exeter Press), pp. 63–75

## 1983

Ed., *Gower's Confessio Amantis: Responses and Reassessments* (Cambridge: D. S. Brewer)

'Affection and Imagination in *The Cloud of Unknowing* and Walter Hilton's *Scale of Perfection*', *Traditio*, 39, 323–66

'"Moral Gower" and Medieval Literary Theory', in *Gower's Confessio Amantis*, pp. 50–78

## 1984

*Medieval Theory of Authorship: Scholastic Literary Attitudes in the Later Middle Ages* (London: Scolar Press)

'*The Cloud of Unknowing* and Walter Hilton's *Scale of Perfection*', in *Middle English Prose: A Critical Guide to Major Authors and Genres*, ed. by A. S. G. Edwards (New Brunswick, NJ: Rutgers University Press), pp. 61–81

'Exegesis, Latin' and 'Exegesis, Middle English', in *Dictionary of the Middle Ages*, ed. by Joseph Strayer, 13 vols (New York: Charles Scribner's Sons, 1982–89), IV, 542–48

'Light on the Interior Eye', review of V. A. Kolve, *Chaucer and the Imagery of Narrative*', in *The Times Literary Supplement*, p. 865

Review of Judson Boyce Allen, *The Ethical Poetic of the Later Middle Ages: A Decorum of Convenient Distinction*, in *Speculum*, 59, 363–66

Review of Glending Olson, *Literature as Recreation in the Later Middle Ages*, in *MÆ*, 53, 109–10

## 1985

'Devotional Readings', review of David C. Fowler, *The Bible in Middle English Literature*, in *The Times Literary Supplement*, p. 884

'Ordering Chaucer', review of Helen Cooper, *The Structure of* The Canterbury Tales, in *Essays in Criticism*, 35, 265–69

## 1986

'Chaucer's Pardoner and the "Office of Preacher"', in *Intellectuals and Writers in Fourteenth-Century Europe*, ed. by Piero Boitani and Anna Torti, The J. A. W. Bennett Memorial Lectures (Tübingen: Gunter Narr; Cambridge: D. S. Brewer), pp. 88–119

'From Medieval to Renaissance? Chaucer's Position on Past Gentility', The 1986 Thomas Chatterton Lecture, *Proceedings of the British Academy*, 72, 205–46

'The Reader to Determine', review of Jesse M. Gellrich, *The Idea of the Book in the Middle Ages: Language Theory, Mythology and Fiction*, in *The Times Literary Supplement*, p. 46

Review of Herbert Grabes, *The Mutable Glass: Mirror-Imagery in Titles and Texts of the Middle Ages and English Renaissance*, tr. by Gordon Collier, in *MÆ*, 55, 120–23

Review of Tim William Machan, *Techniques of Translation: Chaucer's Boece*, in *Studies in the Age of Chaucer*, 8, 225–29

## 1987

Ed., *The Medieval Boethius: Studies in the Vernacular Translations of* De Consolatione Philosophiae (Cambridge: D. S. Brewer)

'"Glosynge Is a Glorious Thyng": Chaucer at Work on the *Boece*', in *Medieval Boethius*, pp. 106–24

'Weight Worn Lightly', review of Joan M. Ferrante, Robert W. Hanning and J. A. W. Bennett (eds), *The Challenge of the Medieval Text: Studies in Genre and Interpretation*, and Douglas Gray (ed.), *Middle English Literature*, in *The Times Literary Supplement*, p. 140

Review of A. C. Spearing, *Medieval to Renaissance in English Poetry*, in *Studies in the Age of Chaucer*, 9, 253–60

Review of Penn R. Szittya, *The Antifraternal Tradition in Medieval Literature*, in *Journal of Theological Studies*, 38, 553–57

## 1988

*Medieval Theory of Authorship: Scholastic Literary Attitudes in the Later Middle Ages*, 2nd edn (Philadelphia: University of Pennsylvania Press; Aldershot: Wildwood House/Scolar Press)

Ed., with A. B. Scott, with the assistance of David Wallace, *Medieval Literary Theory and Criticism c. 1100–c. 1375: The Commentary Tradition* (Oxford: Clarendon)

'Gentil and Generous', review of Nevill Cogill, *The Collected Papers of Nevill Coghill, Shakespearian and Medievalist*, ed. by Douglas Gray, in *The Times Literary Supplement*, p. 674

'The Medieval Match', review of Rosemary Woolf, *Art and Doctrine: Essays on Medieval Literature*, ed. by Heather O'Donoghue, Myra Stokes and T. L. Burton, *Medieval Literature and Antiquities: Studies in Honour of Basil Cottle*, in *The Times Literary Supplement*, p. 142

## 1989

Ed., *Latin and Vernacular: Studies in Late-Medieval Texts and Manuscripts*, York Manuscripts Conferences: Proceedings Series 1 (Cambridge: D. S. Brewer)

Review of Gregory Kratzmann and James Simpson (eds), *Medieval Religious and Ethical Literature: Essays in Honour of G. H. Russell*, in *YLS*, 3, 163–68

## 1990

'*Amor* and *Auctoritas* in the Self-Commentary of Dante and Francesco Da Barberino', *Poetica: An International Journal of Linguistic-Literary Studies*, 32, 25–42

'Commentary as Criticism: A Chapter in the History of Medieval Literary Theory', in *The Medieval Text – Editors and Critics: A Symposium*, ed. by Marianne Børch, Andreas Haarder and Julia McGrew (Odense: Odense University Press), pp. 13–30

Review of Ross G. Arthur, *Medieval Sign Theory and* Sir Gawain and the Green Knight, in *Studies in the Age of Chaucer*, 12, 244–48

Review of Susan Noakes, *Timely Reading: Between Exegesis and Interpretation*, in *Lectura Dantis*, 7, 142–44

## 1991

Ed., with A. B. Scott, with the assistance of David Wallace, *Medieval Literary Theory and Criticism c. 1100–c. 1375: The Commentary Tradition*, rev. edn (Oxford: Clarendon)

'*De Vulgari Auctoritate*: Chaucer, Gower and the Men of Great Authority', in *Chaucer and Gower: Difference, Mutuality, Exchange*, ed. by R. F. Yeager (Victoria: University of Victoria Press), pp. 36–74

'John Gower, *Sapiens* in Ethics and Politics', rev. of 1980 article, in *Gower's* Confessio Amantis: *A Critical Anthology*, ed. by Peter Nicholson (Cambridge: Boydell and Brewer), pp. 158–80

'La teoria medievale dell' autorita', translated extracts from *MTA*, in *I contesti culturali della letteratura inglese: il medioevo*, ed. by Piero Boitani (Bologna: Società editrice il Mulino), pp. 263–337

'Theorizing the Rose: Commentary-Tradition in the *Querelle de La Rose*', in *Poetics: Theory and Practice in Medieval English Literature*, ed. by Piero Boitani and Anna Torti, The J. A. W Bennett Memorial Lectures (Woodbridge: Boydell and Brewer), pp. 13–36

Review of J. D. Pickles and J. L. Dawson (eds), *A Concordance to John Gower's* Confessio Amantis, and Peter Nicholson (ed.), *An Annotated Index to the Commentary on Gower's* Confessio Amantis, in *Review of English Studies*, 42, 564–65

## 1992

Ed., with Charlotte Brewer, *Crux and Controversy in Middle English Textual Criticism* (Woodbridge: Boydell and Brewer)

'The *Accessus* Extended: Henry of Ghent on the Transmission and Reception of Theology', in *Ad Litteram: Authoritative Texts and Their Medieval Readers*, ed. by Mark Jordan and Kent Emery (Notre Dame, IN: University of Notre Dame Press), pp. 275–326

'Authors in Love: The Exegesis of Late-Medieval Love-Poets', in *The Uses of Manuscripts in Literary Studies: Essays in Memory of Judson Boyce Allen*, ed. by Charlotte Cook Morse, Penelope Reed Doob and Marjorie Curry Woods (Kalamazoo, MI: Medieval Institute Publications), pp. 161–91

## 1993

Ed., *Chaucer's* Boece *and the Medieval Tradition of Boethius*, Chaucer Studies 18 (Cambridge: D. S. Brewer)

'The *Boece* as Late-Medieval Translation', co-authored with Tim William Machan, in *Chaucer's* Boece, pp. 167–88

'Chaucer's Commentator: Nicholas Trevet and the *Boece*', in *Chaucer's* Boece, pp. 83–166

'*More Platonico Loquitur*: What Nicholas Trevet Really Did to William of Conches', co-authored with Lodi Nauta, in *Chaucer's* Boece, pp. 1–33

Review of Tony Hunt, *Teaching and Learning Latin in Thirteenth-Century England*, and Cynthia Renée Bland, *The Teaching of Grammar in Late Medieval England*, in *Notes and Queries*, ns 40, 530–32

## 1994

Ed., *Late-Medieval Religious Texts and Their Transmission: Essays in Honour of A. I. Doyle*, York Manuscripts Conferences: Proceedings Series 3 (Cambridge: D. S. Brewer)

'Repainting the Lion: Chaucer's Profeminist Narratives', in *Contexts of Pre-Novel Narrative*, ed. by Roy T. Eriksen (Berlin: De Gruyter), pp. 153–83

Review of James M. Dean and Christian K. Zacher (eds), *The Idea of Medieval Literature: New Essays on Chaucer and Medieval Culture in Honor of Donald R. Howard*, in *Studies in the Age of Chaucer*, 16, 175–78

Review of Siân Echard and Claire Fanger (eds), *The Latin Verses in the Confessio Amantis: An Annotated Translation*, in *Speculum*, 69, 464–65

## 1995

*The Shorter Poems*, Oxford Guides to Chaucer, with contributions by V. J. Scattergood and J. J. Smith (Oxford: Clarendon)

'Late-Medieval Vernacular Literature and Latin Exegetical Traditions', in *Text und Kommentar*, ed. by Jan Assmann and Burkhard Gladigow (Munich: Wilhelm Fink), pp. 309–29

*Lifting the Veil: Textual/Sexual Nakedness in the* Roman de la Rose, Occasional Publications 1 (London: King's College London, Centre for Late Antique and Medieval Studies)

'Medium and Message: Henry of Ghent on Scriptural Style', in *Literature and Religion in the Later Middle Ages: Philological Studies in Honor of Siegfried Wenzel.*, ed. by Richard G. Newhauser and John A. Alford (Binghamton, NY: Center for Medieval and Early Renaissance Studies), pp. 209–35

'The Significance of the Medieval Theory of Authorship', reprinted extract from *MTA*, in *Authorship: From Plato to the Postmodern*, ed. by Seàn Burke (Edinburgh: Edinburgh University Press), pp. 23–30

## 1996

'Anthropologising Alisoun: The Case of Chaucer's Wife of Bath', *The Yearbook of Research in English and American Literature: REAL*, 12, 203–21

'Fifteenth-Century Versions of Thomistic Literalism: Girolamo Savonarola and Alfonso de Madrigal', in *Neue Richtungen in der hoch- und spätmittelalterlichen Bibelexegese*, ed. by Robert E. Lerner with Elisabeth Müller-Luckner (Munich: Oldenbourg), pp. 163–80

'Latin to Vernacular: Academic Prologues and the Medieval French Art of Love', in *Medieval and Renaissance Scholarship: Proceedings of the Second European Science Foundation Workshop on the Classical Tradition in the Middle Ages and the Renaissance (London, Warburg Institute, November 1992)*, ed. by Nicholas Mann and Birger Munk Olsen (Leiden: Brill), pp. 153–86

## 1997

Ed., with Charlotte C. Morse and Thorlac Turville-Petre, *Essays on Ricardian Literature in Honour of J. A. Burrow* (Oxford: Clarendon)

Ed., with Peter Biller, *Medieval Theology and the Natural Body*, York Studies in Medieval Theology 1 (Woodbridge: York Medieval Press, in association with Boydell and Brewer)

'The Author's Two Bodies? Authority and Fallibility in Late-Medieval Textual Theory', in *Of the Making of Books: Medieval Manuscripts, Their Scribes and Readers. Essays Presented to M. B. Parkes*, ed. by P. R. Robinson and Rivkah Zim (Aldershot: Scolar Press), pp. 259–79

'*De Impedimento Sexus*: Women's Bodies and Medieval Impediments to Female Ordination', in *Medieval Theology and the Natural Body*, pp. 109–39

'Looking for a Sign: The Quest for Nominalism in Chaucer and Langland', in *Essays on Ricardian Literature*, pp. 142–78

'A Rose by Many Names: Jean de Meun's Competition of Genres', in *Gattungen Mittelalterlicher Schriftlichkeit*, ed. by Barbara Frank, Thomas Haye and Doris Tophinke (Tübingen: Gunter Narr), pp. 183–99

## 1998

Ed., with Peter Biller, *Handling Sin: Confession in the Middle Ages*, York Studies in Medieval Theology 2 (Woodbridge: York Medieval Press, in association with Boydell and Brewer)

'*A Leur Fez Cousines:* Words, Deeds and Proper Speech in Jean de Meun and Chaucer', in *Medieval Heritage: Essays in Honour of Tadahiro Ikegami*, ed. by Masahiko Kanno, Hiroshi Yamashita, Masatoshi Kawasaki, Junko Asakawa and Naoko Shirai (Tokyo: Yushodo Press), pp. 31–63

### 2000

Ed., with Sarah Rees Jones and Richard Marks, *Courts and Regions in Medieval Europe* (Woodbridge: York Medieval Press, in association with Boydell and Brewer)

'Chaucer's Criseyde and Feminine Fear', co-authored with Eric Johnson, in *Medieval Women: Texts and Contexts in Late-Medieval Britain. Essays for Felicity Riddy*, ed. by Jocelyn Wogan-Browne, Rosalynn Voaden, Arlyn Diamond, Ann Hutchison, Carol Meale and Lesley Johnson (Turnhout: Brepols), pp. 199–216

'"Figures of Olde Werk": Chaucer's Poetic Sculptures', in *Secular Sculpture, 1300–1550*, ed. by Phillip Lindley and Thomas Frangenberg (Stamford: Shaun Tyas), pp. 124–43

'*Quadruplex Sensus, Multiplex Modus:* Scriptural Sense and Mode in Medieval Scholastic Exegesis', in *Interpretation and Allegory: Antiquity to the Modern Period*, ed. by Jon Whitman (Leiden: Brill), pp. 231–56

### 2001

*Magister Amoris: The* Roman de la Rose *and Vernacular Hermeneutics* (Oxford: Oxford University Press)

Ed., *Middle English Poetry: Texts and Traditions. Essays in Honour of Derek Pearsall*, York Manuscripts Conferences: Proceedings Series 5 (Woodbridge: York Medieval Press, in association with Boydell and Brewer)

'"Goddes Speken in Amphibologies": The Ambiguous Future of Chaucer's *Knight's Tale*', *Poetica: An International Journal of Linguistic-Literary Studies*, 55, 23–37

### 2003

'Absent Glosses: A Crisis of Vernacular Commentary in Late Medieval England?', *Essays in Medieval Studies*, 20, 1–17

'Chaucer and the Queering Eunuch', *New Medieval Literatures*, 6, 107–28.

'Making Bodies: Confection and Conception in Walter Brut's Vernacular Theology', in *The Theory and Practice of Translation in the Middle Ages*, ed. by Rosalynn Voaden, René Tixier, Teresa Sanchez Roura and Jenny Rebecca Rytting, The Medieval Translator / Traduire au Moyen Âge 8 (Turnhout: Brepols), pp. 1–16

'Material Swords and Literal Lights: The Status of Allegory in William of Ockham's *Breviloquium* on Papal Power', in *With Reverence for the Word: Medieval Scriptural Exegesis in Judaism, Christianity and Islam*, ed. by Jane Dammen McAuliffe, Barry D. Walfish and Joseph W. Goering (New York: Oxford University Press), pp. 292–308

'Reclaiming the Pardoners', *Journal of Medieval and Early Modern Studies*, 33, 311–34

## 2004

'Absent Glosses: A Crisis of Vernacular Hermeneutics in Late-Medieval England', an expanded version of the 2003 essay of the same title, in *Text and Voice: The Rhetoric of Authority in the Middle Ages*, ed. by Marianne Børch (Odense: University Press of Southern Denmark), pp. 138–67

'Literary Theory and Literary Practice', extracts reprinted from *MTA*, in *Middle English Literature: A Guide to Criticism*, ed. by Roger Dalrymple (Oxford: Blackwell, 2004), pp. 14–19

## 2005

Ed., with Ian Johnson, *The Cambridge History of Literary Criticism*, II, *The Middle Ages* (Cambridge: Cambridge University Press)

*Sources of the Boece*, ed. by Tim William Machan, with the assistance of A. J. Minnis, The Chaucer Library (Athens: University of Georgia Press)

'Acculturizing Aristotle: Matthew of Linköping's *Translatio* of Poetic Representation', *Zeitschrift für deutsche Philologie*, 124, 238–59.

'Dante in "Inglissh": What *Il Convivio* Really Did for Chaucer', *Essays in Criticism*, 55, 97–116

'"I Speke of Folk in Seculer Estaat": Vernacularity and Secularity in the Age of Chaucer', The 2004 Biennial Chaucer Lecture, *Studies in the Age of Chaucer*, 27, 25–58

'Introduction', co-authored with Ian Johnson, in *The Cambridge History of Literary Criticism*, II, *The Middle Ages*, 1–12

'Latin Commentary Tradition and Vernacular Literature', co-authored with Ralph Hanna, Tony Hunt, R. G. Keightley and Nigel

F. Palmer, in *The Cambridge History of Literary Criticism*, II, *The Middle Ages*, 363–421

'Medieval Imagination and Memory', in *The Cambridge History of Literary Criticism*, II, *The Middle Ages*, 239–74

'Piers' Protean Pardon: The Letter and Spirit of Langland's Theology of Indulgences', in *Studies in Late Medieval and Early Renaissance Texts in Honour of John Scattergood*, ed. by Anne Marie D'Arcy and Alan J. Fletcher (Dublin: Four Courts), pp. 218–40

'"Respondet Walterus Bryth …": Walter Brut in Debate on Women Priests', in *Text and Controversy from Wyclif to Bale: Essays in Honour of Anne Hudson*, ed. by Helen Barr and Ann M. Hutchison (Turnhout: Brepols), pp. 229–49

## 2006

'From *Coilles* to *Bel Chose*: Discourses of Obscenity in Jean de Meun and Chaucer', in *Medieval Obscenities*, ed. by Nicola McDonald (Woodbridge: York Medieval Press in association with Boydell and Brewer), pp. 156–78

'The Construction of Chaucer's Pardoner', in *Promissory Notes on the Treasury of Merits: Indulgences in the Late Middle Ages*, ed. by R. N. Swanson (Turnhout: Brepols), pp. 165–91

'John Wyclif – All Women's Friend?', in *Mindful Spirit in Late Medieval Literature: Essays in Honor of Elizabeth D. Kirk*, ed. by Bonnie Wheeler (New York: Palgrave Macmillan), pp. 121–33

'*Nolens auctor sed compilator reputari*: The Late-Medieval Discourse of Compilation', in *La méthode critique au Moyen Âge*, ed. by Mireille Chazan and Gilbert Dahan (Turnhout: Brepols), pp. 47–63

'Purchasing Pardon: Material and Spiritual Economies on the Canterbury Pilgrimage', in *Sacred and Secular in Medieval and Early Modern Cultures: New Essays*, ed. by Lawrence Besserman (New York: Palgrave Macmillan), pp. 63–82

'Standardizing Lay Culture: Secularity in French and English Literature of the Fourteenth-Century', in *The Beginnings of Standardization: Language and Culture in Fourteenth-Century England*, ed. by Ursula Schaefer (Frankfurt am Main: Peter Lang), pp. 43–60

'The Wisdom of Old Women: Alisoun of Bath as *Auctrice*', in *Writings on Love in the English Middle Ages*, ed. by Helen Cooney (New York: Palgrave Macmillan), pp. 99–114

## 2007

*Fallible Authors: Chaucer's Pardoner and Wife of Bath*, The Middle Ages Series (Philadelphia: University of Pennsylvania Press)

Ed., with Jane Roberts, *Text, Image, Interpretation: Studies in Anglo-Saxon Literature and Its Insular Context in Honour of Éamonn Ó Carragáin*, Studies in the Early Middle Ages 18 (Turnhout: Brepols)

## 2009

*Medieval Theory of Authorship: Scholastic Literary Attitudes in the Later Middle Ages*, reissued 2nd edn with a new preface (Philadelphia: University of Pennsylvania Press)

*Translations of Authority in Medieval English Literature: Valuing the Vernacular* (Cambridge: Cambridge University Press)

'Once More into the Breech: The Pardoner's Prize *Relyk*', in *Through a Classical Eye: Transcultural and Transhistorical Visions in Medieval English, Italian and Latin Literature in Honour of Winthrop Wetherbee*, ed. by R. F. Yeager and Andrew Galloway (Toronto: University of Toronto Press, 2009), pp. 287–315

'"Oonly consent of love is sufficiant for matrimonie": Translating John Wyclif's Word of the Mind', in *Lost in Translation?*, ed. by Denis Renevey and Christiania Whitehead, The Medieval Translator/Traduire au Moyen Âge 12 (Turnhout: Brepols), pp. 189–203

'Tobit's Dog and the Dangers of Literalism: William Woodford OFM as Critic of Wycliffite Exegesis', in *Defenders and Critics of Franciscan Life: Essays in Honor of John Fleming*, ed. by Michael Cusato and G. Geltner (Leiden: Brill), pp. 41–52

## 2010

Ed., with Rosalynn Voaden, *Medieval Holy Women in the Christian Tradition, c. 1100–c. 1500*, Brepols Collected Essays in European Culture 1 (Turnhout: Brepols)

'Introduction', co-authored with Rosalynn Voaden, in *Medieval Holy Women*, pp. 1–9

'Religious Roles: Public and Private', in *Medieval Holy Women*, pp. 47–81

## 2011

'1215–1349: Culture and History', in *The Cambridge Companion to Medieval English Mysticism*, ed. by Vincent Gillespie and Samuel Fanous (Cambridge: Cambridge University Press), pp. 69–89

'Ethical Poetry, Poetic Theology: A Crisis of Medieval Authority?', in *Medieval and Early Modern Authorship*, ed. by Guillemette Bolens (Tübingen: Narr), pp. 293–308

'The Trouble with Theology: Ethical Poetics and the Ends of Scripture', in *Author, Reader, Book: Medieval Authorship in Theory and Practice*, ed. by Stephen Partridge and Erik Kwakkel (Toronto: University of Toronto Press), pp. 21–37

'Wyclif's Eden: Sex, Death and Dominion', in *Wycliffite Controversies*, ed. by Mishtooni Bose and J. Patrick Hornbeck II (Turnhout: Brepols), pp. 59–78

## 2013

'Brewer's Chaucer and the Knightly Virtues', in *Traditions and Innovations in the Study of Middle English Literature: The Influence of Derek Brewer*, ed. by Charlotte Brewer and Barry Windeatt (Cambridge: D. S. Brewer), pp. 34–46

'Image Trouble in Vernacular Commentary: The Vacillations of Francesco Da Barberino', *Nottingham Medieval Studies*, 56, being a special issue: *Studies in Medieval Rhetoric in Honour of Mary Carruthers*, ed. by Laura Iseppi de Filippis, 229–45

## 2014

*The Cambridge Introduction to Chaucer*, Cambridge Introductions to Literature (Cambridge: Cambridge University Press)

*Historians on Chaucer: The* General Prologue *to the* Canterbury Tales, ed. by Stephen Rigby, with the assistance of Alastair J. Minnis (Oxford: Oxford University Press)

'Chaucer Drinks What He Brews: *The House of Fame*, 1873–82', *Notes and Queries*, ns 61, 187–89

'Inglorious Glosses?', in *John Gower in England and Iberia: Manuscripts, Influences, Reception*, ed. by Ana Sáez-Hidalgo and R. F. Yeager (Cambridge: D. S. Brewer), pp. 51–75

'The Medieval Bible as Literature', co-authored with A. B. Kraebel, in *The Edinburgh Companion to the Bible and the Arts*, ed. by Stephen Prickett (Edinburgh: Edinburgh University Press), pp. 440–58

## 2015

'Discourse Beyond Death: The Language of Heaven in the Middle English *Pearl*', in *Language in Medieval Britain: Networks and*

Exchanges. Proceedings of the 2013 Harlaxton Symposium, ed. by Mary Carruthers (Donington: Shaun Tyas), pp. 214–28

'Fragmentations of Medieval Religion: Thomas More, Chaucer and the Volcano Lover', The Presidential Address, The New Chaucer Society, Nineteenth International Congress, July 16–20, 2014, University of Iceland, Reykjavík, Studies in the Age of Chaucer, 37, 3–27

'Reconciling Amour and Yconomique: Evrart de Conty's Ambition as Vernacular Commentator', in Traduire au XIVe siècle: Evrart de Conty et la vie intellectuelle à la cour de Charles V, ed. by Joëlle Ducos and Michèle Goyens (Paris: Editions Honoré Champion), pp. 199–221

'The Restoration of All Things: John Bradford's Refutation of Aquinas on Animal Resurrection', Journal of Medieval and Early Modern Studies, 45, 323–42

'Unquiet Graves: Pearl and the Hope of Reunion', in Truth and Tales: Cultural Mobility and Medieval Media, ed. by Fiona Someset and Nicholas Watson (Columbus: Ohio State University Press, 2015), pp. 117–34

## 2016

From Eden to Eternity: Creations of Paradise in the Later Middle Ages, The Middle Ages Series (Philadelphia: University of Pennsylvania Press)

Ed., with Ian Johnson, Mawsuat Kambridj fi al-naqd al-adabī, II, al-Usur al-Wusta, an Arabic translation of the 2005 Cambridge History, tr. by Muhammad Hamdi Ibrahim, Adil al-Nahhas and Hisham Darwish, in two parts (Cairo: National Center for Translation)

'Aggressive Chaucer: Of Dolls, Drink and Dante', in Translation and Authority – Authorities in Translation, ed. by Pieter de Leemans and Michèle Goyens, The Medieval Translator/Traduire au Moyen Âge 16 (Turnhout: Brepols), pp. 357–76

'Figuring the Letter: Making Sense of Sensus Litteralis in Late-Medieval Christian Exegesis', in Interpreting Scriptures in Judaism, Christianity and Islam: Overlapping Inquiries, ed. by Mordechai Z. Cohen and Adele Berlin, with the assistance of Meir M. Bar-Asher, Rita Copeland and Jon Whitman (Cambridge: Cambridge University Press), pp. 159–82

'Other Worlds: Chaucer's Classicism', in The Oxford History of Classical Reception in English Literature, I, 800–1558, ed. by Rita Copeland (Oxford: Oxford University Press), pp. 412–33

## 2017

'*The Prick of Conscience* and the Imagination of Paradise', in *Pursuing Middle English Manuscripts and Their Texts: Essays in Honour of Ralph Hanna*, ed. by Simon Horobin and Aditi Nafde (Turnhout: Brepols), pp. 157–75

## 2018

'Bending Augustine's Nose, or How to Authorize Sexual Pleasure', *The Mediaeval Journal*, 8.2, 1–20

## 2019

'Secularity', in *Geoffrey Chaucer in Context*, ed. by Ian Johnson, Literature in Context (Cambridge: Cambridge University Press), pp. 178–86

Review of Christopher Cannon, *From Literacy to Literature: England, 1300–1400*', in *Spenser Review*, 49.1, n.p.

Review of Rory G. Critten, *Author, Scribe, and Book in Late Medieval English Literature*, in *MÆ*, 88, 164–66

Review of Richard Firth Green, *Elf Queens and Holy Friars: Fairy Beliefs and the Medieval Church*, in *Spenser Review*, 49.2, n.p.

Review of Eleanor Johnson, *Staging Contemplation: Participatory Theology in Middle English Prose, Verse and Drama*, in *Speculum*, 94, 1174–76

Review of Tamás Karáth, *Richard Rolle: The Fifteenth-Century Translations*, in *MÆ*, 88, 420–21

Review of Jonathan Morton, *The* Roman de la Rose *in Its Philosophical Context: Art, Nature and Ethics*, in *Spenser Review*, 49.3, n.p.

Review of Phillip L. Reynolds, *How Marriage Became One of the Sacraments: The Sacramental Theology of Marriage from Its Medieval Origins to the Council of Trent*, in *MÆ*, 88, 146–47

Review of Myra L. Uhlfelder, *The* Consolation of Philosophy *as Cosmic Image*, in *MÆ* 88, 436–37

## 2020

*Hellish Imaginations from Augustine to Dante: An Essay in Metaphor and Materiality*, Medium Ævum Monographs 37 (Oxford: Society for the Study of Medieval Languages and Literature)

Review of John Bugbee, *God's Patients: Chaucer, Agency and the Nature of Laws*, in *MÆ*, 89, 397–98

Review of Megan L. Cook, *The Poet and the Antiquaries: Chaucerian Scholarship and the Rise of Literary History, 1532–1635*, in *MÆ*, 89, 407–8

Review of Brian Donaghey, Noel Harold Kaylor, Jr., Philip Edward Phillips and Paul E. Szarmach (eds), with the assistance of Kenneth C. Hawley, *Remaking Boethius: The English Language Translation Tradition of* The Consolation of Philosophy, in *MÆ*, 89, 392–93

Review of A. I. Doyle, *Hope Allen's Writings Ascribed to Richard Rolle: A Corrected List of Copies*, ed. and extended by Ralph Hanna, in *MÆ*, 89, 172

Review of Philip Knox, Jonathan Morton and Daniel Reeve (eds), *Medieval Thought Experiments: Poetry, Hypothesis and Experience in the European Middle Ages*, in *Speculum*, 95, 270–72

Review of A. Joseph McMullen and Erica Weaver (eds), *The Legacy of Boethius in Medieval England: The* Consolation *and Its Afterlives*, in *Speculum*, 95, 593–94

Review of Sarah Salih, *Imagining the Pagan in Late Medieval England*, in *MÆ*, 89, 404–5

Review of Sebastian Sobecki, *Last Words: The Public Self and the Social Author in Late Medieval England*, in *MÆ*, 89, 402–3

Review of Marion Turner, *Chaucer: A European Life*, in *Spenser Review*, 50.1, n.p.

Review of John O. Ward, *Classical Rhetoric in the Middle Ages: The Medieval Rhetors and Their Art, 400–1300, with Manuscript Survey to 1500 CE*, in *MÆ*, 89, 161–62

Review of Nancy Bradley Warren, *Chaucer and Religious Controversies in the Medieval and Early Modern Eras*, in *MÆ*, 89, 399–400

Review of Cord Whitaker, *Black Metaphors: How Modern Racism Emerged from Medieval Race-Thinking*, in *MÆ*, 89, 383–84

### 2021

*Phantom Pains and Prosthetic Narratives: From George Dedlow to Dante*, Cambridge Elements in Histories of Emotions and the Senses (Cambridge: Cambridge University Press)

Review of John M. Bowers, *Tolkien's Lost Chaucer*, in *MÆ*, 90, 349–50

Review of Dyan Elliot, *The Corrupter of Boys: Sodomy, Scandal, and the Medieval Clergy*, in *MÆ*, 90, 156–57

Review of Kara Gaston, *Reading Chaucer in Time: Literary Formation in England and Italy*, in *MÆ*, 90, 167–68

Review of William F. Hodapp, *The Figure of Minerva in Medieval Literature*, in *MÆ*, 90, 153–54

Review of Megan E. Murton, *Chaucer's Prayers: Writing Christian and Pagan Devotion*, in *MÆ*, 90, 164–65

### 2022

'Demonic Prosthesis and the Walking Dead: The Materiality of Chaucer's Green Yeoman', *New Medieval Literatures*, 22, 114–61

'"We only punish them when they do wrong": Slavery and the St Boswells Bard, John Younger (d. 1860)', *Scottish Local History*, 111, 38–43

## Forthcoming

'John Younger (1785–1860): Marked by Fire and Steel', *The Burns Chronicle*

'Proto-Surgery, Resurrection and Race: Interpreting "The Ethiopian's Leg Transplant" Miracle', *The Mediaeval Journal*

# Bibliography

## Primary Sources

Albertus Magnus, *Alberti Magni Opera omnia ad fidem codicum manuscriptorum edenda*, 40 vols (Münster in Westfalen: Aschendorff, 1951–2019)
  *Book of Minerals*, tr. by Dorothy Wyckoff (Oxford: Clarendon, 1967)
  *De mineralibus et rebus metallicis libri quinque* (Cologne: Birckmannum et Baumium, 1569)
Alexander of Hales, *Doctoris irrefragabilis Alexandri de Hales Ordinis Minorum Summa theologica*, 4 vols in 5 (Quaracchi: Collegio di San Bonaventura, 1924–48)
Alighieri, Dante, *La Commedia secondo l'antica vulgata*, ed. by Giorgio Petrocchi, 4 vols (Milan: Mondadori, 1966–67)
Aquinas, Thomas, *Commentary on Aristotle's Politics*, tr. by Richard J. Regan (Indianapolis, IN: Hackett, 2007)
  *Doctoris angelici divi Thomae Aquinatis Opera omnia*, ed. by Stanisla Eduard Fretté and Paul Maré, 34 vols (Paris: Vivès, 1871–80)
  *In Octo Libros Politicorum Aristotelis Expositio*, ed. by Raimondo M. Spiazzi (Turin: Marietti, 1966)
  *Sancti Thomae Aquinatis doctoris angelici opera omnia iussu Leonis XIII P. M. edita*, Leonine edn, 50 vols as of 2000, with various revised vols appearing since 1987 as *editiones alterae retractatae* (Rome: Vatican Polyglot Press, 1882–)
  *Sancti Thomae Aquinatis doctoris angelici, ordinis Praedicatorum, opera omnia*, 25 vols (Parma: Fiaccadori, 1852–73)
  *Scriptum super libros sententiarum magistri Petri Lombardi Episcopi Parisiensis*, ed. by Pierre Mandonnet and Marie Fabien Moos, 4 vols (Paris: Lethielleux, 1929–47)
  *Summa Theologiae*, ed. and tr. by the English Dominican Province, 61 vols (Cambridge: Blackfriars, 1964–76)
Aristotle, *Aristotelis Politicorum Libri Octo cum Vetusta Translatione Guilelmi de Moerbeka*, ed. by Franz Susemihl (Leipzig: Teubner, 1872)
  *Aristotle's Politics*, tr. by Carnes Lord, 2nd edn (Chicago: University of Chicago Press, 2013)

*De arte poetica: translatio Guillelmi de Moerbeka ...; accedunt expositio media Averrois sive 'Poetria' Hermanno Alemanno interprete et specimina translationis Petri Leonii*, ed. by Lorenzo Minio-Paluello, 2nd edn, Aristoteles Latinus 33 (Brussels: Desclée, de Brouwer, 1968)

*The Metaphysics*, ed. and tr. by Hugh Tredennick, 2 vols, LCL 271 and 287 (Cambridge, MA: Harvard University Press, 1933–35)

*Poetics*, ed. and tr. by Stephen Halliwell, with Longinus, *On the Sublime*, ed. and tr. by W. H. Fyfe, rev. by Donald Russell, and *On Style*, ed. and tr. by Doreen C. Innes, rev. edn, LCL 199 (Cambridge, MA: Harvard University Press, 1995)

*Politics: Books I and II*, tr. by Trevor Saunders (Oxford: Clarendon, 1995)

*Rhetorica. Translatio Anonyma sive Vetus et Translatio Guillelmi de Moerbeka*, ed. by Bernhard Schneider, Aristoteles Latinus 31.1–2 (Leiden: Brill, 1978)

Arnulf of Orléans, *Arnulfi Aurelianensis Glosule super Lucanum*, ed. by Berthe M. Marti (Rome: American Academy in Rome, 1958)

Bacon, Francis, *The Works of Francis Bacon*, III, *Of the Advancement of Learning*, ed. by James Spedding and Robert Leslie Ellis (London: Longman, 1857)

Bacon, Roger, *Moralis philosophia*, ed. by Eugenio Massa (Zürich: Thesaurus mundi, 1953)

*Opus maius*, ed. by John Henry Bridges (Oxford: Clarendon, 1897)

Bax, Earnest Belfort (ed.), *Boethius'* Consolation of Philosophy *Translated from the Latin by George Colville, 1556*, The Tudor Library 5 (London: D. Nutt, 1897)

Beckerlegge, O. A. (ed.), *Le Secré de Secrez by Pierre d'Abernun of Fetcham*, ANTS 5 (Oxford: ANTS, 1944)

Bernard of Clairvaux, *Sermons on the Song of Songs*, tr. by Kilian Walsh, 4 vols (Kalamazoo, MI: Cistercian Publications, 1971–83)

Bernardus Silvestris, *Commentum quod dicitur Bernardi Silvestri super sex libros Eneidos*, ed. by Julian Jones and Elizabeth Jones (Lincoln: University of Nebraska Press, 1977)

*Poetic Works*, ed. and tr. by Winthrop Wetherbee, Dumbarton Oaks Medieval Library 38 (Cambridge, MA: Harvard University Press, 2015)

Boethius (Anicius Manlius Severinus Boethius), *De consolatione philosophiae. Opuscula theologica*, ed. by Claudio Moreschini, 2nd edn (Munich: K. G. Saur, 2005)

*The Theological Tractates. The Consolation of Philosophy*, ed. and tr. by H. F. Stewart and E. K. Rand, with the translation of 'I.T.' rev. by H. F. Stewart, LCL (Cambridge, MA: Harvard University Press, 1936)

Bonaventure, *Doctoris Seraphici S. Bonaventurae opera omnia*, 11 vols in 10 (Quaracchi: Collegio di San Bonaventura, 1882–1902)

Bonaventure, *The Soul's Journey into God, the Tree of Life, the Life of St Francis*, tr. by Ewert Cousins, Classics of Western Spirituality (New York: Paulist Press, 1978)

Bromyard, John, *Summa praedicantium* (Basel: Amerbach, 1484?)

Bruni, Gerardo (ed.), 'The *De differentia rhetoricae, ethicae et politicae* of Aegidius Romanus', *The New Scholasticism*, 6 (1932), 1–18

Burnett, Charles (ed. and tr.), *Adelard of Bath: Conversations with His Nephew, on the Same and the Different, Questions on Natural Science and on Birds*, Cambridge Medieval Classics 9 (Cambridge: Cambridge University Press, 1998)

Caplan, Harry (ed. and tr.), *Rhetorica ad C. Herennium de ratione dicendi*, LCL 403 (Cambridge, MA: Harvard University Press, 1954)

Cassian, John, *Iohannis Cassiani Conlationes XXIIII*, ed. by Michael Petschenig, CSEL 13 (Vienna: Geroldi, 1886)

Cassiodorus, *Expositio Psalmorum*, ed. by Marcus Adriaen, 2 vols, CCSL 97–98 (Turnhout: Brepols, 1958)

Chaucer, Geoffrey, *Chaucer's Boece: A Critical Edition Based on Cambridge, University Library MS Ii.3.21*, ed. by Tim William Machan (Heidelberg: Winter, 2008)

*The Riverside Chaucer*, ed. by Larry D. Benson et al. (Boston: Houghton Mifflin, 1987)

Cicero (M. Tullius Cicero), *Brutus*, ed. and tr. by G. L. Hendrickson, with *Orator*, ed. and tr. by H. M. Hubbell, LCL 342 (Cambridge, MA: Harvard University Press, 1971)

*De oratore*, ed. and tr. by H. Rackham, 2 vols, LCL 348–49 (Cambridge, MA: Harvard University Press, 1942)

Copeland, Rita and Ineke Sluiter (eds), *Medieval Grammar and Rhetoric: Language Arts and Literary Theory, AD. 300–1475* (Oxford: Oxford University Press, 2009)

De Bruyne, Donatien (ed.), *Préfaces de la Bible latine* (Namur: Godenne, 1914)

De Lorris, Guillaume and Jean de Meun, *Le Roman de la Rose*, ed. by Félix Lecoy, 3 vols (Paris: Champion, 1965–70)

*The Romance of the Rose*, tr. by Charles Dahlberg, 3rd edn (Princeton, NJ: Princeton University Press, 1995)

Dodwell, C. R. (ed. and tr.), *Theophilus: The Various Arts (De diversis artibus)* (Oxford: Clarendon, 1961)

Duff, J. Wight and Arnold M. Duff (eds and trs), *Minor Latin Poets*, rev. edn, 2 vols, LCL 284 and 434 (Cambridge, MA: Harvard University Press, 1935)

Feruardent, François (ed.), *Biblia sacra cum Glossa ordinaria nouisque additionibus*, 6 vols (Venice: Giuntas, 1603)

Fetcham, Pierre de, 'De la charte du diable fet a coveytous,' in *The Anglo-Norman Lyric*, ed. by Brian J. Levy and David L. Jeffrey (Toronto: Pontifical Institute of Mediaeval Studies, 1990), pp. 137–41 (no. 28)

Galbraith, G. R. (ed.), *The Constitution of the Dominican Order, 1216 to 1360* (Manchester: Manchester University Press, 1925)

Geoffrey of Vinsauf, *Poetria nova*, tr. by Margaret F. Nims, rev. edn (Toronto: Pontifical Institute of Mediaeval Studies, 2010)

*The Poetria nova and its Sources in Early Rhetorical Doctrine*, ed. by Ernest Gallo (The Hague: Mouton, 1971)

Geoffrey of Vitry, *The Commentary of Geoffrey of Vitry on Claudian*, De raptu Proserpinae, ed. by A. K. Clarke and P. M. Giles (Leiden: Brill, 1973)
Giles of Rome, *De regimine principum* (Rome: Bartolomeo Zannetti, 1607)
  *Rhetorica Aristotelis cum fundatissimi artium et theologie doctoris Egidii de Roma luculentissimis commentariis* (Venice: Giorgio Arrivabene, 1515)
Glei, Reinhold F. (ed.), 'Iodoci Badii Ascensii in Boetium de consolatione philosophiae grammaticalis explanatio liber I', *Neulateinisches Jahrbuch*, 10 (2008), 87–144
Godden, Malcolm and Susan Irvine (eds), *The Old English Boethius: An Edition of the Old English Versions of Boethius's* De Consolatione Philosophiae, 2 vols (Oxford: Oxford University Press, 2009)
Gower, John, *English Works of John Gower*, ed. by G. C. Macaulay, 2 vols, EETS es 81 and 82 (London: Paul, Trench, Trübner, 1900–01)
Gregory the Great, *Homiliae in Hiezechielem prophetam*, ed. by Marcus Adriaen, CCSL 142 (Turnhout: Brepols, 1971)
Grosseteste, Robert, *De cessatione legalium*, ed. by Richard C. Dales and Edward B. King, Auctores Britannici Medii Aevi 7 (London: Oxford University Press for the British Academy, 1986)
Halm, Karl (ed.), *Rhetores Latini Minores* (Leipzig: Teubner, 1863)
Henry of Ghent, *Summa quaestionum ordinarium theologi recepto preconio Solennis Henrici a Gandauo* (Paris: Josse Bade, 1520)
Hesketh, Glynn (ed.), *Lumere as lais*, 3 vols, ANTS 54–55, 56–57, 58 (London: Anglo–Norman Text Society, 1996–2000)
Hobbes, Thomas, *Leviathan*, ed. by Noel Malcolm, 3 vols (Oxford: Clarendon, 2012)
  *The English Works of Thomas Hobbes of Malmesbury*, ed. by William Molesworth, 11 vols (London: Bohn, 1839–45)
Hoccleve, Thomas, *'My Compleinte' and Other Poems*, ed. by Roger Ellis (Exeter: University of Exeter Press, 2001)
Holcot, Robert, *Robert Holcot, Exegete: Selections from the Commentary on Minor Prophets*, ed. and tr. by Ralph Hanna (Liverpool: Liverpool University Press, 2021)
  *Super Sapientiam Salomonis* (Cologne: Winters, before 1476)
Hugh of St Cher, *Opera omnia in universum Vetus et Novum Testamentum*, 8 vols (Lyon: Sumptibus Societatis Bibliopolarum, 1645)
Hugh of St Victor, *Didascalicon: A Medieval Guide to the Arts*, tr. by Jerome Taylor (New York: Columbia University Press, 1961)
  *Hugonis de Sancto Victore super Ierarchiam Dionisii*, ed. by Dominique Poirel, CCCM 178 (Turnhout: Brepols, 2015)
Humbert of Romans, *Treatise on Preaching*, ed. by Walter M. Conlon, tr. by the Dominican Students of the Province of St Joseph (London: Blackfriars, 1955)
Hunt, Tony (ed.), *Rauf de Linham, Kalender*, ANTS Plain Texts Series 1 (London: ANTS, 1983)

(ed.), *Three Anglo-Norman Treatises on Falconry*, Medium Ævum Monographs ns 36 (Oxford: Society for the Study of Medieval Languages and Literature, 2009)

(ed.), *Writing the Future: Prognostic Texts of Medieval England*, Textes littéraires du Moyen Âge 24, Divinatoria 2 (Paris: Classiques Garnier, 2013)

Huygens, R. B. C. (ed.), *Accessus ad auctores. Bernard D'Utrecht. Conrad d'Hirsau, Dialogus super auctores*, rev. edn (Leiden: Brill, 1970)

Isidore of Seville, *Etymologiarum sive Originum libri XX*, ed. by W. M. Lindsay, 2 unpaginated vols (Oxford: Clarendon, 1911)

John of Salisbury, *Policraticus sive De nugis curalium*, ed. by Clemens Webb, 2 vols (Oxford: Clarendon, 1909)

John of Wales, *Summa Johannis Valensis de regimine vite humane seu Margarita doctorum* (Lyon, 1511)

Keil, Heinrich (ed.), *Grammatici Latini*, 7 vols (Leipzig: Teubner, 1857–80)

Lactantius Placidus, *Lactantii Placidi qui dicitur Commentarios in Statii Thebaida et Commentarium in Achilleida*, ed. by Richard Jahnke (Leipzig: Teubner, 1898)

Langland, William, *Piers Plowman: A New Annotated Edition of the C Text*, ed. by Derek Pearsall, 2nd edn (Exeter: University of Exeter Press, 2008)

*Piers Plowman: A Parallel-Text Edition of the A, B, C and Z Versions*, ed. by A. V. C. Schmidt, 2 vols in 3, 2nd edn (Kalamazoo, MI: Medieval Institute Publications, 2011)

*The Vision of Piers Plowman: A Critical Edition of the B-Text*, ed. by A. V. C. Schmidt (London: Dent, 2011)

Lucretius (T. Lucretius Carus), *De rerum natura*, tr. by W. H. D. Rouse, rev. by Martin Ferguson Smith, LCL 181 (Cambridge, MA: Harvard University Press, 1992)

McGinn, Bernard (ed.), *Three Treatise on Man: A Cistercian Anthology* (Kalamazoo, MI: Cistercian Publications, 1977)

Miller, Joseph M., et al. (eds), *Readings in Medieval Rhetoric* (Bloomington: Indiana University Press, 1973)

Murphy, J. J. (ed. and tr.), *Three Medieval Rhetorical Arts* (Berkeley: University of California Press, 1971)

Öberg, Christina Sandquist (ed.), *Versus Maximiani* (Stockholm: Almquist and Wiksell, 1999)

Olivi, Peter John, *La Caduta du Gerusalemme. Il commento al Libro delle Lamentazioni di Pietro Giovanni Olivi*, ed. by Marco Bartoli (Rome: Istituto storica italiano per il medio evo, 1991)

*Petri Iohannis Olivi Expositio in Canticum Canticorum*, ed. by Johannes Schlageter (Grottaferrata: Collegio di San Bonaventura, 1999)

Orengo, Renato (ed.), *Les Dialogues de Grégoire le grand traduits par Angier*, 2 vols (Paris: Société des anciens textes français, 2013)

Osternacher, Johannes (ed.), *Theoduli eclogam* (Urfahr: Collegium Petrinum, 1902)

Ovid (P. Ovidius Naso), *The Art of Love and Other Poems*, ed. and tr. by J. H. Mozley, 2nd edn, rev. by G. P. Goold, LCL 232 (Cambridge, MA: Harvard University Press, 1979)

*Metamorphoses*, ed. and tr. by Frank Justus Miller, 3rd edn, rev. by G. P. Goold, 2 vols, LCL 42–43 (Cambridge, MA: Harvard University Press, 1984)

*Tristia. Ex Ponto*, ed. and tr. by A. L. Wheeler, rev. by G. P. Goold, LCL 151 (Cambridge, MA: Harvard University Press, 1924)

Ovid (pseudonymous), *De vetula*, ed. by Paul Klopsch, Mittellateinische Studien und Texte 2 (Leiden: Brill, 1967)

Pannier, Léopold (ed.), *Les lapidaires français du moyen âge du xii, xiii, et xiv siècles* (Paris: Vieweg, 1882)

Pecock, Reginald, *The Donet ... with the Poore Mennis Myrrour*, ed. by Elsie Vaughan Hitchcock, EETS os 156 (London: Oxford University Press, 1921)

*Reginald Peacock's Book of Faith: A Fifteenth-Century Theological Tractate*, ed. by J. L. Morison (Glasgow: J. Maclehose and Sons, 1909)

*The Repressor of Over Much Blaming of the Clergy by Reginald Pecock, D.D., Sometime Lord Bishop of Chichester*, ed. by Churchill Babington, 2 vols, Rerum britannicarum medii ævi scriptores 19 (London: Longman, Green, Longman and Roberts, 1860)

*The Reule of Crysten Religioun*, ed. by William Cabell Greet, EETS os 171 (London: Oxford University Press, 1927)

Pellegatta, Pietro (ed.), 'Edizione critica del commento *Testatur Servius* alle *Bucoliche* di Virgilio attribuito a Ilario d'Orléans' (unpublished doctoral thesis, Università Ca' Foscari Venezia, 2014)

Peter of Auvergne, *Questiones super I–VII libros Politicorum: A Critical Edition and Study*, ed. by Marco Toste (Leuven: Leuven University Press, forthcoming)

Peter of Celle, *Selected Works*, tr. by Hugh Feiss (Kalamazoo, MI: Cistercian Publications, 1987)

Quintilian (M. Fabius Quintilianus), *Institutionis oratoriae libri duodecim*, ed. by Michael Winterbottom, 2 vols (Oxford: Clarendon, 1970)

*The Orator's Education*, ed. and tr. by Donald Russell, 5 vols, LCL 124–27 and 494 (Cambridge, MA: Harvard University Press, 2001)

Raby, F. J. E. (ed.), *Poems of John of Hoveden*, Surtees Society 154 (London: Andrews, 1939)

Raine, James (ed.), *The Fabric Rolls of York Minster*, Publications of the Surtees Society 35 (Durham: George Andrews, 1859)

Rainolds, John, *John Rainolds's Oxford Lectures on Aristotle's Rhetoric*, ed. and tr. by Lawrence D. Green (Newark: University of Delaware Press, 1986)

Richard de Bury (attr.), *The Philobiblon of Richard of Bury, Bishop of Durham, Treasurer and Chancellor of Edward III*, ed. and tr. by Ernest C. Thomas (London: Paul, Trench and Co., 1888)

Rigg, A. G. (tr.), 'The Eclogue of Theodulus: A Translation', Toronto, Centre for Medieval Studies <https://medieval.utoronto.ca/ylias/web-content/theoduli.html> [last accessed 11 November 2022]

Robert of Melun, *Œuvres. Texte inédit*, ed. by Raymond-M. Martin and R. M. Gallet, 3 vols in 4 (Louvain: Spicilegium Sacrum Lovaniense, 1932–52)

Rolle, Richard, *The Contra Amatores Mundi of Richard Rolle of Hampole*, ed. and tr. by Paul F. Theiner (Berkeley: University of California Press, 1968)

*De emendatione vitae: eine kritische Ausgabe des lateinischen Textes von Richard Rolle ; mit einer Übersetzung ins Deutsche und Untersuchungen zu den lateinischen und englischen Handschriften*, ed. and tr. by Rüdiger Spahl (Göttingen: V&R Unipress, 2009)

*The Incendium Amoris of Richard Rolle of Hampole*, ed. by Margaret Deanesly (Manchester: Manchester University Press, 1915)

*The Melos Amoris of Richard Rolle of Hampole*, ed. by E. J. F. Arnould (Oxford: Blackwell, 1957)

*The Psalter, or Psalms of David and Certain Canticles, with a Translation and Exposition in English by Richard Rolle of Hampole*, ed. by H. R. Bramley (Oxford: Clarendon, 1884)

*Richard Rolle de Hampole, 1300–1349. Vie et œuvres suivies du Tractatus super Apocalypsim*, ed. by Nicole Marzac (Paris: Vrin, 1968)

*Richard Rolle: Unprinted Latin Writings*, ed. and tr. by Ralph Hanna (Liverpool: Liverpool University Press, 2019)

Ruelle, Pierre (ed.), *L'Ornement des Dames (Ornatus mulierum): Texte anglo-normand du XIIIe siècle* (Brussels: Presses universitaires de Bruxelles, 1967)

Ruhe, Ernstpeter (ed.), *Sydrac le philosophe: Le livre de la fontaine de toutes sciences*, Wissensliteratur im Mittelalter 34 (Weisbaden: Ludwig Reichert Verlag, 2000)

Russell, D. A. and M. Winterbottom (ed.), *Ancient Literary Criticism: The Principal Texts in New Translations* (Oxford: Clarendon, 1972)

Russell, D. W. (ed.), *La Vie seint Richard evesque de Cycestre by Pierre d'Abernon de Fetcham*, ANTS 51 (London: ANTS, 1995 for 1993)

Science, Mark (ed.), *Boethius: De Consolatione Philosophiae*, tr. by John Walton, Canon of Oseney, EETS os 170 (London: Oxford University Press, 1927)

Servius (Maurus Servius Honoratus), *Servianorum in Vergilii carmina commentatorium editio Harvardiana*, ed. by E. K. Rand et al., 3 vols (Lancaster, PA: Societatas Philologica Americana, 1946–)

Stanbury, Sarah (ed.), *Pearl* (Kalamazoo, MI: Medieval Institute Publications, 2001)

Studer, Paul and Joan Evans (eds), *Anglo-Norman Lapidaries* (Paris: Champion, 1924)

Sullivan, Thérèse (ed. and tr.), *The Rhetoric of Augustine of Hippo* (Waco, TX: Baylor University Press, 2008)

Trevisa, John, *The Governance of Kings and Princes*, ed. by D. Fowler, C. Briggs and P. Remley (New York: Garland, 1997)

Vico, Giambattista, *The Art of Rhetoric (Institutiones oratoriae, 1711–1741)*, ed. and tr. by Giorgio A. Pinton and Arthur W. Shippee (Amsterdam: Rodopi, 1996)

*De Nostri Temporis Studiorum Ratione di Giambattista Vico. Primo redazione inedita dal. ms CIII B 55 della Bibl. Naz. di Napoli*, ed. by Marco Veneziani (Florence: Olschki, 2000)

*Institutiones oratoriae*, ed. by Giuliano Crifò (Naples: Instituto Suor Orsola Benincasa, 1989)

*New Science*, tr. by David Marsh (Harmondsworth: Penguin, 1999)

*Opere*, ed. by Fausto Nicolini (Milan: Ricciardi, 1953)

*On the Study Methods of Our Time*, tr. by Elio Gianturco (Indianapolis, IN: Bobbs-Merrill, 1965)

Vincent of Beauvais, *Speculum Doctrinale Vincentii* (Venice: Hermann Lichtenstein, 1494)

Virgil (P. Vergilius Maro), *Eclogues. Georgics. Aeneid: Books 1–6*, ed. and tr. by H. Rushton Fairclough, rev. by G. P. Goold, LCL 63 (Cambridge, MA: Harvard University Press, 1916)

Waleys, Thomas, *Diui Aurelii Augustini … de Ciuitate dei contra paganos Libri duo et viginti … Cum commentariis Thome Valois et Nicolai Triueth necnon additionibus* (Basel: Koberger, 1515)

Walther, Hans (ed.), *Proverbia sententiaeque Latinitatis Medii Aevi. Lateinische Sprichwörter und Sentenzen des Mittelalters in alphabetischer Anordnung*, 9 vols (Göttingen: Vandenhoeck and Ruprecht, 1963–86)

Webber, T. and A. G. Watson (eds), *The Libraries of the Augustinian Canons*, Corpus of British Medieval Library Catalogues 6 (London: The British Library with the British Academy, 1998)

Wenzel, Siegfried (ed. and tr.), *The Art of Preaching: Five Medieval Texts and Translations* (Washington, DC: Catholic University of America Press, 2013)

(ed. and tr.), *Fasciculus morum: A Fourteenth-Century Preacher's Handbook* (University Park: Pennsylvania State University Press, 1989)

(ed.), *Summa virtutum de remediis anime*, The Chaucer Library (Athens: University of Georgia Press, 1984)

Wheeler, Stephen M. (ed. and tr.), *Accessus ad auctores: Medieval Introductions to the Authors (Codex latinus monacensis 19475)* (Kalamazoo, MI: Medieval Institute Publications, 2015)

Willemsen, Carl A. (ed.), *De arte venandi cum avibus*, 2 vols (Graz: Akademische Druck, 1969)

William of Conches, *Glosae super Boetium*, ed. by Lodi Nauta, CCCM 158 (Turnhout: Brepols, 1999)

Wogan-Browne, Jocelyn, Nicholas Watson, Andrew Taylor and Ruth Evans (eds), *The Idea of the Vernacular: An Anthology of Middle English Literary Theory, 1280–1520* (University Park: Pennsylvania State University Press, 1999)

Wood, Casey A. and F. Marjorie Fyfe (trs), *The Art of Falconry: Being the* De arte venandi cum avibus *of Frederick II of Hohenstaufen* (Stanford, CA: Stanford University Press, 1961)

Woolley, Reginald Maxwell (ed.), *The Officium and Miracula of Richard Rolle of Hampole* (London: Society for Promoting Christian Knowledge, 1919)

Wyclif, John, *De veritate sacrae Scripturae*, ed. by Rudolf Buddensieg, 3 vols (London: Wyclif Society, 1905–7)

Ziolkowski, Jan M. and Michael C. J. Putnam (eds), *The Virgilian Tradition: The First Fifteen Hundred Years* (New Haven, CT: Yale University Press, 2008)

## Secondary Studies

Adams, Robert, *Langland and the Rokele Family: The Gentry Background to Piers Plowman* (Dublin: Four Courts Press, 2013)

Aers, David, *Beyond Reformation? An Essay on William Langland's* Piers Plowman *and the End of Constantinian Christianity* (Notre Dame, IN: University of Notre Dame Press, 2015)

Piers Plowman *and Christian Allegory* (London: Edward Arnould, 1975)

*Sanctifying Signs: Making Christian Tradition in Late Medieval England* (Notre Dame, IN: University of Notre Dame Press, 2004)

Albin, Andrew, *Richard Rolle's Melody of Love: A Study and Translation with Manuscript and Musical Contexts* (Toronto: Pontifical Institute of Mediaeval Studies, 2018)

Alexander, Gavin, 'Prosopopoeia: The Speaking Figure', in *Renaissance Figures of Speech*, ed. by Sylvia Adamson, Gavin Alexander and Katrin Ettenhuber (Cambridge: Cambridge University Press, 2007), pp. 97–112

Alford, John A., 'Biblical *Imitatio* in the Writings of Richard Rolle', *ELH*, 40 (1973), 1–23

Allen, Judson Boyce, *Ethical Poetic of the Later Middle Ages: A Decorum of Convenient Distinction* (Toronto: University of Toronto Press, 1982)

*The Friar as Critic: Literary Attitudes in the Later Middle Ages* (Nashville, TN: Vanderbilt University Press, 1971)

Alter, Robert, *The Art of Biblical Poetry* (New York: Basic Books, 1985)

Anderson, Harald, *The Manuscripts of Statius*, rev. edn, 3 vols (Arlington, VA: privately printed, 2009)

Armstrong, Adrian and Sarah Kay, *Knowing Poetry: Verse in Medieval France from the Rose to the Rhétoriqueurs* (Ithaca, NY: Cornell University Press, 2011)

Ault, W. O., 'By-Laws of Gleaning and the Problem of Harvest', *Economic History Review*, 14 (1961), 210–17

Backus, Irena (ed.), *The Reception of the Church Fathers in the West: From the Carolingians to the Maurists*, 2 vols (New York: Brill, 1997)

Baldwin, Anna, 'Patient Politics in *Piers Plowman*', *YLS*, 15 (2011), 99–108

'The Triumph of Patience in Julian of Norwich and Langland', in *Langland, the Mystics and the Medieval English Religious Tradition: Essays in Honour of S. S. Hussey*, ed. by Helen Phillips (Cambridge: D. S. Brewer, 1990), pp. 71–83

Baldzuhn, Michael, *Schulbücher im Trivium des Mittelalters und der Frühen Neuzeit. Die Verschriftlichung von Unterricht in der Text- und Überlieferungsgeschichte der 'Fabulae' Avians und der deutschen 'Disticha Catonis*, 2 vols (Berlin: De Gruyter, 2009)

Barney, Stephen A., *The Penn Commentary on* Piers Plowman, v, *C Passus 20–22, B Passus 18–20* (Philadelphia: University of Pennsylvania Press, 2006)

Bastert, Bernd, 'Boethius unter Druck: Die *Consolatio Philosophiae* in einer Koberger-Inkunable von 1473', in *Boethius Christianus? Transformationen der* Consolatio philosophiae *in Mittelalter und früher Neuzeit*, ed. by Reinhold F. Glei, Nicola Kaminski and Franz Lebsanft (Berlin: De Gruyter, 2010), pp. 35–69

Baswell, Christopher, *Virgil in Medieval England: Figuring the* Aeneid *from the Twelfth Century to Chaucer*, Cambridge Studies in Medieval Literature 24 (Cambridge: Cambridge University Press, 1995)

Battistini, Andrea, 'Three Essays on Vico', *New Vico Studies*, 12 (1994), 1–46

Bernau, Anke, 'Feeling Thinking: *Pearl*'s Ekphrastic Imagination', in *The Art of Vision: Ekphrasis in Medieval Literature and Culture*, ed. by Ethan Knapp et al. (Columbus: Ohio State University Press, 2015), pp. 100–23

Berndt, Rainer and Michel Fédou (eds), *Les réceptions des Pères de l'Église au Moyen Âge: le devenir de la tradition ecclésiale: congrès du Centre Sèvres – Facultés j'suites de Paris (11–14 juin 2008)*, 2 vols (Münster: Aschendorff, 2013)

Beullens, Pieter and Pieter de Leemans, 'Aristote à Paris: le systeme de la *pecia* et les traductions de Guillaume de Moerbeke', *Recherches de Théologie et Philosophie médiévale*, 75 (2008), 87–135

Binkley, Peter, 'John Bromyard and the Hereford Dominicans', in *Centers of Learning: Learning and Location in Pre-Modern Europe and the Near East*, ed. by Jan Willem Drijvers and Alasdair A. MacDonald (Leiden: Brill, 1995), pp. 255–64

Black, Robert and Gabriella Pomaro, *Boethius's* Consolation of Philosophy *in Italian Medieval and Renaissance Education: Schoolbooks and Their Glosses in Florentine Manuscripts* (Florence: Società Internazionale per lo Studio del Medioevo Latino, 2000)

Bloomfield, Morton W., 'A Grammatical Approach to Personification Allegory', *Modern Philology*, 60 (1963), 161–71

Boas, Marc, 'De Librorum catonianorum historia atque compositione', *Mnemosyne*, ns 42 (1914), 17–46

Bognini, Filippo, '"O terque quaterque beati" (*Aen.* I.94): Aperçu d'une lecture séculaire', *Interfaces: A Journal of Medieval European Literatures*, 3 (2016), 179–99

Bolens, Guillemette and Lukas Erne (eds), *Medieval and Early Modern Authorship* (Tübingen: Narr Verlag, 2011)

Borroff, Marie, '*Pearl*'s "Maynful Mone": Crux, Simile and Structure', in *Acts of Interpretation: The Text in Its Contexts, 700–1600*, ed. by Mary Carruthers and Elizabeth D. Kirk (Norman, OK: Pilgrim Books, 1982), pp. 159–72

Bose, Mishtooni, 'Two Phases of Scholastic Self-Consciousness: Reflections on Method in Aquinas and Pecock', in *Aquinas as Authority: A Collection of Studies Presented at the Second Conference of the Thomas Instituut te Utrecht, December 14–16, 2000*, ed. by Paul Van Geest, Harm Goris and Carlo Leget (Leuven: Peeters, 2002), pp. 87–107

Brancato, Dario, 'Readers and Interpreters of the *Consolatio* in Italy, 1300–1550', in *A Companion to Boethius in the Middle Ages*, ed. by Noel Harold Kaylor and Philip Edward Phillips (Leiden: Brill, 2012), pp. 357–411

Breen, Katharine, *Imagining an English Reading Public, 1150–1400*, Cambridge Studies in Medieval Literature 79 (Cambridge: Cambridge University Press, 2010)

'Introduction', YLS, 33 (2019), 145–58

Briggs, Charles F., *Giles of Rome's* De regimine principum*: Reading and Writing Politics at Court and University, c. 1275–c. 1525* (Cambridge: Cambridge University Press, 1999)

'MS Digby 233 and the Patronage of John Trevisa's *De regimine principum*', *English Manuscript Studies, 1100–1700*, 7 (1997), 249–63

Brockwell, Charles W., Jr, *Bishop Reginald Pecock and the Lancastrian Church: Securing the Foundations of Cultural Authority* (Lewiston, NY: Edwin Mellen, 1985)

Bude, Tekla, 'Wet Shoes, Dirty Coats and the Agency of Things: Thinking Personification through New Materialism', YLS, 33 (2019), 205–29

Burns, E. Jane, *Bodytalk: When Women Speak in Old French Literature* (Philadelphia: University of Pennsylvania Press, 1993)

Butterfield, Ardis, *The Familiar Enemy: Chaucer, Language and Nation in the Hundred Years War* (Oxford: Oxford University Press, 2010)

Calabrese, Michael, 'Posthuman *Piers?* Rediscovering Langland's Subjectivities', YLS, 32 (2018), 3–36

Camargo, Martin and Marjorie Curry Woods, 'Writing Instruction in Late Medieval England', in *A Short History of Writing Instruction: From Ancient Greece to Contemporary America*, ed. by James J. Murphy, 3rd edn (New York: Routledge, 2012), pp. 114–47

Campbell, Kirsty, *The Call to Read: Reginald Pecock's Books and Textual Communities* (Notre Dame, IN: University of Notre Dame Press, 2010)

Cannon, Christopher, *From Literacy to Literature: England, 1300–1400* (Oxford: Oxford University Press, 2016)

Carruthers, Mary, *The Book of Memory: A Study of Memory in Medieval Culture*, 2nd edn, Cambridge Studies in Medieval Literature 70 (Cambridge: Cambridge University Press, 2008)

'The Concept of *Ductus*, or Journeying through a Work of Art', in *Rhetoric Beyond Words: Delight and Persuasion in the Arts of the Middle Ages*, ed. by Mary Carruthers, Cambridge Studies in Medieval Literature 78 (Cambridge: Cambridge University Press, 2010), pp. 190–213

*The Craft of Thought: Meditation, Rhetoric and the Making of Images, 400–1200*, Cambridge Studies in Medieval Literature 34 (Cambridge: Cambridge University Press, 1998)

'"The Desert", Rhetorical Invention and Prayer in the Augustinian Renewal of the Twelfth Century', in *Prayer and the Transformation of the Self in Early Christian Mystagogy*, ed. by Hans van Loon et al. (Leuven: Peeters, 2018), pp. 393–408

*The Experience of Beauty in the Middle Ages* (Oxford: Oxford University Press, 2013)

*The Search for St Truth: A Study of Meaning in* Piers Plowman (Evanston, IL: Northwestern University Press, 1973)

Caviness, Madeleine H., 'Hildegard as Designer of the Illustrations to Her Works', in *Hildegard of Bingen: The Context of Her Thought and Art*, ed. by Charles Burnett and Peter Dronke, Warburg Institute Colloquia (London: Warburg Institute, 1998), pp. 29–62

Charland, Thomas Marie, *Artes praedicandi: contribution a l'histoire de la rhetorique au moyen âge* (Paris: Vrin, 1936)

Chenu, Marie-Dominique, *Introduction à l'étude de saint Thomas d'Aquin* (Montreal: Institut d'études médiévales, 1950)

*La théologie comme science au XIIIe siècle*, 3rd edn (Paris: Vrin, 1969)

Clark, J. P. H., 'Richard Rolle as a Biblical Commentator', *Downside Review*, 104 (1986), 165–213

Clark, James G., 'The Friars and the Classics in Late Medieval England', in *The Friars in Medieval Britain: Proceedings of the 2007 Harlaxton Symposium*, ed. by Nicholas Rogers (Donnington: Shaun Tyas, 2010), pp. 142–51

Clarke, Amy K. and Harry L. Levy, 'Claudianus', in *Catalogus Translationum et Commentariorum*, III, ed. by F. Edward Cranz and Paul Oskar Kristeller (Washington, DC: Catholic University of America Press, 1976), pp. 141–71

Clogan, Paul M. (ed.), *The Medieval Achilleid of Statius* (Leiden: Brill, 1968)

Coates, Alan, et al. (eds), *A Catalogue of Books Printed in the Fifteenth Century Now in the Bodleian Library*, 6 vols (Oxford: Oxford University Press, 2005)

Cohen, Jeffrey Jerome, *Stone: An Ecology of the Inhuman* (Minneapolis: University of Minnesota Press, 2015)

Cole, Andrew, 'Chaucer's English Lesson', *Speculum*, 77 (2002), 1128–67

'Heresy and Humanism', in *Middle English*, ed. by Paul Strohm (Oxford: Oxford University Press, 2007), pp. 421–37

Cole, Andrew and D. Vance Smith (eds), *The Legitimacy of the Middle Ages: On the Unwritten History of Theory* (Durham, NC: Duke University Press, 2010)

Coleman, Joyce, 'Property and Poverty', in *The Cambridge History of Medieval Political Thought, c. 350 -c. 1450*, ed. by J. H. Burns (Cambridge: Cambridge University Press, 1988), pp. 607–48

'Some Relations between the Study of Aristotle's *Rhetoric, Ethics* and *Politics* in Late Thirteenth- and Early Fourteenth-Century University Arts Courses and the Justification of Contemporary Civic Activities (Italy and France)', in *Political Thought and the Realities of Power in the Middle Ages*, ed. by J. Canning and O. G. Oexle (Göttingen: Vandenhoeck and Ruprecht, 1998), pp. 127–57

Colish, Marcia L., 'The Pseudo-Peter of Poitiers Gloss', in *Mediaeval Commentaries on the Sentences of Peter Lombard*, ed. by G. R. Evans, 2 vols (Leiden: Brill, 2002–10), II, pp. 1–33

Copeland, Rita, 'Academic Prologues to Authors', in *The Oxford History of Classical Reception in English Literature*, I, 800–1558, ed. by Rita Copeland (Oxford: Oxford University Press, 2016), pp. 151–63
  'The Curricular Classics in the Middle Ages', in *The Oxford History of Classical Reception in English Literature*, I, 800–1558, ed. by Rita Copeland (Oxford: Oxford University Press, 2016), pp. 21–33
  'Pathos and Pastoralism: Aristotle's *Rhetoric* in Medieval England', *Speculum*, 89 (2014), 96–127
  *Rhetoric, Hermeneutics and Translation in the Middle Ages: Academic Traditions and Vernacular Texts*, Cambridge Studies in Medieval Literature 11 (Cambridge: Cambridge University Press, 1991)
Copeland, Rita and Peter T. Struck (eds), *The Cambridge Companion to Allegory* (Cambridge: Cambridge University Press, 2010)
Cornelius, Ian, 'Boethius' *De consolatione philosophiae*', in *The Oxford History of Classical Reception in English Literature*, I, 800–1558, ed. by Rita Copeland (Oxford: Oxford University Press, 2016), pp. 269–98
Cornish, Alison, *Vernacular Translation in Dante's Italy: Illiterate Literature*, Cambridge Studies in Medieval Literature 83 (Cambridge: Cambridge University Press, 2011)
Cossack, Hermann, *Über die altenglische metrische Bearbeitung von Boethius*, De consolatione philsophiae (Leipzig-Reudnitz: Max Hoffmann, 1889)
Coulson, Frank T. and Bruno Roy, *Incipitarium Ovidianum: A Finding Guide for Texts in Latin Related to the Study of Ovid in the Middle Ages and Renaissance* (Turnholt: Brepols, 2000)
Courcelle, Pierre, *La Consolation de philosophie dans la tradition littéraire: antecedents et postérité de Boèce* (Paris: Études Augustiniennes, 1967)
Courtenay, William J., *Schools and Scholars in Fourteenth-Century England* (Princeton, NJ: Princeton University Press, 1987)
Crane, Susan, *Animal Encounters: Contacts and Concepts in Medieval Britain* (Philadelphia: University of Pennsylvania Press, 2012)
Craun, Edwin D., *Lies, Slander and Obscenity in Medieval English Literature: Pastoral Rhetoric and the Deviant Speaker*, Cambridge Studies in Medieval Literature 31 (Cambridge: Cambridge University Press, 1997)
Crawford, Jason, *Allegory and Enchantment: An Early Modern Poetics* (Oxford: Oxford University Press, 2017)
Cummings, Robert, 'Classical Moralists and Philosophers', in *The Oxford History of Literary Translation in English*, II, 1550–1660, ed. by Gordon Baker, Robert Cummings and Stuart Gillespie (Oxford: Oxford University Press, 2010), pp. 371–89
Dahan, Gilbert, 'Les classifications du savoir aux XIIe et XIIIe siècles', *L'enseignement philosophique*, 40 (1990), 5–27
  'The Commentary of Thomas Aquinas in the History of Medieval Exegesis on Job: *Intentio et Materia*', *Nova et Vetera*, 17 (2019), 1053–75
  *Interpreter la Bible au moyen âge. Cinq écrits du XIIIe siècle sur l'exégèse de la Bible traduits en français* (Paris: Parole et silence, 2009)

*L'exégèse chrétienne de la Bible en Occident médiéval (XIIe–XIVe s.)* (Paris: Cerf, 1999)
'L'exégèse de la Bible chez Guillaume d'Auvergne', in *Autour de Guillaume d'Auvergne († 1249)*, ed. by Franco Morenzoni and Jean-Yves Tilliette (Turnhout: Brepols, 2005), pp. 237–70
'L'exégèse médiévale de la Bible et les Pères. Tradition, progrès, liberté', *Théophilyon*, 21 (2016), 15–37
*Lire la Bible au moyen âge. Essais d'herméneutique médiévale* (Geneva: Droz, 2009)
'Notes et textes sur la poétique au moyen âge', *Archives d'histoire doctrinale et littéraire du Moyen Âge*, 47 (1980), 171–239
'Les paraboles du chapitre 13 de Matthieu dans l'exégèse du XIIIe siècle', *Annuaire EPHE. Section des sciences religieuses*, 110 (2001–2), 377–80
'Les Pères dans l'exégèse médiévale de la Bible', *Revue des Sciences philosophiques et théologiques*, 91 (2007), 109–27
'Saint Thomas d'Aquin et la métaphore. Rhétorique et herméneutique', *Medioevo*, 18 (1992), 85–117
'Symbole et exégèse médiévale de la Bible', *PRIS-MA. Recherches sur la littérature d'imagination au Moyen Âge*, 26 (2010), 3–31
'Tradition patristique, autorité et progrès dans l'exégèse médiévale', in *Les réceptions des Pères de l'Église au Moyen Âge: le devenir de la tradition ecclésiale : congrès du Centre Sèvres – Facultés j'suites de Paris (11–14 juin 2008)*, ed. by Rainer Berndt and Michel Fédou, 2 vols (Münster: Aschendorff, 2013), I, pp. 349–68
Daston, Lorraine and Katy Park, *Wonders and the Order of Nature* (New York: Zone Books, 1998)
Davlin, Mary Clemente, '*Kynde Knowyng* as a Major Theme in *Piers Plowman* B', *Review of English Studies*, ns 22 (1971), 1–19
De Angelis, Violetta, 'I commenti medievali alla *Tebaide* di Stazio: Anselmo di Laon, Goffredo Babione, Ilario d'Orléans', in *Medieval and Renaissance Scholarship: Proceedings of the Second European Science Foundation Workshop on the Classical Tradition in the Middle Ages and the Renaissance (London, The Warburg Institute, 27–28 November 1992)*, ed. by Nicholas Matt and Birger Munk Olsen (Leiden: Brill, 1997), pp. 75–136
De Hamel, C. F. R., *Glossed Books of the Bible and the Origins of the Paris Booktrade* (Woodbridge: D. S. Brewer, 1984)
De Lubac, Henri, *Exégèse médiévale: les quatres sens de l'Écriture*, 2 vols in 4 (Paris: Aubier, 1959–64)
Dean, Ruth J. with Maureen B. M. Boulton, *Guide to Anglo-Norman Literature: Texts and Manuscripts*, ANTS Occasional Publications Series 3 (London: ANTS, 1999)
Denery, Dallas G., II, Kantik Ghosh and Nicolette Zeeman (eds), *Uncertain Knowledge: Scepticism, Relativism and Doubt in the Middle Ages* (Turnhout: Brepols, 2014)

Donaghey, Brian, 'The Post-Medieval Translation of the *De Consolatione Philosophiae* of Boethius, 1500–1800', in *The Medieval Translator/Traduire au Moyen Âge 5*, ed. by Roger Ellis and René Tixier (Turnhout: Brepols, 1996), pp. 302–21

Dunbabin, Jean, 'The Reception and Interpretation of Aristotle's *Politics*', in *The Cambridge History of Later Medieval Philosophy: From the Rediscovery of Aristotle to the Disintegration of Scholasticism, 1100–1600*, ed. by Norman Kretzmann et al. (Cambridge: Cambridge University Press, 1982), pp. 723–37

Elliot, A. G. '*Accessus ad auctores*: Twelfth-Century Introductions to Ovid', *Allegorica*, 5 (1980), 6–48

Evans, Joan, *Magical Jewels of the Middle Ages and the Renaissance, Particularly in England* (Oxford: Clarendon, 1922)

Feeney, Denis, 'Criticism Ancient and Modern', in *Oxford Readings in Classical Studies: Ancient Literary Criticism*, ed. by Andrew Laird (Oxford: Oxford University Press, 2006), pp. 440–54

FitzGerald, Brian, *Inspiration and Authority in the Middle Ages: Prophets and their Critics from Scholasticism to Humanism* (Oxford: Oxford University Press, 2017)

Flannery, Mary C., 'Response', *YLS*, 33 (2019), 231–38

Fleck, Ludwik, *Genesis and Development of a Scientific Fact*, ed. by Thaddeus J. Trenn and Robert K. Merton, tr. by Fred Bradley and Thaddeus J. Trenn (Chicago: University of Chicago Press, 1979), originally published as *Entstehung und Entwicklung einer wissenschaftlichen Tatsache: Einführung in die Lehre vom Denkstil und Denkkollektiv* (Basel: Schwabe, 1935)

Fletcher, Alan J., *Preaching, Politics and Poetry in Late Medieval England* (Dublin: Four Courts Press, 1998)

Fletcher, Angus, *Allegory: The Theory of a Symbolic Mode* (Ithaca, NY: Cornell University Press, 1964)

Fletcher, J. M., 'The Faculty of Arts', in *The History of the University of Oxford*, 1, *The Early Oxford Schools*, ed. by J. I. Catto with Ralph Evans (Oxford: Clarendon, 1984), pp. 369–99

Flüeler, Christoph, *Rezeption und Interpretation der Aristotelischen 'Politica' im späten Mittelalter*, 2 vols (Amsterdam: Grüner, 1992)

Frank, Robert Worth, 'The Art of Reading Medieval Personification-Allegory', *ELH*, 20 (1953), 237–50

Franklin Brown, Mary, *Reading the World: Encyclopaedic Writing in the Scholastic Age* (Chicago: University of Chicago Press, 2012)

Friedman, John B., 'The Friar Portrait in Bodleian Library MS Douce 104: Contemporary Satire?', *YLS*, 8 (1994), 177–85

Fyler, John M., *Language and the Declining World in Chaucer, Dante and Jean de Meun*, Cambridge Studies in Medieval Literature 63 (Cambridge: Cambridge University Press, 2007)

Galloway, Andrew, *The Penn Commentary on* Piers Plowman, 1, *C Prologue–Passus 4, B Prologue–Passus 4, A Prologue–Passus 4* (Philadelphia: University of Pennsylvania Press, 2006)

Garnsey, Peter, *Thinking about Property: From Antiquity to the Age of Revolution* (Cambridge: Cambridge University Press, 2007)

Getz, Faye Marie, 'Charity, Translation and the Language of Medical Learning in Medieval England', *Bulletin of the History of Medicine*, 64 (1990), 1–17

Gibson, Margaret (ed.), *Boethius: His Life, Thought and Influence* (Oxford: Blackwell, 1981)

Gillespie, Vincent, 'Chichele's Church: Vernacular Theology in England after Thomas Arundel', in *After Arundel: Religious Writing in Fifteenth-Century England*, ed. by Vincent Gillespie and Kantik Ghosh (Turnhout: Brepols, 2011), pp. 3–42

— 'Fatherless Books: Authorship, Attribution and Orthodoxy in Later Medieval England', in *The Pseudo-Bonaventuran Lives of Christ: Exploring the Middle English Tradition*, ed. by Ian Johnson and Allan F. Westphall (Turnhout: Brepols, 2013), pp. 151–96

— 'Thy Will be Done: *Piers Plowman* and the *Paternoster*', in *Late-Medieval Religious Texts and Their Transmission: Essays in Honour of A. I. Doyle*, ed. by Alastair Minnis (Cambridge: D. S. Brewer, 1994), pp. 95–119

Giraud, Cédric, 'Anselme de Laon', in *Histoire littéraire de la France publiée par l'Académie des inscriptions et belles-lettres*, XLIII:2 (Paris: De Boccard, 2014), pp. 239–91

Glei, Reinhold F., '*Quae philosophia fuit, facta philologia est*. Der Kommentar des Jodocus Badius Ascensius (1498) zur *Consolatio Philsophiae* des Boethius', in *Boethius Christianus? Transformationen der* Consolatio philosophiae *in Mittelalter und früher Neuzeit*, ed. by Reinhold F. Glei, Nicola Kaminski and Franz Lebsanft (Berlin: De Gruyter, 2010), pp. 179–215

Glei, Reinhold F., Nicola Kaminski and Franz Lebsanft (eds), *Boethius Christianus? Transformationen der* Consolatio philosophiae *in Mittelalter und früher Neuzeit* (Berlin: De Gruyter, 2010)

Glunz, H. H., *History of the Vulgate in England from Alcuin to Roger Bacon, Being an Inquiry into the Text of Some English Manuscripts of the Vulgate Gospels* (Cambridge: Cambridge University Press, 1933)

Gontero-Lauze, Valérie, *Sagesses minerales. Médicine et magie des pierres précieuses au Moyen Âge* (Paris: Garnier, 2010)

Grafton, Anthony, 'Epilogue: Boethius in the Renaissance', in *Boethius: His Life, Thought and Influence*, ed. by Margaret Gibson (Oxford: Blackwell, 1981), pp. 410–15

Green, V. H. H., *Bishop Reginald Pecock: A Study in Ecclesiastical History and Thought* (Cambridge: Cambridge University Press, 1945)

Griffiths, Lavinia, *Personification in* Piers Plowman (Cambridge: D. S. Brewer, 1985)

Grondeux, Anne, '*Auctorias* et glose: quelle place pour un auteur dans une glose?', in *Auctor et auctoritas: invention et conformisme dans l'écriture médiévale: actes du colloque tenu à l'Université de Versailles-Saint-Quentin-en-Yvelines, 14–16 juin 1999*, ed. by Michel Zimmermann (Paris: École des Chartes, 2001), pp. 245–54

*À l'école de Cassiodore. Les figures « extravagantes » dans la tradition occidentale* (Turnhout: Brepols, 2013)

Gross, Daniel, *The Secret History of Emotion: From Aristotle's* Rhetoric *to Modern Brain Science* (Chicago: University of Chicago Press, 2006)

Gross, Daniel and Ansgar Kemmann (eds), *Heidegger and Rhetoric* (Albany, NY: State University of New York Press, 2005)

Guynn, Noah, 'Authorship and Sexual/Allegorical Violence in Jean de Meun's *Roman de la Rose*', *Speculum*, 79 (2004), 628–59

Hadot, Pierre, *Philosophy as a Way of Life: Spiritual Exercises from Socrates to Foucault*, ed. by Arnold I. Davidson, tr. by Michael Chase (Oxford: Blackwell, 1995)

Hamesse, Jacqueline (ed.), *Les Prologues médiévaux: Actes du Colloque international organisé par l'Academia Belgica et l'Ecole francaise de Rome avec le concours de la F.I.D.E.M.* (Turnhout: Brepols, 2000)

Hanna, Ralph, 'The Difficulty of Ricardian Prose Translation', *Modern Language Quarterly*, 51 (1990), 319–40

— 'Henry Daniel's *Liber Uricrisiarum* (Excerpt)', in *Popular and Practical Science of Medieval England*, ed. by Lister Matheson (East Lansing, MI: Colleagues Press, 1994), pp. 185–218

— 'Langland's Patience and Reading *Piers Plowman*', *Notes and Queries*, ns 64 (2017), 524–30

— *Patient Reading/Reading Patience: Oxford Essays on Medieval English Literature* (Liverpool: Liverpool University Press, 2017)

— *The Penn Commentary on Piers Plowman*, II, *C Passus 5–9, B Passus 5–7, A Passus 5–8* (Philadelphia: University of Pennsylvania Press, 2017)

— 'Sir Thomas Berkeley and His Patronage', *Speculum*, 64 (1989), 878–916

— 'The State of English, *c.* 1335: A Generally Unnoticed Discussion', *Notes and Queries*, ns 64 (2017), 15–19

— 'The Wisdom of Poetry: John of Wales's Defense', *Journal of Medieval Latin*, 27 (2017), 303–26

Harvey, John H., 'Henry Daniel: A Scientific Gardener of the Fourteenth Century', *Garden History*, 15 (1987), 81–93

Haskins, Charles Homer, 'King Harold's Books', *English Historical Review*, 37 (1922), 398–400

Heidegger, Martin, *Basic Concepts of Aristotelian Philosophy*, tr. by Robert D. Metcalf and Mark B. Tanzer (Bloomington: Indiana University Press, 2009)

Herren, M., 'Reflections on the Meaning of the *Ecloga Theoduli*: Where Is the Authorial Voice?', in *Poetry and Exegesis in Premodern Christianity: The Encounter between Classical and Christian Strategies of Interpretation*, ed. by Willemien Otten and Karla Pollmann (Leiden: Brill, 2007), pp. 199–230

Hesketh, Glynn, 'Lexical Innovation in the *Lumere as Lais*', in *De mot en mot: Aspects of Medieval Linguistics. Essays in Honour of William Rothwell*, ed. by Stewart Gregory and D. A. Trotter (Cardiff: University of Wales Press and MHRA, 1997), pp. 53–79

Hexter, Ralph J., 'Shades of Ovid: Pseudo- (and Para-) Ovidiana in the Middle Ages', in *Ovid in the Middle Ages*, ed. by James G. Clark, Frank T. Coulson and Kathryn L. McKinley (Cambridge: Cambridge University Press, 2011), pp. 284–309

Hiatt, Alfred, 'Lucan', in *The Oxford History of Classical Reception in English Literature, 1, 800–1558*, ed. by Rita Copeland (Oxford: Oxford University Press, 2016), pp. 209–26

Hinton, Thomas, 'French and Anglo-French in the Thirteenth Century: A Reappraisal of Walter de Bibbesworth's 'Tretiz', *Modern Language Review*, 112 (2017), 848–74

Hoenen, Maarten J. F. M. and Lodi Nauta (eds), *Boethius in the Middle Ages: Latin and Vernacular Traditions of the* Consolatio Philosophiae (Leiden: Brill, 1997)

Holsinger, Bruce, *The Premodern Condition: Medievalism and the Making of Theory* (Chicago: University of Chicago Press, 2005)

Houghton, Walter E., 'Michael Walpole, Translator of Boethius' *De Consolatione*', *American Journal of Philology*, 51 (1930), 243–48

Hunt, R. W., 'The Introductions to the *Artes* in the Twelfth Century', in *Studia Mediaevalia in honorem Reverendi Patris Raymundi Josephi Martin* (Bruges: De Tempel, 1948), pp. 85–112

Hunt, Tony, *Teaching and Learning Latin in 13th-Century England*, 3 vols (Cambridge: D. S. Brewer, 1991)

Huot, Sylvia, 'Bodily Peril: Sexuality and the Subversion of Order in Jean de Meun's *Roman de la Rose*', *Modern Language Review*, 95 (2000), 41–61

*The* Romance of the Rose *and Its Medieval Readers: Interpretation, Reception, Manuscript Transmission*, Cambridge Studies in Medieval Literature 16 (Cambridge: Cambridge University Press, 1992)

Ingham, Richard, *The Transmission of Anglo-Norman: Language History and Language Acquisition* (Amsterdam: Benjamins, 2012)

James, Montague R., *A Descriptive Catalogue of the Manuscripts in the Library of Jesus College, Cambridge* (London: Clay, 1895)

James-Raoul, Danièle, 'La Personnification dans les arts poétiques médio-latins des XIIe et XIIIe siècles', in *La Personnification du moyen âge au XVIIIe siècle*, ed. by Mireille Demaules (Paris: Garnier, 2014), pp. 35–51

Jameson, Fredric, *Allegory and Ideology* (London: Verso, 2019)

Jasin, Joanne, 'The Compiler's Awareness of Audience in Medieval Medical Prose: The Example of Wellcome MS 225', *Journal of English and Germanic Philology*, 92 (1993), 509–22

'A Critical Edition of the Middle English *Liber Uricrisiarum* in Wellcome 225' (unpublished doctoral thesis, Tulane University, 1983)

Jeudy, Colette and Yves-François Riou, 'L'*Achilléide* de Stace au moyen âge: abrégés et arguments', *Revue d'histoire des textes*, 4 (1974), 144–80

Johnson, Ian, 'The "Goostly Chaffare" of Reginald Pecock: Everyday Craft, Commerce and Custom Meet Syllogistic Polemic in Fifteenth-Century London', in *Religious Practices and Everyday Life in the Long Fifteenth*

Century (1350–1570): Interpreting Changes and Changes of Interpretation, ed. by Ian Johnson and Ana Maria Rodrigues (Turnhout: Brepols, forthcoming)

'Mediating Voices and Texts: Nicholas Love and Reginald Pecock', in *Medieval and Early Modern Religious Cultures: Essays Honouring Vincent Gillespie on His Sixty-Fifth Birthday*, ed. by Laura Ashe and Ralph Hanna (Cambridge: D. S. Brewer, 2019), pp. 127–46

*The Middle English Life of Christ: Academic Discourse, Translation and Vernacular Theology* (Turnhout: Brepols, 2013)

'Walton's Sapient Orpheus', in *The Medieval Boethius: Studies in the Vernacular Translations of* De Consolatione Philosophiae, ed. by Alastair Minnis (Woodbridge: D. S. Brewer, 1987), pp. 139–68

Jones, Peter M., 'University Books and the Sciences, c. 1250–1400', in *The Cambridge History of the Book, II, 1100–1400*, ed. by Nigel J. Morgan and Rodney M. Thomson (Cambridge: Cambridge University Press, 2008), pp. 453–62

Jordan, William Chester, 'The Gleaners', in *Boundaries in the Medieval and Wider World: Essays in Honour of Paul Freedman*, ed. by Thomas Barton et al. (Turnhout: Brepols, 2017), 201–20

Karnes, Michelle, *Imagination, Meditation and Cognition in the Middle Ages* (Chicago: University of Chicago Press, 2011)

Kaster, Robert A., *Guardians of Language: The Grammarian and Society in Late Antiquity* (Berkeley: University of California Press, 1988)

Kay, Sarah, 'Women's Body of Knowledge: Epistemology and Misogyny in the *Romance of the Rose*', in *Framing Medieval Bodies*, ed. by Sarah Kay and Miri Rubin (Manchester: Manchester University Press, 1994), pp. 211–35

Kay, Sarah and Nicolette Zeeman, 'Versions of the Natural', *Journal of Medieval and Early Modern Studies*, 49 (2019), 445–56

Kaylor, Noel Harold, Jr. and Philip Edward Phillips (eds), *A Companion to Boethius in the Middle Ages* (Leiden: Brill, 2012)

(eds), *Vernacular Traditions of Boethius's* De consolatione philosophiae (Kalamazoo, MI: Medieval Institute Publications, 2016)

Keiser, George R., 'Through a Fourteenth-Century Gardener's Eyes: Henry Daniel's Herbal', *Chaucer Review*, 31 (1996), 58–75

Kelly, Henry Ansgar, *Ideas and Forms of Tragedy from Aristotle to the Middle Ages*, Cambridge Studies in Medieval Literature 18 (Cambridge: Cambridge University Press, 1993)

Kempshall, M. S., *The Common Good in Late Medieval Political Thought* (Oxford: Oxford University Press, 1999)

*Rhetoric and the Writing of History* (Manchester: Manchester University Press, 2011)

'The Rhetoric of Giles of Rome's *De regimine principum*', in *Le Prince au miroir de la littérature politique de l'Antiquité aux Lumières*, ed. by Frédérique Lachaud and Lydwine Scordia (Mont-Saint-Aignan: Publications des universités de Rouen et du Havre, 2007), pp. 161–90

Klemm, Elisabeth, *Die illuminierten Handschriften des 13. Jahrhunderts deutscher Herkunft in der Bayerischen Staatsbibliothek* (Wiesbaden: Ludwig Reichert Verlag, 1998)

Knox, Philip, 'Human Nature and Natural Law in Jean de Meun's *Roman de la Rose*', in *The Roman de la Rose and Thirteenth-Century Thought*, ed. by Jonathan Morton and Marco Nievergelt with John Marenbon (Cambridge: Cambridge University Press, 2020), pp. 131–48

Jonathan Morton and Daniel Reeve (eds), *Medieval Thought Experiments: Poetry, Hypothesis and Experience in the European Middle Ages* (Turnhout: Brepols, 2018)

Koivisto-Alkano, Päivi, 'The Vocabulary of Cognition in Early English Translations of Boethius from Chaucer to Preston', *Neuphilologische Mitteilungen*, 98 (1997), 397–414

Kraebel, Andrew, *Biblical Commentary and Translation in Later Medieval England: Experiments in Interpretation*, Cambridge Studies in Medieval Literature 109 (Cambridge: Cambridge University Press, 2020)

'Biblical Exegesis and the Twelfth-Century Expansion of Servius', in *Classical Commentaries: Explorations in a Scholarly Genre*, ed. by Christina S. Kraus and Christopher Stray (Oxford: Oxford University Press, 2016), pp. 419–34

'Modes of Authorship and the Making of Medieval English Literature', in *The Cambridge Handbook of Literary Authorship*, ed. by Ingo Berensmeyer, Gert Buelens and Marysa Demoor (Cambridge: Cambridge University Press, 2019), pp. 98–114

'*Ordinatio:* The Arrangement of Parts in a Book', in *The Unfinished Book*, ed. by Alexandra Gillespie and Deidre Lynch (Oxford: Oxford University Press, 2020), pp. 62–78

'Poetry and Commentary in the Medieval School of Rheims: Reading Virgil, Reading David', in *Interpreting Scripture in Judaism, Christianity and Islam: Overlapping Inquiries*, ed. by Mordechai Cohen and Adele Berlin (Cambridge: Cambridge University Press, 2016), pp. 227–48

Kuhn, Thomas S., *The Road Since Structure: Philosophical Essays, 1970–1993, with an Autobiographical Interview*, ed. by James Conant and Kohn Haugeland (Chicago: University of Chicago Press, 2000)

*The Structure of Scientific Revolutions*, 4th edn (Chicago: University of Chicago Press, 2012)

Kuttner, Stephan, 'Gratian and Plato', in *The History of Ideas and Doctrines of Canon Law in the Middle Ages* (London: Variorum Reprints, 1980), no. XI, pp. 93–118

Lahey, Stephen E., 'Reginald Pecock on the Authority of Reason, Scripture and Tradition', *Journal of Ecclesiastical History*, 56 (2005), 235–60

Landgraf, Arthur, *Écrits théologiques de l'école d'Abélard* (Louvain: Spicilegium Sacrum Lovaniense, 1934)

Lathrop, Henry Burrowes, *Translations from the Classics into English from Caxton to Chapman, 1477–1620* (Madison: University of Wisconsin Press, 1933)

Latour, Bruno, *Politics of Nature: How to Bring the Sciences into Democracy*, tr. by Catherine Porter (Cambridge, MA: Harvard University Press, 2004), originally published as *Politiques de la nature. Comment faire entrer les sciences en démocratie* (Paris: La Découverte, 1999)

Lawler, Traugott, 'The Pardon Formula in *Piers Plowman:* Its Ubiquity, Its Binary Shape, Its Silent Middle Term', *YLS*, 14 (2000), 117–52

—— *The Penn Commentary on* Piers Plowman, IV, *C Passus 15–19, B Passus 13–17* (Philadelphia: University of Pennsylvania Press, 2018)

Lawton, David, 'Psalms as Public Interiorities: Eleanor Hull's Voices', in *The Psalms and Medieval English Literature: From the Conversion to the Reformation*, ed. by Tamara Atkin and Francis Leneghan (Cambridge: D. S. Brewer, 2017), pp. 298–317

—— 'The Subject of *Piers Plowman*', *YLS*, 1 (1987), 1–30

Le Talleur, Guillaume, *Dictionarius familiaris et compendiosus. Dictionnaire latin-français de Guillaume le Talleur*, ed. by William Edwards and Brian Merrilees (Turnhout: Brepols, 2002)

Leach, Eleanor Winsor, 'Georgic Imagery in the *Ars amatoria*', *Transactions and Proceedings of the American Philological Association*, 95 (1964), 142–54

Leclercq, Jean, 'L'idéal du théologien au Moyen Âge. Textes inédits', *Revue des Sciences Religieuses*, 21 (1947), 121–48

—— *The Love of Learning and the Desire for God: A Study of Monastic Culture*, 3rd edn, tr. by Catharine Misrahi (New York: Fordham University Press, 1982)

—— *Otia Monastica: études sur le vocabulaire de la contemplation au moyen âge* (Rome: Herder, 1963)

Lefèvre, Yves, *L'Elucidarium et les lucidaires* (Paris: Boccard, 1954)

Leff, Gordon, *Bradwardine and the Pelagians: A Study of His 'De causa Dei' and Its Opponents* (Cambridge: Cambridge University Press, 1957)

Lewis, Charlton T. and Charles Short (eds), *A Latin Dictionary* (Oxford: Clarendon, 1969)

Lewis, Neil, 'Robert Grosseteste and the Church Fathers', in *The Reception of the Church Fathers in the West: From the Carolingians to the Maurists*, ed. by Irena Backus, 2 vols (New York: Brill, 1997), I, 197–229

Lindenbaum, Sheila, 'London after Arundel: Learned Rectors and the Strategies of Orthodox Reform', in *After Arundel: Religious Writing in Fifteenth-Century England*, ed. by Vincent Gillespie and Kantik Ghosh (Turnhout: Brepols, 2011), pp. 187–206

Little, A. G., 'Provincial Priors and Vicars of the English Dominicans', *English Historical Review*, 33 (1918), 496–97

Logan, F. Donald, *University Education and the Parochial Clergy in Medieval England: The Lincoln Diocese, c. 1300–c. 1350* (Toronto: Pontifical Institute of Mediaeval Studies, 2014)

Luscombe, David E., 'The Authorship of the *Ysagoge in theologiam*', *Archives d'histoire doctrinale et littéraire du Moyen Âge*, 35 (1968), 7–18

—— 'The State of Nature and the Origin of the State', in *The Cambridge History of Later Medieval Philosophy: From the Rediscovery of Aristotle to the*

*Disintegration of Scholasticism, 1100–1600*, ed. by Norman Kretzmann et al. (Cambridge: Cambridge University Press, 1982), pp. 757–70
Machan, Tim William, *Techniques of Translation: Chaucer's* Boece (Norman, OK: Pilgrim Books, 1985)
Macken, Raymond, *Denys the Carthusian, Commentator on Boethius's* De Consolatione Philosophiae, Analecta Cartusiana 118 (Salzburg: Institut für Anglistik und Amerikanistik, Universität Salzburg, 1984)
Madsen, Deborah L., *Rereading Allegory: A Narrative Approach to Genre* (Basingstoke: MacMillan, 1995)
Manitius, Max, *Geschichte der lateinischen Literatur des Mittelalters*, 3 vols (Munich: C. H. Beck, 1911–31)
Mann, Jill, *Langland and Allegory*, Morton W. Bloomfield Lectures on Medieval Literature 2 (Kalamazoo, MI: Medieval Institute Publications, 1992)
Marmo, Costantino, '"Hoc autem etsi potest tollerari . . .": Egidio Romano e Tommaso d'Aquino sulle passioni dell'anima', *Documenti e studi sulla tradizione filosofica medievale*, 2 (1991), 281–315
Marshall, David L., *Vico and the Transformation of Rhetoric in Early Modern Europe* (Cambridge: Cambridge University Press, 2010)
Martin, Conor, 'Some Medieval Commentaries on Aristotle's *Politics*', *History*, ns 36 (1951), 29–44
Martin, Raymond-M., 'Notes sur l'œuvre littéraire de Pierre le Mangeur', *Recherches de Théologie ancienne et médiévale*, 3 (1931), 54–66
Massa, Eugenio, *Ruggero Bacone. Etica e poetica nella storia dell' 'Opus maius'* (Rome: Edizioni di Storia e letteratura, 1955)
McGinn, Bernard, *The Varieties of Vernacular Mysticism, 1350–1550* (New York: Crossroad, 2012)
McMullen, A. Joseph and Erica Weaver (eds), *The Legacy of Boethius in Medieval England: The* Consolation *and Its Afterlives* (Tempe: Arizona Center for Medieval and Renaissance Studies, 2018)
Meyer, Heinz, '*Intentio auctoris, utilitas libri:* Wirkungsabsicht und Nutzen literarischer Werke nach Accessus-Prologen des 11. bis 13. Jahrhunderts', *Frühmittelalterliche Studien*, 31 (1997), 390–413
Middleton, Anne, 'Acts of Vagrancy: The C Version "Autobiography" and the Statute of 1388', in *Written Work: Langland, Labor and Authorship*, ed. by Steven Justice and Kathryn Kerby-Fulton (Philadelphia: University of Pennsylvania Press, 1997), pp. 208–317
   'Narration and the Invention of Experience: Episodic Form in *Piers Plowman*', in *The Wisdom of Poetry: Essays in Honor of Morton Bloomfield*, ed. by Larry Benson and Siegfried Wenzel (Kalamazoo, MI: Medieval Institute Publications, 1982), pp. 91–122
Milan, Paul B., 'The Golden Age and the Political Theory of Jean de Meun: A Myth in *Rose* Scholarship', *Symposium*, 23 (1969), 137–49
Miller, J. Hillis, 'Derrida's Destinerrance', *Modern Language Notes*, 121 (2006), 893–910

Minio-Paluello, Lorenzo, 'Guglielmo di Moerbeke, traduttore della Poetica di Aristotele (1278)', *Rivista di filosofia neoscolastica*, 39 (1947), 1–17
Mooney, Michael, *Vico in the Tradition of Rhetoric* (Princeton, NJ: Princeton University Press, 1985)
Morton, Jonathan, The Roman de la Rose *in Its Philosophical Context: Art, Nature and Ethics* (Oxford: Oxford University Press, 2018)
  '"Where Are the Bodies?": Gender-Bending Voices in the *Roman de la Rose*', *Cahiers de Recherches médiévales et humanistes*, 22 (2011), 123–37
Morton, Jonathan and Marco Nievergelt, with John Marenbon (eds), *The* Roman de la Rose *and Thirteenth-Century Thought*, Cambridge Studies in Medieval Literature 111 (Cambridge: Cambridge University Press, 2020)
Moyes, Malcolm Robert, *Richard Rolle's* Expositio super novem lectiones mortuorum: *An Introduction and Contribution towards a Critical Edition*, 2 vols (Salzburg: Institut für Anglistik und Amerikanistik, Universität Salzburg, 1988)
Mueller, Janel, *The Native Tongue and the Word* (Chicago: University of Chicago Press, 1984)
Mulcahey, M. Michèle, *First the Bow Is Bent in Study: Dominican Education before 1350* (Toronto: Pontifical Institute of Mediaeval Studies, 1998)
Munk Olsen, Birger, '*Accessus* to Classical Poets in the Twelfth Century', in *The Classics in the Medieval and Renaissance Classroom: The Role of Ancient Texts in the Arts Curriculum as Revealed by Surviving Manuscripts and Early Printed Books*, ed. by Juanita Feros Ruys, John O. Ward and Melanie Heyworth (Turnhout: Brepols, 2013), pp. 131–43
  *L'étude des auteurs classiques latins aux XIe et XIIe siècles*, 5 vols (Paris: CNRS Éditions, 1982–2020)
Nauta, Lodi, 'The *Consolation:* The Latin Commentary Tradition, 800–1700', in *The Cambridge Companion to Boethius*, ed. by John Marenbon (Cambridge: Cambridge University Press, 2009), pp. 255–78
  'A Humanist Reading of Boethius's *Consolatio Philosophiae*: The Commentary by Murmellius and Agricola (1514)', in *Between Demonstration and Imagination: Essays in the History of Science and Philosophy Presented to John D. North*, ed. by Lodi Nauta and Arjo Vanderjagt (Leiden: Brill, 1999), pp. 313–38
  '"Magis sit Platonicus quam Aristotelicus": Interpretations of Boethius's Platonism in the *Consolatio Philosophiae* from the Twelfth to the Seventeenth Century', in *The Platonic Tradition in the Middle Ages: A Doxographic Approach*, ed. by S. Gersh and M. Hoenen (Berlin: De Gruyter, 2002), pp. 165–204
  'The Scholastic Context of the Boethian Commentary by Nicholas Trevet', in *Boethius in the Middle Ages: Latin and Vernacular Traditions of the* Consolatio Philosophiae, ed. by Maarten J. F. M. Hoenen and Lodi Nauta (Leiden: Brill, 1997), pp. 41–67

Nederman, Cary J., 'Nature, Sin and the Origins of Society: The Ciceronian Tradition in Medieval Political Thought', *Journal of the History of Ideas*, 49 (1988), 3–26

Newman, Barbara, 'What Did It Mean to Say "I Saw"? The Clash between Theory and Practice in Medieval Visionary Culture', *Speculum*, 80 (2005), 1–43

Obertello, Luca, *Severino Boezio*, 2 vols (Genoa: Accademia Ligure di Scienze e Lettere, 1974)

Oggins, Robin, *The Kings and Their Hawks: Falconry in Medieval England* (New Haven, CT: Yale University Press, 2004)

Oliva, Adriano, *Les débuts de l'enseignement de Thomas d'Aquin et sa conception de la sacra doctrina* (Paris: Vrin, 2006)

Orlemanski, Julie, 'Langland's Poetics of Animation: Body, Soul, Personification', *YLS*, 33 (2019), 159–84

Owst, G. R., *Literature and Pulpit in Medieval England* (Cambridge: Cambridge University Press, 1933)

Pächt, Otto and J. J. G. Alexander, *Illuminated Manuscripts in the Bodleian Library, Oxford*, 3 vols (Oxford: Clarendon, 1966)

Palmer, Nigel F., 'The German Boethius Translation Printed in 1473 and Its Historical Context', in *Boethius in the Middle Ages: Latin and Vernacular Traditions of the* Consolatio Philosophiae, ed. by Maarten J. F. M. Hoenen and Lodi Nauta (Leiden: Brill, 1997), pp. 287–302

Panofsky, Erwin, *Gothic Architecture and Scholasticism* (Cleveland, OH: Meridian Books, 1957)

Pantin, W. A., 'John of Wales and Medieval Humanism', in *Medieval Studies Presented to Aubrey Gwynn*, ed. by J. A. Watt, J. B. Morrall and F. X. Martin (Dublin: Lochlainn, 1961), pp. 297–319

Papahagi, Adrian, '*Glossae collectae* on Boethius's *Consolation of Philosophy* in Paris, BN Lat. MS 13953', *Chôra*, 6 (2008), 291–337

Parkes, M. B., 'The Compilation of the Dominican Lectionary', in *Literarischen Formen des Mittelalters: Florilegien, Kompilationen, Kollectionen*, ed. by Kaspar Elm (Wolfenbüttel: Harrassowitz, 2000), pp. 91–106

'The Influence of the Concepts of *Ordinatio* and *Compilatio* on the Development of the Book', in *Medieval Learning and Literature: Essays presented to R. W. Hunt*, ed. by J. J. G. Alexander and M. T. Gibson (Oxford: Clarendon, 1978), pp. 115–41; reprinted in his *Scribes, Scripts and Readers: Studies in the Communication, Presentation and Dissemination of Medieval Texts* (London: Hambledon, 1991), pp. 35–69

Partridge, Stephen and Erik Kwakkel (eds), *Author, Reader, Book: Medieval Authorship in Theory and Practice* (Toronto: University of Toronto Press, 2012)

Parvulescu, Anca, 'European Kinship: Eastern European Women Go to the Market', *Critical Inquiry*, 37 (2011), 187–213

Paxson, James J., *The Poetics of Personification* (Cambridge: Cambridge University Press, 1994)

Perret, Noëlle-Laetitia, *Les traductions françaises du* De regimine principum *de Gilles de Rome : parcours matériel, culturel et intellectuel d'un discours sur l'éducation* (Leiden: Brill, 2011)

Petrosillo, Sara, 'Predatory Poetics: Reading Weight in Thirteenth-Century Falconry Treatises', *Exemplaria*, 29 (2017), 195–209

Phillips, Philip Edward, 'The English *Consolation of Philosophy*: Translation and Reception', *Carmina Philosophiae: Journal of the International Boethius Society*, 17 (2009), 97–126

Potthast, August, *Wegweiser durch die Geschichtswerke des europäischen Mittelalters bis 1500*, 2 vols (Berlin: Weber, 1896)

Quain, Edwin A., 'The Medieval *Accessus ad Auctores*', *Traditio*, 3 (1945), 215–64

Quilligan, Maureen, *The Language of Allegory: Defining the Genre* (Ithaca, NY: Cornell University Press, 1979)

Quinn, Betty Nye, 'Ps. Theodolus', in *Catalogus Translationum et Commentariorum*, II, ed. by Paul Oskar Kristeller and F. Edward Cranz (Washington, DC: Catholic University of America Press, 1971), pp. 386–408

Raskolnikov, Masha, *Body against Soul: Gender and* Sowlehele *in Middle English Allegory* (Columbus: Ohio State University Press, 2009)

Renevey, Denis, *Language, Self and Love: Hermeneutics in the Writings of Richard Rolle and the Commentaries on the Song of Songs* (Cardiff: University of Wales Press, 2001)

Renouard, Philippe, *Bibliographie des impressions et des œuvres de Josse Badius Ascensius, imprimeur et humaniste, 1462–1535* (Paris: Paul and Guillemin, 1908)

Rice, Nicole R., *Lay Piety and Religious Discipline in Middle English Literature*, Cambridge Studies in Medieval Literature 73 (Cambridge: Cambridge University Press, 2008)

Ricœur, Paul, *La métaphore vive* (Paris: Seuil, 1975)

Rissanen, Matti, 'In Search of *Happiness: Felicitas* and *Beatitudo* in Early English Boethius Translations', *Studia Anglica Posnaniensia*, 31 (1997), 237–48

Rissanen, Matti, et al., *The Helsinki Corpus of English Texts* (Helsinki: Department of Modern Languages, University of Helsinki, 1991)

Robertson, Kellie, *Nature Speaks: Medieval Literature and Aristotelian Philosophy* (Philadelphia: University of Pennsylvania Press, 2017)

Roos, Paolo, *Sentenza e proverbio nell'antichità e i* Distici di Catone: *il testo latino e i volgarizzamenti italiani* (Brescia: Morcelliana, 1984)

Rosenfeld, Jessica, *Ethics and Enjoyment in Later Medieval Poetry: Love after Aristotle*, Cambridge Studies in Medieval Literature 85 (Cambridge: Cambridge University Press, 2011)

Rouse, Richard H. and Mary A. Rouse, *Preachers, Florilegia and Sermons: Studies on the 'Manipulus Florum' of Thomas of Ireland* (Toronto: Pontifical Institute of Mediaeval Studies, 1979)

—— '*Statim Invenire*: Schools, Preachers and New Attitudes to the Page', in *Renaissance and Renewal in the Twelfth Century*, ed. by Robert L. Benson and Giles Constable, with Carol D. Lanham (Oxford: Clarendon, 1982), pp. 201–25

Rubin, Gayle, 'The Traffic in Women: Notes on the "Political Economy" of Sex', in *Toward an Anthropology of Women*, ed. by Rayna R. Reiter (New York: Monthly Review Press, 1975), pp. 157–210

Saccenti, Riccardo, 'The *Materia super libros Sententiarum* Attributed to Peter Comestor: Study of the Text and Critical Edition', *Bulletin de philosophie médiévale*, 54 (2012), 155–215

Salter, Elizabeth, *English and International: Studies in the Literature, Art and Patronage of Medieval England*, ed. by Derek Pearsall and Nicolette Zeeman (Cambridge: Cambridge University Press, 1988)

Sandler, Lucy Freeman, 'The *Lumere as lais* and Its Readers: Pictorial Evidence from British Library MS Royal 15 D. II', in *Thresholds of Medieval Visual Culture: Liminal Spaces*, ed. by Elina Gertsman and Jill Stevenson (Woodbridge: Boydell, 2012), pp. 73–94

—— 'Scribe, Corrector, Reader: The Marginal Drawings of the Morgan Library "Lumere as lais" and their Maker', *English Manuscript Studies, 1100–1700*, 17 (2012), 107–39

Scase, Wendy, *Reginald Pecock* (Aldershot: Variorum, 1996)

—— 'Reginald Pecock, John Carpenter and John Colop's Common-Profit Books: Aspects of Book Ownership and Circulation in Fifteenth-Century London', *MÆ*, 61 (1992), 261–74

Schmidt, Paul Gerhard, 'Jodocus Badius Ascensius als Kommentator', in *Der Kommentar in der Renaissance*, ed. by August Buck and Otto Herding (Boppard am Rhein: Boldt, 1975), pp. 63–71

Schmitter, Amy M., '17th and 18th Century Theories of Emotion', in *Stanford Encyclopedia of Philosophy* (Stanford: Stanford University, 2016). <https://plato.stanford.edu/entries/emotions-17th18th/> [last accessed 1 November 2022]

Scholderer, Victor and L. A. Sheppard, *Catalogue of Books Printed in the XVth Century Now in the British Museum*, VIII, *France, French-Speaking Switzerland* (London: British Museum, 1949)

Schümmer, K., *John Waltons metrische Übersetzung der* Consolatio Philosophiae: *Untersuchung des Handschriftenverhältnisses und Probe eines kritischen Textes* (Bonn: Peter Hannstein, 1914)

Sharpe, Richard, *A Handlist of the Latin Writers of Great Britain and Ireland before 1540* (Turnhout: Brepols, 1996)

Silk, Michael, 'Invoking the Other: Allegory in Theory, from Demetrius to de Man', in *Allegory Studies: Contemporary Perspectives*, ed. by Vladimir Brljak (London: Routledge, 2022), pp. 41–65

Silvestre, Hubert, 'Le schéma « moderne » des *accessus*', *Latomus*, 16 (1957), 684–89

Simpson, James, *Piers Plowman: An Introduction*, 2nd edn (Exeter: University of Exeter Press, 2007)

'The Power of Impropriety: Authorial Naming in *Piers Plowman*', in *William Langland's Piers Plowman: A Book of Essays*, ed. by Kathleen M. Hewett-Smith (New York: Routledge, 2001), pp. 145–65

Skinner, Quentin, *Reason and Rhetoric in the Philosophy of Hobbes* (Cambridge: Cambridge University Press, 1996)

Slotemaker, John T. and Jeffrey C. Witt, *Robert Holcot* (New York: Oxford University Press, 2016)

Smalley, Beryl, 'Gilbertus Universalis, Bishop of London (1128–34), and the Problem of the "Glossa ordinaria"', *Recherches de Théologie ancienne et médiévale*, 7 (1935), 235–62 and 8 (1936), 24–60

'John Ridewall's Commentary on *De civitate Dei*', *MÆ*, 25 (1956), 140–53

'La Glossa Ordinaria: Quelques prédécesseurs d'Anselme de Laon', *Recherches de Théologie ancienne et médiévale*, 9 (1937), 365–400

'Robert Holcot OP', *Archivum Fratrum Praedicatorum*, 26 (1956), 5–97

'Thomas Waleys OP', *Archivum Fratrum Praedicatorum*, 24 (1954), 50–107

Smith, D. Vance, *Arts of Possession: The Middle English Household Imaginary* (Minneapolis: University of Minnesota Press, 2003)

Smith, Jennifer Anh-Thu Tran, 'Reginald Pecock and Vernacular Theology in Pre-Reformation England' (unpublished doctoral dissertation, University of California, Los Angeles, 2012)

Smith, Lesley, 'What Was the Bible in the Twelfth and Thirteenth Centuries?', in *Neue Richtungen in der hoch- und spätmittelalterlichen Bibelexegese*, ed. by Robert E. Lerner with Elisabeth Müller-Luckner (Munich: Oldenbourg, 1996), pp. 1–15

Solmsen, Friedrich, 'The Aristotelian Tradition in Ancient Rhetoric', *American Journal of Philology*, 62 (1941), 35–50 and 169–90

Somerset, Fiona, *Clerical Discourse and Lay Audience in Late Medieval England*, Cambridge Studies in Medieval Literature 37 (Cambridge: Cambridge University Press, 1998)

Spearing, A. C., *Medieval Autographies: The 'I' of the Text* (Notre Dame, IN: University of Notre Dame Press, 2005)

Specht, Henrik, '"Ethopoeia" or Impersonation: A Neglected Species of Medieval Characterization', *Chaucer Review*, 21 (1986), 1–15

Spencer, H. Leith, *English Preaching in the Middle Ages* (Oxford: Clarendon, 1993)

Staico, Ubaldo, 'Rhetorica e politica in Egidio Romano', *Documenti e studi sulla tradizione filosofica medievale*, 3 (1992), 1–75

Star, Sarah, 'The Textual Worlds of Henry Daniel', *Studies in the Age of Chaucer*, 40 (2018), 191–216

Stark, David, *The Sense of Dissonance: Accounts of Worth in Economic Life* (Princeton, NJ: Princeton University Press, 2009)

Strauss, Leo, *The Political Philosophy of Hobbes: Its Basis and Its Genesis*, tr. by Elsa M. Sinclair (Oxford: Clarendon, 1936)

Striker, Gisela, 'Emotions in Context: Aristotle's Treatment of the Passions in the *Rhetoric* and his Moral Psychology', in *Essays on Aristotle's* Rhetoric, ed. by Amélie Oksenberg Rorty (Berkeley: University of California Press, 1996), pp. 286–302

Struever, Nancy, 'Hobbes and Vico on Law: A Rhetorical Gloss', in *History of Rhetoric and the Rhetoric of History* (Farnham: Ashgate, 2009), no. XIX

—— 'The Pertinence of Rhetorical Theory and Practice for Current Vichian Scholarship', in *History of Rhetoric and the Rhetoric of History* (Farnham: Ashgate, 2009), no. I

—— 'Rhetoric and Philosophy in Vichian Inquiry Investigation', *New Vico Studies*, 3 (1985), 131–45

Tachau, Katherine H., *Vision and Certitude in the Age of Ockham* (Leiden: Brill, 1988)

Tanselle, G. Thomas, 'The Bibliographical Concepts of *Issue* and *State*', *Papers of the Bibliographical Society of America*, 69 (1975), 17–66

Tavormina, M. Teresa, 'Uroscopy in Middle English: A Guide to the Texts and Manuscripts', *Studies in Medieval and Renaissance History*, 3rd series, 11 (2014), 1–154

Teskey, Gordon, *Allegory and Violence* (Ithaca, NY: Cornell University Press, 1996)

Thomson, R. M., *Catalogue of the Manuscripts of Lincoln Cathedral Chapter Library* (Cambridge: D. S. Brewer for the Dean and Chapter of Lincoln, 1989)

Toivanen, Juhana, 'The Personal and the Political: Love and Society in the *Roman de la Rose*', in *The* Roman de la Rose *and Thirteenth-Century Thought*, ed. by Jonathan Morton and Marco Nievergelt, with John Marenbon (Cambridge: Cambridge University Press, 2020), pp. 111–30

Toste, Marco, 'The Naturalness of Human Association in Medieval Political Thought Revisited', in *La nature comme source de la moral au Moyen Âge*, ed. by Maaike van der Lugt (Florence: Società Internazionale per lo Studio del Medioevo Latino, 2008), pp. 113–88

Tuck, Richard, 'Hobbes's Moral Philosophy', in *The Cambridge Companion to Hobbes*, ed. by Tom Sorrell (Cambridge: Cambridge University Press, 1996), pp. 175–207

Tyler, Elizabeth M., 'From Old English to Old French', in *Language and Culture in Medieval Britain: The French of England, c. 1100–1500*, ed. by Jocelyn Wogan-Browne et al. (York: Boydell and Brewer for the York Medieval Press, 2009), pp. 164–78

Van der Lugt, Maaike (ed.), *La Nature comme source de la morale au Moyen Âge* (Florence: Società Internazionale per lo Studio del Medioevo Latino, 2008)

Voigts, Linda Ehrsam, 'What's the Word? Bilingualism in Late-Medieval England', *Speculum*, 71 (1996), 813–26

Von Moos, Peter, 'The Use of *Exempla* in the *Polycraticus* of John of Salisbury', in *The World of John of Salisbury*, ed. by Michael Wilks (Oxford: Blackwell for the Ecclesiastical History Society, 1984), 207–61

Wakelin, Daniel, 'Possibilities for Reading: Classical Translations in Parallel Texts, c. 1520–1558', *Studies in Philology*, 105 (2008), 463–86
Walls, Keith, *John Bromyard on Church and State* (Market Weighton: Clayton-Thorpe, 2007)
Walsh Morrissey, Jake, 'Anxious Love and Disordered Urine: The Englishing of Amor Hereos in Henry Daniel's *Liber Uricrisiarum*', *Chaucer Review*, 49 (2014), 161–83
Ward, John O., 'Quintilian and the Rhetorical Revolution of the Middle Ages', *Rhetorica*, 12 (1995), 231–84
Warton, Thomas, *The History of English Poetry, from the Close of the Eleventh to the Commencement of the Eighteenth Century*, 3 vols (London: Dodsley et al., 1774)
Waters, Claire M., *Angels and Earthly Creatures: Preaching, Performance and Gender in the Later Middle Ages* (Philadelphia: University of Pennsylvania Press, 2004)
— 'Loving Teaching: Status, Exchange, and Translation in Pierre d'Abernon's *Lumere as lais*', *MÆ*, 81 (2012), 304–19
— *Translating Clergie: Status, Education and Salvation in Thirteenth-Century Vernacular Texts* (Philadelphia: University of Pennsylvania Press, 2016)
— 'The Voice of the Sluggard: Humanizing Sloth in the *Manuel des pechiez*', *YLS*, 33 (2019), 185–204
Watson, Nicholas, '*Piers Plowman*, Pastoral Theology and Spiritual Perfectionism: Haukyn's Cloak and Patience's *Pater noster*', *YLS*, 21 (2007), 83–118
— *Richard Rolle and the Invention of Authority*, Cambridge Studies in Medieval Literature 13 (Cambridge: Cambridge University Press, 1991)
Watson, Patricia, 'Love as Civilizer: Ovid, Ars Amatoria, 2, 467–92', *Latomus*, 43 (1984), 389–95
Wei, Ian P., *Intellectual Culture in Medieval Paris: Theologians and the University, c. 1100–1330* (Cambridge: Cambridge University Press, 2012)
Wenzel, Siegfried, 'Academic Sermons at Oxford in the Early Fifteenth Century', *Speculum*, 70 (1995), 305–29
— *Macaronic Sermons* (Ann Arbor: University of Michigan Press, 1994)
— *Medieval* Artes Praedicandi: *A Synthesis of Scholastic Sermon Structure* (Toronto: University of Toronto Press for the Medieval Academy of America, 2015)
— *Preachers, Poets and the Early English Lyric* (Princeton, NJ: Princeton University Press, 1986)
Westphall, Allan F., 'Reconstructing the Mixed Life in Reginald Pecock's *Reule of Crysten Religioun*', in *After Arundel: Religious Writing in Fifteenth-Century England*, ed. by Vincent Gillespie and Kantik Ghosh (Turnhout: Brepols, 2011), pp. 267–84
Wetherbee, Winthrop, 'The Literal and the Allegorical: Jean de Meun and the *De Planctu Naturae*', *Mediaeval Studies*, 33 (1971), 264–91
White, Hayden, 'Tropics of History: The Deep Structure of the *New Science*', in *Tropics of Discourse: Essays in Cultural Criticism* (Baltimore: Johns Hopkins University Press, 1978), pp. 178–217

Whitman, Jon, *Allegory: The Dynamics of an Ancient and Medieval Technique* (Cambridge, MA: Harvard University Press, 1987)
Wilmart, André, 'Un commentaire des Psaumes restitué à Anselme de Laon', *Recherches de Théologie ancienne et médiévale*, 8 (1936), 325–44
Wisse, Jakob, *Ethos and Pathos from Aristotle to Cicero* (Amsterdam: Hakkert, 1989)
Wogan-Browne, Jocelyn, 'Time to Read: Pastoral Care, Vernacular Access and the Case of Angier of St Frideswide', in *The Texts and Traditions of English Pastoral Care: Essays in Honour of Bella Millett*, ed. by Cate Gunn and Catherine Innes Parker (York: Boydell and Brewer for the York Medieval Press, 2009), pp. 62–77
Wood, Anthony A. and Philip Bliss, *Athenae Oxonienses: An Exact History of All the Writers and Bishops Who Have Had Their Education in the University of Oxford, to Which Are Added the Fasti, or Annals of the Said University*, new edn, 4 vols (London: Rivington, 1813–1820)
Wood, Sarah, *Conscience and the Composition of Piers Plowman* (Oxford: Oxford University Press, 2012)
Woods, Marjorie Curry, *Classroom Commentaries: Teaching the Poetria nova across Medieval and Renaissance Europe* (Columbus: Ohio State University Press, 2010)
  'The Teaching of Poetic Composition in the Later Middle Ages,' in *A Short History of Writing Instruction: From Ancient Greece to Modern America*, ed. by James J. Murphy, 2nd edn (Mahwah, NJ: Hermagoras Press, 2001), pp. 123–43
  *Weeping for Dido: The Classics in the Medieval Classroom* (Princeton, NJ: Princeton University Press, 2019)
Zeeman, Nicolette, *Arts of Disruption: Allegory and* Piers Plowman (Oxford: Oxford University Press, 2020)
  Piers Plowman *and the Medieval Discourse of Desire*, Cambridge Studies in Medieval Literature 59 (Cambridge: Cambridge University Press, 2006).
  'Response: Not Peter or Perkyn, but Piers', *YLS*, 30 (2016), 297–305
  'Willing', in *Middle English Literature: Criticism and Dissent*, ed. by Holly Crocker and D. Vance Smith (London: Routledge, 2014), pp. 470–79
Zetzel, James E. G., *Critics, Compilers and Commentators: An Introduction to Roman Philology, 200 BCE–800 CE* (New York: Oxford University Press, 2018)
Zimmermann, Albert (ed.), *Antiqui und Moderni: Traditionsbewusstsein u. Fortschrittsbewusstsein im späten Mittelalter* (Berlin: De Gruyter, 1974)
Zonta, Mauro, 'Le origini letterarie e filosofiche delle versioni ebraiche del *De Consolatione Philosophiae* di Boezio', in *Boethius Christianus? Transformationen der* Consolatio philosophiae *in Mittelalter und früher Neuzeit*, ed. by Reinhold F. Glei, Nicola Kaminski and Franz Lebsanft (Berlin: De Gruyter, 2010), pp. 397–429

# Index

*accessus*, 9, 15, 19, 24–46, 59, 71, 89
    Aristotelian template, 42–46, 48, 60
Adam of Dryburgh, 209
Adelard of Bath, *De avibus tractatus*, 53
Aers, David, 190, 198–200
Alan of Lille, *De Planctu Naturae*, 187
Albert the Great, Saint, 168
    *Summa theologiae*, 69
Alcher of Clairvaux, *De spiritu et anima*, 207
Alexander of Hales, 69
    *Summa theologica*, 67–68
Alexander the Great, 51
al-Farabi, 64–65
al-Ghazali, 65
Alighieri, Dante, *Divine Comedy*, 214
allegory, 164, 180–81, 204
Ambrose, Saint, 90
Andrew of St Victor, 114
Angier of Oxford, translation of Gregory's *Dialogues*, 45
Anselm of Laon, 1–2, 5, 11, 99
anxiety, 209
Apostles' Creed, 147–50
*argumentum*, as a kind of writing, 31, 38
Aristotle, 19, 42–44, 51, 79, 219, 266–67
    and branches of knowledge, 62–64
    on communal and private property, 169–73
    *Metaphysics*, 42, 212–13
    *Nicomachean Ethics*, 92, 160, 251–52, 254–55
    *Organon*, 63–64, 69
    *Physics*, 42
    *Poetics*, 14–15, 42, 62, 76
    *Politics*, 22, 161–62, 168–72, 252, 254
    *Rhetoric*, 23, 249–58
Aristotle, Pseudo-, *Secreta secretorum*, 51
Augustine, Saint, 66, 70, 89, 105–6, 127, 130
    *De civitate Dei*, 106
    *De doctrina Christiana*, 124–25, 130
authority
    inspired authority of the Fathers, 106–9
    and kingship, 50–52
    and natural knowledge, 55
Averroes, 65
    Commentary on Aristotle's *Poetics*, 64
Avianus, *Fables*, 26–27, 37–39
Avicenna, 64–65, 120
    *Canon Medicinae*, 123

Bacon, Francis, 257
Bacon, Roger
    *Moralis philosophia*, 65
    *Opus maius*, 65
Badius Ascensius, Jodocus, Commentary on Boethius, 227, 231–32, 243, 245
Bartholomew the Englishman, *De proprietatibus rerum*, 139
Berkeley, Thomas, lord, 254
Bernard of Clairvaux, Saint, 22
    *Sermons on the Song of Songs*, 208, 210–11
Bernardus Silvestris, 9, 12
    *Cosmographia*, 180
Bible
    biblical commentary, 9, 94–98, 100, 106–15, *see also* exegesis
    Aristotelian prologues to, 106
    Books of
        Daniel, 73
        Ecclesiastes, 72
        Esther, 79–80
        Exodus, 107
        Galatians, 66, 83
        Genesis, 55, 58, 60
        I Corinthians, 66
        I Timothy, 66
        Isaiah, 73
        Job, 72, 74
        John, 110
        Lamentations, 73, 76, 84–85
        Luke, 128
        Psalms, 13, 15, 76, 139
        Romans, 66

# Index

Song of Songs, 13, 16, 72, 75
Wisdom, 20, 78, 86, 107
figures in Bible
  Esther, 79–80
  Hagar, 82
  Judith, 80
  Moses, 107
  Sarah, 83
modes of writing in, 71–74
scientific and poetic language, 66–71
study of its poetics, 62–77
Boethius, 187
  *Contra Eutychen*, 230
  *De consolatione philosophiae*, 15, 220–47
    commentaries on, 3–4, 12
    history of translation into English, 23, 220–26, 245–46
    print history of, 226–28
Bokenham, Osbern, *Legendys of Hooly Wummon*, 60
Bonaventure, Saint, 72, 95, 138
  *Itinerarium mentis in Deum*, 206–8
  *Lignum vitae*, 208
Bradwardine, Thomas, *De causa dei*, 21
Brancato, Dario, 245
Brecht, Bertolt, *Mother Courage and Her Children*, 180–81
Briggs, Charles, 258
Bromyard, John, 123, 132–34
  *Summa praedicantium*, 116–18
Bruno the Carthusian, 71

Calabrese, Michael, 189
calendars, treatises on, 56–58
Carruthers, Mary, 18
Cassian, 11
  *Collationes*, 12
Cassiodorus, 62
causes, four, 42, 44
Cawoode, John, 221
Chaucer, Geoffrey, 21, 60
  *Boece*, 23, 221, 225, 236–42
  *Canterbury Tales*
    *Nun's Priest's Tale*, 21
    *Parson's Tale*, 143
    *Squire's Tale*, 214–16
  *House of Fame*, 180, 188
  *Legend of Good Women*, 136
Chenu, M.-D., 109
Cicero, 166
  *De Inventione*, 160
  *De optimo genere oratorum*, 66
  *De oratore*, 184
  *Orator*, 185

Cicero, Pseudo-, *Rhetorica ad Herennium*, 125, 130, 184–85
Claudian, *Rape of Proserpine*, 26, 37, 41
Coleman, Janet, 254
Colvile, George, 221–26
  Translation of Boethius, 23, 228–46
  and Chaucer's *Boece*, 236–42
  Latin edition used, 242–45
*compilatio*, 138, 157–58
conduct literature
  *Distichs of Cato*, 27–30
Conrad of Hirsau, *Dialogus super auctores*, 184
*Consolation of Philosophy*. *See* Boethius
Constantine the African, 59, 120, 126
Constantinople, 88
cosmetics, 59
Craun, Edwin, 189

Daniel, Henry
  *Herbal*, 120
  *Liber Uricrisiarum*, 20, 119–29, 131–36
delight, 90
Demetrius, *On Style*, 185
Denys the Carthusian, commentary on Boethius, 228, 232, 235
Derrida, Jacques, 154
Descartes, René, *Discours de la méthode*, 259
dicing, 84
Dickens, Charles, *Bleak House*, 180–81
Dionysius, Pseudo-, 11, 66, 68–70, 73
disquiet, 206–19
dissonance, 137, 157–58
*Distichs of Cato*, 26–31, 41
*divisio textus*, division of the text, 4, 15, 37, 139
Dominicans. *See* Order of Preachers
Donatus, Aelius, 10, 220
  *Ars grammatica*, 184
Du Pré, Jean, 242
Durham, 88

*Eclogue of Theodulus*, 26–27, 30–34, 41
eclogues, 32
Eden, 174
*eidolopoiia*, 186
Elizabeth I, queen of England, 245
Emotions, history of, 249–68
*enargeia*, 183
*episteme*, 219
Erghome, John, 93
ethics, 33, 39–40
Evax, king of Arabia, 51, 53
exegesis, 62–63, 71–77, 94–115
  inspiration of Church Fathers, 106–9

exegesis (cont.)
    and poetic language, 70–71
    and public declamation, 81–93
*explanatio*, 125

fable, 31–33, 38
falconry
    and natural knowledge, 54–55
    treatises on, 53–55
*Fasciculus morum*, 143
Feeney, Denis, 17
Fleck, Ludwik, 48
*forma tractandi*, 16, 44
*forma tractatus*, 10, 16, 44, 139
Francis, Saint, 206–8
Frederick II, of Hohenstaufen, 50, 53
French language, rise of writing in England, 47–48

Galen, 59, 120
Gawain. *See Sir Gawain and the Green Knight*
Geoffrey of Vinsauf, *Poetria nova*, 39, 186
George of Trebizond, *Rhetoricorum libri quinque*, 257
Gerard of Cremona, 64
Gilbert of Poitiers, 15
Gilbert the Englishman, 120
Gilbertus Universalis, 12
Giles of Rome, 16, 23, 250
    Commentary on Aristotle's *Rhetoric*, 252–53
    Commentary on the Song of Songs, 145
    *De differentia rhetoricae, ethicae et politicae*, 257
    *De regimine principum*, 172, 249, 253–57, 267
*Glossa ordinaria*, 1, 9, 79
Golden Age, 159–68, 172–76
Gossuin de Metz, *Imago mundi*, 59
Gower, John, 60
    *Confessio Amantis*, 121
Gratian, *Decretum*, 163
Gray, William, 93
Gregory the Great, Pope and Saint
    *Dialogues*, 45
    *Homiliae in Hiezechielem*, 204
    *Moralia in Job*, 109
Griffiths, Lavinia, 189
Grosseteste, Pseudo-, *Marriage of the Nine Daughters of the Devil*, 57
Grosseteste, Robert, 106
Guillaume de Deguileville, 61
    *Pelerinage de vie humaine*, 180
Guillaume de Lorris. *See* Jean de Meun
Guillaume de Machaut. *See* Machaut

*habitus*, 123, 145
Hanna, Ralph, 189
Harold Godwineson, king of England, 54
Heidegger, Martin, 251
Hélinand of Froidmont, 89
Henry II, king of England, 53
Henry of Ghent, *Summa quaestionum ordinarium*, 70, 110–11
Herbert, William, 93
Herbert of Bosham, 9
Hermannus Alemannus (Herman the German), 14, 62, 64–65
Hildegard of Bingen, *Scivias*, 218
Hippocrates, 59
History, as a kind of writing, 31–32, 38
Hobbes, Thomas, 23, 249–50, 257–62
    *A Brief of the Art of Rhetorick*, 258–59
    *De homine*, 258
    *Elements of Law*, 258
    *Leviathan*, 257–62, 264
Hoccleve, Thomas, 21
Holcot, Robert, 20–21, 128–29
    *Super Sapientiam Salomonis*, 78–84, 88
Honorius of Autun, *Elucidarius*, 43, 49, 59
Horace
    *Ars poetica*, 65
    *Odes*, 14
Hugh of St Cher, 73
Hugh of St Victor, 11–12, 107, 209
Humbert of Romans, 124, 130–31, 133
    *De eruditione praedicantium*, 129
Hunt, R. W., 15, 19
Huot, Sylvia, 168

inspiration, 94–115
    and patristic writers, 106–9
intention, 24, 27–30, 33, 36, 38, 42
Isaac Judaeus, *De urinis*, 135
Isidore of Seville, 10

Jacobus de Fusignano, 124, 127
Jean de Meun, 61
    *Roman de la Rose*, 22, 161–69, 173–80, 187
    Translation of Boethius, 239
Jerome, Saint, 105
John III Vatatzes, emperor of Nicaea, 89
John of Hauville, *Architrenius*, 84
John of Howden, 46
John of Maroeuil, 107
John of Salisbury, *Polycraticus*, 81, 91
John of Varzy, 72
John of Wales, 81, 91–93, 140
    *Breviarium de virtutibus*, 92
    *Communiloquium*, 91
Joyce, James, *Ulysses*, 180–81

# Index

Kafka, Franz, *The Castle*, 180–81
Kay, Sarah, 175
Kilwardby, Robert, 122, 138
kingship
  and authority, 50–52
  and *philosophus* figures, 51
Koberger, Anton, 226
Koivisto-Alanko, Päivi, 225
Kuhn, Thomas, 48

Lactantius Placidus, commentary on the *Thebaid*, 8
Langland, William, 60
  *Piers Plowman*, 22, 180, 182–205, 214
    Anima, 193
    *clergie* in, 192
    Conscience, 195–96, 200–2
    Haukyn, 200–4
    Pacience, 196–98, 201
    Piers as personification, 193–94
    priesthood and ordination in, 198–204
    Wil, 195, 214
lapidaries, 51–53
  and secular and sacred knowledge, 52–53
Lathrop, Henry Burrowes, 223, 225
Latini, Brunetto, *Li Livres dou Tresor*, 47, 139
law, its study opposed to theology, 82–84
Lawler, Traugott, 191, 203
*Le Livre de Sidrac*, 49–50, 59
  translation history of, 50
Leland, John, 99
*Liber Catonianus*, 25
literary theory, 250, 267
  in the Middle Ages, 15–17
Lollardy, 142
London, 141
  distance to Rome, 155
  Dominican *studium* at Blackfriars, 123
Longinus, *On the Sublime*, 15
Lucan, 6, 8
Lucretius, 159

Machaut, Guillaume de, *Remede de Fortune*, 187
Machiavelli, Niccolò, *Il Principe*, 257
Macrobius, 90
Maire, Johannes, 258
Mandeville, John, his *Livre* or *Book*, 60
Manitius, Max, 220
*Mankynde*, 180
Mann, Jill, 188
*manuductus*, 19, 68, 73
Marbode of Rennes, *De gemmis*, 51
Mary, queen of England, 223
Maximian, *Elegies*, 26–27, 37, 40
McGinn, Bernard, 96

medicine
  critique of physicians, 132–34
  uroscopy, 120, 131–35
  and vernacular translation, 126–28
meditation, 208–11
*Medulla Grammatice*, 237–38
metaphor, 70, 73
metonymy, 184
Minnis, Alastair, 6, 14, 18, 43, 117, 137–39, 183, 249–50
  *Fallible Authors*, 176
  *Medieval Theory of Authorship*, 15, 160, 250
mirrors for princes, 50
*modus agendi* or *tractandi*, 42, 70, 71
  *modi* of the Bible, 71–74
de Montmoret, Humbert, 228, 230
Morton, Jonathan, 161
Murmellius, Johannis, 227, 231–32, 235
mythography, 6–8

Neckham, Alexander, 31
Nicholas of Lyre, 107, 139

Old English *Boethius*, 221
Olivi, Peter John, 75
orality, 10, 45
Order of Preachers, 122–24
  as 'dogs of God', 134
  Dominican education at *studia*, 122–23
*ordinatio*, 10, 21, 138–40, 157–58
*Ornatus Mulierum*, 59
Ovid, 88, 90, 179, 188
  *Amores*, 85
  *Ars Amatoria*, 160
  *Metamorphoses*, 74, 159, 167
Ovid, Pseudo-, *De vetula*, 20, 81, 84–90

Palasinus, Raymundus, 228, 232, 242
Parkes, Malcolm, 137–38
*pastoralia*, 43
*Pearl*, 216–19
Pecock, Reginald, 21, 137–58
  on the Apostles' Creed, 147–50
  on the Decalogue, 150–53
  *Donet*, 142, 146–53, 157
  and God's infinitude, 153–56
  and natural reason, 142, 144
  and scholastic textuality, 140
  *Repressor [of Overmuch Blaming of the Clergy]*, 142
  *Reule of Crysten Religioun*, 153–56
  virtues, 142–46
personification, 180–95, 204–5
  and *prosopopoeia* in Latin rhetorical theory, 183–87

Peter Abelard, 71
Peter Comestor, 107, 113
  *Historia scholastica*, 43
Peter Lombard
  *Magna glosatura*, 9, 15, 95, 97, 99, 112
  *Sentences*, 108
Peter of Auvergne, commentary on Aristotle's *Politics*, 171–72
Peter of Celle, 210
Philippe VI de Valois, king of France, 51
*Philobiblon*, authorship of, 86
Pierre d'Abernon de Fetcham
  as God's notary, 47
  *Lumere as lais*, 19, 43–47, 49, 59–60
  Translation of the *Secreta secretorum*, 51, 59
Plato, 171
  *Republic*, 162, 164, 168–70
poetry
  as aid to understanding, 74–76
  and biblical exegesis, 70–71
  and biblical language, 62–77
  and knowledge, 56
  poetics, 14
  and the sciences, 63–69
  and scientific language, 66–71
Porphyry, *Isagoge*, 64
preaching, 81, 93, 116–18, 128–33
  arts of preaching, 118
  and delight, 89–90
  and medical speech, 117
  and style of language, 129–31
Priscian, *Praeexercitamina*, 186
prologues. *See accessus*
property, 162–64
  and erotic desire, 167–68
*prosopopoeia*. *See* personification

Quentell, Henry, 227
Quintilian, *Institutio oratoria*, 186, 209–10

Rainolds, John, 257
Ralph de Lenham, *Art de Kalender*, 56–59
*ratio discurrens*, 149, 157
Remigius of Auxerre, 230
Rice, Nicole, 199
Richard de Bury, 85
Richard de Fournival, 84
Richard of St Victor, 109, 209
Ricœur, Paul, 70
Ridewall, John, 78, 106
Rissanen, Matti, 225
Robert of Basevorn, 89–90
  *Forma praedicandi*, 130
Robert of Melun, *Quaestiones de Epistolis Pauli*, 107
Rolle, Richard, 20, 94–115

Commentary on the Apocalypse, 99
Commentary on the Song of Songs, 98
*Contra Amatores Mundi*, 100–1
*Emendatio Vitae*, 100
English commentary on the Psalter, 95
*Incendium Amoris*, 96, 98, 100, 112
Latin commentary on the Psalter, 97
and magisterial authority, 109–12
*Melos Amoris*, 96, 98, 102–3, 108
as *modernus*, 101–5
and mystical interpretation, 96–115
*Roman d'Eneas*, 212
*Roman de la Rose*. *See* Jean de Meun
Roscelin of Compiègne, 71
Rubin, Gayle, 194

Schedel, Hartmann, 25
Schmidt, Paul Gerhard, 227
scholasticism, and the vernacular, 61
*scientia*
  and *ars*, 67
  and authority, 50
  division into four parts, 64
  and fiction, 53
  and the history of science, 48–49
  and poetics, 63–69
Scott, A. B., 6
Seneca, 90, 129
  commentaries on, 10
Servius, commentary (attr.) on the *Aeneid*, 4–5
similitudes, 65, 73, 91, 129
*Sir Gawain and the Green Knight*, 212
Skinner, Quentin, 258
Smalley, Beryl, 1, 20, 78, 81
Socrates, 162, 169, 172
*Speculum stultorum*. *See* Wireker
Spenser, Edmund, 246
  *Faerie Queene*, 180
Stark, David, 137
Statius
  *Achilleid*, 26–27, 37, 41
  *Thebaid*, commentaries on, 8
Stephen of Tournai, 108
Strauss, Leo, 258
style, 31, 66
*Summa virtutum de remediis anime*, 143

Tanzo, Anselmo, 245
*techne*, 209, 219
Tempier, Étienne, 253
Ten Commandments, 150–53
theology
  definition of, 67
  and scientific language, 66–71
Theophilus, *De diversis artibus*, 213–14

theory, 11–14
Thomas Aquinas, Pseudo-, commentary on
    Boethius, 226–32, 235–36, 238–42, 244
Thomas Aquinas, Saint, 70, 72–73, 109, 145,
    149, 168, 252
  Commentary on Aristotle's *Politics*, 169–70
  Commentary on Job, 74–75
  Commentary on the *Posterior Analytics*, 64
  Commentary on the *Sentences*, 66, 68–69
  *De regno ad regem Cypri*, 259
  *Summa theologica*, 163, 178, 253
  translation, in preaching and medical writing,
    125–29
Trevet, Nicholas, 10, 106, 109
  Commentary on Boethius, 221, 226, 230,
    235–36, 238, 240
Trevisa, John, 254
*trivium*, 63
Trota of Salerno, 59

Ulysses, 85
uroscopy, 120, 131–35

Valerius Maximus, 90
Varchi, Benedetto, 245
vernacularity, 43, 48
  and authority, 51
  and knowledge, 60–61
  and specialised translation, 125–29
  and style, 124–25
Vico, Giambattista, 23, 249–50, 262–67
  *De nostri temporis studiorum ratione*, 262
  *Institutiones oratoriae*, 263–64

*New Science*, 262, 264–67
Vincent of Beauvais, 140
  *Speculum doctrinale*, 186
Vincent, Simon, 228
de Vingle, Jean, 227
Virgil, 10, 31, 188
  *Aeneid*, 180
  commentaries on the *Aeneid*, 1–5, 8–10
  *Eclogues*, 90
Vives, Juan Luis, *De ratione dicendi*, 257

Waleys, Thomas, 106, 123, 127, 132, 134
  *De modo componendi sermones*, 123, 125
Wallace, David, 6
Walpole, Michael, commentary (attr.) on
    Boethius, 245–46
Walton, John, translation of Boethius, 221
Waters, Claire, 43
Watson, Nicholas, 98, 197
White, Hayden, 265
Whittington College, 141
William de Bougevilla, 88
William of Auvergne, 73
William of Conches, 10
  Commentary on Boethius, 3, 12, 230
William of Moerbeke, 22, 62, 168, 252
Wireker, Nigel, *Speculum stultorum*, 84
Wolff, Thomas, 228
wonder, 211–12, 215, 218
Wood, Sarah, 195, 200
Wyclif, John, 20

*Ysagoge in theologiam*, 12, 14, 64

For EU product safety concerns, contact us at Calle de José Abascal, 56–1°, 28003 Madrid, Spain or eugpsr@cambridge.org.